SPEAKING IN AMERICA

SPEAKING IN AMERICA

Harold Barrett

California State University, Hayward

Harcourt Brace Jovanovich College Publishers

Fort Worth   Philadelphia   San Diego   New York   Orlando   Austin   San Antonio
Toronto   Montreal   London   Sydney   Tokyo

Editor in Chief	Ted Buchholz
Executive Editor	Bill McLane
Acquisitions Editor	Janet Wilhite
Developmental Editor	Terri House
Project Editor	Kelly Riche
Senior Production Manager	Ken Dunaway
Book Designer	Melinda Huff
Photo Permissions Editor	Lili Weiner
Cover/Part Opener Illustration	John Nelson

Address for Editorial Correspondence
Harcourt Brace Jovanovich, 301 Commerce Street, Suite 3700, Fort Worth, TX 76102

Address for Orders
Harcourt Brace Jovanovich, 6277 Sea Harbor Drive, Orlando, FL 32887
1-800-782-4479, or 1-800-433-0001 (in Florida)

Photo credits begin on page 438 and constitute a continuation of the copyright page.

ISBN: 0-03-076117-4

Library of Congress Catalog Card Number: 92-71197

Printed in the United States of America

3 4 5 6 7 8 9 0 1 2   043   9 8 7 6 5 4 3 2 1

To Lee

PREFACE

I want to open with a word about rhetorical invention, specifically on the writing of textbooks. *Speaking in America* has grown out of my earlier textbooks and retains a good deal of their substance. Beyond that, it's the culmination of classroom experience and growth in certain perceptions on teaching speech communication. Thus do we grow, all of us.

But there's another factor to consider in understanding the forces that work to bring about such change. Besides being influenced by their daily discoveries and scholarly activity, most authors find themselves adapting to conditions of their time. Recall that after Sputnik we saw books begin to reflect the new competitive spirit in the country and to include topical references to that startling occurrence. Then came monumental events like the first trip to the moon, two major wars, the emergence of the computer age, and the end of the cold war; all required responses by writers, including those in the speech communication field.

But the most dramatic and insistent development has been in areas other than war and technology. Bearing directly on everyone's life in recent years is an extraordinary social and political evolution. Standing out for its influence on our communications with others has been a clear transformation in the shape of the American *audience:* new people; people acquiring new freedoms and opportunities—educational, political, and professional; new thinking; and the acceptance of new perspectives on roles, orientations, and relationships. Along with these have come new responsibilities. And with greater awareness and endorsement of social, religious, and cultural pluralism, we have moved toward more widely shared power in the community.

Implications for communication are enormous, and I have allowed them to lead me in the preparation of this public speaking book. Have we ever known a period when each person's voice counted for more? Have we ever known an age when competent speaking and listening were more essential? When have the burdens of saying and responding been more distributed across all cultures? Truly, these are exciting times.

However, there's a sobering side. One is reminded of the great moment when the Greeks of the fifth century, B.C., gained democracy but came to know that having it was not enough. They learned that their enjoyment of democracy depended on their rhetorical ability, on their use of the arts of persuasion. Real empowerment in the Assembly, law courts, and elsewhere was based on speaking ability. So it is in this day. Skill and sophistication are required for taking advantage of opportunities now available in the community. One of the jobs of instructors in speech communication is to prepare students to function successfully in the changed and demanding communicative environment. It's a dynamic, stimulating world, sometimes frightening, and we must do our part in preparing people to participate.

Participation involves relating to others. The *fact of others,* of our audiences, has exerted much influence on the writing of this book. My mentor, Bower Aly, used to say—after Aristotle—that the act of speaking is about knowing and addressing *audiences.* We find means of securing a hearing for our ideas only insofar as we know, respect, and adapt to audiences.

The American audience has become much more diversified. With demographic transformations have come modifications in the character of the speaker–listener relationship, and, consequently, an urgency for awareness of the variety to be found in personal conditions and identities. We have a lot to learn about each other. Therefore, I've worked into this book a multicultural theme. The fact of diversity in America is recognized throughout. Communicators from various cultures are acknowledged. Three new model outlines are based on topics of special importance to minority cultures. The same goal guided selection of illustrative material. Moreover, I have sought a balanced treatment, for *Speaking in America* is dedicated to unity among us. The book stresses, from the beginning, cultural empathy and the value of knowing and respecting the people with whom we want to—and must—communicate.

A related truth, as I know it, is one highlighted convincingly by Kenneth Burke in many of his works on rhetorical topics: The process of identification provides the explanation of success in interaction with others. As he cogently observes, and as we surely know, the human condition is characterized by difference and distance. Therefore, to communicate with others, we must discover and acknowledge kinship. It's as simple as that—and as complex and challenging. Included in the process of locating points of unity, bases for identifying, is the understanding of conditions that work to keep us apart. From this view on the theory of human interaction, I hope the reader will appreciate the emphasis given to the audience in this book and to strategies of securing identification with the audience.

Moreover, readers will observe that the book addresses certain interpersonal elements that are basic to the act of public speaking, in other words, the person-to-person nature of effective public speaking. The book seeks to make the student communicator aware of the importance of being sensitive to human qualities and conditions that are central to *all* interaction: trust, apprehension, fear, defensiveness, alienation, the need to be acknowledged by others, and so on. This content augments and happily co-exists with tried-and-true rhetorical theory, the standard methodology that is the foundation for all ideas in the book.

Also, I've made use in the book of my extensive study of a central element of the human condition, *narcissism,* both favorable and unfavorable.[1] This topic, here a very light sprinkle, customarily is not included in public speaking texts. It concerns the self as a prime factor in communication: How do the speaker and listener feel about themselves? Are they self-occupied, or are they actively involved and attuned? As Burke would find, narcissism provides motivation for acts of communication. We as individuals feel a need to join with others, and thus do we attempt communication. But unfavorable narcissism, such as defensiveness (a form of self-protection arising from personal insecurity), is the enemy of unity, of communication, for it exacerbates isolation. This content belongs in the basic public speaking class, for the self and its status are central factors in acts of communication. My treatment of this phenomenon is rather subtle, I feel, and I trust it will be welcomed as a useful perspective on communication.

Note also the discussion of the "good audience" in Chapter Eight, on persuasion, and Chapter Ten, on listening. Favorably self-interested, the good audience seeks its own ends and constrains speakers in positive ways. The good audience is the model of a mature audience—purposeful, fair, free, demanding, alert, and productively responsive to a speaker's exertions of influence.

Also, I would like my colleagues to take a good look at Chapter Nine, on critical thinking. I'm pleased with it. You'll note a couple of unusual features. First is the focus on critical thinking in *communication,* on participants' *thinking together.* Second, the chapter covers, and moves well beyond, ordinary formal reasoning and cognitive structures, getting into personal and emotional bases of problems and fallacies in thinking. The *human self* is made central here, showing how excessive self-interest and ordinary human narcissism can be counter-productive, threatening critical thinking.

Other features of *Speaking in America* include a recognition of the past and current importance of public speaking in the building of our country, and an appreciation of our democratic heritage and cultural richness as they are inextricably connected to opportunity and adequacy in speechmaking. Found in the book are many model outlines, both for speeches and small group discussion. I feel good about the chapter on organization, a basic and vital matter in public speaking instruction. The chapter on listening and the section on transitions, also very important matters in speech communication, give me similar satisfaction. It should be mentioned, also, that the approach to delivery is holistic, adhering to the view that presentation is essentially tied to content. As said by that wise teacher of us all, James Albert Winans, the final composition of a speech takes place at the moment of utterance.

---

[1] See Harold Barrett, *Rhetoric and Civility: Human Development, Narcissism, and the Good Audience* (Albany: State University of New York Press, 1991).

In each of the model speech outlines of Chapters Six, Seven, and Eight, you'll see that bracketed information is given to indicate the placement of supporting materials in the speech. This information is placed *outside the outline.* Thus outlines are kept "clean," comprised of premises only, while revealing the location of materials.

The Glossary is designed to be clear and comprehensive, a particularly useful tool.

One of the most important messages that I want to convey to colleagues is that I know that no book can satisfy each individual instructor's thinking on sequencing of chapters. I have found that opinions diverge greatly on that issue. Thus, I have worked to allow for instructor options in sequencing student experience. Most professionals seem to agree on adoption of a progressively challenging structure and a "one thing at a time" approach, as I would call it. Remember the lesson of progymnasmata? But one instructor will do it this way, another will do it that way. Though I have my own favorite step-by-step pattern, I have been ever mindful of the need here to accommodate differing instructional strategies, to maintain modular integrity of the chapters. Instructors can use them in an order of their choice.

I've also prepared an instructor's manual. In it are many exercises, suggestions and aids, sample syllabi and class schedules, discussion questions, test questions, and other helpful items.

Finally, I've made a conscientious effort to create a book that is both useful and appealing to the student, readable as well as reliable in theory. The theory is seasoned and sound, and I believe the handling of it here will help in making it accessible to readers. *To write for the student* has been my constant goal.

In making decisions on content and form, I had questions that required consultation with people who have special knowledge or expertise. The following persons helped in one way or another: Rhoda L. Agin, John E. Baird, Denise L. Brady, James V. Carroll, Rueling Chuang, Tam Duc Do, Elizabeth A. Ginno, John C. Hammerback, Jean Holzman, Barbara P. Kwan, Nancy Lau, Sally K. Murphy, Hibbatul M. K. Omar, Daniel S. Prentice, Anne Pym, David Rojas, Jack A. Samosky, Linda Schneider, John Sepolin, Jon Sharp, Shellie Stauber-Haygood, Florence A. Stronck, Tracy Thomas, Charlene B. Tompkins, Charles Wanjie, Kathleen Wong, and Eric Woodford. Also, I must give blanket thanks to my students in Speech 1000, scores each year, who served unwittingly as teachers of the teacher.

Gale S. Auletta has influenced the ethos of the book more than she knows, with her knowledge, enthusiasm, and dedication to the facilitation of communication among people of all backgrounds and cultures.

Karen L. Fritts, characteristically generous with findings from her years of successful experience, provided innumerable suggestions for strengthening the chapter on small group discussion. I hope she likes the finished product.

Margaret S. Morrisson, "Maggie," gave information and inspiration that resulted in the chapter on critical thinking of which I am proud.

Ruth Gilbert, Jake Scott, and Ed Wende shared useful editorial counsel at important points in my writing. I appreciate their support.

Several reviewers wrote extensive reports on strengths and weaknesses of the manuscript as first written. I gave close attention to all of their criticisms, finding them of exceptional value. I am indebted to these good colleagues: Norma Landa Flores, Golden West College, Huntington Beach, California; JoyLynn H. Reed, Saint Edward's University, Austin, Texas; Miriam Zimmerman, University of San Francisco, San Francisco, California; Rebecca Johns, Weber State University, Ogden, Utah; Lee Tiberghien, Garden City Community College, Garden City, Kansas.

Thanks, too, to that other group of stalwart professionals, those at Harcourt Brace Jovanovich. I'd like to thank my editors: Janet Wilhite, Kelly Riche, and Terri House. Many thanks also to Karen E. Bolin, Mary Pat Donlon, Ken Dunaway, Melinda Huff, Laura Lashley, and Lili Weiner.

As always, Carol has been there with me, from the earlier days when I pushed a No. 2 lead pencil across page upon page of legal-size yellow pads or pounded the old faithful Underwood, to now, as I peck at a compatible computer's keys. She's the alpha and the omega of everything, a self-contained editorial department, a one-person support group, a grand partner in life-sustaining communication.

Harold Barrett

TABLE OF CONTENTS

SPEAKING IN AMERICA

I

SPEAKERS AND AUDIENCES: UNITY AND COMMUNICATION

1

★ **LOOKING AHEAD** ★

1. What does it mean to say that difference and distance between speaker and audience motivate communication?

2. Why has speaking in America been so important?

3. What careers involve speaking?

4. Why do we remember great speakers?

5. Why do we think of everyone as a speaker?

6. What part do communicators of diverse backgrounds play in the building of America?

7. What does it mean to say that all of us have a culture?

8. Why should speakers learn about audiences?

9. How are accommodation and civility related to communication?

Below is a condensed version of an interesting discussion that took place in a speech communication class recently.

Bud: Sure, I know that people in the United States have many different personal interests, lifestyles, and cultures. That's OK. Just let them go their way, and I'll go mine.

Rena: That's a broad-minded attitude, Bud. But the problem is that doing things in this country means we've got to work together. We have to *communicate*.

Bud: Nobody says we don't need to communicate. It's that I don't see any particular difficulty in people talking to each other, *whoever* they are. Hey, just do it!

Jamal: Well, communication isn't that easy. To bring it off, we have to understand who we're talking to and have a real feeling for where they're coming from.

Gilbert: That's right. We all have our own sets of feelings and priorities and ways of acting. And many of these things come out of our backgrounds and whether we're male or female, of this ethnic group or that, and so forth.

Rena: After all, communication is sharing, back and forth. It depends on knowing each other and connecting that way. There's no other way to do it.

Bud: Well, I do want more unity in this country. I'm for that.

AUDIENCES AND COMMUNICATIVE MOTIVATION

The above discussion is about *audiences,* and it previews a subject of enormous importance to us. **When communicating with others, our diversity is a major factor.** Whether small or great, difference and distance exist between speaker and audience. Meeting that condition is the essential challenge in communication. According to widely accepted theory on communication, our *separateness* is a condition that we humans cannot tolerate in our lives and which we spend tremendous effort to overcome. The need is so pressing that **bridging the gaps that set us**

apart is the prime motivation in communication. If we had no differences among ourselves, we would not be motivated to seek unity.[1] Such is the most basic motive of every speaker, whether talking at a neighborhood gathering or to a group of strangers across town. It's not too much to say that no speaker ever achieved his or her purpose with an audience without finding a way to meet difference and distance, without discovery of some kind of unity, some basis for sharing thoughts and feelings. Even members of our own families have their separate ways and ideas, and we need to remember these particular features as we talk with them. Since speech communication is an exchange between one person and *others,* it's as much about audiences and their characteristics as it is about speakers and methods. In the process of communication, both speaker and audience are primary factors. **The quest for unity between them, which we call identification, is the one absolute in our communicative experience.** It's a true *imperative,* a ''command'' that cannot be denied. This truth of human interaction provides the underlying spirit and theory for the beginning and ending of this chapter, as well as a practical perspective for the entire book. It's good theory.

A COUNTRY OF SPEAKERS

Before returning to the basic theory of communication, let's set up a perspective on the prevalence of speaking. For example, it's important to remind ourselves that the United States is a country of speakers and always has been. Think of any area of national life and you'll find speakers and

listeners—people involved with others in communication. Legislatures and law courts, school boards, and city councils are obvious examples. There are the many and varied clubs, places of worship, classrooms, and occasions for ordinary decision making. Add to these situations all sorts of formal and informal gatherings that you know about. **Talk is everywhere. We believe in it, and we use it freely.**

BUILDING THROUGH TALK

We're a busy country, always building things. We build by bulldozing dirt, pouring concrete, and linking steel girders. And we build by talking. It takes lots of talk to develop a policy or plan a program. What do we ever accomplish without people speaking to people? **It takes speech to get things started and speech to carry them out.** In a real sense, talking is a part of social architecture, a basic and necessary element in the structuring of a community. It's a central and vital function in the conduct of all daily affairs and in the achievement of social good.

What are the goals of these active speakers in our society? They vary, of course. In addition to all those who talk to get their plans adopted or lay the groundwork for various projects, there are those who want specific changes in the community, such as the enactment of new laws or the establishment of new policies or systems. There are campaigners with advertising programs to carry out or candidates to elect. Consider also the

César Chávez, president of the United Farm Workers union, speaks to members in 1979.

participants in social movements. Countless men and women exist in the vanguard of events, endlessly talking, spending energy and time promoting rights, benefits, and programs.

Professions and Careers

All professions and careers make use of talking. First to come to mind are law, politics, teaching, sales, the clergy, business management, investment consulting, and public relations. But that's just a start. Former students reporting back tell me about the many opportunities for using oral communication skills in their work. Here are a few of their careers, all requiring competence in speaking: flight operations director, mental health association coordinator, school district business manager, head reference librarian, physician, administrator of a disabled student services center, personnel director, field consultant for a large restaurant chain, case systems administrator, corporation executive, head of a human services department, account representative, police officer, coordinator of a science and engineering department, educational director of a large hospital, conductor of assertiveness workshops, and radio and television broadcaster. **In the building of a career, whether that takes one to the lab, out in the field, or to the office, speaking ability is essential.**

GREAT SPEAKERS

While recognizing that speaking is prevalent, we ought to set some of it apart from the ordinary. What about the great speakers? History books give special note to a few. Though their moments in time have vanished and their excited audiences have dispersed, some of them said things that led to significant betterment in human life. Their speaking, often a courageous act, resulted in extended freedoms and an improved lot for all. Occasionally a speaker has come along whose words have become acknowledged as great and worth repeating or preserving. These are the speakers and speeches we study in school and want our children to remember. We quote those with great ideas that have served nations and contributed to the development of civilization. In the United States, we think of the speeches of Abraham Lincoln, Franklin D. Roosevelt, Susan B. Anthony, and others. Among those remembered elsewhere are José Martí of Cuba and Benito Juárez of Mexico. Simón Bolívar was a great leader and orator in South America as were Jawaharlal Nehru in India, Giuseppe Garibaldi in Italy, and Carlos P. Romulo in the Philippines. Winston Churchill, of the United Kingdom, is respected around the world for his speaking and leadership during a critical time in history—World War II. These names represent the eloquent and determined people whose speaking led to improvement of conditions in the world.

A Speech Is For Now

Very few speeches are kept and published for later generations to appreciate. That isn't surprising, for most speeches do not have relevance outside the context of their moment in time—even presidential addresses. **A speech isn't created for posterity, but for a current occasion and particular need.** When a speaker thinks beyond the immediate purpose, he or she often fails—the result of neglecting the primary goal. Good speeches are functional and designed to accomplish goals. Rarely are they remembered or cherished as words of literature.

AMERICAN SPEAKERS

Some early builders and speakers of America were native to the continent. Sequoyah the Cherokee and Satanta the Kiowa were both fine orators. Many others came from across the Atlantic Ocean. Historians tell of their accomplishments and those of their descendants. Among the names of American speakers with European ancestry are Adams (several of them), Andrew Jackson, Daniel Webster, Jacob Riis, Lucy Stone, Carl Shurz, Woodrow Wilson, Margaret Sanger, Fiorello LaGuardia, Eleanor Roosevelt, Bernard Baruch, John F. Kennedy, Paul Sarbanes, and Zbigniew Brzezinski.

The African continent also contributed builders of our nation. Some of these were former slaves, but most were their offspring, the sons and daughters of people brought in bondage to America beginning in the seventeenth century: Frederick Douglass, Harriet Tubman, Booker T. Washington, W. E. B. DuBois, Martin Luther King, Jr., Shirley Chisholm, Barbara Jordan, and Benjamin Hooks. People of numerous other cultures added their voices: Larry Itliong, César Chávez, José Angel Gutiérrez, Reies Tijerina, Jamake Highwater, Ralph Nader, Mike Masaru Masaoka, Daniel Inouye, Patsy Mink, and Hiram Fong. The speaking and building symbolized by these individuals constitute significant parts of the history of this nation.

> *E pluribus unum:*
> *One out of many.*
>
> *Motto of the United*
> *States of America*

Ordinary Speaking

While honoring the great ones, let's keep in mind that the speaking required in the shaping and maintenance of society cannot be handled by a select list of famous personalities. Ordinary citizens must be responsible for the bulk of activity. **Many voices are needed, many talkers to initiate and propose, meet and confer, advocate, stimulate, and persuade.**

Of course, some ordinary speaking may seem trivial or of scant value to society. But who knows what purpose a given speech may serve. Perhaps it provides the speaker with emotional release. Goals and results vary, and sometimes we can't be certain about them.

Moreover, we must acknowledge that some speaking is undesirable, deceitful or prejudiced and against the social good. A person's speaking frequently reveals personal intent and respect for others—or lack of it. But what can we do about seemingly irresponsible speaking? Suppress it? What of the nation's commitment to free speech? What are the criteria of good and bad speaking? And who is to decide?

Ordinarily, the immediate audience decides. Regardless of your position on the issues inherent in this discussion, one conclusion appears certain: **Responding to the messages of others is one of our chief roles in this society.** The reason is that in a democracy, all of us are speakers, even when we are silent. Saying nothing may be taken as saying "yes."

COMMUNICATING IN A DIVERSE AMERICA ▬▬▬▬▬▬▬▬

Though I've spent much time here discussing speechmaking of the past, it can be said truthfully that **never before has speaking been more important in America.** All people—in the community, within the family, and at work—have messages to be heard. As speakers and audiences, these communicators differ in background, habit, age, interest, race, physical characteristics, sexual orientation, and gender. They live in every part of the country, in all neighborhoods and cities, and they represent all philosophies and points of view. It's clear that in our time, people place high value on the need to have a voice. **This speaking up and taking part involves persons of all cultures, origins, and walks of life.**

As I read the daily newspaper of my own region, I am reminded of the diversity of community leaders. In the town to the south, the mayor is of Asian-Pacific ancestry. The town next to that has an Irish American mayor. In the larger city to the north, the mayor is African American. Three different races are represented on the board of supervisors in my county. Hispanic citizens are active at all levels of government, local and state. All of these people make public addresses, participate in round-table discussions, appear on radio and television broadcasts, and contact others in purposeful conversation. They use speech to advance their causes and work for the welfare of the community. This is speechmaking in America today.

ALL OF US HAVE A CULTURE

Sociologists and other experts observe that our particular cultural attributes are evident in our characteristic patterns of behavior, our clusters of beliefs, concepts, and values.

Our Democratic Heritage

A most notable part of the general culture in the United States is our democratic heritage, the bedrock of values and equitable procedures for conducting affairs of the nation. Traceable to the beliefs and experiences of the earliest newcomers on this continent and to their forebears, this cultural treasure provides the foundations of justice and the principles for working together responsibly and humanely. Without this solid base of rights, privileges, and processes of fair play, civil and equitable interaction would be impaired. Indeed, respecting our democratic heritage is a chief source of hope for communicative success in this country. It can facilitate our ability to relate to others and to cross the boundaries of individual identities. As daily newspapers remind us, many nations are experiencing difficulty in reaching solutions to ethnic and social conflict. To some degree, they are experiencing communication problems! If we, as citizens of the United States, can acknowledge the democratic institutions of our common culture and use them effectively and wisely, they will give us creative power in learning to communicate better.

Family Culture

More specifically, **each person's culture is reflected in individual families and reference groups, where he or she learns different ways of doing and saying.** Some of these practices show up as social norms and values—lessons on right and wrong behavior, distinct ways of celebrating holidays, or traditions at the dinner table. As one of my students said, "My family life has given me my culture." How do you define your culture?

A Nation of Immigrants

Some of the features of our individual cultures we can trace back to other lands. As John F. Kennedy observed, we are "a nation of immigrants." With the exception of Native Americans, everybody has roots traceable to other lands. A sampling of students in my speech communication classes this year suggests the great cultural diversity of the United States. Of course, many have ties to Europe, though some are so distant that they do not acknowledge them. As one of them put it, "I'm plain American, I guess." Others in my classes are more specific, naming their backgrounds as Vietnamese, Chinese, Japanese, Korean, Filipino, Hispanic, African, or Middle-Eastern. On my class rosters I find these names: Jensen, Nguyen, Rosenberg, Becker, Vu, Asano, Kim, Koutsoukis, DeCaro, Boorsma, Schwartz, Pedersen, Kitchel, Carman, Holzman, Archer, Bray, O'Conner, Chuang, Martinez, Thomas, Padua, Tran, Lam, Rivera, England, Nabavi, Stauber-Haygood, and Wanjie. They represent all continents of the world. **Cultural identity is a part of being *somebody* in America.**

   The names I have mentioned are those of the current wave of builders, the ones who will lead social, political, educational, and economic developments in the decades ahead. They are names of people studying speech communication, which will serve them well. As they build careers and community programs, they will be speaking, just like Americans of centuries past. Topics may differ from those of prior generations, but most of the issues will be the same as they always have been. They will be related to problem solving and getting the job done, to matters relating to taxation, civil rights, community welfare, marketing and production, negotiations of labor and management, power of the media, family problems, war and peace, and so forth. Most basic issues of human existence continue over time. My speech students may not be aware of it at every waking minute, but they are indeed getting ready to take those important places out there, outfitting themselves with the arts and skills of oral communication and the methods of informing, persuading, and discussing. They'll have ample opportunity to use them.

LEARNING ABOUT AUDIENCES

Students of speech communication may not initially realize that **a fundamental goal of a speech class is to learn about audiences**. This is a rare and valuable opportunity, as you shall see in class interaction and in discussions on audience in subsequent chapters. In communication, it's as important to know listeners as it is to know theory. That's a fact. Neither speaker nor listener acts alone. Communication occurs only when participants work together in a transaction. As noted by Aristotle, Greek writer on speechmaking, and as confirmed by others since his time, the listener ultimately judges the acceptability of a message. Thus, the audience makes the decisions in our democracy and establishes public policy. **When freedom flourishes, speaking flourishes, because listeners with the right of choice have the power.** Free persons make critical choices on whose ideas to believe and which plans to adopt.

Here's a truth of democratic participation: Knowing and respecting the people—appreciating the audience—is the first necessary criterion for success in speaking and achieving good works in the community.

Diversity of Audience

Successful speakers always have recognized differences in background and orientation in their audiences. In our own day, it's our responsibility to dedicate ourselves even more to understanding the diverse others with whom we speak, to accept a wide variety of cultural expression, and to relate to others with appreciation of that variety. First of all, it's the right thing. Second, it's practical, for varied are the people with whom we will be communicating for the rest of our lives. Sincere accommodation to others leads to a return in kind and to a genuine meeting of minds. I've seen it happen over and again, as you have, surely.

While honoring our different selves is a necessary act, effectiveness in communication comes from emphasizing commonalities: values, ideals, hopes and dreams, behaviors, and other things shared. Relating and closing the gaps requires being accommodative and adaptable. **How else can we achieve real community—cohesion and unity with one or** many—than through communication that is both purposeful and respectful.

BEING WITH AUDIENCES: ACCOMMODATION AND CIVILITY

In general terms, accommodation means interacting cooperatively and agreeably with people as they become our audiences. In specific terms, it means not allowing ourselves to be distracted by the accent of a communicator whose native language isn't English. It means bearing with others as they struggle to make sense of American values and behaviors. It means being patient with a person who stutters or one whose physical impairment necessitates slower movement. **Interacting with others, regardless of differences, often requires much empathy—feeling how they feel. It requires civility.** Civility is a kind of maturity, shown in one's capacity to respond to others as people with distinct and valid personalities, needs, interests, and values. Some key attributes of civility when relating to audiences are courtesy, knowledge, awareness, support, respect, responsibility, patience, and reciprocity.

Necessarily, *unity* is the aim of communicators. That truth pervades the writings of wise thinkers on communication from the ancient Greeks to modern Americans. Without unity of speaker and listener, a message will not be shared, whether to a single person in private conversation or to a group in a college classroom. No precept is more basic in communication theory. Sharing and bringing people together is what communication is all about. Consequently, the theory of this book rests on the conviction that a diverse people, representing variety in color, ancestry, physical condition, religion, moral value, and gender, as well as in personal, political, and social orientation, can together discover the means of getting along with one another. **Understanding leads not only to mutual appreciation but also to creation of grounds for making contact with others—the bases for communicating effectively.** We are in this society together. That's a fact we cannot deny. But we do have options, which is what the study of communication teaches: exploring useful theory, learning about ourselves and others, and discovering how to make good communication choices. We cannot deny social necessity. So perhaps we should ready ourselves for living well and relating well in this dynamic society so as to enjoy the best of it—together.

LOOKING BACK

Speakers are to be counted among the builders of America and of civilization. Included are great orators and ordinary talkers. In the many eras of our nation's growth and development, these speakers have represented all backgrounds and identities.

We are a land of numerous cultures and varied individuals, and as we relate to one another, each of us stands on the ground of our own particular culture and individual nature. This is a fact. It's also a promise of potential effectiveness in speaking with others and enrichment of communicative relationships.

Thus arises the great challenge: to know and be who we are while knowing and accepting others as they are, as we work together to discover *common ground*. This common ground provides the basis for the unity and accommodation necessary for effective, satisfying communication.

NOTE

1. This is the theory of identification, as developed by Kenneth Burke. See Phillip K. Tompkins, *Communication as Action: An Introduction to Rhetoric and Communication* (Belmont: Wadsworth, 1982), 43–49. If you wish to explore further the theory of motivation for communication, consult the works of Kenneth Burke directly (*A Rhetoric of Motives* and others) or commentaries on his writings. Your instructor may have specific articles or books to recommend on this fascinating subject.

FOUNDATIONS OF SPEAKING

II

STUDYING SPEECH COMMUNICATION

2

One day just before class, Tonya was talking to herself, trying to solve a difficult personal problem. In this important "interior" conversation, two of her inner selves, Protective Priscilla and Gutsy Gertrude, were debating.

Protective Priscilla:	Let's drop this speech class! Why suffer for three months?
Gutsy Gertrude:	Hey, we have to take it eventually, Priscilla.
Protective:	But, I'm afraid.
Gutsy:	Of what?
Protective:	You know, being looked at up there and feeling awkward. Everyone else is *so* good. I wasn't made to be a *public speaker*.
Gutsy:	Now listen, there are two things to know about us. First, we can do it. The instructor has seen thousands like us make it through, and we're not all that unique. Second, at the end of the term we'll feel great about hanging in there.
Protective:	You're a real cheerleader, aren't you!

The question of fear in speaking is something to be faced in a speech class. Has it been on your mind? We'll return to the topic later on, but first let's see what it means to study speech communication.

SPEECH COMMUNICATION: TWO DIMENSIONS

Speech communication is the theory and practice of people talking with others. We will focus on the topic in two intertwined and compatible ways, and neither should be neglected.

1. *The practical and formal:* the discipline, the rhetorical theory of discovering ideas, selecting among them, and supporting them; arranging ideas; and using appropriate language and methods of presentation.

2. *The interpersonal:* the personal and social behavior of people and the choices available to them as they speak to audiences. Involved in the interactive process are trust, credibility, respect for feelings and needs, self-concept, role-taking, and other elements.

Naming these dimensions shows the interdependence of rhetorical and interpersonal principles in communication, with the second augmenting the first. The characteristic theme of both is people affecting people. This public-speaking book stresses oneness in these principles and regards them as harmonious elements.

SPEAKING: SOCIAL ACTION

Necessarily, our lives are tied to those of others. In our daily existence, as we work, learn, and play, we follow our social sense and participate as members of an organized society. Functioning socially, we affect others in various ways: a father laughing at his daughter's funny Halloween costume, a girl kissing a boy, an alert driver dimming the headlights of his car, a politician deciding to run for office. All are examples of people involved in social acts. Speaking is also a social act, one of the most common and significant. **People use speech to do things *with* people and sometimes *to* people.** An employer may use speech to acknowledge a deserving worker; a parent may console an unhappy child; a legislator may induce a senate to vote for a clean air bill. What we say does affect others. "Sticks and stones will break my bones, but words will never hurt me," shouts little Terry bravely. But Terry is wrong, for words *can* hurt.

And Linda says to Don, "Nothing that you say, only what you do, will bring us together." She, too, is wrong, because saying *is* doing.

Roles

In relating to others through speech, we assume many roles. Sometimes we may play the role of father or teacher, mediator, comedian, rebel, psychologist, child or lawyer. Parts of ourselves developed over the years become strategies for communication: ways to be effective with others. We all have an array of roles that we choose or seem to fall into in specific situations that will depend on who we are, who the others are, and our immediate purposes. What are some of the roles that are useful to you in communication? Some people find themselves at their communicative best as advisor or teacher. Others assume roles as supporter, activist, advocate, questioner, or dissenter. You may discover that one benefit of speech training is further development of communication roles; breadth is of great value in interaction with others. **Whatever the role, to speak is to affect others. It's social action.**

SPEECH COMMUNICATION: A DYNAMIC PROCESS

The act of speaking with people is a *dynamic* and ongoing interpersonal *process*. As such, there may be intricate and sometimes unpredictable conditions that involve the ever-changing and fascinating behavior of people. Oral communication is never static, and it's so complex that to discuss it is to oversimplify the process. Nevertheless, we will review certain basic elements, to provide a foundation for later consideration.

When one person greets another, the sender of the greeting, the speaker, encodes a cordial message. The speaker puts language symbols together, using words, vocal expressions, and perhaps physical movement. The symbols may be words such as "Good morning," a warm voice, and a wave of the hand. The receiver, understanding the symbols, decodes or interprets the message. But the interaction doesn't stop there; the receiver will usually make a response, also with words, vocal expressions, and possibly physical movement. The response of the receiver is called *feedback:* the message being sent back, the other person's reaction. It's the facial expression that implies "I don't understand," the lowered head that indicates "I'm sorry," or the little word "Wow!" that may stand for "What a nice thing to do!" Feedback lets the speaker know if the audience understood, and it gives cues on what to say or do next.

In giving feedback, even with grunts or nods, receivers become senders. The communication goes back and forth, sending and receiving, messages sent and messages sent back, on and on. It *is* an extraordinarily lively process.

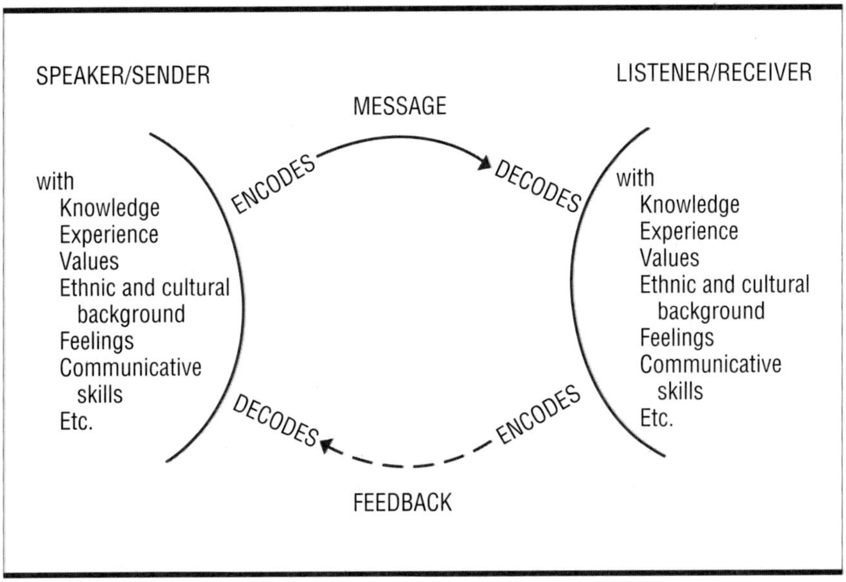

Figure 2-1

The communication process

Figure 2-1 *The communication process*

People send their messages and receive feedback in three ways: **verbally,** with words; **vocally,** with utterances of the voice like "Hm-mm," "Eee!," or "Sss!" and dozens of other expressions that cannot be reproduced with our regular alphabet; and **visually,** through gestures, body movements, winks of an eye, smiles, and other physical action.

All three modes are vital to communication; all carry message content, that is, they say something, and they have a positive or negative influence on the final effect of the interaction.

Communication involves much more than the use of words and sounds. **All behavior contributes to the act of shaping messages.** Sometimes, as the old saying goes, "Actions speak louder than words"; that is, nonverbal acts, such as a twinkling of the eyes, may be more powerful than verbal ones. Therefore, in relating to others it helps to be aware of all parts of a message: a hand gesture that serves as punctuation, a sad look that contradicts the happy words, extending an arm into the air that communicates joy, and so forth. Understanding requires sensitivity to all stimuli and their meanings. We will examine nonverbal communication more fully in other chapters.

Variables

Effectiveness in communication depends on any number of conditions: the knowledge of the listener and speaker; their various experiences; social values; ethnic or cultural background; feelings of the moment; verbal, vocal, and visual skills in communication; and other variables.

Figure 2-1 is a graphic representation of the process as it's initiated. It can be used to explain interactions ranging from public speaking to conversation. The basic ingredients are the same in all speech communication. Note the six key variables that may affect the sending and receiving of messages.

One variable is *knowledge:* How much does the speaker know about the subject at hand, how much does the listener know, and what knowledge do they share?

Similar questions can be asked about the variables of *experience, values, ethnic and cultural background, communicative skills,* and *feelings.* For example, how many listeners have *experienced* a soccer game? What are their views on the general worth or *value* of the game? Do their *feelings* play a part in their reactions to the subject? Many people who grew up in Europe, Latin America, and other countries are as devoted to soccer as Americans are to football. *Cultural background* influences interests and behaviors, and *ethnic background*—race, native language, family history or features—is also a primary influence. For example, in America there are now great numbers of people whose first language is not English.

These and other variables affect the sending and receiving of messages. Basic questions in communication are what relevant experiences, values, backgrounds, and feelings do speakers and listeners share and what are the differences? As we interact with one another, how are these differences met?

Communication skills refer to the fundamentals of effective speaking and listening, for example, skill in organizing ideas or use of language that is respectful to both genders. Various skills are vital in the process, of course; a message may never be communicated if people are untrained in communication.

The *Etc.* on both sides of the model covers "everything else"—all other variables, for example, the physical or psychological: a physical disability, hearing loss, or mood of depression can be factors affecting speaking and listening. There are many conditions at work in the process of communication.

Noise

Communication is a demanding process, and failure may occur at any point. **Any problem or condition that appears as an obstacle to communication is called *noise,*** a term borrowed from scientific communication theory. Insufficient knowledge, multiple and unreconciled perspectives on events, conflicting values, ethnic and cultural backgrounds, feelings, and experiences may all enter in as noise. Of course noise may be actual physical noise, such as a low-flying airplane, or it may be less obvious, perhaps a listener's dislike of a topic, the threat of a controversial proposal or unusual lifestyle, a speaker's lack of interest or withholding of vital information. Noise refers to any physical or psychological condition that interferes with communication, and it may be caused by the size of room, conditions of climate, or the time of day. It may arise out of a social, religious, political, or educational reference, or the context of the occasion. All possible influences must be taken into account when considering factors that affect communication. With such a view, one can begin to understand the interactive features and complexity of oral communication.

THE HUMAN CONDITION

A number of scholars of rhetoric and communication, among them Kenneth Burke, believe that interactions of people are motivated by the human condition. Our messages to others are in response to the way things are in this life and because we are *individuals,* apart from others. **Our individuality arises from our distinctness, the differences that separate us**: age, gender, ethnicity, family history, and religious, moral, political, and social views—all of those variables discussed previously. Think of this diversity as you relate to members of your speech communication and other classes. Difference can foster alienation, aloneness, isolation, estrangement, or unconnectedness. These are harsh words, suggesting considerable pain, and all of us have felt it. What hurts more than not to belong, to be out of touch with people, to be on the outside? Think of the many words in the English language used to refer to this condition: gap, disunion, detachment, cut off, divorced, foreign, parted, breach, disengagement, split, division, and discord. A good thesaurus includes hundreds more.

When Denied Communication

People want to be in harmony with others; societies work vigorously to achieve that, to secure and maintain cohesion. In most societies, individual behavior that threatens cohesion is the greatest wrong, and people may be ostracized in one way or another. For serious misbehavior, convicts in prison may receive solitary confinement, be shut off from contact with others and alienated. Cadets in some military schools impose the "silent treatment" to punish someone for violation of a social code or rule. All of us know people who use the silent treatment against others and thereby deny them the sustenance and joy afforded by communication. "Excommunication" takes many forms. It hurts to be ignored, as we all know.

IDENTIFICATION

Again, we are different from each other; we are apart from each other, and we need each other (even at those moments when we're not able to handle human characteristics that differ from ours). Let's relate the human condition to ordinary communication and the theory of identification.

Unwilling to endure the condition of separation, people take

action to relate, to *communicate*. Speech communication is a reaching out, an act to close the distance between ourselves and others, to bridge the gaps, to unite. To succeed in communicating is to locate a base of common interest, to find ways of *identifying* with others, to discover and use foundations for *mutual* understanding and build a cooperative relationship. To communicate, it is necessary to appreciate and know as much as we can about others, their cultures and values, outlooks on life, interests and inclinations.

Furthermore, we must respect and appreciate our own identity and culture, our beliefs and feelings about things. We cannot understand the meaning of another unless it in some way relates to us. One might say that **to communicate is to find something of ourselves in our audiences, to discover, and build from, the reflections of our selves in the selves of others.** We see others in terms of our own experience; we abstract reflections of ourselves. What do we have in common, and what can we share? Those are vital questions for communicators.

In Practical Terms

Let's discuss the theory of identification in terms of practical speaking. In affecting others through the social act of speech, we seek ways to reach them, to meet them, to get together and share with them, to confirm them. Indeed, to *communicate* can be defined as "causing another or others to partake of or share in." **Speech communication is a study of the means of sharing messages and of the reciprocal influence of people that occurs in the process.** Though the messages vary in each situation, the basic process remains the same. For example, a student explains a certain theory of music to the speech class, and it will be fundamentally similar to the well-prepared lecture of the instructor. Both speakers want to be effective, influential, in sharing an informative message.

During a critical time in the nation's history, Henry Clay, in 1850, spoke before the U.S. Senate to convince colleagues that his compromise proposals should be adopted *for the good of the entire nation.* He was successful in finding ways to cause a majority to share his ideas and to be aware of the probable *common* good that would result. Similarly a group of student leaders discovered a way to show the administration and faculty of their college how parking problems might be solved. The success of the students came from their ability to demonstrate benefits to be gained by *the entire college,* and by showing that goals and interests were shared widely.

Newspapers reported the success of a young man, a college student, who, on the ledge of a high building, was able to communicate the value of living to an old man bent on suicide. Though separated by two generations, they found *something held in common.*

These are examples of useful speech employed to accomplish a purpose. They reveal an indispensable condition of communication, a shared foundation on which speaker and listener stand, for thinking and acting together. A person separated from another in idea or attitude, at a loss to find ways to connect, cannot hope to achieve communication. The essential problem is the inability to locate a basis on which minds can meet. This difficulty partly explains the obstacle to communication sometimes faced by people of different world views, of persons in different cultures, of two lovers who have drifted apart, of you and someone with whom you cannot seem to make contact. You see, speaker and listener must shape thought together. As French author Joseph Joubert once said, you cannot talk about poetry with people unless they bring a little poetry with them. **The fundamental question is, on what bases can speaker and listener identify and thereby communicate?** Most chapters of this book are planned to offer you theory, methods, and experience in answer to that question.

> *I am the shadow of the words I cast.*
>
> *Octavio Paz, novelist*

USES OF SPEECH

All of the principal uses of speech communication can be classified as either (1) speech for personal and social growth or (2) speech to get things done.

For Personal and Social Growth

"Every child is born into a life with others, and it is only in exchange with others that personal and social competence can come about."[1]

    It's only with others that we become *somebody*. Influenced by parents and other caregivers, we develop a self that will represent us in all events of our life. Processes of communication facilitate that development; regardless of gender, race, or physical attributes, the patterns of growth are shared by everyone. Moreover, our communication with those important others begins immediately at birth. From earliest infancy we send out signals in quest of self-information, seeking to know who we are and where we fit in. We interpret the signals sent back by caregivers and objects in the environment and then learn our place or status in our small world. All those with whom we interact and communicate in those first months and years provide our very first and most vital feedback. We thereby gather information regarding abilities, roles, opportunities, and potential. In exchanges with others we have choices to make in creatively shaping a self; we become a person different from all other persons. We build dimensions of the self and learn culture, establishing perceptions, verbal and nonverbal behaviors, values, and a philosophy of life. Not the least important construction is the foundation for becoming an effective and respectful communicator.

    It's no exaggeration to say that a major function in living is the pursuit of identity. The process of shaping and reshaping the self goes on and on, through social interaction and self-analysis. We develop our personal

President Abraham Lincoln

communicative roles and strategies and learn social form: how to interact successfully with other human beings. Because a major use of communication is for personal and social growth, a class in speech communication should offer useful experiences in sharpening relevant sensitivities and adding to powers of perception and empathy, in encouraging recognition and acceptance of one's unique, individual self, and in fostering an awareness of oneself in relation to others.

To Get Things Done

Speaking is appropriately viewed as a practical art and a means of accomplishing specific tasks. The history of the United States is replete with illustrations of practical people in their careers and in their political, social, and spiritual lives making frequent use of speaking. **The story of nearly every great man or woman in history is in some measure the story of purposeful speaking.** Roles of Abraham Lincoln come to mind: the backwoods politician and lawyer influencing those who were also pioneers in the land; Abe, the young legislator arguing bills in state and national assemblies; then as the stump campaigner effectively engaging the mighty Stephen A. Douglas in the famous debates that bear the names of both men; and as the president seeking in his Second Inaugural Address "a just and lasting peace among ourselves and with all nations." On all occasions, Lincoln spoke *for a purpose*. Even the memorable

Gettysburg Address is an example of practical work. Lincoln did not speak at Gettysburg just to say a few words or to set down a speech that eventually would appear in anthologies of literature. No, he was imbued with an immediate purpose, and he used speech to accomplish it. At the dedication of the Gettysburg cemetery, while the Civil War raged on, Lincoln wanted to pay homage to dead soldiers of that war and to remind the nation "that government of the people, by the people, for the people, shall not perish from the earth." His message was that the people must carry on.

Another great American who uses speech for functional ends is Thurgood Marshall. A lawyer and graduate of Howard University Law School, Marshall was prominent in the fight to abolish segregation in the public schools and in other struggles to secure civil rights for all citizens. He served as a justice of the Supreme Court from 1965 to 1991, continuing to use his speaking powers to support causes of minorities and women.

Great persons handle only a small portion of the daily speaking chores to be done. Consider all the speaking that keeps the airlines operating and helps run the Department of the Interior, the City of Atlanta, the First Methodist Church, as well as South Dakota State University and the IBM corporation. The volume of required talk is indeed astounding. That's why executives of business and other organizations say over and over again: "Skill in oral communication is prerequisite to success with us."

Speech has a purposeful, practical function: it's used to get the work done.

SPEAKING SITUATIONS

The specific situation is a constraint on the kind of communication that can occur there. The purpose of the event, level of formality, physical and psychological distance separating the participants, numbers of people present, physical setting, the structure of the event, and expectations of participants are only a few of the elements that characterize a situation. From their interpretation of each situation, speakers decide such matters as what clothes to wear, how long to talk, where to place themselves with the audience, what kind of humor to use (if any), how much personal information to disclose, and so forth. Listeners, too, have decisions to make, for example, how to respond, whether to applaud at a given point, whether it would be appropriate to leave an event before it's over, and whether to believe the speaker. **Sensitivity to features of various situations is essential for successful functioning in this society.**

This Class As Situation

The speech communication class is a situation. The people involved with you in it are a collection of individuals placed together quite arbitrarily, through the registration process. Mentally put yourself in your favorite seat in the class, and look around the room. You'll note that the individuals differ in gender, age, and ethnic identity. Though you can't know everything about them, you know that they also differ in social background, academic major, political view, religion, life-style, hopes and aspirations, and so on. Each has a distinct personality. One of the individuals is the instructor, whose purposes, cultural background, knowledge, set of values, and training will affect the experiences of everyone in the group.

Add to your analysis of the situation the room as decorated, shaped, ventilated, and arranged; the time of year and hour of day; and the textbook and other instructional materials. Include the events that take place on the occasion of your meetings, planned and unplanned, formal and informal, brief and lengthy.

Next, think about interactive activity in the class. Note the development of cohesiveness and a spirit of working together, as students get to know one another. Observe that this collection of separate individuals begins to become a group, but the interactions of this group will differ from those of other groups, for example, of chemistry, history, or English classes. While all classes across the campus have their own beneficial character, in a speech communication class the unity that occurs has a special quality: a "we're-in-this-together" feeling that works for the good of all.

The experiences in this class are different in other ways. First, a lot of the work will be oral. Certainly that's no surprise to you. Although one can learn much about communication without actually talking, full benefits of the investment of time and energy come only from the speaking experience. In this sense *one learns to speak well by speaking.*

A second distinguishing feature of the speech class is its social character. You'll have relationships with others in this "situation." You'll talk with the class and receive feedback from them in the form of ideas or direct suggestions, and you, too, will provide feedback. In short, speaking involves a direct exchange with others; it's social. The class gives you the opportunity and the reason for speaking, and it will serve you in a variety of ways as a "reflector," helping you to answer such vital questions as "Who am I?" and "How am I doing?"

A third feature, and very important one, gets right to the heart of the nature of speech communication. Speaking is *interaction with others,* not a solo performance. Speaking is not "performing," contrary to what one sometimes hears; it involves people with messages, *purposefully working together,* relating and transacting their communicative "business." It's not an exhibition by an individual person, nor is it a display for its own sake. **The tone is not "look at me"** but *"we're doing it together."*

Speech is different from other classes in another way. One speech student summed it up well when he said, "In this course you really learn more than how to be a better speaker. You have a chance to learn about people and their thoughts and experiences. By hearing them discuss their ideas, you seem to develop a greater respect and appreciation for them."

In other words, you have the opportunity to increase your sensitivity to the feelings, attitudes, and diverse backgrounds of others and become more perceptive and considerate. You learn to adapt to differences, a valuable lesson for us, individuals that we are. Such gains lead to more effective and more satisfying speaking.

OBJECTIVES

A word on objectives and expectations for the class. Wide experience of students and teachers in speech communication suggests that the following are realistic and worthwhile prospects.

1. A major objective of the class is to achieve **greater mastery of time-tested principles of speech communication**. Most of these principles are by no means new, having been formulated by great minds centuries ago and then augmented in more recent history. We have taken the theories, added to them, and interpreted them for modern use. The resulting body of rhetorical principles forms the cornerstone of practical speech communication. Among the giant theorists, all of whom have influenced the writing of this book, are the following:

Aristotle (384–322 B.C.)—Wrote the *Rhetoric,* the major work of all time on speaking, with decided significance and influence in our time.

Cicero (106–43 B.C.)—Wrote several books in which he formulated and interpreted rhetorical theories, to meet needs of his time. He was the greatest orator in Rome.

Quintilian (A.D. c.35–95)—The author of the most exhaustive work on speaking ever written, the twelve-volume *Institutes of Oratory,* that prescribes the training for speakers from infancy to old age. He was the greatest teacher in Rome.

George Campbell (1719–1796)—His *Philosophy of Rhetoric* provided new insights in speaking theory, for example, in audience psychology and analysis.

Hugh Blair (1718–1800)—A Scotsman, like Campbell, whose *Lectures on Rhetoric and Belles Lettres* was the most popular book for students of speech in nineteenth-century America.

Richard Whately (1787–1863)—British author of *Elements of Rhetoric,* also a popular text in America. Stressing logical proof and sound argument, the book continues to influence debating and argumentation to this day.

George Herbert Mead (1863–1931) and Charles Horton Cooley (1864–1929)—Americans who were among the first to determine that the self of each individual is developed in interaction with others; identity is built through communication.

James A. Winans (1872–1956)—An American who followed the concepts of psychologist William James, emphasizing the gaining and holding of attention in effective speaking; he established a norm for speaking extemporaneously.

Kenneth Burke (1897–)—An American whose writings have introduced rich dimensions into the theory of speaking, particularly in regard to the central function of identification in the process.

The Discipline of Speech Communication

Speech communication is a discipline having to do with ideas and feelings, with preparing messages and relating to audiences, with interacting purposefully and respectfully, in all types of speaking situations. It's about determining useful strategy in organization and development of ideas as one relates to an audience, and it's about responding effectively to messages. The following discusses some of the other areas relating to the principles emphasized in a speech communication class.

Language and Presentation. Principles of language and presentation are given attention in the speech class, as are skills of presentation. The language usage of most people can be improved, in the interest of more effective communication. Vocabularies can be strengthened. Distracting practices in pronunciation can be discovered and altered. In matters of language usage and speech delivery, the goal is presentation of clear and cogent thought and avoidance of distraction. Matters such as grammar, word choice, and posture are directly related to *communication of ideas;* nothing should work against that purpose.

Most people recognize that **verbal language alone is insufficient to the task of oral communication.** Messages are also sent, reinforced, or developed by bodily actions, vocal variations, and other nonverbal usages. Every apparent visible element plays some part in the process of communication: a person's appearance, including posture, clothing, jewelry, and hairstyle; facial expressions; foot movements; any object held or manipulated; and so forth. Remember, too, things that are heard. I mean words, yes, but also consider nonverbal utterances such as clicks of the tongue, groans, laughter, and vocal expressions of all kinds—or the resonation of sound-making objects and musical instruments that may be used as aids in developing ideas.

Critical thinking. This area, also tied to the study of speech communication, has become an important part of curricula in many colleges and universities across the country. It's stressed in speech classes because communication requires sound reasoning. Thinking critically helps in making appropriate decisions on selecting subjects and purposes, organizing and developing ideas, and in making other preparations for speaking.

Listening. Listening is related to critical thinking; the two processes are inseparable actually. Most people probably consider themselves good listeners, when they want to be. Although it's true that desire helps, it's also true that most untrained listeners are rather inefficient. Whether to appreciate the speech of another student, to answer the persuasive appeal of a politician, or to understand a lecture on economics, good listening is essential, and it *can* be learned.

2. Increased self-awareness as a speaker. Since speech communication involves a person relating to others, attention must be given here to some of the psychological and social factors that have bearing on the process. **Effective participation, understanding others and being understood, depends on how people think of themselves in the speech environment.** People can't be free to function to the fullest of their capabilities until they feel sufficiently comfortable with themselves in the speech setting. For example, one cautious member of a speech class had to be convinced (more accurately, she had to convince herself) that she really did belong in the "role of speaker." "This is not for me," she declared after class one day in the first week. But when she discovered that she indeed wanted to be a speaker, when she accepted the role, her speaking improved.

One goal of the class is to increase your self-awareness: sensitivity to your needs, values, and feelings that are relevant to the role. The course is designed to accomplish this, and to foster growth in coping, self-perception and confidence, independence, and respect for listeners. Everything people know about themselves and their interpersonal behaviors relates directly to communicative competence. As you gain self-knowledge, information on who you are, your status and roles, your special self, you will be more accepting of yourself, which leads to improvement in speaking with other people. The process works the other way as well: When the aptitude for communicating grows, the total self is positively affected. **Speaking is a central and vital part of the self; when a part is strengthened, the whole is strengthened.** The possibilities for expanding personal insights are exciting.

3. Increased self-assurance as a speaker. Most people feel fear in speaking, even those who may appear confident. Actually, **apprehension is a normal response that occurs when danger is perceived.** Many people, until they become confident, visualize a speaking situation as hazardous; they feel alone and unsure. Feeling uneasy and anticipating personal loss or harm, people have a tendency to withdraw or fight back in some way. This phenomenon is sometimes called the "flight or fight" option. It explains the discomfort that is experienced. Also, it may explain possible feelings of hostility toward the situation, which is mistakenly perceived to be the cause of the discomfort. Some apprehensive people become self-critical, taking their fears out on themselves.

A Defensive Response

Regardless of the way we explain it, the basic issue is self-esteem. Feeling secure leads to positive self-regard and readiness to take risks, while feeling insecure promotes defensive responses. Communication apprehension is a defensive response. Counterproductive though it may be, it's natural. How can this natural fear be approached?

Though tempted to take flight, one who knows the value of speaking skill and is determined to improve can muster the resolve *to stay and relate.* Making this choice shows a determination to face the situation, do the work and gain strength, and go through the program of planned experiences in speaking. It does take courage for many to put themselves up in front of other people. In their first speech in a speech communication class as many as half of the students are somewhat hampered by apprehension. But compare the first speech with the one presented at the end of the course, when confidence is up. What a difference!

I have never known a student to be sorry that he or she stayed on to finish the class, to stick it out.

The following are six positive and practical responses to fear and defensiveness in a speaking situation.

- *Put the speaking experience in perspective.* Some speakers find it assuring that the audience does not perceive the extent of their feelings. Though a speaker may feel out of control, that's very rarely the case. Even under great pressure, humans can control outward appearances very well. We somehow rise to the occasion and carry things off satisfactorily.

  Remember that everyone in the class probably feels some insecurity in a speaking situation, even those who claim otherwise. Your instructor is sensitive to the feelings of speakers and will do as much as possible to create a safe environment.

  Perhaps you have heard that fear is useful in keeping speakers motivated and alert. That's true. A degree of stimulation is needed to bring an adequate response to the challenge. Perceived this way, apprehension can be a source of personal power that contributes to success in communication.

- *Know and accept your role.* A major source of fear is misplaced emphasis on oneself. Speaking is *communicating,* an act involving oneself *with others.* It's an exchange of thoughts and opinions. It's not a "one-person show," nor is it an exhibition of speaking techniques. Maturity in speaking is marked by suitable purpose, knowing the needs of the audience, and using ideas and methods to create an interaction with the audience. Growth comes from taking the message and listeners more seriously than oneself. As Socrates advised, "Know thyself." In part, this means knowing "thy" role as one with a piece of work to do.

- *Choose comfortable subjects.* Select a subject that fits you. The right topic can help reduce apprehension. You'll feel more secure with a favored subject, one that you know and like. The next chapter includes more information on this matter.

- *Prepare fully.* **To achieve confidence, there's no substitute for preparation.** Knowing and "owning" the ideas of your message, and having a reliable plan for presenting them will add immeasurably to your security as a speaker. Much of the theory in this book is based on this point of view.

- *Practice your speeches.* Rehearse aloud, as though speaking to the actual audience, and for as many times as necessary to make the speech yours and comfortable to you. Additional suggestions are in Chapter Three. See also the use of speaking notes in Chapter Four.

- *Find support for your work.* After planning a speech, tell a friend, family member, or speech classmate about it. Explain your purpose, the main ideas, and how you intend to develop them. You can receive encouraging feedback with this consultation.

Talk to yourself about the speech, if no one is available. Go through the speech and stop to commend yourself on particularly promising features, and tell yourself how to strengthen any part in which you do not have confidence. Keep talking to yourself, checking elements, and supporting yourself, until you view the speech as entirely positive and all doubts are gone.

4.   **Increased personal congruence in communication.** The goal is to become more congruent, for the rewards can be very satisfying, and success in communication may depend on it. **To be congruent is to act in a way consistent with your beliefs and attitudes, that is, free to act and be as you believe.** This is an ideal well worth the effort needed to pursue it. Congruence is an internal harmony between your world view and your expression of it. It's unity of your personal components, realized when you relate to others. This topic is important because the more congruent the beliefs and feelings of an individual, the clearer and more certain communication will be with others. Because we seek greater competence in in*ter*personal relationships, one fundamental aim is to work toward a happy in*tra*personal condition, being "together with oneself." Trying to match experience with an awareness of the experience is the test of congruence. Through speech instruction, you can sharpen self-perception, achieve greater consistency in behavior, and eliminate ambiguity or contradictions in internal orientation and external expression.

Check Yourself

Being congruent is acting in accord with the way you view yourself. It's presenting yourself and your ideas clearly and directly, a kind of personal honesty. For example, should you say "Thank you" at the end of a speech? I don't think so, except when a group has provided speaking time as a favor to you. Should you apologize for some "weakness" in your speech? Would doing so be congruent behavior on your part? I doubt it. If you are a native of a foreign country and have an accent, should you be ashamed? Of course not! The same advice applies to most dimensions of your identity. In fact, **acceptance of who you are is a positive act and a definite source of power in communication**. Think about it!

Opportunities to test congruence will appear frequently in the speech class. For example, when choosing a subject for a speech, you may ask, "Is this subject really appropriate for me? How do I feel about it?" Or if you're tempted to use a speech from a magazine that is ready-made, ask yourself, "Does this choice accurately depict me? Is it consistent with my self-concept? What good would using this speech do for me?" On other occasions you may decide to adopt a certain voice pattern, or to be open in expressing your opinion about some social issue or to be silent and safe. Self-checking, asking and answering such questions, can lead to harmony between self and action—and to greater congruence.

Trust

Congruence leads to better communication with audiences. People who are able to function consistently with their beliefs and values relate better with people. Interaction is more productive when we allow others to experience ourselves as we believe ourselves to be. **As self-confidence and trust grow, people are able to engage with others openly and less defensively.** Trust reduces anxiety and creates more satisfying communicative interactions. For most people, the growth process is gradual, but it's something we must attend to continually.

As trust increases and distractions appear less often, listening abilities are strengthened. A person who is not threatened by constructive criticism, one who can *listen* to suggestions, may learn from other people. With less attention given to defending behavior, more effort can be directed toward communication, to solving problems in preparing a speech or setting up a discussion.

Speech students can test their perceptions of self and others, derive security from appreciating their capabilities, and realize that they can make successful choices when sharing their ideas with others. Major steps in improving the speaker-audience relationship are self-awareness and self-acceptance. They lead to congruence, the building of trust, and a readiness to confidently engage other people.

Remembering Our Social Nature

We can't forget our social existence. We are communal beings, and we are of at least one culture. To function satisfactorily and aim for a good life, we put ourselves into a variety of societies. We belong to family units, clubs, interest groups, and religious organizations; we put ourselves in a sizeable number of less intimate, ever-varying social locales. Belonging is a big thing in our lives.

"No man is an island," declared John Donne. At least no one *wants* to be an island, to be alone. People are motivated to connect with others. How can we relate satisfactorily in this world full of people? How can we understand others and be understood by them? By communication. **Communication can topple the walls that separate people and prepare**

the way for respect and understanding. There's an urgent need today for better communication among people. That's a major reason for this class.

5. Added general education. This important objective is relevant here because it starts in the speech communication class. I refer to the general education that's useful in living and working: a strengthening of the processes of reasoning, testing intellectual and critical powers, undergoing the rigors of handling ideas, and similar mental disciplines. Methods learned in speech have applicability in other areas of daily life. For example, speech communication students report that problem-solving methods learned in class were useful outside of class, that the pattern of organizing ideas for speeches worked well in writing papers, and methods of evaluating evidence and selecting supporting materials proved invaluable. One former student said, "The plan for structuring speeches was a big help in writing essays. My grades in English show it!" Testing ideas that are learned in speech class is a personal asset that can serve almost anywhere. Admittedly, preparing speaking assignments is hard work, but the dividends are great, not only immediately but later, when training in speech communication is put to use.

Another enhancement of general education is called the "cosmopolitan dimension." **While interacting in the multicultural classroom, listening to new ideas and fresh perspectives, students have a marvelous opportunity to expand their personal scope and breadth, to gain a special kind of maturity.** To be cosmopolitan is to be wise in the ways of the world. "Cosmopolitan" suggests an attitude of confidence and security, a willingness to share in the richness of the minds of others. Seeking dialogue with men and women, younger and older, of different orientations and physical conditions, with a myriad of customs, patterns of behavior, professional interests, and philosophies is the opposite of being parochial and narrow. **To be cosmopolitan is to be unafraid of the unfamiliar and to value diversity.** Such sophistication is one basis for joyful human interaction and true general education—a questing for unity while confidently welcoming variety.

Achieving the Objectives

The objectives of the speech communication class are demanding. They require thought, work, and commitment to self-improvement. In this regard, there are some key questions to ask that arise out of the experience of hundreds of students in speech communication and from the thinking of many instructors. Consideration of them will help you make the most of your efforts in this class.

Questions About You   1.   How can you make the most of the opportunity? Consider your purposes and interests in the class. What do you seek here? Are your expectations reasonable, fair and realistic? How can you take advantage of the available experiences, sharing your

thoughts and feelings when opportunities arise? Answering these questions will help you create a useful perspective for advancement.

The successful application of any principle is based on knowledge of it. This is especially relevant in speech communication. Careful study of subject matter leads to more successful speaking. The question "Which should be emphasized, theory or practice?" is not often debated among scholars of communication. **Principle and practice are essential in this kind of learning.** They are interdependent.

You will have definite responsibilities in the speech class. For example, there will be reading and speaking assignments and student participation in class discussions. Fundamentally, your job is to assimilate the theory and put it to practice. Yet beyond that obligation is your participation in an exciting adventure, if you'd care to look at it that way. The idea of adventure suggests risk, risks in relating to others, when one dares to involve oneself in new communicative experience. But the rewards far outweigh the risks both in the course and in the years ahead.

2. How should you react to comments on your work? Criticism is a vital part of a course in speech communication. Your work will be criticized, and perhaps you will be expected to offer criticism on the work of other students.

Criticism is like a coin; it has two sides and may refer either to strengths or to points needing improvement. We tend to think of criticism as only negative, whereas criticism can be positive and constructive. It's something we all need, helpful feedback on how we're doing. Your work may be criticized in several ways, either by the direct comments of the instructor in class or by written suggestions. If the instructor analyzes your work orally, the goal may be to help teach the entire class, to draw attention to a feature of your speaking from which others can learn. When the instructor talks about the speaking of another student, some of the references may apply to your work as well. **Learning from the experience of others is one of the benefits of the class.** You may have an opportunity to have your work criticized by other class members. On these occasions you'll have a chance to learn something about communication.

Comments on your speaking should be positive, designed to further your development. It's natural for people to resent criticism of their work, especially when they have made a full and sincere effort, yet, any human product can be improved, and good criticism makes improvement possible. **Constructive feedback obviates unfavorable defensive reactions.**

Try the following to see if you can take a positive point of view when receiving criticism:

- Listen to or read the criticisms offered, seeking to understand them.
- Ask for clarification of any comment that's not clear.
- Remember that criticism is not rejection of your work; the time taken in criticism indicates recognition of actual or potential merit.

- Be as objective as you can; take criticism maturely and get some good out of it.
- After full and reasonable deliberation, apply the suggestions made to you.

Questions About You and the Group

On its first day together, a speech class is a loose collection of persons. But soon the class begins to assume features of a special culture. As you observe growing cohesiveness, consider reasons for this development. The instructor plays a role, as well as the actions of all the individuals who meet at this time and place. Unconnected persons at the beginning, they begin to take on a collective identity. They become a group, and that involves you.

1. How will you participate? Everyone will benefit by choosing to become a part of the class and making a contribution to it. Perhaps you can achieve some kind of positive identification with the group on terms that you and the group can accept. Ways to participate are by speaking, listening, and entering actively into class discussions.

2. What are the time limits for speeches? Realistically, for the benefit of the class, speaking time will have to be limited. The instructor has a number of assignments that must be covered, so the observance of time limits contributes to group objectives.

For formal speeches, accepting time constraints is a beneficial part of speech education. It's one of those requirements that can help a speaker make good choices when preparing. And as the wife of a famous politician said to her husband, "To be immortal a speech doesn't have to be eternal."

3. How will you respond to the work of others? We all want audiences who will give careful attention to our thoughts and views. We appreciate listeners who follow along and understand what we have to say. The chances for success by speakers are increased greatly if listeners are interested in the messages and are willing to interact.

In the speech communication course, there's a marvelous opportunity to positively affect others—and yourself at the same time. You can also continue to refine your sensitivity to the ways of others and be aware of clues that tell you how a person feels or what he or she means.

Questions About You and Society

Your society is all the people with whom you will be speaking throughout your entire life.

1. Do you recognize the power of the spoken word? Speaking moves people. **Much of what we buy, how we vote, what we do and think can be traced to the influence other people have had on us.** People rely heavily on speech to gain influence.

You are also an influence in the lives of people, and with increased speaking proficiency you will strengthen that power to influence. Consciously or not, people speak to affect others. Usually, those with more ability and training are more effective. As the course unfolds, notice the effect you have on the other people in class. Notice reactions of the audience, evidence of the power of speech.

2. What are the two primary choices as a communicator? They are pragmatic and ethical, having to do with choices on (a) being effective and on (b) how to treat people in the process. When speakers choose ideas, test lines of reasoning, and apply methods of communication, they ask themselves the question, "What will work to reach my goal on this occasion?" This is not the only concern of most people who relate to others. Besides striving for effect, they recognize the dignity of those with whom they speak, and they show awareness of the needs and feelings of others as they engage interpersonally. Most speakers who are successful over the years operate with a social sense, though some speakers find reason to challenge the established order. Those who achieve their goals show social sensitivity. That is, they recognize the values of relating humanely to others. Civility and respect are bases of effectiveness in communication.

In the final analysis, effectiveness and ethics are intertwined. Effective speaking is social speaking. As we noted earlier in this chapter, speech communication is based on finding and establishing points of contact between speaker and listener. That's the concept of identification. Perceptive speakers know that listeners need assurances on the sincerity and intent of a speaker. Often, listeners can sense antisocial behavior, somehow feeling the lack of concern a speaker has for their welfare. **We can't separate practical purpose from respect for others.**

We see that the speaker makes a twofold choice: not only how to succeed but also how to relate to listeners. Consider the case of hypothetical student X who, while preparing a speech for class is faced with a big choice, whether or not to include appealing but untrue material. The choice of X bears on a personal code of ethics.

Will you think only of immediate gain, or take the broader view and remind yourself that personal success in life is not dependent on the outcome of one ten-minute speech? Those few minutes of speaking may be a single act in your life, but what of the future, and your perception of self over the long term?

Nearly all important decisions in life are those that affect others, for good or ill. The decisions of the communicator are no exception.

LOOKING BACK

We have discussed several fundamental topics in practical communication.

1. Speech communication has two dimensions: the practical and formal and the interpersonal.

2. Speaking is social action.

3. Communication is dynamic, with a number of basic variables.

4. The human condition provides motivation for speaking.

5. Identification, the quest for unity with audiences, is the primary goal and central to the process of communication.

6. Speech communication is used to grow personally and socially and to get things done.

7. Speaking situations vary.

8. Objectives of a speech class help to give direction to the work.

Guided by your instructor, **this course is designed to facilitate your growth and take you step by step toward greater competence.** For some, improvement will be more rapid than for others. Remember that the rate of improvement doesn't always indicate the quality of improvement. Be patient as you do the work; take first things first, and keep in mind the words of Quintilian, the eminent speech teacher of ancient Rome:

Nature has herself appointed that nothing great is to be accomplished quickly, and . . . difficulty should precede every work of excellence.

By difficulty, Quintilian made reference to the decisions that speakers face. **Here at the *beginning*, think of the *end*. You're going to be a stronger, more effective person if you're ready to make those good choices.**

NOTE

1. Harold Barrett, *Rhetoric and Civility: Human Development, Narcissism, and the Good Audience* (Albany: State University of New York Press, 1991), 13.

STARTING RIGHT

3

★ **LOOKING AHEAD** ★

1. What is an appropriate subject? Where is one to be found?

2. How is a *subject* different from a *topic*? Why and how should one narrow the subject to a topic?

3. What is the general objective of a speech?

4. What is the thesis of a speech?

5. What are the characteristics of a good thesis?

6. What is the extemporaneous method of speech preparation and presentation? What are its values?

CHAPTER 3

STARTING RIGHT

When the time comes to prepare that first speech, a conversation like this is often heard.

Speech Student #1: I have no idea what to talk about: I've got nothing to say.

Speech Student #2: What do you mean?

Speech Student #1: Well, I'm not an expert on anything, that's what.

Speech Student #2: OK. But are you happy with that CD player you bought recently?

Speech Student #1: Yeah. I shopped around and found the right one. But what's that got to do with a speech subject for me?

Speech Student #2: So you know how to buy a CD player and you work in a drug store and you like to take pictures and you hate to ride city buses and you go camping every year and . . . and you have nothing to talk about?

The second student is being very helpful because many speech students do need to be reminded of their personal supply of promising subjects. The selection of a subject, the starting point in preparing a speech, will be explored in this chapter along with other first steps.

MAKING CHOICES

Speaking is an act of making choices about what to say and how, and sometimes about where, when, or with whom. Sometimes deciding never reaches the conscious level of our minds, or so it seems. In conversation and other informal interaction, it doesn't seem to take much thinking to make decisions about purpose and effective strategy. A basic premise of this book is that experiences requiring conscious choice and careful preparation and planning of talks will add to your effectiveness as a communicator; therefore, you will face a number of conscious choices in completing speaking assignments for this class.

SUBJECTS

In preparing a talk, the first task, and sometimes the most perplexing, is choosing a subject. "What should I talk about?" is a question that most speech students seem to have the greatest difficulty answering, especially in early assignments.

The answer instructors most frequently give is "The choice is *yours;* talk about what you would like to talk about."

In the final analysis, the choice *is* yours. After all, who knows your mind better than you? Who must direct the planning, the practicing, and the presentation? And who is responsible for the final outcome? Again, speaking is necessarily tied to decision-making. All basic decisions are yours, from beginning to end. Realizing that this first choice may be the hardest, **consider three factors in deciding on a subject: yourself, the audience, and the occasion.**

What's Right for You?

What do you want to talk about? What are your interests? What are your favorite subjects of conversation? When you talk to friends, what subjects do you bring up? What subjects mentioned in the media or elsewhere get your attention? What ideas have the highest priority in your thinking?

As discussed in Chapter Two, congruence relates to harmony between oneself and personal choice, that is, being right with oneself. With what subjects are you congruent? What subjects are right for you? What subjects will allow you to speak congruently, comfortably, and in accord with the way you think and feel? Certain subjects don't fit certain people. If you feel that a subject will cause you to hold back and limit your freedom to handle it, look for another. For example, why pick the subject of abortion if you would be uncomfortable discussing it? Many other good subjects are available. Again, the choice is yours.

Speech students find this a difficult decision because what one chooses to talk about represents one's self to the group. The choice of subject is autobiographical in that it tells something about the speaker, and people are concerned about the judgments of others. In the final analysis, deciding is a matter of being honest with yourself and respecting your interests, feelings, and principles.

What subject will work for you? Foreign travel? Family? Weekend experiences? Musically inclined people have possibilities ranging from the guitar to Bach. You may be interested in government, protection of wildlife, literature and culture, sports, frontiers in science, or rights and freedoms.

Brainstorming   To remind yourself of subjects that are right for you, you might try brainstorming, an open-minded process of freely naming and writing down subjects, one after the other, without critical comment.

Separate the generation of ideas from the evaluation of ideas, not yet allowing yourself to reject any subject. Give your mind freedom to go in any direction it wishes. Be nonjudgmental and spontaneous. Start with a subject, for example, "computers." What follows may be "wordprocessing." From that you may think of "term paper," and then "bibliography," and then "my method of building a master bibliography." Is any of that promising? If not, try again. Let your mind go where it will. "Chicago" may suggest "the Cubs," which may suggest "baseball." "Baseball" may suggest "homerun," which may suggest "professional success," which may prompt the subject of "a career in finance." Let the brainstorming continue to produce ideas without ruling any out. You can also brainstorm for subjects with the assistance of a friend, going back and forth as each of you name possibilities.

After making such explorations, ask yourself how much you know about the subjects listed. Probably a subject that you find interesting will be one about which you have considerable information. It is safe to say that if you like it, you know enough about it to discuss it in a short talk.

We know that almost everyone has some apprehension about speaking. An appropriate choice of subject can help reduce the problem. Recall from Chapter Two the *positive* approaches to fear. There's no more positive way to meet fear than by selecting a good subject. **Speaking on a familiar subject will allow you to be more self-assured and confident than if you were talking about something you didn't like, know, or feel secure in handling.** People are more at home in their own territory, with familiar subject matter. When dealing with ideas that they like and ones that they know, people are more efficient and relaxed, better adjusted to the speaking situation.

What of Your Audience?

Think about your audience, the people with whom you speak and interact. In this class, audience size will vary. You may talk one to one or in a small group, but often you will speak with the entire class.

Does your audience want an inspirational address equal to those of our great orators? Do they expect to hear a Martin Luther King, Jr., or a John F. Kennedy? If your subject is consumer protection, do they expect you to be as sophisticated in the subject as Ralph Nader? Of course not. They know that the class is a learning situation. Everyone certainly expects you to do your best, but no one expects you to have all the information on any given subject. You may be an expert in some field, but people will not be critical of you if you are not. This does not relieve you of the burden of adequate preparation.

Often, pleasing yourself in the choice of a subject will please your audience. They want you to present familiar and personally appealing ideas. People tend to respond positively to congruent speech, that which is consistent with the feelings and beliefs of the speaker. This is important for you to know and accept in the early stages of your work. Remember that

interest and comfort are contagious. **If you care about what you say and express it freely, listeners will sense your feelings about the subject and will react accordingly.**

As you progress you will probably become more attentive in adapting to an audience. Most students speak better when they think beyond the completion of a speaking assignment and earnestly try to reach their listeners. **Your assignments become opportunities to *communicate* important thoughts, not merely *exercises,* and the experiences will help increase your effectiveness and build your competence for future speaking.** As you become competent, you will heighten your awareness of the characteristics of an audience and enlarge your understanding of other people. The process starts with an audience analysis that includes age, gender, cultural and ethnic identity, general background, beliefs, attitudes, and interests. Become acquainted with the listeners.

Age

Speakers need to discover the age levels of their prospective listeners. Are there any children or adolescents in the group? Are most adults? What's the mix? Though many subjects appeal to everyone, frequently the response of one age group will vary from that of another. Aristotle noted in *Rhetoric,* his book on speaking, that older audiences are not good listeners when young people talk on matters in which they lack experience. The lesson is probably useful today. From the ancient Greeks to modern authorities on speaking theory, the advice is that the search for subjects for given age levels is best directed to a study of people and their preferences, habits, and needs.

Continue to develop sensitivity toward individual and collective behavior and give serious thought to age levels that might suggest differences in interests or attitudes. For example, it would be useful for speakers to study characteristics of people in the young-adult range and compare them to those in the middle-age or old-age range. Although such research would be beneficial, you need to be ready for the exceptions, as there are people who refuse to fit the mold.

Gender

Do you sense that gender ought to be a criterion in choosing your subject? Speakers should recognize variables in a given audience, but also be careful of stereotyping, for most topics cannot be classified as feminine or masculine. Certain topics might be inappropriate, depending on the gender of listeners, but not necessarily.

Though subject choice is a critical part of oral communication, success sometimes depends more on how well you adapt the subject to the audience. Adaptation beyond choice of subject is a topic for other chapters. At this point, remember that the responses of listeners to a subject may be related to their gender.

Cultural and Ethnic Identity

Each of us represents a culture. For some, the designation is distinctly related to ethnicity, for example, Asian-Pacific, African American, and Hispanic. The fact that each of us has family roots provides us with a basis for thinking of cultural traits. Our family culture determines much of our identity, the kinds of people we are. You, as a speaker, will want to be aware that the personalities of listeners and world views arise from family customs, rules, standards and values, practices in rearing the children, traditions, and so forth.

By understanding cultures, perhaps by focusing on family, **speakers can know variations in audience psychology, values, ways of thinking, and predispositions regarding certain subjects.** For example, people of many Asian-Pacific families try not to be confrontational in relating and communicating. Instead they are motivated to avoid open conflict, even being reluctant to say "no" in response to the requests of others. Generally speaking, most Americans are decidedly more assertive.

General Backgrounds, Beliefs, and Attitudes

What are the educational, social, political, and religious backgrounds of your audience that need to be considered? What about sexual orientation? What subjects will appeal to your listeners, and what subjects, if any,

should be avoided? How does the audience feel about your prospective subject? Will you be able to make graceful adaptations?

What do you know about the attitudes and outlooks of the listeners on issues of the day? What subjects might you feel personally obliged to talk about, even though they may conflict with an audience attitude? Because identification of speaker and listener is key to communication, this is a dangerous question, but it seems appropriate in a society dedicated to freedom of speech. If your moral or social convictions compel you to speak on a subject that may oppose the beliefs of much of your audience, perhaps no one should dissuade you. The greatest challenge to a leader is speaking out against a popular war. Even World War II brought out a number of people who protested the involvement of the United States. Perhaps you have "wars" to speak for or against. Then speak, giving special care to your strategies.

Listeners' Fears   As you make basic decisions, keep in mind the discussion in Chapter Two about fear and defensiveness. Listeners can get fearful and defensive, too. When that condition creates a distraction from your thesis, it's a problem in communication. As far as you can ascertain, are the attitudes of your listeners' toward your subject favorable or unfavorable? Consider that thought and the possibility that your subject may be threatening. Once again, much depends on the approach of the speaker to a subject. Most subjects, with proper handling and on certain occasions, will probably lead to acceptable speeches. Above all, don't forget that your purpose is *communication,* not mere self-expression. You'll be successful only if you make accommodations for the thinking and feeling of your audience. That's the only way to relate to others effectively.

History may ultimately support your position, but you face people here and now. The present opportunity to communicate may be the only one. Assess the odds and decide.

Respecting the backgrounds, beliefs and attitudes of your audience will uncover subjects that you and they consider worthwhile. Chapters Five and Eight will cover the topic of audience understanding.

Interests

What subjects will appeal to the immediate interests of your listeners? What are their professional interests? What are the current issues and topics that they talk about? You may want to capitalize on the topical and appealing subjects of the moment. A certain popular song may give you a clue, or a local campus event, or a major news story, or a recurring popular expression. Is your audience sports-minded? If so, along what lines? Do they like literature or movies? What about fashion and design, travel, or foreign affairs?

Some speakers fail to discover the level of sophistication or comprehension of the listeners. They are speakers whose subjects are too esoteric and specialized for a general audience, for example, speeches on quantum theory or hydrogeography to groups unable to appreciate them. And they are speakers whose subjects are too far below the level of awareness of their listeners, for example, serious speeches on sharpening a pencil or dusting a table.

What of the Occasion?

What subject is fitting for the occasion? In class, the occasion probably remains the same unless your instructor chooses to vary it. Ordinarily, you meet in the same room, at the same time, and for the same purpose. Therefore, the demand is that imposed by any social situation. What idea will be appropriate for communication in this occasion? Good taste is important, for both speaker and audience want to avoid embarrassment. Does your view of the occasion meet the perceptions of others? It's true that classroom speakers have much freedom; however, a certain amount of discretion is needed when dealing with people in social settings. Everyone wants respectful treatment. On future occasions, outside the class, you may be restricted by the purpose of the gathering, the season of the year, or the time of day. For suggestions on meeting special demands, see Chapter Fourteen, "Preparing for Special Occasions."

Remember that the classroom occasion becomes "real" only when speakers think of it as an opportunity to *communicate* with people. Thus, view the occasion as a chance for *real communication* of ideas and feelings on a chosen subject. This and all occasions are a time and place for practical interaction with others. Such a positive approach to your work will produce the best results.

__More than anything else, to start right in speech preparation means to choose the right subject.__

FROM SUBJECT TO TOPIC

Imagine the tremendous ambition of a speaker who tells an audience, "Today I'll discuss the history of Australia." Is it possible in a single speech to cover the subject or even the history of the State of Queensland in Australia? Of course not. The breadth is too great. Writers have written hundreds of books and articles on Australia, and that country has been the subject of countless motion pictures and television programs. Yet no one has covered the entire subject. Even the most informed and loyal of Queenslanders would be unable to tell you all about their state in one sitting, despite their knowledge and enormous enthusiasm for it.

__Subjects must be limited—cut down in size, to meet demands of time, purpose, and other realities.__ It's a matter of narrowing the *subject,* a broad area of interest, to a *topic,* a specific subdivision. A topic limits the scope, clearly implying boundaries by its wording. Furthermore, the wording of a topic may reflect the attitude of the speaker toward it or his position on it.

To prepare a talk on Australia, we would need to discover a part or dimension of the subject, a topic, and give attention to that part only. The state of Queensland is a part of Australia, but it is too vast. What about focusing on a certain town? Take the northern city of Cairns, for instance, or even more specifically, the tourist attractions in Cairns. Now we're getting closer to a real topic. Tourist attractions might be the division we decide to treat. But if its scope is too great for the time available, we must narrow the topic further, perhaps by deciding on *one* kind of attraction. And what might that be? Boating? Fishing? Off-shore coral islands? Local architecture? Let's say that the speaker does narrow the topic to off-shore coral islands, and by reducing it one more step arrives at "How the off-shore coral islands were formed."

By reviewing, we can visualize our planning in a general-to-specific order of movement:

From Australia, we "funneled down" to the state of Queensland,
　To the city of Cairns,
　　To tourist attractions of Cairns: boating, fishing, off-shore coral islands, and local architecture,
　　　To off-shore coral islands,
　　　　To "how the off-shore coral islands were formed"—the topic of the speech.

Here are other examples of necessary narrowing:

1. The subject as first conceived: Television
   First limiting: Educational Television
      Second limiting: Educational Television for Preschool Children
         Topic: Educational Effects of Mr. Rogers' Neighborhood on Preschool Children
2. The subject as first conceived: Unemployment
   First limiting: Unemployment in the Cities
      Topic: Some Causes of Unemployment in the Cities
3. The subject as first conceived: College newspapers
   First limiting: Usefulness of College Newspapers
      Second limiting: College Newspapers as Sources of Information
         Topic: Our College Newspaper as a Source of Sports Information
4. The subject as first conceived: Choosing a College Major
   First limiting: Criteria for Choosing a College Major
      Second limiting: Choosing a College Major on the Basis of Career Opportunities
         Topic: Career Opportunities for Majors in Geography

Depending on personal choice and the demands of the occasion, any one of the above topics might prove to be adequate for a speech of six to eight minutes. Might be! But sometimes a speaker is satisfied too soon. As you go through the selection process, ask yourself these questions:

1. Can I cover the topic in the allotted time?
2. Does the topic suggest a definite and promising direction for the speech?

And since mere coverage is not communication, the next question is:

3. Can I cover the topic adequately, without having to neglect any important points or hurry myself?

FROM TOPIC TO GENERAL OBJECTIVE

During this discussion on limiting subjects you have wondered about the possible goals of speeches. For example, what would be the general objective of speaking on the topic "Our College Newspaper as a Source of Sports Information"? One answer is that the speaker wants the audience to share ideas and respond favorably to them. That may be the overall goal of most speeches; however, it does not specify any kind of emphasis. In other words, though a fundamental aim of any speech is to *affect others,* speakers usually plan for a *particular* result, and speeches are often classified in this way.

As rhetorician George Campbell wrote in the eighteenth century, "In speaking, there is always some end proposed, or some effect which the speaker intends to produce on the hearer."[1] Writing later in the century, his fellow Scotsman Hugh Blair noted, "Whenever a man speaks or writes, he is supposed as a rational being, to have some end in view: either to inform or to amuse or to persuade, or, in some way or other, to act upon his fellow creatures."[2] How do you want "to act upon your fellow creatures"? In preparing a speech, determine the response you want and plan accordingly. **Decide whether your general objective is to *inform*, to *persuade*, or to *entertain*.**

Though pursuing one objective in a speech, speakers often find that one or another of the remaining two objectives will be apparent. To illustrate, a speech designed to *persuade* people to see a certain movie may be *informative;* while giving *information* on training a collie to heel, a speaker may include *entertaining* commentary here and there; in telling *how* one arrives at a philosophy of life through experience, a speaker is likely to tell or suggest *what* to do, that is, to try persuasion.

As you see, the general objectives of speeches are typically intertwined; nonetheless, it's advantageous to examine them individually: to inform, to persuade, and to entertain.

To Inform

People in your class will prepare speeches designed to give information. Talks with this general objective are common. When informing, the speaker intends to enlighten the audience, to tell listeners how to do something, to explain the characteristics of some person, place, thing, or concept, to describe or make clear or unfold. The following ends are essentially informational:

To define the term *jive* as it's used by some members of the African American culture

To describe life on a typical small American farm

To distinguish among types of allergies

To discuss the history of the engagement ring

To point out origins of jazz

To explain how to make lumpia

To relate ways to trim houseplants

To Persuade

Although some theorists distinguish between the general objectives of persuading and convincing, I will take them as one. Thus, **to persuade is to affect beliefs, to establish new ones in the minds of listeners, to reinforce those held, or to cause their abandonment.** In this sense, persuading is convincing; furthermore, to persuade is to influence behavior, to influence one to do something, to stop doing something, or to do something in another way. Therefore, in persuasion you appeal to people to believe something or to take some action. Not everyone in the audience may be moved to believe immediately, nor may any action be immediate; nevertheless, the goal of the speaker is to convince or to secure action at once or for some future time.

Some theorists restrict *persuasion* to the goal of *action,* for example, to persuade listeners to go out to see a professional football game. To these theorists *conviction* is apart from persuasion and has the general objective of *influencing belief,* when specific listener action is not urged. To convince listeners that the San Francisco Forty-Niners were the best football team of the 1980s is an example.

The following objectives are persuasive, some to influence belief and some to influence behavior. Can you distinguish between them?

To show why divorce laws should be amended

To develop an appreciation for the Native American's historic unity with nature

To advocate a change in the jury system

To encourage people to go backpacking

To give reasons for supporting the basketball team

To prove that the greenhouse effect can be countered in this century

To call upon listeners to conserve water

To prove that *Hispanic* is the right word for distinguishing people of Spanish-speaking backgrounds

To Entertain

Any speech, regardless of its end, may have elements of entertainment and humor. There are speeches, however, that are planned primarily for entertainment. These are not as common in the classroom as speeches that inform and persuade. Talks to entertain are difficult, and it takes a special flair to sustain humor and carry it off well. Many teachers of speech communication believe that speech training will have greater value if the oral assignments are completed with more serious goals in mind; nonetheless, you may find an opportunity to give an entertaining speech, either during this course or in another situation. The following might represent the aim of entertainment:

To categorize three kinds of comedians

To describe someone's first experience in wind-surfing

To characterize the typical new counselor at the end of the first day at camp

To discuss the antics of a three-year-old

To describe the latest fads

To tell the fun I had teaching my friend to use chopsticks

In summary, as speakers choose a subject and narrow it to a topic, they give serious thought to the general objective of the talk, which helps them to keep their focus steady. Here is a sample layout, from subject to general objective:

Subject: Feminine Gender
Topic: Names Used to Refer to Persons of the Feminine Gender
General Objective: To persuade listeners to use appropriate names when referring to persons of the feminine gender.

FROM GENERAL OBJECTIVE TO THESIS

With a topic and general objective in mind, the next step is wording a *specific* purpose. **The specific purpose, or *thesis,* is a central and vital part of the talk. It's a complete sentence that indicates to the audience what you plan to discuss with them.** Perhaps in other communication courses you called the purpose sentence "central idea," "proposition," "theme statement," or "key idea." Regardless of the name, its function is to make known your intent. It sets forth the ground that you will cover, and where you are going. To prevent misunderstanding and vagueness, the thesis must be a purposive, complete sentence and include only one idea. Moreover, it should be stated briefly and designed to interest the audience in your proposal.

Let's digress momentarily to put the all-important thesis in its place as a member of the four-part speech. In Chapter Four, you will see that a speech is made up of an introduction, a thesis, a body, and a conclusion, and each has a major function. **The introduction leads to the specific purpose of the talk; the thesis states it; the body works to attain it; and the conclusion clinches attainment of it.** The thesis is the heart of the message, the point to be conveyed.

Little wonder, then, that the thesis requires so much care in phrasing. A faulty thesis can cause the entire effort to go awry. What are the weaknesses of these theses?

1. Women's hairstyles of the 1980s.

2. I intend to describe high points of my trip to London and tell you how to travel on $30 a day.

3. It's my purpose to explain the various functions of a gasoline internal-combustion engine designed to offer maximum efficiency when the spark plugs have been either thoroughly cleaned or replaced with the best on the market today.

4. Let me tell you about family education.

5. Students who hold down full-time jobs while going to school can't possibly get a decent education.

All these theses have serious faults. Thesis 1 is incomplete. Actually, it's an undirected *topic,* not a purposively worded thesis. What about hairstyles of the 1980s? Is it the aim of the speaker to criticize them? To describe them? To show that they are coming back now? We don't know, for a definite purpose hasn't been stated.

The speaker can prevent the problem with a complete sentence that clearly reveals intent:

My objective is to discuss some features of women's hair styles of the 1980s that would have appeal today.

>   or

Women's hairstyles of the 1980s are receiving much attention in three movies now being shown locally.

Thesis 2 is a full sentence but too confusing. What is the purpose? Actually, the thesis is two-headed: It indicates two purposes. A speaker would be overly ambitious to suppose that both aims could be accomplished. It's hard enough to realize *one* objective. Listening to any talk can be difficult, without adding complications. **The good speaker is the good guide who takes listeners in only one direction.** When you find yourself with a two-headed thesis, discard one of the ideas. Perhaps you can save the extra one for another speaking occasion. An improved thesis would be:

I want to describe the high points of my trip to London.

>   or

These are the outstanding places of interest in London, I believe.

or

To travel abroad on $30 a day, follow four simple rules.

Thesis 3 is ambiguous because of its extreme length and involvement. It should stop after "engine." Explanations and necessary ramifications can be made later in the speech. The job at this point is to state the purpose, briefly and simply.

In addition to discarding the words about spark plugs, et cetera, another refinement seems necessary for a short speech. The speaker should use qualifiers to limit the extent of the "contract" with the audience. For example:

It is my purpose to explain just two functions of a gasoline internal-combustion engine.

or

Today I'll explain the function of the carburetor in a gasoline internal combustion engine.

What other theses seem to be inherent in that complex original statement?

Thesis 4 is also ambiguous. What *about* family education? What *of* family education? What is the speaker's intent? Is it to discuss family planning, contributions of family members, economic issues? It's a sign of danger whenever a thesis includes such phrasing as "talk *about*" this or that or "talk *on*" or "tell *of*." Words like *about, on,* and *of* tend to generalize and flatten statements of purpose. They give a scattershot feeling and destroy any intent to be specific. These statements show improvement:

You should be aware of the family counseling available at the Community Clinic.

or

My aim is to develop one useful definition of the term good father.

Thesis 5 is faulty because it could alienate the audience. The speaker may have good reasons for holding the stated position on employment, but willing listeners are needed before any convincing can be done. **The thesis should be *rhetorical,* that is, worded to interest listeners.** Since many students find it necessary to work while going to college, thesis 5 is potentially threatening and may provoke resistance. Perhaps it would be better to employ a less confrontational thesis. The speaker can still make the point, but tactfully. These theses are better:

Here are some ways to get the most out of your time in school.

or

Think carefully before taking on a demanding full-time job.

A well-phrased thesis, then, gets the speaker off to a good start by specifying a definite objective. A good thesis is

A complete sentence

Purposive

Composed of a single idea

Uninvolved and reasonably brief

Designed for audience acceptance

Recalling the main terms discussed so far, we have the following steps in planning a talk:

1. Selecting a fitting *subject,* for example, "Need for Career Planning"

2. Limiting the subject to a *topic,* for example, "Need for Career Planning in Elementary School"

3. Determining a *general objective* from the topic, for example, "To convince the audience of the need for career planning instruction in elementary school"

4. Shaping a *thesis* from the general objective, for example, "I'd like to give you several reasons for including career planning in the elementary school curriculum"

USING THE EXTEMPORANEOUS MODE

When you have devised a promising thesis, and have made certain decisions on the development of the message, you face the problem of "handling" your message—the method of containing and presenting it. What is the best method? Writing it out and memorizing it? Writing it out and reading it word for word? Or using the extemporaneous mode? Speakers in the past relied more on memory than speakers do today. Many of them used to memorize long passages or even entire speeches. Historians of public address relate that some of the most effective and praiseworthy speakers were often those with the best memories. They trained themselves in memorizing, as part of the art of speechmaking.

Memorization has lost its place in our culture. Today we don't hear many heavily memorized speeches, except at speech contests, in club rituals, and so forth. There are good reasons for the change. Few people can memorize a speech word for word without showing awkwardness. Memorization almost seems unnatural to audiences now. **Too often a memorized talk is impersonal, stiff, and at a distance from the audience, as though presented by a robot.** There is also the ever-present fear of forgetting a word, which causes a speaker to be on guard, struggling to come up with that elusive word, with the resulting disruption of the flow of thought. Such pressures cause even more tension and stiffening.

Another method of presenting ideas is from manuscript, that is, reading the entire speech. At times, this system is used by politicians, government officials, some business executives, and members of the clergy. For these people, it is needed occasionally. When it's well done, it can be effective; when done poorly, communication suffers. Unless very skilled, the speaker never gets the message off the page and out to the audience. There is no meeting of the eyes and, consequently, no meeting of the minds. Manuscript reading can lower the probability of success in building a bond between speaker and audience, in identifying.

Because of hazards inherent in memorization and manuscript reading, speech instructors emphasize the *extemporaneous mode.* Don't confuse this use of the term with the "extemporaneous" speaking contest, that allows a participant 45 minutes to an hour for preparation. Also, extemporaneous isn't synonymous with *impromptu.* An impromptu speech is one prepared on the spur of the moment.

When you use the extemporaneous method, you fully prepare, but you don't memorize your speech, nor do you write it word for word. Good extemporaneous speaking does require a clear and sound conception of the speech, but in *outline* form. Here are five successful strategies for using this method:

1. **Starting with the subject of your speech, select familiar and interesting ideas that you have a desire to communicate and want your listeners to hear.**

2. **Use brief notes, either mental or written.** If your notes are cluttered with too much detail, they become almost a verbatim representation of your speech and too hard to handle. It's better to have only the skeleton of your talk, just enough detail in your notes to help you carry the thought along. For more information on use of speaking notes, see Chapter Five.

3. **Develop the speech gradually, over time.** It takes time for speakers to retain speech ideas. The content of speeches needs to be sifted, sorted, evaluated, *and* assimilated. The process involves speakers searching their minds for relevant and reliable pieces of information, maybe doing some background reading, and talking to people about the topic. Some thoughts they discard; some they keep, by jotting down new ideas that they discover. Gradually they *incorporate* data, from any and all sources, and *encompass* the whole. **In making the speech all their own, they free themselves *to give it to others.***

   With this excellent system, there's no real need to memorize or read a speech, for in possessing the thoughts, you'll be congruent with it.

4. **Practice the speech.** That is, say it out loud. Some people do it in seclusion. Others practice before family or friends or try out ideas in dinner-table conversation. Practice helps to gain confidence which comes from "owning" the thought, from *really knowing* what you are saying and where the thought is going. The advice is to practice purposefully, with your thesis uppermost in mind, and as often as necessary to prepare yourself to communicate your ideas.

5. **Speak conversationally.** The accepted mode of speech today is one of naturalness, of conversational ease. Audiences want speakers to be open and to talk *with* them in a friendly manner. **So *talk with* them. They are human, you are human, and together you are engaging in an interpersonal sharing.** See if you can keep it that way, an unmechanical, free, and willing exchange of thought. "True speech is a dialogue," said James Albert Winans, one of America's great speech teachers of years ago. "Better than talking to us is talking *with* us. It's conversation with an audience."[3]

   The poet Robert Frost was once asked how he produced a feeling of ease and freedom of expression in his poems, even while conforming to structured forms and conventions of poetry. How is it possible to be *free* and *disciplined* at the same time? Frost, who had an interest in horses, attributed his freedom to "working easy in harness." This could be your goal with the extemporaneous method. It's a matter of accepting the form, the "harness," or purposeful design, and coming to "work easy" through preparation, attention to necessary revision, and useful practice.

LOOKING BACK

There are five fundamental steps in speech preparation:

1. Choosing an appropriate subject
2. Narrowing the subject to a topic
3. Determining the general objective
4. Wording the thesis carefully
5. Using the extemporaneous mode

And of course, in speaking extemporaneously, ample practice is needed.

Finally, note that, with a well-prepared speech in hand, the most important factor in speaking is the relationship you have with your audience. It suggests that showing an interest in the well-being of the audience and having a desire to communicate something worthwhile to them will benefit all involved. **Most listeners are willing to interact with a speaker who is sincere, mindful of their welfare, and well prepared.**

SUBJECTS FOR TALKS

Following are subjects recommended for this book by students in recent speech communication classes. All of them can be changed to suit speaker interest.

Buying clothes	Caring for the environment
Family fun	Corridos, folk ballads
Part-time work	Job preparation—the basics
Recording technology	Selection of conversation topics
Travel abroad	Business ethics
Financing education	Professional football and networks
Interpersonal sensitivity	My ancestors
Available scholarships	Communication in management
Learning from my father	Knitting
Pretty places nearby	Caring for plants
Favorite food back home	Learning English
Cultural pride	Physicians at work
Students' relationships	Career opportunities in government
Biking on mountain trails	Alcohol problems of teenagers
Uses of solar energy	World food supply
Achieving physical fitness	The best pets
Music I grew up on	Living with a friend
A world champion	Dancing in my family
My favorite place to relax	Customs of my neighbors
	Survival in the desert
	"The spice of life"—my choice

Importance of exercise   Saving money
Betting on horse racing   Improving study habits
Living at home   Direction of the economy
Doing it my way   Motorcycling
New laws to know about   Patterning your life after someone
Parking problems   Keeping up with current events
Studying photography   Personal adventures and experiences
Home entertainment   A good hobby for older people
Television commercials   Recreation in the city
Gymnastics   Farming—a way of life
My kind of wedding   Commuting to school
Learning shorthand   Available low-cost housing

NOTES

1. George Campbell, *The Philosophy of Rhetoric* (London: William Tegg, 1850), 1.

2. Harold F. Harding, ed., *Lectures on Rhetoric and Belles Lettres* (Carbondale and Edwardsville: Southern Illinois University Press, 1965), II:2.

3. James Albert Winans, *Public Speaking* (New York: Century, 1917), 38.

ORGANIZING THE SPEECH

4

ORGANIZATION

Organization is a major "secret of success" in oral communication (and, incidentally, a secret to getting a good grade on a speech). Speech instructors emphasize organization in their classes because they know that **clarity and orderly unfolding of the parts of messages are essential to effectiveness in communication.** An analogy may be useful in explanation of this point: A river can be directed into channels to provide the greatest good for all people, or it can be allowed to run at will. So it is with the flow of ideas. Ideas can be channeled for ease of reception by audiences, or they can be allowed to ramble aimlessly, unmanaged and wasted.

Experienced speakers are aware that listeners expect messages to be organized in some way. Thus, they devise a *plan,* a way of ordering the elements of their messages. **Proceeding systematically, speakers are able to accommodate their thinking to the listeners' need for order.** By so doing, they provide one more basis for a meeting of minds, for connecting and identifying. Patterning ideas to fit the mental framework of listeners answers a human requirement; it satisfies by eliminating the frustration of disorientation.

Think of it in very practical terms. **Listeners want guidance and direction**; they find structure and arrangement helpful and disarrangement baffling. Literally, a speaker must "parcel out" thoughts to an audience. Knowing the ever-present possibilities for misunderstanding and confusion, the good speaker follows a set plan of distribution when addressing the audience. Good organization helps the listener because the exchange is methodical, first things first and part by part. And of course, good organization helps the speaker accomplish the purpose of the speech. This structuring of parts can be compared to a lawyer's brief, which is necessary to help a jury think clearly and logically. A plan guides the speaker's thinking on the subject matter. Furthermore, knowing how to manage the message increases the speaker's confidence. In sum, good organization leads to effectiveness in communication, a fact that all other accomplished speakers know.

PREPARING OUTLINES

Preparation of an outline for your speech is basic to achieving good organization. As a "blueprint," the outline clearly reflects your choices in the placement of ideas and contributes significantly to final speaking results. But before making specific applications to the speech outline, let's review the general mechanics of outlining.

Headings and Indentations   The mechanics of outlining require care in choosing symbols for headings and in indenting. Use numbers and letters alternately to indicate points and divisions of points. Indent each subdivision of a point to show graphically its relationship to the point. On a standard typewriter or word processor, keyboard indentations are usually three or more spaces. Spacing for handwritten work is comparable, perhaps somewhat greater.

Head the first point with a Roman numeral. Then, to label a division of the first point, indent and use a capital letter. To head a division of that point, indent and use an Arabic numeral. If it's necessary to subdivide the latest point, indent and use a small letter; then, if necessary, alternate an Arabic numeral in parentheses with a small letter in parentheses. The system does provide for further division, but those details are of no real value to us, or to the great majority of outline users. Rarely will any points in a practical speech outline be subdivided beyond the small letter stage, the fourth level.

The following incomplete outline is included to illustrate the use of symbols for headings and indentations. Observe, in the gradations from Western Hemisphere to Boston, how indenting shows progressive "funneling" of thought from a very *general* point to more *specific* points.

I.   Western Hemisphere
   A.   North America
      1.   United States
         a.   Northeastern United States
            (1)   Massachusetts
               (a)   Boston
               (b)   Springfield
            (2)   Maine
         b.   Southeastern United States
      2.   Canada
   B.   South America

What addition to the outline would be required to include your favorite American city?

Coordinate Points   Outlines consist of coordinate and subordinate points. The coordinate points in an outline are those of equal weight, those of the same approximate value or nature. Symbols for their headings are also of the same class. North America and South America, in the preceding partial outline, are coordinate points. The contents of the headings are equal in substance, and the symbols reflect the equality, both being large letters. Note that four additional points in the outline have parallel points, for example, Boston and Springfield. To illustrate further, the following types of coniferous trees are listed as coordinate headings:

    I.   Pine
   II.   Fir
  III.   Cedar

The following points are also coordinate, in complete sentences this time:

    I.   Lake Tahoe is deep.
   II.   Lake Tahoe is cold.
  III.   Lake Tahoe is beautiful.

Subordinate Points   Divisions of larger points are called *subordinate* points. They are secondary to, and are parts of, the larger points. They either explain the larger heading or enumerate its contents: a leg (subordinate) is part of a person (larger point), and room is subordinate to house. In the preceding geographic outline, North America and South America are subordinate to Western Hemisphere; the United States and Canada are directly subordinate to North America. Observe other subordinate geographic relationships in the outline. Selected subordinate headings under the previously mentioned types of conifers could be as follows:

    I.   Pine
        A.   Jeffrey
        B.   Sugar
        C.   Ponderosa
   II.   Fir
        A.   White
        B.   Red
  III.   Cedar
        A.   Incense
        B.   Western red

In outlining, we find that every point can have a subordinate point, and every subordinate point can have a point immediately subordinate to it. This is illustrated by the children's song "And the Green Grass Grew All Around."

In the woods there grew a tree; on this tree there was a limb; on this limb there was a branch; on this branch there was a bough; on this bough there was a twig; on this twig there was a nest; in the nest there was a bird. . . .

Each succeeding part is subordinate to the preceding one, and we observe a movement from the general to the specific. Here is a layout of the "Green Grass" excerpt, showing the funneling of thought:

```
—Woods
 —Tree
  —Limb
   —Branch
    —Bough
     —Twig
      —Nest
       —Bird
```

Preparation of a good speech outline is hard work, but it's a necessary step in getting set for clear and effective communication. The models that appear at the end of the chapter illustrate sound outlining technique.

THE SPEECH OUTLINE

The basic form of a speaking plan is the outline. It's the framework of the entire speech, and shows the principal points and subpoints to be covered, the order in which they will be covered, their relationship to one another, and often their relative weight or importance.

For certain speaking assignments, your instructor will probably ask for an outline before you speak. A soundly prepared outline requires rigorous effort, but the effort is well spent. The outline is your master plan for speaking, a physical representation of your carefully conceived pattern of thought. From this full outline, you can abstract your speaking notes: a brief list of the main points of your outline. The notes can be mental or written, depending on your choice or your instructor's request.

The outline will indicate what you set out to do in a given speech and your plan for proceeding. Also, it will be useful to your instructor in ascertaining your progress and your needs. Class requirements will prescribe the type of outline to be prepared, and whether it's to be in topical or sentence form.

At the end of this chapter, you'll find a section on preparing outlines and speaking notes, with information on the differences between the two and suggestions on using speaking notes.

ANALYSIS: THE FOUR PARTS OF A SPEECH

Let's look carefully at the four parts of a speech outline.

The Introduction

The introduction is the beginning of the talk, and speakers use it to accomplish two important goals: to establish common ground and to guide the audience to the thesis.

1. To establish a common ground—bases of identification—with the audience. To arouse attention and develop interest, many speakers begin by referring to an area of common interest or concern. Relating in this way is so much a part of our life that we often include such a reference without consciously realizing its full value in setting the ground for communication. **Seeking mutuality, togetherness, is a basic motive of people,** and it applies to both conversation and formal speaking. Ordinary questions such as "What do you think of the weather?" or "Is it hot enough for you today?" testify to the motivation in social interaction of discovering conditions of mutual concern. We look for grounds of identification, *common* ground. This is social strategy, the way we function with one another.

Applying this social lesson in class, you might begin a talk by referring to an incident (or person or thing or belief) that you think will have meaning to the audience. Perhaps there's an event that can be tied in with your topic and thus serve as an example in your introduction. For instance, say that you plan to discuss "Hazards of Underwater Exploration" and that a major investigation of the ocean's depths occurred recently. Some kind of reference to that known event could help to unite your audience with your subject. You might begin "You may have been among those glued to the TV last week when underwater explorers removed treasures from that sunken Spanish galleon. . . ."

You can start your speech by referring to a classmate's speech, an event experienced in common. Use that base, already set down, to help you get started. If on Wednesday, Anthony showed the importance of saving endangered species of birds, and on another day you plan to talk on "Why Everyone Should Have Regular Physical Examinations," you might begin by saying, "On Wednesday, Anthony told us of the benefits of saving birds. Today I'll change that to saving humans."

Sometimes a dramatic statement, question, or statistic will touch on a topic of general interest and thus get a response. If your purpose is to explore infant mortality, begin with a probing question and statistics: "Why does the richest nation in the world rank twentieth in keeping infants alive; why do babies in the United States of America die at such alarming rates?"

A word of caution about using startling statements. Some discretion may be needed. In one campus speech contest an enthusiastic speaker, wanting to ensure attention at the outset of his speech, pulled out a track pistol and fired it. Needless to say, it produced a shock—so much of a shock that no one was able to listen for the balance of the program.

A talk on the purposes of higher education might start with quoted material, as in this introduction:

The famous American educator Clark Kerr once said, "The University is not established to make ideas safe for students; the University is established to make students safe for ideas." Now, before agreeing or disagreeing with that provocative statement, you ought to have a very good understanding of what it means. What does it mean to you? I believe that the message is vital and of much more importance than its length suggests. Therefore, I'd like to give my interpretation of it, especially as it applies to us here today. Specifically, I intend . . . [balance of the thesis follows].

Of course, humor is a favorite way for speakers to reach their audiences. An appropriate story or funny expression in the introduction can be helpful in identifying with and uniting people. For further discussion of humor, see Chapter Fourteen, ''Preparing for Special Occasions,'' the section on the after-dinner speech.

The more the speaker and listeners seem to be separated in customs, interests, or beliefs, the more attention the speaker should give to finding areas of shared concern. In communication, the speaker strives to show some fundamental bond with the listeners. The opening words of a recent speech by Queen Elizabeth II of England illustrate her attempt to stress the similarities and shared sympathies of people in her audience. You may never find yourself in an identical speaking situation, but be assured that the principles of audience adaptation demonstrated in her speech can be applied by any speaker to any occasion.

Queen Elizabeth made the speech to the United States Congress in May of 1991 after the successful end of the war in the Persian Gulf region. Britain and the United States had cooperated closely in that military operation, united in aim and spirit. Her purpose was to urge continuation of that spirit. Here are words of her introduction.

Mr. Speaker, Mr. President, Distinguished Members of Congress, I know what a rare privilege it is to address a joint meeting of your two houses. Thank you for inviting me.

The concept so simply described by Abraham Lincoln as "government by the people, of the people, for the people," is fundamental to our two nations. Your Congress and our Parliament are the twin pillars of our civilizations and the chief among the many treasures that we have inherited from our predecessors.

We, like you, are staunch believers in the freedom of the individual and the rule of a fair and just law. These principles. . . .[1]

Now for the second goal of an introduction.

2. To guide the audience to the thesis. After establishing rapport, lead your audience to the thesis. Said another way, you need to prepare them for the announcement of your purpose. If you've given appropriate preliminary background or explanatory material, the audience will be ready for your proposal. Because you want your listeners to respond favorably to your thesis, justify its importance by building up to it. If your purpose is to discuss the reasonableness of raising bridge tolls, it may be necessary in the introduction to meet negative feelings about drivers paying more money. If you are advocating a compulsory biology class, careful audience preparation should precede your purpose statement. Almost all topics, especially controversial ones, require some kind of preparatory commentary to facilitate listening.

The following introduction was used successfully to introduce a short speech to a class. Relying primarily on definition, the speaker in approximately 30 seconds caught the listeners' interest and laid out a pathway to the door of her thesis.

> *Most people know what initials like MPH, SOS, and RSVP stand for, but the other day when one of my instructors mentioned the initials GDP, I noticed that a lot of people in the class looked puzzled. Do you know the initials? Though they affect the lives of every American, too few can explain them. Economists say the GDP—gross domestic product—is the total value of goods and services produced inside a nation. GDP is the country's domestic worth, economically. "Yes," you say, "but what does GDP mean to me?" That's just the question I hope to answer today. [The thesis then follows.]*

Here is another introduction, one leading to a thrilling discussion of an American problem and solution. Standing before nearly 250,000 people in Washington, D.C., in 1963, Martin Luther King, Jr., gave his inspirational speech, "I Have a Dream." In a message that is now a classic, Dr. King eloquently envisioned the realization of freedom and brotherhood in America.

> *Five score years ago, a great American, in whose symbolic shadow we stand today, signed the Emancipation Proclamation. This momentous decree came as a great beacon light of hope to millions of Negro slaves who had been seared in the flames of withering injustice. It came as a joyous daybreak to end the long night of their captivity.*
>
> *But one hundred years later, the Negro still is not free. One hundred years later, the life of the Negro is still sadly crippled by the manacles of segregation and the chains of discrimination.*
>
> *One hundred years later, the Negro lives on a lonely island of poverty in the midst of a vast ocean of material prosperity. One hundred years later, the Negro is still languished in the corners of American society and finds himself an exile in his own land. So we have come here today to dramatize a shameful condition.*

Of the four parts of a speech that I have discussed, the introduction comes first because, of course, it's the first part that you deliver to the audience. But it should not be the first part that you prepare. Does that seem odd? Actually, the best time to plan the introduction is *after* you have prepared the rest of your speech. You can't make final decisions about your opening remarks until you've laid out the main part. Only then will you know what it is you are to introduce. That's logical, isn't it? Practical expe-

Martin Luther King, Jr.

rience using this method is the best means of discovering its value. It's an old notion, advised by the Roman statesman Cicero over 2000 years ago, and it still works.

Then comes the thesis.

The Thesis

The thesis follows naturally from the introduction. It's the thesis that you work toward and lead up to in the introduction. **After a good introduction, the thesis will fall into place in a position of central and continuing importance.**

Recall from Chapter Three that the thesis is a complete sentence and, being purposive, states your objective clearly. Furthermore, it must include only one idea, be short, and be designed for audience acceptance. Here are examples of acceptable theses:

Let me point out the advantages of attending a community college.

I'd like to show you how to read a fingerprint.

These are my reasons for urging that everyone be a television critic.

Three logical arguments led to my decision to move back to the city.

The Body

The body is a discussion of the thesis; it's made up of the main ideas to be presented. In the body you develop your purpose, that is, you tell your audience what you told them you would tell them.

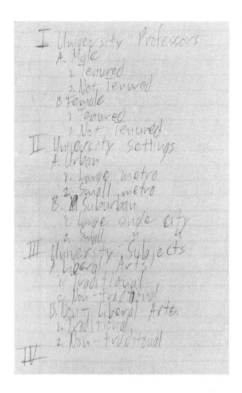

But *how* do you tell them? First, you tell them in an orderly manner, knowing that it doesn't make sense to cast ideas in all directions hoping that by some mysterious means listeners will pick up the thoughts. Communication is too important to be treated so haphazardly. Speakers must be purposeful and discerning in making structural decisions.

Structural Decisions 1. **First, analyze your thesis to determine its contents.** A thesis can be broken down into units of thought. "What are its divisions or sections?" you should ask. "What are the inherent parts? When I 'open up' the thesis, what will I find?" The divisions of the thesis are the chief points in the body of your speech. We call them *main heads*. Examine the following sample theses and main heads.

Thesis
Here's how I explain the greatness of Frank Sinatra's long career.
Body
    I.   He's a marvelous singer.
   II.   He has a keen "show-business" sense.
  III.   He chooses the right songs to sing.

Speakers sometimes like to use an "organizational preview," often called "partition," immediately following the thesis, to announce the main heads that will be covered in the speech. Notice the preview in italics in this thesis:

Thesis

    I'd like to describe the steps to follow in applying for a scholarship: *getting a list, determining the best ones,* and *submitting applications.*

Body

    I.   Get a current list of available scholarships.
    II.   Determine which ones seem best suited to you.
    III. Submit a number of applications.

As you can see, the main heads are parts of the thesis. The thesis is like a pie, and the body is made up of pieces of the pie, that are discovered in the process of analysis.

Analysis is critical to speech preparation. For one thing, it helps the speaker to think straight. Through careful examination of the thesis, the speaker comes up with the chief ideas, the main heads, to present to the audience.

Second, a conscientious analysis of the thesis will help to assure audience understanding. How much communication would take place if the speaker threw the whole "pie" at the audience without giving thought to arrangement and purposeful distribution? Probably very little. On the other hand, when the speaker makes clear what the whole pie will be and then proceeds to present it piece by piece, confusion is reduced appreciably. A listener can more easily pay attention to a thesis when it's laid out in sections, one section at a time. **People understand and assimilate information better when they are able to see it as pieces and how each relates to the whole.**

   2.   Choose only two, three, or four main heads. Divide your thesis into at least two parts. In fact, there are many theses that lend themselves to being analyzed into just two main heads. You've heard speeches, for example, that have dealt with the pros and cons, the advantages and disadvantages, the right and wrong, the east and west, or the before and after.

Only in rare cases should you have more than four main parts. Regarding numbers of main heads, Roy C. McCall found in his important research on the speaking of Harry Emerson Fosdick, that "Audiences cannot grasp more than three at one sitting; four, perhaps, if the speaker exercises special care in keeping the outline constantly before them." Fosdick told of once giving a speech with six main heads: "It came out like a broom, in a multitude of small straws."[2] Listeners are able to manage only a few thoughts at one time. A point of diminishing returns is sometimes reached in speaking at which the listener can absorb no more new ideas. Changing the metaphor from straws to rocks, one might say that delivering a speech is like shoveling gravel onto the flat bed of a truck. You reach a point when you may as well stop. The added gravel merely rolls down from the high pile as fast as you shovel it on.

Finding yourself with more than four main heads may tell you that your topic is too broad. In that case, you obviously must limit the scope. Another possible solution is to find fewer but broader divisions of the proposition. Your solution in this instance is to combine certain main heads or to reclassify them. For example, assume that in planning a speech on sources of news in the media, you have these main heads:

     I.   Daily metropolitan newspapers
    II.   Weekly magazines
   III.   Nightly TV news programs
   IV.   Monthly magazines
    V.   Occasional radio documentaries
   VI.   Weekly radio programs of interviews and commentary
  VII.   Weekly TV programs of interviews and commentary
VIII.   Occasional TV documentaries
   IX.   Weekly newspapers
    X.   Hourly radio news

Anticipating your listeners' problems in grappling with ten separate thoughts, you seek a better way to handle the ideas. You decide to regroup into three main heads.

    I.   Daily sources of news
       (with daily metropolitan newspapers, nightly TV news programs, and hourly radio news as subheads)
   II.   Weekly sources of news
       (with weekly magazines, weekly radio programs of interviews and commentary, weekly TV programs of interviews and commentary, and weekly newspapers as subheads)
  III.   Occasional sources of news
       (with occasional TV documentaries and occasional radio documentaries as subheads)

Once again, for the sake of your audience and purpose, choose only two, three, or four main heads.

   3.   Balance your main heads. After analyzing the thesis, **test the chosen main heads to determine if they are coordinate.** Are they of equal weight or nature?

Because main heads are the primary parts of the thesis, they must be coordinate and parallel. Notice the balance and parallel structure in the following set of main heads:

    I.   A class in small group discussion will teach you group process.
   II.   A class in small group discussion will teach you group sensitivity.
  III.   A class in small group discussion will teach you group problem solving.

As you see, the following change upsets the coordinate relationships. The main heads are no longer balanced.

I. A class in small group discussion will teach you group process.
II. A class in small group discussion will teach you group sensitivity.
III. A class in small group discussion is not as easy as it seems.

Do you see what happened? I and II refer to specific benefits, whereas III comments on the difficulty of the process. III does not belong because it's of a different nature, and not parallel to I and II. In handling such a problem, the speaker must choose which unifying characteristic the main heads are to have, and then make certain each one assumes that characteristic.

4. **Eliminate any overlapping of your main heads.** Each unit of the thesis should be mutually exclusive of every other unit; that is, it should only be concerned with a single and separate point. **Each main head represents a limited area of thought, distinct from that of every other main head.** Overlapping indicates that one main head is part of another, and the outline should be arranged to show that part as subordinate. In the following set of main heads, IV is part of III and does not deserve main head status.

I. Win-win is one type of conflict resolution.
II. Win-lose is another type.
III. Lose-lose is another.
IV. The third type may be the least desirable.

Here is another example of overlapping.

I. Psychology is a study of human behavior.
II. Psychology is a study of human experience.
III. Psychology is a study of human reaction.

What's the difficulty here? I and III are very closely related, but because *reaction* is a type of *behavior,* III is subordinate to I and should be placed as a subhead to I.

Overlapping can intrude quite easily if the speaker is not alert. Avoiding it helps to prevent confusion in listeners' minds.

5. **Maintain unity of form in shaping main heads. If the main heads are unified, they will be of a single form: ordered by time, space, reason, topic, problem-solution, or some other structure.** Your choice of form will be prescribed by your overriding purpose in the speech. Organization is related directly to purpose, and well-chosen structural elements, such as the basic pattern of the message, will help achieve the purpose. In a word, form should conform to goal.

To determine the dominant unifying order of your analysis, you need to examine the thesis and answer some fundamental questions about it. Get a feeling for its inherent nature: "What sort of structural perspective will help me achieve the stated purpose? Does my purpose call for laying out ideas in a step-by-step order? Do I plan to be descriptive? Do I plan to deal with causes and effects of some condition? Do I propose to deal with

> Nothing *contributes more to effectiveness in speaking than the hard work of devising a plan to achieve the purpose!*
>
> *Heard at a conference of speech communication instructors*

value judgments, for example, issues concerning goodness or usefulness? Do I want my audience to *visualize* elements of my message, to perceive them spatially?" Keeping your perspective before you, select the available unifying options.

Time   The first option is order of *time*. Because events and ideas have meaning in time, a thesis or proposition can be analyzed chronologically. Is chronological order a relevant frame of reference for discovering meaning in your thesis? When elements follow each other in steps or in process, or when sequence is central, time is doubtless the organizing force.

When ordered according to time, the main ideas of the body often suggest something to do with the clock; the calendar; or periods, eras, seasons, decades, steps in the development of something, and so forth. For example:

Thesis
   Let me tell you how one boy, James I'll call him, grew up at Kid's camp.

Body
   I.   He arrived in early June as a typical spoiled brat.
   II.   By mid-July he was making an effort to get along.
   III. When he left in August, he was a "good kid," no longer a baby.

Thesis
   I'm going to show you how to help an injured wild animal.

Body
   I.   Carefully cover the animal with a blanket or coat.
   II.   Place it in a sturdy box with shredded paper or rags.
   III. Keep it warm and quiet, in darkness.
   IV.   Get assistance from a veterinarian or wildlife specialist.

Space   The second option is *space* order. Do you visualize divisions of the thesis as having a definite spatial character of some kind? Do they refer to placement or location? Do you see the divisions as part of a pattern or in some way related to distance—close and far, up and down, and so forth? Or possibly in terms of comparative dimensions?

To unify your main heads in terms of space, you must discover the locus of your thesis in areas: in geographical places, in regions, districts, or zones, or according to physical layout. The spatial divisions may refer to areas microscopic in size or universal in proportion.

Thesis
   In tennis, the basic differences between doubles and singles can be explained in reference to the court.

Body
   I.   In doubles, players use the entire court.
   II.   In singles, they do not use the alleys.

Thesis

    Do you know how much geography played a part in the development of distinct cultures?

Body

    I.   Mountain ranges separated peoples.

    II.   Bodies of water separated peoples.

    III. Great distances separated peoples.

Reason   Speakers use *reason* order to characterize main heads that they plan for a message designed to uphold a point of view. That a person has a point of view suggests that others have their points of view, perhaps opposing ones. In other words, we are now discussing controversy: issues, argumentation, and persuasion. If your thesis is carefully designed and satisfactorily states your position, the first step in the analysis is to determine the issues that are relevant to the thesis. **Issues are points of disagreement; thus, all issues are controversial.** Your thinking on the issues will suggest your reasons for supporting the thesis. These *reasons* will be your *main heads*, commonly called the *arguments* of your case.

    Each of the following questions points up one kind of general or stock issue: Is there a *need* for the idea or policy proposed in the thesis? Is the plan *practical* and does it have *advantages?* People take sides on such issues. For example, which side do you take on increased aid to foreign countries? Do you believe that there is a *need*, that a certain plan is *practical,* and that the plan offers *advantages,* or do you disagree in some way? Whether for or against the idea, what specific reasons—arguments—will you choose to build your case?

In the type of thesis in which *value* is the main issue, you'll find the "pros" and "cons" relating to such matters are usefulness, goodness, and effectiveness. Then you'll choose particular arguments for your case. For example, if you take the side that computer skills are of value to college students, what are your reasons? You may say that they are valuable because they are *useful.* But why, specifically? Let's say you have three answers to that question: because they help save time in writing papers, because they allow for easy correction of mistakes in all written work, and because they facilitate storage of data. These are the derived arguments that constitute your case, the main heads expressed as reasons.

To repeat, while reflecting on the large, stock issues such as need, practicality, advantages, and value, you'll discover your arguments, the main heads of the thesis. Thus, the thesis does control the entire analysis.

When properly worded, each argument for your case will remain intelligible if the word *because* is placed before it. That's a way to test the wording of an argument, to see if it fits the thesis as a clear, true, distinct *reason.*

Thesis
This nation must make provision for its at-risk children.

Body
I. [because] Families of these children cannot meet the children's nutritional needs.
II. [because] The families cannot meet the children's educational needs.
III. [because] The families cannot meet the children's psychological needs.

Thesis
Benjamin Cardozo was a great American jurist.

Body
I. [because] He worked tirelessly to simplify the law.
II. [because] He advocated cooperation of the judiciary in making effective laws.
III. [because] His view of law placed social effect above abstract logic.

Topical   **When you divide your thesis *topically,* you select mere subtopics of the thesis, parts not tinged by time, space, or reason.** Structuring ideas by *topic* is probably the most common analysis. Note in the following patterns how the main heads seem to "fall out" naturally from the theses.

Thesis
  I'd like to introduce you to some basic terms in biotechnology.
Body
  I.   Bioenergy is that produced from living organisms.
  II. Bioengineering is application of engineering knowledge to the fields of medicine and biology.
  III. Biomass refers to material, mainly living material, present in an organism.
  IV. Biocide is any substance that kills or inhibits growth of microorganisms.

Thesis
  Here are some ways that householders can save water.
Body
  I.   Take short showers.
  II. Replace or remove "thirsty" grass and other plants.
  III. Install "stingy" plumbing devices.
  IV. Use water-saving settings on automatic dishwashers.

Problem-Solution   A fifth pattern that your main heads might assume is *problem-solution*. If this form suits the potential development of your thesis, you'll have only two main heads. The first will discuss a problem, its extent, causes, or effects. The second will present one or more solutions. Of course, you would use this order only if your purpose were to present a problem and to solve it.

Thesis
  The matter of insensitivity to psychological needs of the elderly should concern us all.
Body
  I.   The problem is serious.
  II. There are solutions.

Thesis
  The increasing incidence of pregnancy in early adolescence must be faced.
Body
  I.   Let's examine the kind of problem that exists.
  II. Here are possible solutions.

Other Forms   Additional systems of analysis for producing main heads follow. As you can see, some are merely adaptations of those discussed earlier.

  Cause and effect (or effect, then cause)

  Climactic (ordering from least significant to most significant)

Biographical (a topical form used when a person is discussed; ordered with main heads like Early Life, Goals, and Accomplishments)

Need-plan-benefits (used extensively in argumentation and debate)

Series of critical questions (for example, Where are we? How did we get here? Where do we go from here?)

In summary, at this point the thesis is to be divided into two, three, or four parts, or main heads, that should be balanced and coordinated. Your thesis can be analyzed with emphasis on time, space, reason, topic, problem-solution, or some alternate order, in accordance with your purpose and perspective. But consistency is important. If you start with *time,* stay with it, and word all your main heads in terms of time. When you avoid mixing elements, you'll prevent confusion and keep listeners on track.

The Conclusion

The conclusion, of course, is the final phase of the speech and is your last opportunity to accomplish your purpose: to have the audience react favorably to your thesis. **Neglect of the conclusion is a common failing of inexperienced speakers**, as teachers of speech communication will tell you. A talk on a good subject, clear in purpose and well conceived in other ways, deserves a carefully planned conclusion. A more important reason is that **communication may depend on the way the closing remarks are handled.** The conclusion has two essential functions: to remind listeners of the main ideas and to end the speech fittingly.

    1.   To remind listeners of the main ideas. It's usually a good idea to include a summary of the main points you have covered. Listeners forget more readily than we realize, and a perceptive speaker doesn't take it for granted that they have retained all of the message.

Then there's another human characteristic, semantic confusion, where words have different meanings for different people. A person can express a thought in one way and receive very little response, whereas expression of the same thought in different terms may cause a noticeable reaction. In summarizing the main heads, speakers often choose new wording. Assume that a woman in the class decides to discuss problems of dog ownership by developing three main heads: financial, social, and dietary problems. She could add meaningful variety to her speech by summarizing the points with synonyms, as problems of *money, neighbors,* and *food.* Even if one single listener is enlightened as a result of the varied wording, it may be worth the effort.

As the course progresses, you might try various summary techniques. Some student speakers have been successful using examples. For instance, after discussing three baseball skills, one speaker summarized by citing a famous National League player as an example of someone who possesses all three skills: he could hit, field, and run the bases. You might include an effective quotation to remind the audience of your message. If you choose "Freedom in a Democracy" and "Social Control in a Democ-

Chief Joseph

racy" as your two main heads, this quotation by George Sutherland could provide the right kind of summary: "Liberty and order are the most precious possessions of man, and the essence of the problem of government is reconciliation of the two."

2.   To end the speech appropriately. After the summary comes the ending, to round out the speech and give a feeling of completeness. You should avoid both abrupt and drawn-out endings, and never make apologies. **Above all, finish in a way that's consistent with your purpose.** Your purpose may indicate that you should make an appeal at the end, or possibly you should leave the audience with a challenge or a provocative thought.

Once again, a fitting story or example, or well-chosen words of an authority are often appropriate ways to finish. Some speakers like to conclude by returning to their opening words. This method can work well by giving a feeling of unity and successful completion. In any case, the key is to adapt your ideas to your listeners so that *they are mindful of your thesis.* Your specific purpose will help you decide on the content of a closing.

Assume that Ted, a member of a speech class, is interested in the speechmaking of Native Americans. He began studying the subject in high school and now decides to give his next speech on it. This was his thesis: "My purpose today is to acquaint you with three great American orators."

After composing the body of his speech, Ted began to plan the conclusion. "I've got the summary worked out," he says to himself, "but how should I end the talk? I could tell a story about one of the leader's effective speaking. Or give some of my statistics on the reduction of the Native American population since the 1870s." Ted continues, "No, such statistics won't be relevant to my thesis. What I really want to do is end by conveying a feeling of respect for those orators. After all, that's what my speech is about!"

Having reminded himself of his purpose, Ted found the way to complete his speech. These were his words, as he rehearsed the closing, using very brief speaking notes.

Today I have asked you to go back in time and get to know three of America's outstanding orators: Red Jacket, Chief Joseph, and Kicking Bird. There are many others, and someday you may want to look into the lives of those who interest you. They were real people—most were chiefs. Though doing what they thought was best for their people, they came to realize that with the intrusion of the white people, the old way of living was gone. I'll let Kicking Bird speak for all: "I am as a stone, broken and thrown away—one part thrown this way, and one part thrown that way. I am a chief no more but that is not what grieves me—I am grieved at the ruin of my people; they will go back to the old road, and I must follow them."

One additional conclusion to a speech may be helpful. Martin Luther King, Jr., ended his "I Have a Dream" speech with great hope. Using metaphorical language, words from a familiar patriotic song, words from a spiritual, much reiteration, and geographic points of identification, **he kept his thesis before the audience**, enforcing his plea for freedom and brotherhood. Though few will have occasion to deliver such a splendid speech, all can profit from observing Dr. King's approach.

I have a dream that one day every valley shall be exalted, every hill and mountain shall be made low, the rough places will be made plain, and the crooked places will be made straight and the glory of the Lord shall be revealed and all flesh shall see it together.

This is our hope. This is the faith that I go back to the South with.

With this faith we will be able to hew out of the mountain of despair a stone of hope. With this faith we will be able to transform the jangling discords of our nation into a beautiful symphony of brotherhood.

With this faith we will be able to work together, to pray together, to struggle together, to go to jail together, to stand up for freedom together, knowing that we will be free one day. This will be the day. . . . when all of God's children will be able to sing with new meaning—"My country 'tis of thee; sweet land of liberty; of thee I sing; land where my fathers died, land of the pilgrim's pride; from every mountainside, let freedom ring"—and if America is to be a great nation, this must become true.

> *So let freedom ring from the prodigious hilltops of New Hampshire.*
> *Let freedom ring from the mighty mountains of New York.*
> *Let freedom ring from the heightening Alleghenies of Pennsylvania.*
> *Let freedom ring from the snow-capped Rockies of Colorado.*
> *Let freedom ring from the curvaceous slopes of California.*
> *But not only that.*
> *Let freedom ring from Stone Mountain of Georgia.*
> *Let freedom ring from Lookout Mountain of Tennessee.*
> *Let freedom ring from every hill and molehill of Mississippi, from every mountainside, let freedom ring.*
>
> *And . . . when we allow freedom to ring, when we let it ring from every village and hamlet, from every state and every city, we will be able to speed up that day when all of God's children, black men and white men, Jews and Gentiles, Protestants and Catholics—will be able to join hands and sing in the words of the old Negro spiritual, "Free at last, free at last; thank God Almighty, we are free at last."*

> *Order is power.*
>
> Henri Frédéric Amiel,
> *writer*

USING SPEAKING NOTES

The outline should not be used as speaking notes. The purpose of the outline is to serve as a complete design, with all main structural elements revealed. It's too detailed to serve as a memory aid. When speaking from a full outline, speakers often neglect the audience, and lose contact. They yield to the temptation to rely on the outline, becoming dependent on it and separating themselves from the listeners. There's also a tendency to look down at the outline "just because it's there."

A more reliable aid is speaking notes, an abstraction of the outline: a "barebones" representation. Here are some suggestions on preparing and using speaking notes.

1. Place them on a 3-by-5- or 4-by-6-inch card or piece of paper.

2. Make the notes legible by using large letters.

3. Limit the notes to main ideas; avoid cluttering with nonessential words.

4. Organize the notes in accordance with the outline.

5. When speaking, place the notes on the speaker's stand or hold them in your hand, whichever is more comfortable and less distracting.

6. Use them openly, without embarrassment. There's no need to conceal them, even if that were possible.

7. Try not to let them get in the way. With adequate practice, you'll refer to them infrequently, only when you must check the next

thought. Then calmly look down, pick out the thought quickly, and speak as long as possible before having to look down again. Remember, overuse of notes can create distance between speaker and audience and reduce effectiveness in communication.

8. You probably should read long quotations and complicated or specific data, statistics, for example, but this is no reason to neglect eye contact. Practice to ensure successful presentation.

9. Learn eventually to free yourself from using notes on *every* speaking occasion. You may surprise yourself by progressing to the point of rarely needing to consult them. Work toward real independence.

MODEL SPEAKING NOTES

In giving the talk represented by Model Speech Outline 2, speaking notes, if you use any, might include the points in Figure 4-1, placed on a 3-by-5-inch card.

LOOKING BACK

To reach and identify with listeners, speakers build messages on a practical, reliable plan. In this manner they are able to achieve a purpose and, at the same time, be faithful to their trusting, expectant listeners. Therefore, both functional and interpersonal ends are served. Purposeful communication is more likely to occur when speakers:

1. Prepare a first-rate outline.

2. Formulate a promising thesis.

3. Analyze the thesis carefully so as to discover two, three, or four coordinate main heads that do not overlap.

4. Follow a well-conceived pattern of organization.

5. Establish rapport with listeners in the introduction and guide them to the thesis.

6. In the conclusion, summarize to keep the thesis and main heads before the audience, and make appropriate final remarks.

7. Speak with notes, mental or written, not the full outline.

MODEL SPEECH OUTLINES

Model Speech Outline 1 (In sentence form)
Confucianism
Introduction
    I.   You may have heard of Confucianism.

```
INTRO.
Many do not consult instructors, e.g. fearful person.

THESIS
Simple procedures for cons.

BODY
    A. Office hours
            Choose time; knock; be clear; listen; time (e.g.)
    B. Before class
            Come early; meet in front; be clear; time (e.g.)
    C. Appointment
            Arrange (e.g.); suggestions of  "A" above

CONCL.
Not difficult; summary; try — instructors expect; a matter
of knowing how
```

Figure 4-1

Sample of a three-by-five-inch card containing speaking notes based on Model Speech Outline 2.

II. As a philosophy or as a way of living, Confucianism has been at the center of daily life for millions of people.

III. I have studied it a little.

Thesis

I'd like to introduce you to Confucianism.

Body

I. As the name suggests, this way of thinking and behaving originated with Confucius.
  A. Confucius is the most revered man in Chinese history.
  B. He was born in the sixth century, B.C., a hundred years before Socrates.
  C. He was a self-educated and wise man.
  D. He was the first professional teacher in China.
  E. He believed that all of his students were capable of learning.
    1. In his eyes, all had abundant potential.
    2. He sought to develop the total person.

II. Over the centuries, Confucianism grew in cultural significance.
  A. It prospered under various Chinese dynasties.
  B. Its influence spread to other lands.
    1. Confucianism became a powerful cultural force in Japan.
    2. Confucianism became a powerful cultural force in Korea.
    3. Confucianism became a powerful cultural force in Vietnam.
    4. Other countries in Asia were profoundly affected.
  C. It is taught in Asian schools and homes to this day.

This speaker, discussing certain "factors of influence," has three main heads to develop.

III. Confucianism stresses interpersonal harmony.
    A. The most basic principle is the idea of *jen*.
        1. Jen is the essence of human interpersonal goodness.
            a. Followers strive to adhere to the "Do unto others" rule.
            b. They accord elders great respect.
            c. They value reciprocity in relating to others.
            d. They practice civility in all forms.
            e. They seek to be empathic with others.
        2. Followers try to keep jen as their focus throughout life.
            a. It's said that growth as a human being never ends.
            b. One's jen will continue to be a model for others.
    B. Basic to the Confucian outlook is the placement of self in proper perspective.
        1. Community good has the highest value.
        2. Individualism is subordinate to common welfare.
        3. Interdependence among others is stressed.

Conclusion
    I. This has been a brief introduction to Confucianism.
        A. A man of great wisdom laid the foundation.
        B. Confucianism grew and spread over time.
        C. It continues as a vital interpersonal force.
    II. We as Americans would benefit from studying this practical and humane philosophy of life.

Model Speech Outline 2 (In sentence form)

Office Hours

Introduction

    I.   You'd be surprised how many students go through a whole school year needing instructors' extra help but never taking steps to get it.

        A.   Some apparently don't know that instructors set up office hours specifically for student conferences.

        B.   Some may be afraid for one reason or another, like the student who believed that confessing lack of knowledge could result in a low grade for the course.

   II.   Seeing an instructor is really very easy.

Thesis

    Follow these simple procedures for consulting with an instructor.

Body

    I.   Arrange to see the instructor during office hours.

        A.   Choose a time when both of you are free.

        B.   Knock before entering.

        C.   Express clearly the purpose of your visit.

        D.   Listen carefully to the instructor's comments.

        E.   Don't take more than your share of time.

            1.   Remember, as one student unfortunately did not, that other students may be waiting.

            2.   Respond to nonverbal clues that "tell" when time is up.

   II.   Arrange to see the instructor just before class, if it's not possible during office hours.

        A.   Arrive a few minutes earlier than usual.

        B.   Meet at the front of the room.

        C.   Once again, be clear and precise in stating your purpose.

        D.   Avoid conferring beyond the class's starting time, unlike the person who went on for twenty minutes while the class waited.

  III.   Arrange for a special appointment, should other times be unsatisfactory.

        A.   Telephone or see the instructor personally to make arrangements, as I did just this week.

        B.   Follow suggestions for office-hour consultation.

            1.   Show courtesy by knocking.

            2.   Be clear and purposeful.

            3.   Listen carefully.

            4.   Leave when your time is up.

Conclusion

    I.   You see, it's not difficult.

        A.   Determine the instructor's office hours.

        B.   Meet the instructor before or after class.

        C.   Arrange for an appointment.

II.   Instructors expect you to come by.

III.   "It's all a matter of knowing how."

NOTES

1. Elizabeth II, Queen of England, "Striving Toward Peace Together," *Vital Speeches of the Day,* LVII (July 1, 1991): 546.

2. Roy C. McCall, "Harry Emerson Fosdick, A Study of Sources of Effectiveness," *American Public Address,* ed. Loren Reid (Columbia: University of Missouri Press, 1961), 66.

USING PRIMARY PROCESSES

5

★ **LOOKING AHEAD** ★

1. What does it mean to say that oral communication is "direct interaction"?

2. How does interpersonal awareness relate to public speaking?

3. What are the forces at work against identification?

4. What are primary processes?

5. Specifically, how do these processes—transition, repetition and restatement, definition, and explanation—serve ideas? What are the best ways of using them to one's advantage in speaking?

DIRECT INTERACTION

In trying to communicate face to face—being clear and keeping listeners involved—all of us have had the experience of being frustrated by distracting and competing influences. Occasionally we may even throw up our hands and say, "Why bother? It's impossible." Indeed, communication may be impossible in some situations, given human circumstances and the complexity of ideas. Yet we keep trying. In a few pages, you'll find some specific methods that can help in communication, including transitions. But first, let's see how speaking differs from writing as a communicative act. Making the contrast will help us appreciate our tasks as speakers.

Oral Versus Written Communication

It should not astonish anyone that **with all the competing forces at work, speaking is such a demanding activity.** To heighten that point, contrast oral and written communication. In written communication, conditions are quite different. The contact between originator and receiver is indirect, with the receiver of the message controlling the experience. Put yourself in the role of reader. When distracted by an emotional or physical factor, you can reread a sentence or an entire paragraph, and you can move to a better environment when something bothers you. But a listener usually must stay in the same place. When as reader you become tired or disinclined to continue, you can put the book aside and go back to it. An indisposed listener has only the present opportunity to receive the message.

As public speaker, you are the director of events. You are the one who makes decisions about how fast to go and when to review. You have ideas that you want to convey, and to do so, you must anticipate and contend with the existent emotional and physical distractions. You are obliged to **find ways to keep your listeners ever mindful of your "whereabouts," to clarify what you are saying and to enforce your thoughts, to be interpersonally alert.** How can you bring a wayward listener back into the stream of your thought? Answering that question as well as investigating the conditions that prompt it are the aims of this chapter.

INTERPERSONAL AWARENESS
IN RELATING IDEAS

Of the various reasons for so-called "communication breakdown," none is more prevalent than lack of interpersonal awareness. All too often people who set out to relate to an audience do not take into account basic needs of listeners and certain very human tendencies. They talk on, *believing* that they are communicating, assuming that they are identifying with one another. They don't know how far they're missing the mark. In talking with people we need to take care to be clear in purpose and in the organization of messages.

Recognizing some fundamentals of interaction can help, too. Imagine yourself sitting on a rooftop overlooking a city sidewalk. You spot two people going their separate ways, unaware of each other. Each is unique, on a different "track of existence," we might say. One wants fame, comes from a big family, hates cats, likes baseball, has an Asian background, and has traveled around the world. The other has radically different wants, likes and dislikes, background and experiences. Let's assume that fate causes these two people to meet in a few blocks and somehow begin a conversation. Will these "opposites" be able to communicate? Perhaps, if they find some area of common interest and if they're *sensitive, respectful, and willing to accommodate to each other's way of being.* There's no other way to succeed in communication, whether in public speaking or conversation.

Any audience, large or small, is made up of an ever-changing, highly complex combination of elements. Imagine a conventional speaking situation, possibly in your own class: It's Monday and a woman in the back row volunteers to be the first speaker of the day. She walks to the front of the room and looks out at the audience. What does she see? Does she see a group of robotlike creatures, each assuming exactly the same appearance and position? Of course not. She sees a diverse array of individual persons with a variety of outward characteristics. Some are sitting up straight in their chairs; some are semireclining; two are looking out the window; one is looking at the wall and another at a neighbor. She sees smiles and frowns, looks of anticipation, looks of lassitude, and signs of unrest.

The speaker begins, and soon observes changes in her audience. The man in the third row, who at the outset seemed rather gloomy, smiles now at one of her comments. The one who was slouching down is now sitting more erectly, and the woman in the back is looking out the window. Things are happening, but only the obvious happenings can be noticed by the speaker.

What does the speaker not know? What can she not see? Like viewing the tip of an iceberg, but to a much greater degree, **the speaker sees only a fraction of audience dynamics.** She doesn't know that one of her listeners worked all night and is plagued by drowsiness, that one has to

> *Speech is a joint game by speaker and listener against the forces of confusion.*
>
> *Norbert Wiener, pioneer in cybernetics*

hurry home to act as translator for her mother who doesn't speak English, that another is worried about failing a history test, that another is thinking about tonight's basketball game, that another is remembering the appointment he forgot, and that another feels excited about having a new boyfriend. It would be absurd to expect you as a speaker to know all such details about your audience, but it's imperative that you realize the prevalence and power of the forces of confusion with which you must deal.

Empathy

Success in the act of oral communication, wherever and with whomever it occurs, depends in part on one's sensitivity to the specific cues and various modes of behavior shown by the other participants. **Empathy**—that very special kind of deep awareness of how another feels and a sharing of the feeling—**is a precious asset for communicators who are able to develop it in themselves.** What does the facial expression tell about the state of mind of a certain person at that time? What does the posture tell about the person's comfort or general feeling? What does shifting in the chair say about a person's involvement in the message? Through their bodies, people convey messages regarding their condition and degree of interest in events. Therefore, speakers are advised to be aware of the signals and their possible meanings, for communication's sake. The subject of bodily movement in communication will be discussed more completely in Chapter Twelve.

FORCES AGAINST IDENTIFICATION

Let's turn now to a discussion of a number of intruding forces with which communicators must contend. Among the multitude of human conditions that may intrude on communication, seven appear most frequently. These phenomena, most of them typifying kinds of audience behavior, introduce "noise" into the circuits of communication. Noise is any kind of interference. It can show up in any situation, in formal settings as well as in informal, one-to-one communication. Note that **many sources of noise are narcissistic conditions, those to do with concern of *self*.** Such are the challenges that each of us faces in our daily communicative lives as we interact and attempt to identify with others to establish a meeting of minds.

    1.   Preoccupation. Not infrequently a person's mind will become fully unavailable to others, captured either by worry over some problem or by anticipation of some pleasure. One may be "a thousand miles away," as the saying goes. Communication is in*tra*personal at that moment, taking place inside oneself—alone, and not in*ter*personal. Later in the chapter I will offer some suggestions for meeting this condition.

2. Apathy. Occasionally, some people in your audience will be apathetic. They may not identify with you or your message or feel a need to make an effort. Your solution to apathy starts with the choice of subject and continues through all phases of preparation. Possibly your thorough planning will stimulate interest in your proposal. That's one way to show you care, and **people who genuinely care usually get a response.**

3. Fatigue and discomfort. Your listener may be tired or not feeling well. In either case, that person will not be in top form. On another day, this same person may be willing and able to engage actively with you. To compensate for this condition, you will need to make your best efforts in the arts of communication.

4. Confusion. Even intelligent people, college students, for instance, can lose track of a train of thought or become perplexed by specialized words or terms. All of us, as speakers, sometimes digress and occasionally cover thoughts too quickly. At times we use phrases that are totally foreign to other people. They may be the right words for us to use, the only ones to carry the idea, but as speakers we are obliged to clarify them.

5. Lack of confidence. A rarely acknowledged problem in communication is that **bewilderment can result when people lack confidence in their ability to understand.** Now and then, though not knowing it, a speaker may face one or two listeners who truly question their own powers to comprehend and consequently are not able to focus on the message. "Why try?" the unconfident person silently asks. "I'm not able to understand it." The problem may be incongruence, feeling uncomfortable in the role of listener, or not comprehending certain kinds of ideas. You know how some people feel about math, for example. What can the speaker do to help them comprehend? The answer lies in caring enough to make the message clear and nonthreatening. Means are available.

6. Resistance. By resistance I mean reluctance of audience members to listen, a holding back. Resistance, different from apathy, may be a conscious "dragging of the feet," an unwillingness to participate in the identification process that is basic to successful interaction, or it may represent a "show me" attitude. An extreme form is common in controversy. It manifests itself as hostility and may indicate fear of a threatening idea or antipathy toward the speaker or the occasion. Defensive and disinclined to accept the message, perhaps unable to trust the speaker, this person actively resists the union of minds that is necessary for communication.

7. Physical noise. In addition to understanding interpersonal conditions, **every speaker needs to be aware of the physical surroundings, especially those that compete with efforts to communicate.** Let's go back to the woman speaking to the class. As she talks, someone drops a book and attention is lost momentarily. Somewhere outside a truck is backing up: beep, beep. Carpenters are working next door. Someone comes into the room. The room is stuffy or cold. The seats are uncomfortable and poorly arranged. Again, forces of confusion are at work; this time they're physical forces. An unpleasant or uncomfortable physical atmosphere works against communication.

Sometimes the people present can do something to improve the environment. Sometimes listeners and speaker must simply adjust to the environment the best they can. When it's necessary to live with the existing distraction, they'll get the best results by asserting their powers of attention and refusing to be drawn away. But there are strategic processes that can work to keep the purpose and main ideas highlighted; a speaker can lead an audience to transcend competing physical forces.

So much for the problems. What specific methods can one use to counter preoccupation, apathy, fatigue and discomfort, confusion, lack of confidence, and resistance among listeners, not to mention poor environmental conditions? We'll go now to an exploration of communicative processes that are particularly helpful in meeting the kinds of conditions we've been examining. You may wish to note that the chapter on persuasion extends the topic of adapting to audiences.

PRIMARY PROCESSES: FOR COHESION, MEANING, AND EMPHASIS

Given the conditions we've been discussing, **the main ideas of any message are always "at risk,"** so to speak. Confusion is an ever-present threat. The message may be handled in ways to get desired results, or be lost along the way. Recognizing the existing "dangers out there" and knowing the perils of neglecting thought, successful speakers turn at key points to primary processes to enforce their ideas. They're called *primary* processes because they're *basic* to the building of a point. Often they're *preliminary* measures, used *before* turning to full support of an idea with developmental materials such as visual aids or examples (topics of the next two chapters). Wherever used, their function is essential to, and yet subordinate to, the laying out of the important thought of a message. **They** are foundational strategies, selected to **provide required cohesion, extra meaning, or due emphasis to ideas.** They are especially useful when it's vital that the audience might

lose the track of thought,

or be unaware of the relationships among main heads,

or miss a particular connotation,

or disregard a significant idea.

Primary processes serve ideas: They're to be used at key points along the way. Four primary processes at your disposal are *transition, repetition and restatement, definition, and explanation.*

Transition

One way to reduce confusion and to work toward clarity, cohesion, and greater certainty in communication is to make apparent the relationships of your ideas. **By linking one thought with another, you keep your audience continually identified with your message and aware of what you are saying and where you are going.** This technique involves connecting and integrating new parts as you add them to the whole. Thus you achieve "formal identification," as noted theorist Kenneth Burke would term it, when your listeners are caught up by the structural logic of your speech—moved by the form, by the interrelating of ideas, and by the patterning that gives prominence to some points and downplays others.

Form is an influence on listening and final outcome. For example, if the first main head of your speech is on weight reduction and you're about to take up the second (weight maintenance), indicate to your audience that you're moving to another main head. Put the new one in perspective by showing how it fits in. You might say, "From the all-important matter of weight reduction, let's turn now to weight maintenance, an equally vital concern." Note how the connecting and relating are accomplished.

How Transitions Help
These connectors or stepping stones between points are called *transitions*. And except for ideas, transitions are the most important elements of speakers' messages—and too often neglected. **Without such rhetorical processes, many ideas in speeches would not be perceived by listeners.** Though they rarely add much new thought, they are essential strategies in effective speaking, for they serve to show listeners the progression of thought, how one idea is associated with another, and which ideas are emphasized and which subordinated. Further, **transitions help to build bonds of trust between speakers and their partners in interaction** because they indicate that speakers are aware of the listeners' need for guidance in communication.

Transitions also provide a flow to speeches and seem to give life to ideas. They help a speaker avoid giving a speech that sounds like an outline, an unconnected stack of points. To achieve coherence and understanding, use transitions to guide your audience throughout the entire talk.

Where to Make Use of Transitions
1. To the thesis. Lead from the introduction to the thesis so that your purpose sentence falls into place and logically seems to be the next thing to say. To illustrate:

> *This example of success in losing weight takes me to my purpose [the last words of the introduction]: I want to put before you the chief factors in a weight-control program [thesis].*

Keep the speech "on the road."

2.   To the first main head. At this point, tie in the first main head by merely repeating the essential thought of the thesis as you present the main head statement. To illustrate:

The initial point to keep in mind in managing your weight [restated thesis idea] is weight reduction [the first main head].

3.   To subheads. These are not major transitions, and I mention them only to indicate that as speakers we link minor ideas, too. We use transitional aids to relate subheads of thought many times a day without realizing it, for example, in connecting clauses of sentences. Usually, these are brief—often one-word conjunctions. Examples are *and, also, but, although, because, then, and finally, therefore, in addition,* and *besides.*

4.   To each new head. You can avoid considerable misunderstanding if you keep your listeners aware of your main points and their relationships. **Let the audience know where you have been and where you are going.** When you approach a new main head, show how it relates to the thesis and prior main heads. You many be able to fit in the new main head with a few words or a sentence. At other times you may need a longer statement to integrate the idea. To illustrate:

Along with weight reduction [the first main head restated], another critical element in any program [the thesis restated] is weight maintenance [the second main head].

And then to connect to the final main head:

Though you cut down your weight [*the first main head restated*] *and keep it level* [*the second main head restated*], *all is for nothing unless you have a sound weight conception* [*the third main head*].

5.   To the closing remarks. As they begin the conclusion—in moving to their final comment—many speakers seem hard pressed for words. How many times have you heard the trite phrase "In conclusion . . ."? It's easy to avoid such overused expressions, if you will *allow your purpose to dictate your wording.* Ask yourself what final feeling or attitude you want to convey: "What parting tone will help me to realize my goal?" Let the answer lead you to find the right words.

A person with an informative speech will accomplish the transition—a summary of the thesis and body of the speech—merely by restating the thesis and then the main heads. This restatement is the first part of the conclusion, a link to the very last remarks. To illustrate:

Remember, then, the three vital aspects of weight control [*thesis restated*]. *They are weight reduction, weight maintenance, and weight conception* [*main heads*].

A person with a persuasive speech on the same topic, perhaps with the same thesis, might begin the conclusion quite differently. To illustrate:

Now, I have an excellent program to recommend, one that satisfies the inherent requirements of all three critical factors [*thesis restated*]: *losing it, keeping it off, and thinking right about it* [*main heads*].

Once again, the transition to the closing remarks—the first words of the conclusion—is a summary, a review of principal points of the speech as presented.

Following is an illustration of the placement and wording of transitions in an abbreviated outline (without subpoints). Only major transitional statements are included, and they are italicized. In the column to the right are brief explanations of the process at each point.

Introduction
  I.   Jazz is an American art.
 II.   The music called jazz has many meanings.   **Here italicized is the transition,**
III.   *More than music, jazz is a*   **the lead or stepping stone to the**
       philosophy of life.   **thesis.**
Thesis
       This is an interpretation of
       jazz as a philosophy of life.

Speakers also "underline" ideas, to guide listeners.

Body

I. *Philosophically, jazz* has to do with the fundamental rhythms of life.

II. *Its expressiveness of truths of life is one interpretation;* also, it has to do with reassessing traditional values.

III. *Besides reflecting a nature of humans and establishing norms,* jazz has to do with survival, which may be the most basic *of these principles.*

Conclusion

I. *More than music, jazz is philosophy.*
   A. *It's about who we are.*
   B. *It's about change and freedom.*
   C. *It's about staying alive and continuing on.*

(balance of conclusion omitted)

The italicized words are a restatement of the thesis, a transition to the first main head: fundamental rhythms.

The italicized words are transitional, a restatement of the thesis and main head I. Note variety in thesis restatement: "truths" for "philosophy."

Again, italics show a review of all prior main points, including the thesis: "principles." Note the slight subordination of I and II to III.

The speaker summarizes the thesis (I) and main heads (A, B, and C). Note variety in word choice, providing interest and possibly adding to the meaning of the message.

How would you finish the speech?

There are few hard rules of oral communication that apply to all speakers, all speeches, all audiences, and all occasions. One, however, will always apply: *Your purpose and your listeners' needs will indicate why, where, and how frequently you should use any speaking method.* This rule is relevant to the use of transitions. The following specific suggestions are also pertinent.

1. Vary your word choice occasionally when relating one thought to another. A synonym used in place of a frequently mentioned word can add variety and new understanding to a given thought. For instance, *philosophy* might at times be called *a guide to the meaning of life.* Consult your dictionary or thesaurus for synonyms, and try enlivening your speech with variety.

Some of the overused transitional words and phrases are *but, so, besides, in addition to,* and *another.* It's advisable to try different ways to relate thoughts creatively, letting the thought and your purpose tell you what pattern of words will be effective.

2. Be free and unmechanical in the employment of transitions. People tend to be rigid and mechanical when trying something for the first time—like driving a friend's car or handling a new tennis racquet. They feel a bit rigid or awkward because the object is not familiar. This is true also with the initial conscious use of transition. At first you may feel restricted, self-conscious, or otherwise insecure, but **with practice and the resulting familiarity, you'll soon appreciate transitional methods.** You'll be able to use them gracefully and weave them into the total fabric of your message. Your audience will be grateful.

Repetition and Restatement

Repetition and restatement are other types of primary processes available to ready listeners to grasp main points of the message. *Repetition* refers to repeating a term or sentence in the same form as first expressed. *Restatement* refers to expressing the thought again but with altered wording or form.

The value of these rhetorical processes lies in achieving emphasis or clarity. If a listener is unimpressed with a vital point, repetition may bring out its significance. Repetition serves to emphasize or to accent. When used purposefully, that is, for a reason, it's a recommended method for underscoring and strengthening thought. But repeating for the sake of repeating probably would be distracting and is not recommended.

If a listener's mind has wandered, restatement of an important point may bring that person back to the discussion. If a point is not clearly understood, restatement may illuminate and clarify it. Also, because of the appeal of variety, restatement can bring freshness or a new dimension to an idea.

Probably the most commonly repeated or restated thoughts in a typical talk are the key ideas. Through use of these primary processes—at any point, not only when making a transition—speakers can give a special interpretation of meaning or emphasis to a major idea before developing it with more specific materials. It's something like making a short but useful comment on the side, like an enforcing highlight.

Repetition. Notice how repetition—reuse of identical words—strengthens the following thoughts.

> *We have also come to this hallowed spot to remind America of the fierce urgency of now. This is no time to engage in the luxury of cooling off or to take the tranquilizing drug of gradualism.* Now is the time *to make real the promises of democracy.* Now is the time *to rise from the dark and desolate valley of segregation to the sunlit path of racial justice.* Now is the time *to lift our nation from the quicksands of racial injustice to the solid rock of brotherhood.* Now is the time *to make justice a reality for all God's children.*
>
> —*Martin Luther King, Jr., "I Have a Dream"*

> We're going to teach them about *this system, the economic problems.* We're going to teach them about *the legislation that is rotten and corrupt.* We're going to teach them about *the politicians that are using our people.* We're going to teach them about *the welfare system that perpetuates itself in order to keep people in bondage.* We're going to teach them about *the different government finance programs that take our best leadership.*[1]
>
> —*Rodolpho "Corky" Gonzales, political leader*

Restatement. The following samples show the effect one can achieve by restating a point: recasting with new words.

> *Every expressive act is ultimately a persuasive act.* Anything that is written that another person can read, anything spoken that another person can hear, any picture etched that is hung in a gallery or TV set is potentially persuasive.[2]
>
> —*C. Ray Penn, college professor*

> *Today, blacks are no longer limited to the periphery of the political system. After more than a century of struggle,* they have gained access to the political system; *after decades of painstaking organizing,* they have built a formidable base. . . . [3]
>
> —*Eddie N. Williams, educational leader*

Repetition and Restatement Combined. The following speech passage shows repetition and restatement working together. Can you spot samples of the two and distinguish between them? After emphasizing the way the media like to report bad news over good news, the speaker said,

> *And the problem with all that is that this is not reality. It is only someone's interpretation of reality. The fact is that not everything in the world is bad. Not every bank or public school or hardware store is*

failing, or incompetent. Not every public official is on the take; many
actually are giving, caring people who do a lot of good for the world.
    Not every black hates and distrusts whites, and not every white
hates and distrusts blacks.
    Not every Wall Street broker is a crook.
    And not every professional athlete is a selfish, overpaid, lout.[4]
                        —William L. Winter, journalist

Definition

Certain words that are very familiar to us may be strange to members of our audiences. When we include them in our speaking, the result is confusion and possible resentment. Consequently, given ideas don't have a chance of being communicated. Let's look into the problem and then discuss one kind of primary process that offers a solution: appropriate definition.

All of us develop individualized modes of expression, assuming that they will be understandable to every listener. That's an error on our part. Often we don't realize that a favorite word or phrase may not mean anything to someone else or that our meanings may differ. One explanation is the human tendency to follow patterns of groups to which we belong. We communicate with the language codes of those groups. Thus we impose a form of isolation on ourselves and consequently experience difficulty in communication with those outside of our group. Here are some examples of separation by group.

Family Culture

Take the case of the family unit, whose members learn to use distinct terms all their own. Some terms used in one family may not be used at all by the family across the street or in another part of town. Many families have retained terms that members coined as babies, cute phraseology that caught on and continues to be used for years. Consider, for instance, the so-called "potty terms," euphemistic expressions that parents use with their children when talking about "going to the bathroom," (another euphemism). Also, in reference to a vacation trip, family members may say, "We're going to *the beach*," meaning a *particular* place by the sea, not just *any* ocean beach, not a lake beach, but *the* beach. From experience in your family, can you think of examples of individualized speech and built-up cultural patterns of meaning? More than adopting unique phrasings, families over generations accrue great complexities of meaning. These become traditional; they're absorbed and passed on as elements of a heritage and distinct culture. Yours is yours, and mine is mine.

Ethnic Culture

Second, ethnic groups can be powerful influences on word usage of members. **Language practices of all groups are governed by rules, constraints on what a word means and how, to whom, or when it's said.** A member of one ethnic group talking with a member of another must be ever conscious of his or her linguistic behavior, for the patterns of each is reflective of a background ruled by well-set conventions that may be relatively unknown to the communicators. Awareness of these differences has two dimensions: respect for the distinctness of others and effectiveness in communicating our thoughts and feelings.

The General Culture

Third, in response to the accelerated pace of living and the more impersonal aspects of society, or to other needs for identity, we put ourselves in other kinds of groups and develop a sense of belonging with them. Ordinarily the rules of these associations exert less power on us, and they are not as lasting. We join car clubs, service clubs, and alumni associations; we regularly attend kaffeeklatsches, swim-club parties, and sessions of the weeknight study group. Certain groups, especially those in which a common interest and purpose are deep, often become marked by their unique language. Individualized language usage seems almost to be a ritual. Members of a commune, inner circle, or age group may set themselves apart and speak a language different in significant ways from those of the larger society to which they are reacting.

"In" Words and Taboo Words. Some words are "in" with young adolescents; some are used only by "nerds" (or whatever the current term is

for that type), rollerbladers, or bungee enthusiasts. Other classifications of persons have their special vocabularies.

Almost any group with some cohesion has both "in" words and taboo words. Use of the former and avoidance of the latter give a person identity and status within the group. The status derives partly from the uniqueness of the group, that is, from the fact of its being *apart from* the larger society. The existence of certain groups represents a wish to reject the unattractive features and imposed standards of the general society— to be free from its force. Language patterns of groups further their separation from the general society and act as instruments to accomplish the rejection. With these specialized vocabularies, some groups seem to say, "Get away, world. This is our realm, you can't belong, you're not one of us."

Other Barriers

Further, in this age of intense specialization, **we isolate ourselves in fields of interest and professional activity.** We adopt the language of our specialties and occasionally find it difficult to communicate with people in other fields. We talk "computers," "information systems," "dungeons and dragons," "postmodernism," "space station," and, I must admit, "communication."

Geography also separates. We learn to use words having meaning in the region in which we live. What are called breakfast rolls in some parts of the country may be Danish in another place, or even snails somewhere else.

To be able to talk with people, it's first necessary to recognize personal or cultural dissimilarities and then discover grounds of unity through identification. This takes us to the services of definition. Each of us needs to remember that not everyone shares the "codes of our personal world"; therefore, we must project ourselves beyond the limited confines of the "territory of self" and define when necessary. As a primary process—a base for building thought—definition is an indicated strategy at any point in a speech when the meaning of an idea would otherwise be lost to the listener. The following are among the various ways to define.

1. **Classification.** Defining by naming the class to which the word or phrase belongs.

Fiction is a class of literature comprising works of imaginative narration, especially in prose form.

An *icebox cake* is a confection made from such prepared ingredients as cookies and whipped cream that requires no additional baking but is chilled in a refrigerator before serving.

Culture is the behaviors and beliefs characteristic of a particular social, ethnic, or age group.

2. **Etymology.** Defining by giving information on the history or derivation of the word or phrase.

Shang-hai is a nineteenth-century term referring to the use of force, liquor, or drugs to obtain a sailor for the crew of a ship.

Gringo is a term originating in the mid 1800s, used in Latin America to refer to a foreigner, especially British or American; probably from the word *greigo,* Greek.

Gay has been used since the 1600s in reference to kinds of sexual conduct; the homosexual connotation goes back to the early twentieth century.

3. Example. Defining by giving a case or example.

Boat person: Perhaps I can define boat person best through use of an example. My neighbor Thuan Nguyen became a boat person. Late in 1975, as a young man in his 20s, he found it politically expedient to flee his Vietnamese homeland. Joining others in a small boat headed east, he became a refugee; without sufficient provisions, he cut himself off from family and friends to seek a safe and free life elsewhere. He was a boat person.

4. Negation. Defining by telling what the term is not.

By *pride,* we don't mean showing off or bragging a lot. It's not always needing to be flattered or craving to be well-liked, nor is it being praised at the expense of someone else.

5. Statement of criteria. Defining by listing the conditions or requirements that are necessary to qualify a term for use. A definition stating the necessary criteria often follows definition by classification and is more specific.

> *We [women] are managing the demands of work, marriage, home-making, children and the community. We worry about finances, career moves, take new courses and tackle new issues constantly. More and more women are sensing mastery of self, finding joy in self-expression and a happiness that comes from involvement, commitment, and putting it all together. That's a definition of* success.
> —*Cecile M. Springer, business executive, Seton Hall College Commencement*

At times, speakers may find more than one type of definition valuable in clarifying a term. For instance, observe the strength resulting from a combination of classification and negation in this definition:

> *Basically, the standard documentary today misunderstands the meaning of the word,* objectivity. *Objectivity means judging each case or story or situation on its own merits, applying a powerfully schooled and disciplined judgment.*
> *Objectivity does not mean what present documentarians think it does: balancing each thought or statement with its opposite.*
> —*Howard K. Smith, broadcaster*

Good definitions unite people in thought by putting them on common ground, thus providing a basis for understanding and identification.

Explanation

Explanation is another *primary* process—foundational strategy—for purposefully contending with challenging conditions and predispositions of audiences. Often comprised of more than one sentence, an explanation is a statement to clarify through interpretation or elucidation, and so on, to make something understandable. **Speakers often find explanation valuable when discussing principles, conditions, concepts, or the operations of something**; for example, to simplify the workings of a system, give explication on the development of a theory or why a certain natural phenomenon occurs. Also, on controversial topics, a full explanation may help listeners handle their fears or analyze their objections. The speaker may be able to show that no difference of opinion exists after all, that speaker and listener share the same beliefs. Once during a speech course a student spoke on a very controversial topic, and when he sat down, he had to answer a great number of challenges to his ideas. After he clarified his position with an *explanation* of what he had meant, the group responded, almost in unison, "Why didn't you *explain that in your speech?*" Speaker and audience, it seemed, were not at odds on essential points.

We often assume that listeners understand us or that it's unnecessary to extend an idea or explain. Since technicalities and other features may require *explanation,* we should check our messages and elaborate when necessary. Following are examples of the use of explanation. In the first instance, financial analyst Andrew B. Wilson wants to explain an idea before developing it.

> *Depreciation is opposite of appreciation. It reflects decline in the value of long-term assets as a result of normal wear-and-tear. It is a cost under operating expenses . . . a non-cash cost . . . reducing reported income.*[5]

In the following explanation, like Wilson's above, economist David Reed wants to clarify a point, before giving supporting examples. His point relates to diminishing sources of electrical power. (Note also the repetition that helps the explanation.)

> *What does this mean? I think it means a number of things for the country overall. It certainly means that we're going to have difficulty sustaining economic growth. It means that some areas of the country that have better access to electrical generating capacity are going to prosper, while other areas of the country that lack that capacity are going to find themselves having economic difficulties.*[6]

A carefully phrased explanation can be very useful in setting up an idea, by reducing uncertainty, ambiguity, or possible negative reaction.

> *First learn the meaning of what you say, and then speak.*
>
> Epictetus, Greek philosopher

LOOKING BACK

Faced with forces of confusion, speakers work hard to reach and identify with audiences. Among useful points to keep in mind are the following:

1. Oral communication involves direct interaction of speaker and listener.

2. Interpersonal awareness is essential to success in speaking.

3. The forces at work against identification of speaker and listener are prevalent and strong.

4. Reliable primary processes—particularly transitions, repetition and restatement, definition, and explanation—are available to serve speakers in sustaining ideas, to meet forces opposing communication.

Communication involves caring about your ideas and the needs of your audience. Fortunately, **strategies are available to use in "showing that you care."** They are basic to the task of setting up an idea. The next two chapters will lead into development of ideas.

MODEL SPEECH OUTLINES

Model Speech Outline 1 (In sentence form and *with major transitions italicized*; note also occasional use of other primary processes, as indicated in parentheses outside sentences of the outline)

Owls

Introduction
- I. I've observed that many people have a favorite bird.
  - A. It may be from the waterbird group.
  - B. It may be a perching bird.
  - C. It may be a hawk type.
- II. *I like owls, all of them.*

Thesis

And now I want you to meet three owls that are distinctive.

Body
- I. *Become acquainted with* the great horned owl.
  - A. You'll find this one all over North America.
  - B. It's a large gray and brown bird.
  - C. It measures between 18 to 25 inches, from tip of bill to tip of tail.
  - D. It has ear tufts that are set wide apart.
  - E. The great horned owl eats rabbits, rodents, birds, and certain crawling creatures.
    1. Like most owls, it preys at night.
    2. Its hunting skills are unbelievable. (explanation)

II.   *I'm also partial to* the spotted owl, a bird slightly smaller than *the one with "horns."*
    A.   It measures between 16 to 19 inches, from bill to tail.
    B.   It's dark brown with white spots.
    C.   It has no tufts; no pointed feathers. (restatement)
    D.   The spotted owl goes after rodents and rabbits, and other lagomorphs. (definition)
    E.   One reason for favoring this bird is that its numbers are declining.
        1.   It lives in the forests of the northern Pacific Coast, great timber country.
        2.   Its habitat is being destroyed.
           a.   Timber cutting diminishes the territory that the owl needs for survival.
           b.   Other construction adds to its plight.
III. *Alongside the great horned owl and the spotted one,* the whiskered owl is tiny, *and I find it appealing.*
    A.   Measuring but 6 to 8 inches from tip to tip, it's tiny, to be sure.
    B.   Giving this bird its name are long bristles (whiskers) at the base of its bill.
    C.   The whiskered owl lives in the southern parts of Arizona and New Mexico.
    D.   It has gray plumage.
    E.   Its menu is somewhat different from the other two.
        1.   Taking smaller, daintier bites, it goes for insects, spiders, centipedes, and the like.
        2.   Only rarely will it eat rodents.

Conclusion
    I.   The night knows many kinds of owls, *but these are three that stand out for one reason or other.*
        A.   There's *the big one with horns,* found everywhere on this continent.
        B.   There's *the one with spots,* coming closer and closer to extinction.
        C.   And there's *the little one with whiskers.*
    II.   Very likely few people will ever see an owl up close, except in nature shows on TV.
    III. That's too bad, for they're one of nature's great living wonders.

Model Speech Outline 2 (In sentence form and *with major transitions italicized;* note also occasional use of other primary processes, as indicated in parentheses outside sentences of the outline)

Narcissism

Introduction
    I.   Narcissism is a major psychological condition of these times.

     A.   It affects all relations and relationships.
        1.   It's prevalent in the business world.
        2.   It's prevalent in government.
        3.   It's prevalent in homes of all communities.
     B.   No one is immune from its effects.
  II.   But there are two "kinds" of narcissism, favorable and unfavorable. (explanation)
  III. *Maybe you'd like to know more about unfavorable forms.*

Thesis

My purpose is to help you understand narcissism as a personal problem.

Body

  I.   Outward manifestations *of the problem* are apparent to everyone.
     A.   Abuse of others is common.
     B.   Rage and violence are not uncommon.
     C.   Among other unsocial behaviors are lying, greed, and intolerance.
     D.   At the same time, seemingly contradictory behaviors will be seen; actions may conflict sharply with goals. (restatement)
        1.   Intense effort toward seeking approval is an example.
        2.   Avoidance of shame is another.
  II.   Inward expressions *of narcissism* differ *from the more overt.*
     A.   Depression is a common condition, very common. (repetition)
     B.   Sufferers may feel empty and unfulfilled.
     C.   A malaise is frequently upon them.
        1.   They become enervated. (definition)
        2.   They may lack intellectual curiosity. (explanation)

Conclusion

  I.   *Narcissism is both an interpersonal and intrapersonal force.*
     A.   *It is seen and felt by society.*
     B.   *Sometimes the expression is more intrapersonal.*
  II.   Given its influence on the course of our lives, we should be aware of the workings of this prevalent condition.

NOTES

1.   Rodolfo "Corky" Gonzales, "Social Revolution in the Southwest," in "The Rhetoric of La Raza," an unpublished manuscript by Robert Tice, Chicano Studies Collection, Arizona State University, Tempe, 1971, appendix, p.2.

2.   C. Ray Penn, "A Choice of Words is a Choice of Worlds," *Vital Speeches of the Day,* LVII (December 1, 1990): 116.

3.   Eddie N. Williams, "The Future of Black Politics," *Vital Speeches of the Day,* LVII (March 15, 1991): 349.

4. William L. Winter, "Putting the World in Perspective," *Vital Speeches of the Day,* LVII (March 15, 1991): 336.

5. Andrew B. Wilson, "Developing Business Savvy," *Vital Speeches of the Day,* LVII (May 15, 1991): 475.

6. David Reed, "Electricity Supply Shortage," *Vital Speeches of the Day,* LVII (April 15, 1991): 399.

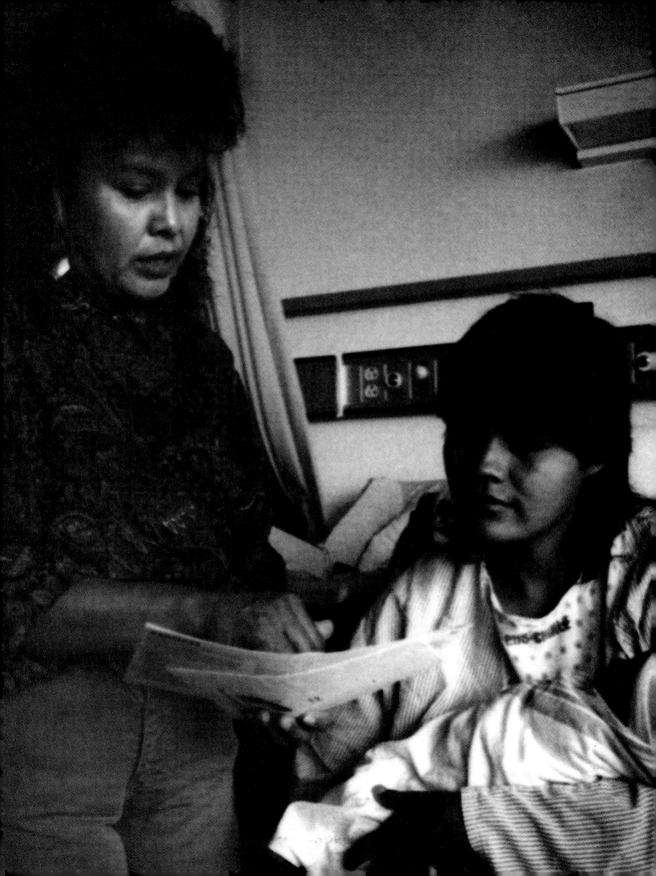

DEVELOPING IDEAS WITH VISUAL AND AUDIO MATERIALS

6

VERBAL AND NONVERBAL ELEMENTS

We use lots of words in speaking: single words, phrases, figurative expressions, and words in all varieties of combinations and patterns. But there are other signs and symbols for communicating, other ways to say things. Accompanying our words are components of sight and added sound. We make sounds with our hands and mouth or other instruments; we change the pitch of our voices; we move the eyes this way and that. Even such behaviors as wearing a new dress or standing very close to someone or being on time or being late give out messages, though wordless.

We communicate *verbally* and *nonverbally*, with words and without words, but typically with these two elements in combination. Ordinarily their working together occurs without conscious thought on our part, for example, wrinkling the forehead when talking about our problems. Other chapters in this book will take up such incidental, less formal usages. The focus here is on the *planned* use of nonverbal aids, visual and audio, to enhance and support the words of a speech and thereby communicate ideas.

DEVELOPMENT OF IDEAS

As a preliminary to the discussion, examine the following partial speech outline. Notice in particular that, like all outlines, it's nothing more than an arrangement of generalizations. As you look it over, what's your first reaction? Do you have a feeling about it?

Thesis
    In the world of art, what was impressionism?

Body
    I.   Devotees of this way of painting departed significantly from established schools.
        A.   The artists sought to depict transitory visual impressions.
            1.   They used broken color to achieve luminosity, a fullness of light.
            2.   They excelled in representing sunlight.
        B.   Yet, the very visualness of the impressionists' program limited the length of its life.

II. Names of artists in the movement are well known.
   A. The most consistent as impressionists were Monet, the plein-air painter; Pissarro; and the gentle, sunny Sisley.
   B. Then there is the lyrical Renoir.
      1. He combined exquisite color with rhythmic line.
      2. He is perhaps best known for remarkable pictures of women and children.
   C. Degas belongs in the canon of greats.
      1. His oils are daring in composition.
      2. His beautiful paintings exercised a liberating influence on other artists, including Gauguin and Picasso.
   D. Add the sterling names of Manet and Cezanne to the list.

Now, one of your reactions as a receiver of a message on impressionism may be that you'd like to *see* some of those ideas. You may want to *see* "transitory visual impressions," "luminosity," Monet's "plein-air" effects, Renoir's lyrics and "rhythmic line," Degas' "daring" composition, and so forth. The outline has well-organized statements: general and unexplained headings. It includes the main *ideas* of the speech: primary headings and subheadings that represent the message's essential substance. When you read the outline, you get a general notion of the content as planned by the speaker. But you can't perceive the brightness, richness, and color inherent in the subject matter. This isn't the complete speech, obviously. It would take a speaker several minutes or perhaps a full half-hour to deliver the body of this speech, and yet you can read the two parts of the outline aloud in one minute. A lot is missing; it's bare and bland, all bones, no flesh.

This brings up a key term in the chapter title: *developing*. **To develop means to unfold more completely and to give fullness and meaning.** Therefore, when speakers develop ideas, they expand on them and heighten or enhance or magnify. They support and fill out their thoughts, giving backing and appropriate elaboration.

The outline on impressionism is undeveloped. The points have not been supported. It's only a skeleton, lacking the specific details it needs to give it life and deserved quality. But that's what outlines are supposed to be. The point is that there are two primary types of data to be found in any message: (1) the general and (2) the specific. ***General data* are the points of outlines, the *framework* of thought. *Specific data* are those concrete *materials* that make the generalizations clear, important, or believable; they fill out the thought.** In speech communication theory, the word *materials* is used specifically in reference to content that backs up and fills out points.

MATERIALS

Materials—specific data—are either physical or verbal. In the next chapter, a continuation of the topic of developing ideas, the focus is on the use of *verbal* materials: examples, statistics, and quotations. Verbal materials, made up of words or numerical data expressed with words, help speakers reach audiences, identifying with them while supporting points. In contrast, physical materials are those that can be seen and sometimes felt, tasted, smelled, or heard. They make strong appeals to the senses. To give adequate information on the painters called French impressionists, you probably would need a lot of visual material: large color prints of representative paintings, possibly some of the artists' preliminary sketches, and other such items. You would develop the thoughts of the outline by referring often to details of their work when making points about it. Imagine how much more effective than telling alone would be the addition of a *showing* of features: the colors, rhythms, effects of light, and the boldness—all in the interest of communicating the full force of impressionism! On this topic, and lots of others, words would not be enough. When visual aids are used appropriately, listeners see the speech as well as hear it. Thus another sensory avenue is made available in communication.

VISUAL AND AUDIO MATERIALS

Most able speakers know the limitations of words alone and realize that people have become dependent on graphic devices. They recognize the value of well-chosen physical materials and make free use of them. Yet occasionally, one will hear a speech that has real poten-

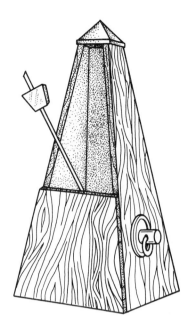

tial but is deficient because of a lack of visual or audio aids. Sometimes such materials are indispensable. Here are some values:

1. Audio-visual aids help create identification with listeners. Relevant materials can bring the minds of communicators together, an achievement that may not be possible with words alone. To begin with, these aids command attention. In some instances, attention may be generated by colors or by the visible texture of an object of unusual shape that may be used to catch interest and secure response. Or perhaps sound could be added to enliven ideas, for example, the tick-tick of a metronome in a talk on rhythm. Also, people respond to movement, a fact known for a long time by safety engineers. An American roadway with its variety of blinkers, flashing lights, and animated arrows is a pertinent example. Such stimuli grab attention because they are strong and demanding. Speakers can help listeners remain involved by using materials that appeal directly to the senses.

2. Audio-visual aids clarify. Again, because words are not always sufficient to the task of communication, it may be necessary to represent an idea physically. Try this experiment on two friends: Describe to one, with words only, how to go to a certain place. Take the same amount of time in giving your directions to the second person, but this time use a sketch or drawing to help communicate the information. Ask each friend to give the directions back to you. I've done it and invariably find that the second person's version is more correct. It's because of the clarifying map.

3. Audio-visual aids help listeners retain ideas. More than making your ideas clear, interesting, and related to the listeners' lives, you may want the audience to retain them. When your listeners leave the speech setting, you usually hope that they will take some of the message with them. Methods are available to accomplish that. A photograph of mountain climbers making a mighty effort to scale Mount Everest may cause people to remember the speaker's point about the climbers' great courage and endurance. After a number of years, several people who were members of one audience still recall the history of the famous McClellan horse saddle because the speaker had an actual saddle to refer to as he talked. Visual or audio support for thoughts can help make it easier for people to retain them.

4.   Audio-visual aids can help reduce apprehension. When asked why she always used a pointer while speaking, one woman replied, "The pointer helps me feel relaxed. I have something to hold and manipulate." Although, because of possible distractions, I don't advocate using a pointer when delivering all speeches, the woman's comment does make sense. Having something to do, for example, showing an object, does reduce tension for most speakers. Being active helps them to loosen up and be more at ease and, therefore, better speakers. Also, an aid may remind speakers of sections of their speeches that they intend to cover, serving like notes, you might say. In that way, their use adds to security in speaking.

Now, let's remind ourselves of certain uses of these materials. First, we'll take the visual.

Using Visual Aids

Distinguished from aids that strictly involve the use of sound, **visual aids are materials that can be seen.** Recall your own communication experiences, and make a mental list of some materials you've seen speakers use. Your list will probably include such items as charts, graphs, maps and globes, blackboard sketches, models, moving pictures, projected slides, and photographs. In addition, you may remember objects of different types that were used as special aids to support ideas. A list of such special aids would be at least as long as a list of topics. The biology teacher who shows the underside of a leaf to show cell structure uses a special visual aid, as does the mechanic who manipulates and describes a customer's worn-out fuel pump. In other words, visual materials are any and all supporting objects that an audience is able to see.

Guidelines for Use   1.   **Use visual materials to serve a purpose. The only justification for including any item in a speech is that it will support a purpose of the speech.** Speakers don't sketch on the blackboard just to be active or because the book says that some sketching may help. They draw or write on the blackboard because there's a point to make, and well-planned sketching will help make the point. An unnecessary aid is not only valueless but also a possible·distraction. Keep this in mind as you prepare oral assignments requiring some use of visual aids.

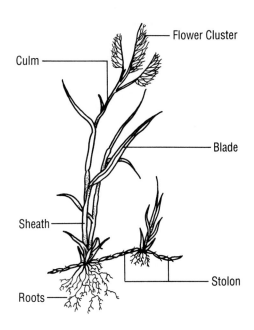

Culm — Flower Cluster

Blade

Sheath

Roots — Stolon

Your grasp of the needs of communication will guide you in being purposeful.

2. Be certain that all listeners can see and appreciate the aid. When sketching, it's advisable to move aside occasionally to allow everyone a clear view. Also, if you've been sketching and referring to the board from the left side for some time, perhaps you should move to the right side. You can return soon, should the left side be more comfortable for you. In any event, remember the sightlines. The listeners most often neglected by speakers are those in back and those in the front rows at the ends. *Always check to see that the speaker's stand does not block anyone's view* of your material, whether you are holding it or have it fixed to a wall or other surface. That's a major violation!

Sketch or write with large and broad lines; keep the drawings and charts simple and not too detailed. Thorough preparation outside of class will contribute to good results.

Also, an object should be used in such a way as to allow easy viewing. It should be large enough for all to appreciate. Photographs present a particular problem. Most pictures from magazines are too small; people in the back rows can't see them adequately. A photograph under 8x10 inches in size should not be used. If you have a promising one but it's too small, see if you can have it enlarged. Moreover, an object should be held at a satisfactory viewing height. Chin height is about right. That's only a general rule because other factors, such as your height and room conditions, may prescribe special handling.

And tell yourself to hold it at that good height, patiently, for as long as its presence is necessary. Have you noticed that some speakers are too quick in putting aside their materials? They show an aid as they would a

Simple devices such as maps help to convey your message.

United States

Atlantic Ocean

GULF OF MEXICO

Mexico

Cuba

Puerto Rico

Pacific Ocean

Caribbean Sea

Central America

South America

flash card and thus lose its potential power. **If an aid is important enough to be included in the speech, it ought to be used carefully and well.** Also, speakers occasionally find it wise to walk out to the audience and move along in front of them as they manipulate or display an object. That kind of attention to listeners' needs can help communication.

3.   Maintain contact in use of the aid. Ordinarily it's advisable to make fitting comment as you use visual material. Verbal support may be both appropriate and necessary. Words can help to explain key points and also maintain interest. At times, pauses in talking are unavoidable and even beneficial, but frequently they offer excuses for listeners to become restless and even to engage in side conversations. Keep the thought flowing and interest growing by having enough to say as you present the visual content of your speech.

Eye contact, too, should not suffer when you're employing a visual aid. There's a tendency when sketching or demonstrating to give attention to the aid and neglect listeners. The solution is simple: **Talk to the people, not to the aid.** Good planning and practice can help prevent loss of valuable eye contact.

4.   Control use of the aid. Using visual materials does have its risks. For example, consider the danger of inadvertently diverting attention to something extraneous, for example when you find no chalk in the room or you can't locate the wall socket. Planning is the answer to that problem, as it is in meeting most problems in communication.

First of all, when you bring objects to a speaking situation, put them in some convenient location near the speaking area or keep them with you at your seat. The point is to **have your materials handy and ready to**

be introduced at the proper place, available yet inconspicuous. And even though you find it necessary to keep them in a bag or box, avoid having them so securely contained that you must struggle to remove them.

Next consider the question of timing. In planning how and where to use a given item, ask yourself if this item should be shown before that other one and when a certain one should be brought out, and so forth. Introduce your object or sketch at the point in your speech where it will best serve to support the message. Early "unveiling" may destroy some suspense value or be a distraction; late showing may provide nothing but a weak anticlimax. Timing can be important to accomplishment of purpose. Again, the importance of rehearsal cannot be overemphasized. And if possible, rehearse in the room where you'll be giving the speech.

When you've finished with an object, put it aside (or in the case of sketching, erase the board), unless you want to leave it on display for certain reasons, and if it will not interfere with another person's speech. Any aid can be overused. **Only on rare occasions should you risk distracting the audience by passing an object among them during your speech.** All too often the passed object gets attention while the speaker's ideas at that moment are not received. While looking at it or anticipating its arrival, an audience member is not a good listener.

If you want to support your ideas with objects that require more space than the room provides, it'll be necessary to arrange for an outside speaking scene. Many teachers of speech communication report that at least once during the course a student will bring in a visual aid of unusual proportions. In this category are such prodigious supporting materials as automobiles, jet skis, motorcycles, archery equipment, athletic gear, and even horses.

Control of visual aids has a humorous side. For a class speech on raising pigeons, a student brought two of the birds with him. At one point, he took the pigeons out of the cage but neglected to close the large opening when he put them back. They got out and flew to a corner of the room, causing great excitement. Eventually they were returned safely to the cage, though not before the audience had completely forgotten the purpose of the speech.

Incidentally, you should check with your instructor about the suitability of some visual aids. For example, firearms or other questionable materials may not be allowed.

Using Audio Aids

Devices that produce sound can be useful in oral communication. These are audio aids. Chiefly, they are tape recorders, cassette and disc players, musical instruments, and so forth, but they could be any sound-producing device, for example, drums, castanets, and whistles. Possibly a speaker plans to discuss how a certain band gets its great sound. Why not illustrate the effects by playing recorded fragments at appropriate spots in the

> *We are less convinced by what we hear than by what we see.*
>
> *Herodotus,*
> *Greek historian*

development of the ideas? Of course, such recorded support should not take up an undue portion of the speaking time. Let your purpose guide you in this.

A speaker, while telling how to play a chord with a guitar, would certainly strum the instrument occasionally, to enhance verbal commentary. In the conclusion, the audience might be treated to an entire short selection serving as a summary—a musical recapitulation of the thesis and main heads discussed in the talk.

Suggestions and guidelines for using an audio aid are essentially the same as those for using a visual aid. First, employ the device to help you reach your goal. Then plan its use and sustain audience contact. In some cases, the level will need careful control, so that the sound is loud enough for all to hear, but not too loud. Finally, be fully and comfortably acquainted with your device, and practice sufficiently to avoid wasteful pauses and any distracting activity.

TYPICAL SITUATIONS

Put yourself in these typical speaking situations, and consider possible solutions to the problems posed. *You'll note that most of the advice given in any one of the situations will apply to other occasions as well.*

1.   **Graphs.** Let's say you plan to point out in a class speech the comparative percentages of student body money spent on athletics, the newspaper, special programs, student council activities, and so forth. How can you convey your points graphically? Why not *show* the percentages? Use a visual aid to help the audience understand your ideas immediately and also *retain* them. A simple, carefully prepared pie graph, boldly drawn, may be the answer.

The line graph and bar graph are examples of other kinds of graphs that may be useful on occasion.

Some Advice

- Make the graph large, easy for all to see, perhaps with contrasting colors.
- Position the graph for convenient viewing. Explore the room in advance to discover appropriate spots for placing your aids. You may need to bring tacks or masking tape for fixing them to a wall or board.
- Plan and rehearse the presentation well, to coordinate the talking and showing.
- A pointer may help to focus listener attention on some feature.

2.   **The real thing.** Suppose that in planning a speech on period furniture you decide to discuss the design of Chinese Chippendale chairs. You can imagine listener dissatisfaction if you tried to make do by pre-

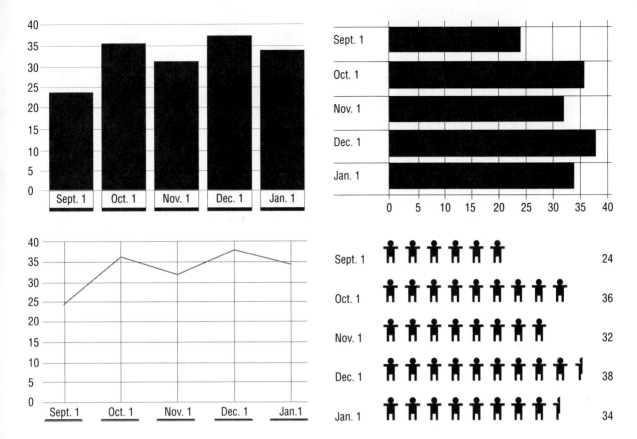

Attendance patterns of the Art Club shown in different types of graphs.

tending that a classroom chair were a Chinese Chippendale chair, even if you had photographs or drawings. It's highly unlikely that pretending would be adequate. No, on this and other such occasions, **bring the real thing.** Though going over to your aunt's house to get the chair may take time out of a busy day, the results would justify the effort.

Some Advice

- Have your object handy, ready for use, and perhaps covered.
- If you want the audience to take special note of some particular detail, as you most likely do, display the object on a table, tilting it this way and that to reveal characteristics.
- Talk to the people, not to the aid.

3. Display. Assume that as a department store display artist you decide to discuss techniques of designing appealing window displays. Obviously visual aids would be needed, but what kind? What about drawings? Perhaps. Should you show pictures of decorated windows? Yes, they would help. Possibly the best of all visual support would entail your setting up a display, like the real thing but in miniature. As you talk, you would move the tiny objects here and there to show various effects.

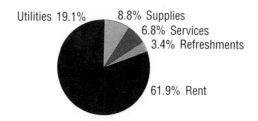

Circle graph of Art Club expenditures for March.

Utilities 19.1%   8.8% Supplies
6.8% Services
3.4% Refreshments

61.9% Rent

Let's say that Thanksgiving is near and you are preparing a talk on how to arrange a dining table centerpiece. You realize that visual aids would be helpful, but you haven't decided on the kind. Should you show magazine pictures of different arrangements? What about a blackboard sketch? Better yet, bring in a bag of the appropriate objects—gourds, ears of corn, pretty leaves, and so forth—and get your points across as you lay out a nice well-planned display.

Some Advice

- Plan for working space within everyone's visual range; an inclined surface may help.
- Make relevant comments about the process, as you handle the physical materials.
- As you speak, maintain eye contact with the audience as much as possible.

4.   Sketches. As an employee of United Parcel Service, you find that choosing the subject for your speech is easy, as is choosing supporting aids. With the purpose of showing the path of a parcel from reception to delivery, you decide to draw a sketch of its travels. You can add to the sketch, let it build, as you progress in your verbal presentation.

Some Advice

- Focus on main points only, excluding minor details or unnecessary complexity.
- Do not apologize for your sketching. At least 50 percent of the speakers in speech communication classes will say something like "I'm a terrible artist, so bear with me." Be with the *other* 50 percent, those who are more concerned about being effective speakers than revered artists.
- Keep in touch with the listeners, visually and verbally.

5.   Charts. With a thesis such as "I intend to show you the management structure of a typical American corporation," you would find a chart valuable. Perhaps you can discover one in a textbook or encyclopedia. Either use a copy machine or printer to enlarge it, or copy it yourself onto a piece of poster board of ample size, using a dark felt marker. Such a chart would be better than a blackboard sketch, neater and more professional.

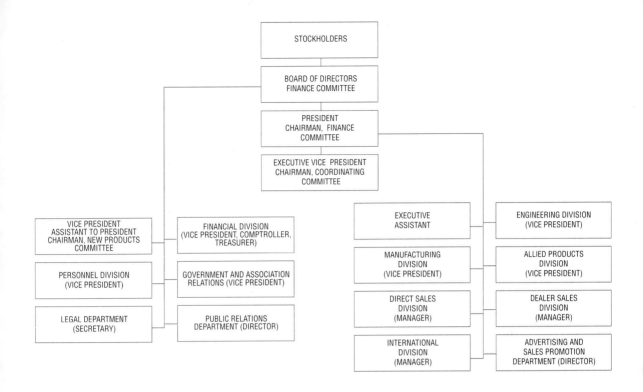

An organizational chart visually explains a corporation's structure.

Also, a chart may give you greater freedom—and the opportunity to have more eye contact with the audience.

Perhaps you want your audience to understand a progression of ideas: the unfolding of a plan or a system's stages of development. To help in communication, you could use a device called a flip chart. It's made up of a set of paper or cardboard charts arranged in sequence and hinged at the top. You flip the sheets over as you speak.

Some Advice

- Place it high enough for all to see.
- If you plan to display the sketch by leaning it against something, be sure it's rigid enough to stand by itself, with no chance of curving and falling (that happens too much!).
- Rehearse!
- During the speech, stand clear of your aid as much as possible, using a pointer to draw attention to details.

6. Various Materials. Let's imagine that a fire occurred in nearby mountains. Having followed the event and being familiar with the fire-fighting equipment that the fire crew used, you decide to speak on that topic. What supporting materials might prove useful? A forest service map of the burned area? Slides or overhead projections of scenes? Photographs of principal air and ground vehicles used in fire control? Typical pieces of hand equipment? Protective clothing worn by the fire crew? The answer, of course, is that any or all of these aids may serve at given places to make the message clear. Once again, **your purpose at any point will dictate the mode of development and materials to use.**

Some Advice

- Introduce the aids at points where they will serve best.
- Resist the temptation to pass articles around during the speech. If time allows, you may arrange to let people handle the articles when you finish speaking.
- Practice sufficiently to coordinate all elements.
- Be sure the photographs are large enough to be appreciated from the back of the room.

7.   Models. If your purpose is to have your listeners understand the principles governing a helicopter's flight, why not use a model helicopter? *Show* the functions and dynamics of the rotating wings and blades on their axes and the creation of lift, and so forth. Sketches or charts might also be of help.

Similar types of aids would be useful in giving information on the mechanics of various kinds of engines, an electric cell, or solar energy systems.

Some Advice

- Avoid hurrying over ideas. Take pains to clarify the principles and show applications.
- Remember the value of restating and reshowing.
- As you talk, be wary of the temptation to digress to an interesting but unrelated dimension of theory. It happens to speakers, especially those who are wrapped up in their subjects and who sense high audience interest! That's what we call a dilemma.

8.   Demonstration, and so forth. Perhaps you have decided to discuss the cultural significance of a folk dance that's familiar to you. Besides ideas to relay, there will be footwork to show and other movement. If relying on words alone, you might resort to analogy, saying that the dance is somewhat like a waltz, except that you don't do this little part and you sort of slide to one side after twirling, and so forth. But don't you agree that a demonstration would be far better? Prevent confusion by actually performing the steps, with realism.

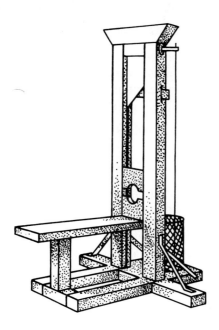

Using a Feltboard. To add to the demonstration and to clarify parts that the audience might have missed because of sightline blocking or fast action, you could reshow the steps with a feltboard. Cut out pieces shaped like the bottom of feet; place and move them appropriately on the feltboard as you explain.

The feltboard method, or any other system involving the use of moveable pieces that adhere to a surface, has many uses for speakers whose presentations require the placing, moving, and removing of elements. Besides introducing listeners to a dance and its movements, you can illustrate bowling techniques, game rules, layouts of towns or buildings, the history of a word's development, comparisons and contrasts of a great variety of phenomena, the component parts of a large design, and countless other subjects. I know a speech instructor who uses a feltboard to explain outlining to her students.

Some Advice

- Work where people can see everything going on. You may have to rearrange the chairs into a circle or half circle.
- Repeat complicated parts of the demonstration.
- If you use a display board, have it set up before you start.
- A slight tilt backward will help assure that the adhering pieces, whether backed with felt, flannel, or sandpaper, or magnetized, will cling to the board.

LOOKING BACK

In communicating their main ideas—the thesis, main heads, and subpoints—speakers call upon *materials*: specific elements of development.

Visual and audio aids are materials that help the development of ideas by:

1. Furthering the process of identification.
2. Clarifying ideas.
3. Helping listeners retain ideas.

And, they assist in reducing apprehension in speaking.

Yes, audio and visual aids are of real value, but only if:

1. They're used purposefully.
2. Listeners are able to see and hear them.
3. They contribute to contact of speaker and listener.
4. The speaker controls their use.

Of the many types of physical materials available, speakers should choose those that fit the requirements of their speech plan. In this regard, you might note the techniques employed by some of your instructors and other good speakers whom you have a chance to observe.

The next chapter is a companion to this one because it covers the other type of specific material of support, the verbal. It will complete our discussion of developing ideas.

MODEL SPEECH OUTLINES

Model Speech Outline 1 (In sentence form and with developmental materials indicated in brackets outside the outline)

Pyramids of the Americas

Introduction

    I. The pyramids of the Americas are marvels of pre-Columbian architecture. [show photographs]

        A. They served as foundations for temples.

            1. They were built to honor the gods.

            2. Unlike the pyramids of Egypt, most were not tombs.

        B. They were constructed of adobe, earth, and rubble. [show drawing]

        C. Facings varied.

            1. Some were painted and decorated.

            2. Some were faced with river stone.

    II. We in North America should know more about them.

Thesis

    I'd like now to distinguish between the two types of pyramids built in the Americas.

Body
  I.   Most of the pyramids have a rectangular or square base.
      A.   They have stepped platforms, raised in stages. [do sketching]
      B.   These are found in various regions. [use map]
          1.   The Incas built them in Peru.
          2.   You'll find them in Honduras.
          3.   The pyramid at Tikal in Guatemala is noteworthy.
              [show drawing]
          4.   El Salvador has a number.
          5.   The Pyramid of the Sun in Mexico is spectacular.
              [show drawing]
              a.   The base is 700 by 700 feet.
              b.   It stands 210 feet high.
  II.   Contrast the square Sun Pyramid with those having a circular base.
      A.   They were built on a round plan with conical layers. [show drawing]
      B.   They are less common than the rectangular or square type.
          1.   The round pyramid at Cuicuilco in Mexico is fascinating. [show drawing]
          2.   The round pyramid at La Venta is fluted. [show drawing]

Conclusion
  I.   This has been a brief introduction to those magnificent structures called pyramids—pyramids of the Americas.
      A.   Remember that most are rectangular or square.
      B.   But some are circular.
  II.   You may wish to learn more about the fabulous story of the architectural genius behind the creation of the pyramids.
      A.   Good books are available.
      B.   Travel tours can be arranged.

Model Speech Outline 2 (In sentence form, with major transitions italicized and developmental materials indicated in brackets outside the outline)

Taking Pictures

Introduction
  I.   Photographs are a universal language whereby experiences, thoughts, and feelings can be conveyed to others.
      A.   Pictures can inform, stimulate the imagination, or persuade vividly. [contrasting photos]
      B.   If you enjoy taking pictures, *you should have an understanding of composition so that your pictures will communicate the right message.*

Thesis
    Let's examine three of the components of good picture composition.

Body
    I.   *Composition can be built around* geometric forms.
        A.   They determine the shape or design.
           1.   Circles will frame the picture and direct attention. [photo]
           2.   Triangles give strength and stability to a composition. [photo]
           3.   Radiation suggests growing movement. [photo]
        B.   They add strength. [refer back to photos]
   II.   *Regardless of the shapes exploited, good picture composition* will have a center of interest. [photo]
        A.   Group the most interesting things near each other.
        B.   The chief point of interest should show the most contrast. [photo]
        C.   Tell one story at a time. [reference to photos]
  III.   *Together with form and point of attention,* consider the illusion of depth, *one of the most vital phases of picture building.*
        A.   Contrast dark objects against light objects. [photo]
        B.   Have lines converge to a point in the distance. [sketching]
        C.   Overlap the edges of objects. [photo]

Conclusion
    I.   *Understanding the effect of geometric shapes, centering interest, and realizing the values of depth can make your picture communicative.*
   II.   Photography is a very expressive form of communication.
  III.   As a photographer, willing to learn, you can be an artist and your camera a medium of expression.
  IV.   Your pictures can speak for you.

Model Speech Outline 3 (In sentence form with major transitions italicized and developmental materials indicated in brackets outside the outline)

A full text of this speech, as rehearsed, is in Appendix A.

What is an Average?

Introduction
    I.   Often we are bombarded by statistics.
        A.   We hear or read about the percentages of this or that.
        B.   We are also informed about averages.
   II.   We can be tricked by someone's use of the term "average."

Thesis
    Today I would like to describe three ways of looking at "average."

Body
    I.   *The first and most common kind of average* is the arithmetic mean.

     A.   Finding the arithmetic mean involves two steps.
         1.   First, sum all the data points in the data set.
         2.   Then, divide by the number of things you counted.
     B.   Let's see what we get. [blackboard sketching of cases]

II.   *In addition to the mean,* the median *is another common form of average.*
     A.   The median is the middle point in the data set.
     B.   Exactly half the points are above this point, and half are below.
     C.   Again, let's see what we get. [blackboard sketching of cases]

III. *While the mean and the median are frequently used forms,* the mode is a third *important average.*
     A.   The mode is the most frequently met-with number in a data set.
     B.   To remember mode, think of *most.*
     C.   Let's see what we get. [blackboard sketching]

Conclusion
   I.   Can you see how I've packaged the data differently?
     A.   *First, I used the mean.* [reference to sketching]
     B.   *Then, I used the median.* [reference to sketching]
     C.   *Finally, I used the mode.* [reference to sketching]
  II. When you hear that something is "average," I hope you'll know how they differ.

DEVELOPING IDEAS WITH VERBAL MATERIALS

7

★ **LOOKING AHEAD** ★

1. What are verbal materials? What are their uses?

2. What is an example?
   a. How are some examples different from others?
   b. How do examples benefit speakers?
   c. How are they to be used?

3. What are statistics?
   a. For what purposes do speakers use statistics?
   b. How are statistics to be checked for reliability?
   c. How are they to be handled in speaking?

4. What are quotation and authority?
   a. For what purposes do speakers use quotation?
   b. How are quotations to be checked for reliability?
   c. How are they to be handled in speaking?

5. What are the principal criteria for selecting developmental materials for speeches?

6. Where does one find materials for speeches?

7. How should one cite sources of materials used in speeches?

A conversation like the following might be heard on any college campus around the country.

He:	Yes, I believe that William Shakespeare is the best writer to have written in the English language.
She:	That's a very big statement. Why do you think so?
He:	I have a bunch of reasons. The first one is his genius in building the character of his people. Take Hamlet, for instance. Has there ever been a truer example of how complex humans are? In Hamlet, we have . . . [He describes Hamlet.]
She:	OK, good example. Any more?
He:	Sure. What about Othello and Macbeth? Let me tell you what Shakespeare does with their characters. First, Othello . . . [description]
She:	You know, you're making a good point.

Analysis of the Dialogue

The "good point" that she refers to is a *reason,* the first point in the other person's case. And apparently his case, resting on well-chosen examples, is beginning to sound convincing to her. She's right; he has made a promising start, but he'll need more reasons and then more supporting examples to back them.

Notice three things about the Shakespeare student's approach. First, he starts with a major *contention,* a *thesis* we'd call it: Shakespeare is the best. Second, he gives a *reason* for his contention, a *main head* we'd call it: Shakespeare's a genius in characterization. Then, he begins to supply *proof*—in the form of *examples,* such as Hamlet and Othello.

VERBAL MATERIALS

And that's what this chapter is about: making assertions—stating points—and backing them. The emphasis here is on the backing, on the "proof." It's on developing the points, generalizations, with specific materials, examples, statistics, and quotations.

In the prior chapter, we concerned ourselves with visual and audio aids, those specific supporting materials that can be seen, felt, or heard. Being concrete and tangible, they serve as excellent developers of ideas in speeches and means of relating them to listeners' lives. They help the speaker anchor thoughts to reality and make abstractions believable, vivid, and clear. The current topic is very closely related. In fact, it's merely a continuation and completion of the study of methods for developing ideas. Our attention will now be turned to those specifics that we call *verbal materials*.

Like their visual and audio counterparts, verbal developers of thought add meaning and proof to assertions in a speech. They help an audience visualize the idea and appreciate its merits; they help the listener understand or be moved by what the speaker is saying. Serving the same general purpose as visual and audio aids, they are useful in these ways:

1. In developing interest and establishing bases for understanding
2. In clarifying thought
3. In moving listeners to respond to thought
4. In causing listeners to remember important thought

In a word, they facilitate identification with audiences. The following discussion of verbal developmental materials will elaborate on the value of the three main types: examples, statistics, and quotations.

> *In speaking, you have to draw a simple picture and color it in.*
>
> César Chávez,
> speaker–activist

Examples

In my favorite book of synonyms, *Roget's International Thesaurus,* 4th edition, revised by Robert L. Chapman, you'll find the following synonyms (and more) for the word "example": instance, exemplification, illustration, specimen, sample, and case in point. As indicated by these words, an example is used to illustrate or exemplify, to serve as a specimen or sample. In oral communication, an example is used to give strength and significance to general points.

Point: *Winter days are great study days.*
Example: *For example, let me tell you about last Saturday afternoon. Remember the downpour? Rain pounded rooftops for five hours without stopping and roared noisily down metal drainpipes, while gusts of wind made tall trees sway and whip. But I was studying in warm satisfaction in my bedroom, on the north side of our house on Bishop Street. Piled on my old brown desk were all the resources that I needed to make the day profitable—history and psychology textbooks, a dictionary, the* Columbia Encyclopedia, *pencils, a notebook or two, and other assorted tools of the student. "Let it rain," I said. In those four or five hours I did the work of 10 ordinary hours.*

Point: *Snorkeling is exciting.*

Example: *My first snorkeling experience was at Green Island on the Great Barrier Reef. After 15 minutes' instruction by a patient and experienced friend, I went off on my own to explore underwater life. You just can't imagine the tremendous varieties of shapes and sizes of fish down there: huge and tiny, fat or slim like a pencil, and with so many different designs of the mouth, eyes, body, and tail. And the colors of their markings! Stripes of pure white or red, yellow and violet dots on pink, chartreuse configurations combined with gorgeous patterns in blues, oranges, and greens of many hues. Also, they come right up to you, looking you in the eye and brushing against you. Some smile, some frown, but I never once felt threatened. It's unreal; I love it!*

There's a kind of magic in examples; they bring speaker and listeners together. Intrigued by a good example, the listeners will get a mental picture of the speaker's idea and make some kind of connection to their own personal experience. The power of an example comes from special features, for example, as shown in the two preceding samples. The appeal is in its:

1. Concreteness
2. References to the familiar
3. Color and variety
4. Stimulation of curiosity
5. Humor (if included)
6. Appeals to personal needs and emotions

The example can assume two basic forms: the long, relatively complete form, which is called an *illustration,* and the short, undeveloped form, which is called an *instance.*

The Illustration   Speakers use the *illustration,* a full example, when they need to include considerable detail in order to allow listeners to participate extensively in development of the thought. Skillful speakers know that to bring the audience "into the speech," their supporting material must in some way be related to listeners' experiences. **A good illustration with its specific details, concreteness, and human interest has broad and immediate appeal.** Thus, it helps make the point.

Description. In the following development of a thought, the illustration capitalizes on elements of *description* to achieve its effect as a supporting aid.

> Point: *The cities of New Zealand are beautiful.*
> Illustration (full example): *One of the most beautiful is Christchurch on the South Island, which I visited one year in the summer months of December, January, and February. Gently flowing through the city is the Avon River, on its way to the Pacific a few miles away. As the name Avon suggests, Christchurch is English in character, with gardens and architecture reminiscent of sites in Hertfordshire and Surrey. In the town center is the magnificent Square and Cathedral. Close by is Hagley Park, a huge expanse which includes playing fields, trees, and acres of green grass; also it encompasses the Botanic Gardens and other attractions. Close by is the Arts Centre, where every imaginable artistic creation is produced and displayed for purchase, everything from leather belts to fine paintings. All this is merely the "top layer" of Christchurch. There is much, much more to experience in this lovely city.*

Narrative. The illustration supporting the next point is a *narrative,* a story. **We all enjoy hearing well-told stories,** and they can be an effective means of supporting points in speeches.

> Point: *One should listen to voices of experience.*
> Illustration (full example): *Last summer as I began working for the Post Office as a mail carrier, I was advised by other carriers about a particular problem at 5129 Blossom Way, that is, about an animal that lived there. It seemed that this dog, a small terrier named Victor, was always waiting inside the gate, on the front porch. Sarah, the carrier who had preceded me on that route, said that she had never been able to get as far as the mail slot, not once. "Ah, come on!" I said to myself, "Afraid of a little dog?" So, on my first day out there, I was determined to reach the slot and push the mail through—the bills, junk mail, and all the rest. As I approached the gate, there he*

> *When one's proofs are aptly chosen, four are as valid as four dozen.*
>
> Matthew Prior,
> writer and speaker

was, the hostile one, lying on the porch. We eyed each other, grimly beginning our battle of wills. He growled, and I growled back, letting him know that I spoke his language and would not be intimidated. I took two steps toward the house; he began to rise. I took another step, and up he jumped with his "Yip, yip, yip!" I turned in a flash and took a mighty leap over the fence, leaving a piece of my right sock in Vicious Victor's mouth. That was it, no more for me! Victor and his master—no one masters that beast!—got zero pieces of mail from me that summer. I should have listened to my predecessors.

In support of a point, C. Ray Penn of Radford University found a useful example, an illustration as *narrative*, in the experience of a friend.

Point: *We must watch our analogies.*
Illustration: *A friend of mine was attempting to build a new housing development and was applying for all of the permits that such a task requires. The local newspaper sent out a reporter to interview him about the project. When the story appeared, it said "Williams is going to have an uphill battle on his hands as he begins his new housing development." The fact that this project—no more difficult than any other—was described with a military analogy almost became a self-fulfilling prophecy. Battles—be they uphill or down—result in bloodshed, create winners and losers, make enemies of innocent bystanders and often expand into wars. The fact that the reporter did not intend to create ill feelings between builder and city council members does not lessen the reporter's responsibility.[1]*

As you see, **illustrations give strength and concreteness to assertions. By providing amplifying detail, they help audiences to share in the thought.** One person has described such examples as the "wings that carry ideas into listeners' minds."

The Instance   The form of example called *instance* is shorter than the longer example, the illustration; it includes less detail. Frequently speakers use instances in a series, as a chain of brief examples. **Linked together, instances will give an idea more believability than will a single short example;** there is force and power in numbers. Note this use of a series of instances by Mary Hatwood Futrell, speaking in Cleveland when she was president of the National Educational Association.

Point: *Cooperation of business and schools is beneficial.*
Instances: *Let me give you some examples of the cooperation that's already taking place all over the United States.*
    In the school district next door to where I teach—Fairfax County, Virginia—a business-school partnership is helping teachers understand the high-tech world so they can better identify the skills needed for a changing work force.

A hospital in St. Louis has developed a curriculum on drug abuse and other health-related subjects for that city's middle schools.

In Florida, the Suncoast Chamber of Commerce set up a partnership with the Pinellas County Public Schools to create an economics education program called "Educational Excellence: A Shared Commitment."

Several San Francisco teachers have received paid internships in the business community under the "Corporate Action in Public Schools" program.[2]

The following point is developed with a number of specific instances.

Point: *American speech is sprinkled with words of Spanish origin.*
Instances: *Here are some examples.*

The word aficionado, *or devotee, is taken directly from the Spanish, but Americans generally put in an extra "f" in spelling it.* Cafeteria *meant coffeemaker or coffee store in the Spanish of early California.* Lariat *is from* la reata.

Guerrilla, a type of warfare, originated during the time of Spain's resistance to Napoleon's aggression. The American slang word hoosegow *is derived from* jusgado *which once was the Mexican name for jail. The word* patio *is courtyard in the Spanish language. A* peccadillo *is a minor sin, hardly punishable.* Macho, *or aggressive manliness, comes from* masculino, *male.*

Reinforcing the Illustration with Instances   An illustration coupled with a group of instances provides stronger support than is possible when either is used without the other. The result can be a highly effective sequence of thought. After stating your point, (1) give a rich illustration to support the point; (2) then bolster the point further with a series of specific instances, short and relevant examples. The following set of examples, an illustration backed by three closely related instances, is from Howard Runkel's speech "Making Lincoln Live" that is printed in full in Appendix A.

Point: *Lincoln was a humble man.*
Illustration: *Do you remember how Lincoln drove out of Washington after a wearying day behind the desk in the White House to confer with his subordinate, General McClellan? The arrogant McClellan, aware of his commander-in-chief's presence, loftily instructed his orderly to tell the President that no interview was possible any more that evening; that he had gone to bed and was not to be disturbed. A witness to the embarrassing scene indignantly besought Lincoln to "pull his rank." "Are you going to tolerate such insubordination?" he pleaded. That stooped and worn figure merely shrugged and answered: "I'd hold McClellan's horse if that would give us victories." History records that on that evening the immortal had waited upon the mortal.*

Instances: *Then there was the time that a high government official discovered Lincoln in the act of blacking his own boots. "Mr. President, gentlemen don't black their own boots," was the protest. Lincoln looked up and replied innocently: "No? Whose boots do they black?"*

Almost touching was that priceless little autobiography Lincoln submitted upon request for a minor "Who's Who" of his day. It is well worth reading again. Here is what this humble man wrote:

> *My parents were of "second families." I can read, write and cipher to the rule of three, but this is all. I was raised to farm work. I became postmaster at a very small post office. There is not much of this autobiography for the reason, I suppose, that there is not much of me.*

Such a man must inevitably recognize the omniscience of his Creator. Hence, when a lady pushed through to him at a public gathering and cried: "Oh, Mr. President, do you think God is on our side in this terrible war?" Lincoln could only reply gravely: "Madame, I'm more concerned with whether or not we are on God's side."

Notice how all four examples in the Lincoln passage, the illustration and three instances, are to the *one* point: Lincoln's humble nature. Such concentration of unified supportive power is to ensure that the point will be enforced in listeners' minds, that listener-speaker identification will be achieved at that moment in the speech. Such **a focused battery of examples gives a point the benefit of both appealing detail and strength of numbers.** It's in this way that the speaker's and listener's minds meet.

Special Characteristics of Examples   1.   **Examples to compare.**

The analogy is one of the most common and most fascinating of all materials of speechmaking. Much of our thinking and speaking is based on analogy—the resemblance of things. For example, we hear statements like these every day: "As a financial consultant, I like to use baseball as an analogy in dealing with my clients. When preparing to advise someone on investing money, I look at the person and try to decide in what 'inning they're playing.' If it's early innings in their productive life, I'll recommend one type of investment. If it's their ninth inning, that's another matter."

To communicate is to discover common ground. The job of the speaker is to choose, organize, and develop ideas in such a way as to invite the listener to share the experience.

To use an analogy is to compare phenomena, to communicate by taking advantage of similarities: games, territory, events, principles, objects, systems, or any number of other things. If the two items are of the same class, the analogy is *literal*; if they are of different classes, the anal-

Is a horse analogous to a zebra?

ogy is *figurative*. Analogies like the following might help you in your next speech. The first one is literal, a comparison of workers' salaries.

Point: *Those who serve are those who deserve.*
Literal Analogy: *Americans love baseball and admire the excellence of the players. Moreover, they pay them well for their work. For what they provide the nation, baseball players deserve our praise and support. And most people would agree that the nation's schoolteachers, likewise talented and well-trained, are also deserving for what they provide. So why do we value teachers so much less? How many players on the rosters of the Oakland A's or New York Mets earn no more than $35,000 a year? Silly question! That's a level of compensation that many teachers in the United States will never reach, even at age 60! How many ball players, most of whom are in their 20s, annually earn five, six, or seven times that salary?*

Here's an example to compare, an analogy from a speech by business analyst Andrew B. Wilson. His analogy is figurative.

Point: *There's no mystery in bankruptcy.*
Figurative Analogy: *You sometimes hear of companies disappearing in a kind of Bermuda Triangle. They will be cruising along with good reported earnings—everything looking a-okay—and then, suddenly, wham—they declare bankruptcy. But there is really no mystery here. The explanation is they ran out of cash.*[3]

Here's another sample use of analogy.

Point: *Analyze the pluses and minuses of your relationships with others.*
Figurative Analogy: *All relationships have pluses and minuses. Be your own accountant, and weigh the "gains against losses," as Robert did. In the first few months, he and Carla were very happy together. She was just right for him in so many ways, and vice versa. But Robert paid a lot for the good times with Carla. He began to feel that she wanted "all of him," every minute, and that she gave him very little time to himself. For a while, he paid gladly, but eventually*

he added things up and came to the conclusion that the costs were beginning to outweigh the benefits. Maybe a realistic accounting will tell you something about one of your relationships.

Be careful in using analogies. Ask yourself if the two elements, such as business practices and human relationships, are enough alike to justify the paralleling. Can the two things be compared? Further, since no two items of any kind are identical in every respect, **an analogy alone usually does not "prove" a point conclusively.** Use of analogy is a characteristically human, colorful, and interesting means of development, yet it serves only to clarify or to provide a base for sounder proof.

2.   Examples to contrast. Illustrative material to show contrast is formed of two or more elements that have basic *dissimilarities*. The contrasting elements are put side by side to make the relevant thought interesting, graphic, or compelling, to further the identification of speaker and audience and thereby facilitate communication. Research director Rosalyn Wiggins Berne provides this sample of effectiveness in making a contrast between myth and reality.

> Point: *The scenario of the perfect career, wife, and mother is a brutal myth.*
> Example to Contrast: *It is the myth of Clare Huxtable. Wife on the popular T.V. Cosby show, Clare Huxtable—a successful lawyer . . . returns home at the end of a day in court to a beautiful, clean, orderly house, to greet happy, well adjusted, smiling children. She is a devoted and loving wife with an adoring, supportive husband. Clare Huxtable, a woman with a beautiful physique, a radiant smile, and a demeanor always relaxed and in control. There she is, greeting us every Thursday night at 8:00—the epitome of perfect grace, representing the perfect balance so many of us desperately aspire to achieve. The reality is, she does not, and cannot, exist.*[4]

Here's an example to contrast from a student speech.

> Point: *Think before wanting to turn back the clock.*
> Example to Contrast: *Whenever my dad starts longing for the "good old days," I ask him if he's ready to give up all the benefits of the 1990s: supermarkets that are open twenty-four hours, medicine to keep his heart rhythms right; three-hour air service to Denver where his grandkids live; a clean fishing stream, not far from his house, which was completely polluted ten years ago; extraordinarily high-quality recordings of his favorite music, and so forth.*

3.   Hypothetical examples. Hypothetical cases are not actual, nor should you present them as such. Instead, ask the audience to imagine a possibility, and introduce the example with "Let's imagine" or "Suppose that" or "We will assume . . . ." When used appropriately, the hypothetical example can help connect an idea to the experiences of listeners, causing them to relate to it. The following is a case in point.

Point: *Who can know the plight of a homeless person?*
Hypothetical Example: *It won't be easy, but see if you can put
yourself in this situation: You lose your job; you lose your car; your
savings account is wiped out; you've no house or apartment to go to.
Every night you sleep under a freeway bridge or in an old car or in a
park. Most of the time you're hungry, dirty, and tired. You're
constantly in deep despair and can see no way out of your
predicament. Hope is gone. Can you picture yourself there? Probably
not, unless you're one of the lucky ones who has returned from the
street, from the bleak and depressing world of the homeless!*

Checking the Reliability of Examples   How can a speaker know if
his or her examples can be relied on to provide adequate backing for an
idea and evoke the desired response from listeners? It's probably fair to
say that **the more critical or controversial the idea, the more careful
a speaker should be in checking the value and trustworthiness of
an example to support it.** Remember that the listener is the final judge
of reliability.

   1.   First, note the number of examples. Do you have enough to
justify a conclusion? For instance, are two verifiable cases of embezzle-
ment by city officials enough to conclude that the city government is cor-
rupt? How many cases of poor gasoline mileage are needed to generalize
that a certain make of car is a "guzzler"? What part does mere coincidence
play in these reckonings? Let good reasoning be your guide in deciding
on the number of examples necessary. For more suggestions on reasoning and concluding with examples, turn to Chapter Nine, "Thinking
Critically."

   2.   Second, determine if the examples are representative. That
is, are they typical cases? Effective though they may be, some should not
be counted. What of speakers who draw major conclusions from selected
examples of college students' behavior? Are excessive drinkers representative of all students? Are significant numbers of students in college escap-
ing from the "real world"? Do they spend great amounts of their time in
protest demonstrations? Individual behaviors vary. The question to ask of
each is: "Is the example representative of the whole?" And be careful of
using examples that merely reinforce preconceived views. Again, **the
final judge of the worth of an example is the listener—** a questioning
listener, one would hope.

   **3.   Third, if contradictory examples appear, can they be
explained?** Can you account for exceptions to the rule; what variable(s)
might be operating to produce a negative instance? For example, studies
show the likelihood that babies who are neglected by parents in their formative years will develop psychological problems. Yet some neglected
children become mentally strong, healthy adults. Why? How do experts
explain exceptions?

   Along with reminding you again to consult Chapter Nine, "Thinking
Critically," I have one last word on the topic of working with examples.

Regardless of efforts to secure foolproof examples and develop unanswerable arguments, speakers must realize that a degree of *probability* is all that can be established ordinarily in communicating a point. In the fascinating realm of supplying proof for ideas, certainty is never to be found. When it comes to those issues in life that matter most, there's always an exception. Thus, there's always an opposing view, and all the more reason to check examples well. **A high degree of probability is the best we can come to in our research and reasoning, and in communicating ideas.**

Statistics

Have you noticed that many people seem to be confused about "facts" and "statistics"? A fact may be statistical, or it may not be. A statistic may be factual, or it may not be. Statistics are numerical data that someone has collected for some purpose; something factual may be expressed either in statistics or in the form of a statement or actual example.

This is a "statistical age" that we live in, a time of much quantification. Look at almost any speech in *Vital Speeches* (a periodical that publishes speeches of the day) and somewhere you'll find at least one numerical compilation used by the speaker to help develop a main head. Everyone uses statistics daily. When we make a point about certain mileages and distances, comparative amounts of money, how much things weigh, a football team's yardage in a certain game, how many days are left in a month, salaries, percentages, and so on, we are in the realm of statistics.

These **numerical materials can give weight and authority to generalizations.** Some points mean little to an audience without supporting statistics.

Speaking at a public affairs council meeting in Pomona, California, Eddie N. Williams wanted to show that African Americans have made great strides in politics in America. He found statistics necessary to his purpose.

> Point: *African Americans are established as political leaders.*
> Statistics: *From less than 500 black elected officials in 1965, there are now more than 7,400 officials. In the capital of the old confederacy, L. Douglas Wilder serves as governor. In our nation's two largest cities—New York and Los Angeles—and in Philadelphia, Detroit, Washington, D.C., and more than 300 other cities across this country, black men and women serve as mayors. In the aftermath of the 1990 elections, there are now 26 black members of the U.S. House of Representatives, including the first black republican in more than half a century. . . . so far only the presidency and vice presidency have eluded blacks.*[5]

Family service executive Geneva B. Johnson is deeply concerned about children in poverty.

Numbers may be critical in speeches also.

Point: *Poverty among children is increasing.*
Statistics: *One in five American youngsters under the age of 18 lives in poverty today. . . . Among children below the age of six, 25 percent live in poverty. Among the nation's poor population as a whole—40 percent—some 13 million individuals are children.*[6]

Following is an excerpt from a speech by political observer George S. Mitrovich, making good use of statistics. Note, by the way, that the whole piece comprises six examples: an illustration and five instances (recall our earlier discussion of examples).

Point: *Political incumbents have fund-raising advantages.*
Statistics: *In the New Jersey Senate race, featuring one of the major presidential hopefuls of the Democratic party, Senator Bill Bradley, ex-Princeton University All-American, ex-NBA star with the New York Knicks, ex-Rhodes Scholar, running in what was thought to be a slam-dunk contest, the Senator spent more than $12 million, while his little-known opponent had only $645,000 to spend—which is not exactly a full-court press.*

In West Virginia, Senator Jay Rockefeller raised more than $3.6 million. His opponent, $21,341.

In Texas, Senator Phil Gramm raised more than $15 million. His opponent, $1.7 million. At the end of the campaign Senator Gramm had more than $4 million in the bank; his opponent $1,581.38.

In one Colorado congressional race the incumbent raised $372,205, while his opponent was only able to raise $2,295. One hundred and sixty-three to one hardly qualifies as fair and equitable odds.

In California congressional races last year more than $30 million *was raised. Forty-three incumbents raised more than $24 million, while their opponents raised less than $5 million. Four California incumbents, facing no opposition, still raised $1.4 million.*[7]

Checking the Reliability of Statistics

Before putting them to use, give your statistical data rigorous examination, with the help of these criteria.

1. Check sources of data. Look into the qualifications of sources. Are they authoritative and credible? Specifically, are they expert, free from bias, and of good reputation? Do their data agree with those of at least one other reputable source? A few years ago a visiting lecturer cited statistics of a "certain study" to conclude that within 50 years a high percentage of people in the United States will suffer a major psychological breakdown. Students in the audience wanted to know who the source was and how the conclusion was reached. Their questioning was entirely proper, for listeners need to know if a speaker's data are derived from a crystal ball or a more reliable source.

For more help in evaluating sources of statistics, you might jump ahead to Checking the Reliability of Authorities because suggestions offered in that section also apply here.

2. Note the size of the sample on which the statistics are based. Is the sample large enough? For instance, what conclusions can you draw from the seemingly astounding observation that in the past six general elections, 100 percent of the registered voters of a certain eastern American town cast ballots? It means very little, really. Because the town's population is only 94, you can't use the case to draw conclusions about the voting habits of people elsewhere. Another town, another *small* town, had a 200 percent rise in its crime rate one year. The number of cases of criminal behavior climbed from two to six. Again, the lesson about the size of the sample is obvious.

3. Note the age of the statistics. Old numerical data must be questioned, unless your interest is in some projection over a period of time or in a certain historical feature of the topic. Statistics on murder rates in the United States in 1955 may be helpful in making comparisons, but they are useless in reckoning the extent of the problem today.

4. Determine the character of units counted. Much confusion arises when people attempt to use ambiguous or undefined material. For instance, one group that compiles statistics on drinking problems counts alcoholics as those whose current drinking habits have certain negative effects on themselves and others. Another group includes those people *and* all those who have a high *potential* for becoming problem drinkers. Which is the "larger" college, the one with 12,000 students in attendance or the one with 15,000? The answer may depend on a definition of "attendance." The college of 12,000 may have 10,000 full-time students, whereas half of the 15,000 attending the second college may be taking only one or two courses.

Suggestions for Handling Statistics **1. Use round numbers when they're suitable.** If it's not important that the exact number be given, simplify and lighten your listeners' burden. The statistics of Eddie N. Williams cited above are in round numbers. He did not need to give the exact number of elected African American officials. It was appropriate for him to specify 500 for 1965 and 7,400 for the current time. Although it's vital to report exactly the number of seconds and tenths of seconds that elapsed in an Olympic athlete's 100-meter run, it's sufficient to say that the smoking toll is 390,000 deaths per year and that smoking costs our society over $52 billion annually. These statistics, incidentally, are from Louis W. Sullivan, Secretary of Heath and Human Services, an authoritative source on the subject of national health.

2. Use statistics sparingly. A sure way to lose listeners is to give an endless stream of numbers: pounds, dollars, people unemployed, gallons, miles, hours, and so forth. Would you be willing (or able) to listen to a speech that went on and on like this one?

> *Every six to seven months, actually about every eight to ten weeks in the summer, we invite all car owners to attend one of our workshops on home-servicing. Of the 674,367 owners who live in the region of twenty square miles that includes the four incorporated cities and the six unincorporated towns, 7,967 typically attend during one of the days of each three- to four-day event, with the doors open between 10 a.m. and 10 p.m. (except for Sunday when we close at 8 p.m.). Of these 7,967, we find that 49.6 percent, or 3,951.632, own cars manufactured abroad, 3,429 of which were built between 1989 and 1993. Of the other 15.4 percent, those owning cars built wholly in the United States, 3,391 were built between the years 1987 and 1993. We plan in the next three to five years to spend between $50,000 and $100,000 more on promotion, in the attempt to increase attendance by at least 19.6 percent during any of the three to four average days of the schedule.*

Boring, right? Right! And why not use round figures?

3. Give your statistics meaning. Interpret or explain them, providing appropriate context; anchor them to a point. For example, what's the *point* in the big paragraph of statistical material above?

Also, you may be able to **find a way to dramatize your statistics or relate them to something familiar.** Instead of giving your audience the rather meaningless piece of knowledge that 132 million feet of cable was used in constructing a new bridge, tell them that this figure equals approximately 25,000 miles of cable—enough to circle the earth. Look for such useful interpretive expressions. Here's another one: "The amount of water used at the nuclear plant in a day is enough to supply all the homes in Revere, Massachusetts, for three years."

In my newspaper today was a story about a chemical spill in the Sacramento River. The paper noted that at this moment, the spill has reached Shasta Lake and is "about a half-mile long and the width of two football fields." *The width of two football fields.* What would Americans do without the use of the football field as a way to interpret measurements, or the distance from home to first base in baseball (ninety feet), or the distance from San Francisco to New York (3,000 miles), or a stack of something said to be as tall as the Empire State Building (1,250 feet)?

Sometimes it's good strategy to put selected statistics on the blackboard, when you want the listeners to fix certain numbers in their minds. A big chart can also accomplish this purpose. The extra effort may be well worth it.

4.   Use statistics judiciously. By judiciously, I mean cautiously and respectfully. Someone once said that handling statistics in speaking requires one's best, not only in intelligence but also in respect for standards of ethics. Figures can lie, or at least give false impressions. A town with an average per capita income of $14,000 would seem to be prosperous; a family of four—husband, wife, and two children—would have $56,000 for the year. But remember what an *average* is. An average is found by getting a total and dividing by the number of units, of people. To get a $14,000 average you may be dealing with hundreds of per capita incomes below $8,000 and not many in the higher ranges.

Look carefully at your statistics. Ask yourself if you really know what you have there. What is the inherent meaning and significance of the material? A student in a speech communication class once cited an authority who held that 97 percent of all American juveniles were law-abiding people—good kids. "This figure," said the speaker, "proves that America has no problem with kids getting into trouble with the law. Why worry about 3 percent?" "Why worry?" asked the people in the class. They suggested to the speaker that he ought to do some multiplying with the remaining 3 percent. Three percent of an estimated 25 million juveniles equals 750,000!

During basketball season the sports page of a college newspaper gave player Stan Clark's weight as 187 pounds. People acquainted with Stan Clark knew that his true weight was closer to 157 pounds. Magazines or newspapers, as well as most other sources, are not always accurate. Even "experts" can slip up. Verification, though difficult and time-consuming, may spare embarrassment or other problems in communication.

5.   Use recent statistics. If your point is to show the need for more state parks for recreational use, your case would not be strengthened if you used 1980 census figures. Nor, perhaps, would your ethical consciousness leave you alone if you included those outdated statistics to prove that no need exists for more parks.

Quotation and Authority

Speakers quote experts, poets, and prominent persons because the **words of qualified others can lend authority and add meaning and appeal to messages; they can give weight to thoughts and help speakers express them more effectively.**

Talking at Yale University on the subject of a national culture of character, Louis W. Sullivan had occasion to call upon authority to support a point. Note that he imbedded his quotations in examples.

Who is the man on the left? Clue: a lot of speakers quote him.

Point: *Character is the source of personal strength.*
Authority: *Frederick Douglass . . . worked not only to abolish the social circumstance of slavery; he also sought to build better individuals, by emphasizing the importance of character. "With character we can be powerful," he proclaimed. "Nothing can harm us so long as we have character."*

"Dr. Martin Luther King, Jr., resolutely . . . worked to prepare people for the day when they would be judged by the content of their character."

"Similarly, Jesse Jackson's quest for social and economic change in the larger society is joined inseparably to a call for personal reform, for better character. As he put it, 'When you drink liquor, and when you take drugs, and when you sell *drugs, and when you shoot people, and when you rob people . . . nobody can save* you *but* you *from yourself.'"*[8]

Writer Gale E. Klappa went to West Georgia College to talk to students and faculty on improving newspaper reporting. On that occasion she used quoted material to good advantage, very likely enjoying success in enlivening her ideas and reaching her listeners. At one point, she borrowed the words of George Bernard Shaw, famous literary figure.

Point: *We need journalists with a sense of perspective.*
Quotation: *George Bernard Shaw once complained that newspapers were "unable to discriminate between a bicycle accident and the collapse of civilization."*

At another place in the speech she again made use of a short quotation, this one of unknown origin.

Point: *Report the good news, too.*
Quotation: *In recent years, the news media appear to have inverted the saying, "No news is good news." They've made it read—"Good news is no news."*[9]

When speaking before the College Entrance Examination Board, educational leader Harold Howe helped make a thought provocative with the words of philosopher John Gardner.

Point: *Our society must appreciate a variety of talents.*
Quotation: *John Gardner pinpointed this neatly for us when he wrote: "An excellent plumber is infinitely more admirable than an incompetent philosopher. The society which scorns excellence in plumbing because plumbing is a humble activity and tolerates shoddiness in philosophy because it is an exalted activity will have neither good plumbing nor good philosophy. Neither its pipes nor its theories will hold water."*

To get a feeling for the use of quotation and authority, it might be profitable to approach it from the opposite direction, by starting with a quotation and imagining what to do with it. Let's try that. What point could you make with the quotations below? How would they help you communicate with listeners?

"The worst thing about new books is that they keep us from reading the old ones."

—*Joseph Joubert, philosopher*

"I reject the romantic notion that the rich have money and the poor have friends. People with resources acquire other resources. Advantage breeds advantage."

—*Claude Fischer, sociologist*

"Dogs are people-pleasers, and much more amenable to training than a cat is, so train the dog to ignore the cat. When it's no longer being chased, the cat will eventually come around and accept the dog, even though they may never be lifelong friends."

—*Donna Brimer, animal behavior specialist*

"It is the manner of use that should determine obscenity. It is the conduct of the individual that should be judged, not the quality of art or literature."

—*Chief Justice Earl Warren*

*"Quarrels could never last long,
If on one side only lay the wrong."*
—anonymous

Checking the Reliability of Authorities   Since speakers often rely heavily on the words of others, the quoted material they select ought to pass tests of reliability. No one should doubt that humans are fallible; **not all judgments and findings, even of experts, are beyond question.** Therefore, testing ought to be a matter of policy. A related reason is that experts do disagree—even eminent experts. Some authorities in criminal justice will tell us that capital punishment deters crime; others, of equal stature, will say that it doesn't. That's where we come in, when we decide to talk on the subject—the point at which we must use *our* minds. The following checks will help.

   1.   Determine the qualifications of your source. It's not enough to know that a certain quotation is from a new book by someone named Paula Hinkley. More information is needed, especially if her subject matter is controversial. Who is she? Does she have expertise or status that gives her ready access to information? What is her title and job? How much experience has she in the field? In a word, is she in a position to know? But beyond knowing, is she reasonably unbiased on the relevant issues? What is her motive in offering the information? Whom does she represent? Does she have a reputation for accuracy and objectivity? Those are difficult questions but good ones.

   2.   Get a firm grasp of the quotation. By so doing you'll be able to decide if it's relevant to your point. I have found that all-too-often the quotations that speakers use to back up a point aren't really *to the point.* For example, President Franklin Roosevelt's statement, "We have nothing to fear but fear itself," doesn't mean that no one should have fears.

   Basic to a good understanding is knowledge of the context in which the quoted authority wrote or spoke. Knowing the facts of who, what, where, why—all the pertinent data—helps greatly in determining the meaning and its significance. For example, why would a long-time conservative leader suddenly take a decidedly liberal view on some important issue of the day? That does happen. Background material may be essential in interpreting such a person's opinions.

   3.   Compare the authority's data against those of others. Are the data corroborated by material from the other sources? If you find disagreement among authorities, can it be accounted for in some way? In areas of doubt or controversy, uncorroborated testimony is usually suspect, as it should be. **If a thorough challenge of questionable material leads to a stronger speech, both you and the audience benefit.**

Suggestions for Handling Quotations   1.   Establish the author's credibility. If the author is not commonly known, give the quoted words extra weight by telling your listeners who the person is and, if necessary, why the material is sound and reliable.

Some occasions will require a sentence or two of biography, but often a parenthetical statement like "Attorney General for the State of Kansas" or "20 years an editor, starting with the Holt company in 1973," will suffice.

2.   Be fair in handling the author's words. Respectful treatment isn't too much to ask. Be faithful to the exact words of a quotation. If you're tempted to "touch up" the wording, look for another quotation, one that supports the desired meaning more aptly. Should you decide to paraphrase (at times necessary with long quotations), be careful. Avoid twisting the words around to the point of losing the shape of the original thought. For instance, is it correct to say that the Bible authorizes capital punishment? Perhaps, but the quotation that includes the phrase "eye for eye, tooth for tooth" is sometimes extended or bent to suit particular needs. **Altered wording creates altered meaning,** in many cases.

3.   When taking quoted words out of context, be careful not to destroy the author's intent. This relates to the suggestion immediately above. When abstracting from a passage, note what came before and after. Those surrounding words may affect the meaning; all are parts of a larger "picture" of thought. *Picture,* incidentally, is a good analogy because indiscriminately taking words out of context may be like showing someone the picture of cousin Tom that you have cut out of a family portrait. Viewing Tom alone, out of the family "context," one doesn't know that Aunt Ella is smiling approvingly at Tom, or that Tom's wife has a very worried look as she stands next to him, or that the family dog is licking Uncle Carlos' boots. The whole picture is a *different* picture.

A biased speaker might quote Abraham Lincoln as having said, "Force is all-conquering," but that speaker would do an injustice to the sixteenth president of the United States unless the complete quotation were given. The statement in full is "Force is all-conquering, but its victories are short-lived."

4.   Vary your wording in introducing and closing quotations. Of course an audience wants to know when a quotation begins and ends, but the expressions "quote" and "unquote" or "I have a quotation" can be overused. To introduce a quotation appropriately, some speakers say, "In the words of W. E. B. DuBois . . ." or "the president expressed it this way . . ." or "Listen to Juárez's statement . . ." or "As Madison said . . . ." Quotations may be closed with "That's the end of Gandhi's comment" or "So much for the view of Wilson." Look for fresh expressions. Changes in vocal pitch or quality or use of other nonverbal modes can be effective in setting off quoted words; this skill can be perfected.

5.   Maintain eye contact while using a quotation. Although it may be necessary to read a quotation, be sure to preserve visual contact. Ample practice is the solution to that problem. The resulting familiarity with the material will give you the confidence and freedom to lift your eyes to the listeners now and again.

CRITERIA FOR SELECTING MATERIAL

In the final analysis, materials should meet the demands of the speech, audience, and occasion.

1. Select material that allows adequate development of the message. Above all, select material that furthers your purpose and relates directly to the point being developed. The only justification for using a supporting aid is that it backs up or clarifies a thought; therefore, it should be relevant to the idea of the moment and thesis.

Make sure that you have enough material to give full support to the idea. A major mistake in speaking is to stop short of satisfactory development, which is like leaving a job before it's done. Another error, though less common, is belaboring ideas with too much material. Answering the question "How much?" starts with knowing your purpose and keeping it uppermost in mind.

2. Select material that helps achieve identification with the audience. This requires knowing the audience, their interests in the subject and feelings about it, and it requires knowing the peculiarities of your material and fitting it to the audience. In this regard, **good materials are those that not only do the supporting job for you but also invite listening.** Thus, they must be relevant to your goal *and* nonthreatening, that is, adaptive and conducive to furthering the speaker–audience relationship.

Remember the diversity of views and backgrounds in your audience. Before settling on any example, statistic, or quotation, ask yourself these questions: Will it appeal to the interests and motives of my listeners? Will it be immediately understood by my listeners? Will it provide a base of common interest with my audience and contribute to unity of thought? Is it in all ways reliable and congruent with my code of ethics and fair play?

3. Select material that meets demands of the occasion. Observe the purpose of the setting and follow the occasion's theme, if there is one. In other words, make preparations that will be consistent with the atmosphere and arrangements established by the person or persons who planned the meeting. This suggestion will be especially important should you ever be called on to talk to a group that is meeting for a special purpose. Speeches should relate to the overall design of the occasion. Chapter Fourteen, "Preparing for Special Occasions," will be helpful in this regard.

FINDING MATERIAL

Though we have raised this question in other contexts, it bears repeating here: Where does one find materials—examples, quotations, and statistics—to use in speeches? The main source, of course, is your reservoir of personal experience. What you have heard, seen, read, and done, and have spent time thinking and learning about are part of you now, to some extent at least. Bits of this background in the form of stories, illustrations, vivid descriptions, and remembered phrases of others can be used to develop the ideas you want to convey. **Dip into that valuable personal store of material, and continue to observe and accumulate data for the future.**

Occasionally you may not have the exact wording of a quotation that supports a given idea, or you may need some fresh statistics. In such cases, you can go to a common reservoir, the library. Again, your thesis and specific needs in development of ideas will guide you in your search.

In addition to the standard books, magazines, and newspapers at your disposal, there are many specialized references, such as encyclopedias of various kinds, books of important statistics, and books of quotations. For more on gathering materials, turn to Appendix B, ''Doing Research on a Topic.''

CITING SOURCES

Suitable acknowledgment of the source of a piece of material can increase its effect, by virtue of the authority that the name may carry. The mention of Lester Therow or Milton Friedman as sources of statistics on some point in economics, or Jane Goodall on the behavior of chimpanzees, will add weight to the data. Also, acknowledgment indicates to listeners that you are a considerate borrower of material, a person of credibility who is willing to recognize properly the work of others. **But be brief in citing a source.** Give just enough information to satisfy essential needs. For example, ordinarily it would be sufficient to say, ''This is what Filipino literary figure N. V. M. Gonzalez declares in his recent book.'' If the topic is controversial, to the point of requiring very careful documentation, you might say, ''This statement is from Gonzalez' book *A Filipino in the World,* published in 1990.'' Only rarely would you need to add, ''by Kalikasan Press of Manila'' or such biographical facts as ''He is a well-known short-story writer, essayist, critic, and winner of numerous prestigious literary awards.'' Though such extensive citations are not needed often, I think you would agree that it can be comforting to a speaker to know a lot about a given important source.

A very well-known source would require the barest of information. For instance, ''As Mayor Thomas said'' or ''Declared Prime Minister John Majors in Parliament'' or ''According to author and philosopher Carlos Fuentes'' would be adequate citations for most situations.

LOOKING BACK

Speakers cannot expect an audience to accept ideas or participate in the development of a speech unless they justify their ideas with carefully chosen supporting data. Alert, thinking listeners ignore or challenge mere generalizations; they want specifics; they need grounds for responding favorably. When hearing a flat and unsupported assertion, they mentally ask, "So what?" Through conscientious discovery of materials, successful speakers find ways of sharing thoughts and facilitating the process of identification. Thorough preparation provides a good chance of setting up a relationship of trust and mutual respect.

The advice, then, is to:

1. Know the nature and value of verbal developmental materials: examples of all kinds; statistics, and quotations.

2. Know how to handle them effectively.

3. In your search for suitable materials, look first to your background, personal experience, and learnings of life. Also available are the library and other handy sources.

4. It's right and beneficial in speaking to acknowledge sources of developmental material used.

For effectiveness in communication, to get a hearing for your ideas, there's no substitute for a full supply of sound supporting materials.

MODEL SPEECH OUTLINES

Model Speech Outline I (In sentence form, with developmental materials and some primary processes—definition, restatement, and explanation—indicated in brackets outside the outline)

Note that development of ideas in this speech relies heavily on examples, some of which have considerable statistical content.

Running Free

Introduction
    I. People face the question of physical fitness in different ways.
        A. Some don't think much about fitness.
        B. Others have development or improvement programs of one sort or another.
            1. We all know people who like swimming. [illustration]
            2. Game sports attract many. [instances]
            3. Specialized activities involve others. [instances]
    II. I like to run or jog. [definition]
Thesis
    For me, running (or jogging) is the best means of staying physically fit.
Body
    I. To begin with, running is an efficient way to keep my body healthy.
        A. By "efficient," I mean getting desired results with minimum expenditure of resources. [definition]

B. It's the yield that comes from the standard "30 minutes, 3 miles, 3 days a week" formula. [quotation]

C. Findings of authorities support my view on gains received. [quotation]

D. In running, I spend less time than required in most other popular forms of exercise to get the same benefits.
    1. Compare running to swimming. [illustration]
    2. Compare running to bicycling. [instance]
    3. Compare running to walking. [instance]
    4. Compare running to handball. [instance]

E. I spend less money.
    1. There are no charges. [instances]
    2. No expensive gear is required. [instances]

II. More than having an output-rewards advantage, my form of staying in shape is convenient. [restatement]

A. A nearby site is the main essential.
    1. Neighboring schools have adequate tracks. [instances]
    2. I have a number of street routes, all starting at my front door. [illustration and instances]

B. Also, I can run when I want.
    1. I don't worry about opening and closing hours of facilities. [instances]
    2. I can run with or without daylight.
    3. I don't need to carry around lots of heavy equipment or paraphernalia. [instances]

III. So, my physical fitness returns are high with low cost; I can take part when and where I want; and to top it off, I get a psychological bonus. [explanation]

A. The feeling of getting out and running free is wonderful.
    1. I find joy in gradually increasing my distance. [instances]
    2. "In a good running program, before long your mountains become molehills." [quotation]
    3. Also, bettering my time is satisfying. [statistics]

B. Running helps me to realign my mind. [definition]
    1. It has helped me to counter depression. [illustration and instances]
    2. I've solved nagging problems. [instances]

C. Arriving back from a good run, I have a personal sense of well-being, of feeling "up" for the day. [restatement]

Conclusion

I. These are my reasons for choosing running.
A. I get excellent bodily benefits from what I expend.
B. Everything is handy and easy.
C. The emotional and mental lift is a plus.

II. Also, it's reassuring to know that experts agree with me. [quotation]

Model Speech Text (Full text, based on the foregoing Model Speech Outline 1, with developmental materials indicated)

Can you spot primary processes, for example, transition, definition, explanation, and restatement?

Running Free

People face the question of physical fitness in different ways, if and when they do. Of course, some don't think much about fitness. But others have development or improvement programs of one sort or another. We all know people who like to swim, right? My friend Ted is a good example. He's twenty years old, not all that athletic, but a guy who's in the water during every free minute, almost, and he's had that love for swimming for all of the four or five years that I've known him. They have a pool at his house, and it's his goal to do two-thousand yards a day with a mixture of strokes. Game sports like baseball, touch football, and basketball attract other friends of mine. Among the more specialized activities people get involved in are weight lifting, folk dancing, jazzercise, and rock climbing.

Illustration

Instances

Instances

But I like to run or jog. How do you define these words? One writer on the subject calls it jogging if a beginner does it and running if it's done faster than eight minutes to the mile. Another calls it jogging when it's for exercise alone. As a matter of fact, many so-called experts use the terms interchangeably.

For me, running (or jogging) is the best means of staying physically fit.

To begin with, running is an efficient way to keep my body healthy. By "efficient" I mean getting desired results with minimum expenditures of resources. It's the yield that comes from the standard "30 minutes, 3 miles, 3 days a week" formula. Findings of authorities support my view on gains received. Dr. Kenneth Cooper confirms that running gives best results. He quotes one of his running clients who says, "You get more for your money and quicker." In running, I spend less time than is required in most other popular forms of exercise to get the same benefits. Compare other activities to running. I made some informal comparison tests of my own on this question and then did research on it, consulting several books and a physiologist who specializes in

Quotation

Quotation

Illustration

comparative values. Even Ted, my swimming friend, had to agree with me as we analyzed some of the scientific data last week and talked to coaches at school. One conclusion was that to receive the same benefits that I get from running one mile in less than eight minutes, I would have to swim twenty-four laps in less than fifteen minutes. Alternatively, I would have to cycle five miles in less than twenty minutes or walk two and a half miles in less than thirty-six minutes or play handball for thirty-five minutes. Not only that, I spend less money, for there are no charges, as in golfers' green fees at $25 or more a day, use of a racquetball court at $6 an hour, or pool fees of a dollar or two. Moreover, no expensive gear is required: a $300 set of golf clubs and $2 balls, a $250 bike or $50 racquets, and so forth.   *Instances*

More than having an output-rewards advantage, my form of staying in shape is convenient. Everything I need is at hand. A nearby site is the main essential, and neighboring schools have adequate tracks, like the quarter-mile ovals at Westside High and Washington Middle School, both two minutes' running time away. In addition, I have a number of street routes, all starting at my front door. My favorite is a three-mile course that takes me down quiet Madison Avenue, onto busy Heyer (but for only thirty seconds), down shady Alana, east around Marshall School, through the Payless lot, and back the full length of Forest Avenue—an enjoyable, peaceful stretch—then Heyer and Madison again and home. Other three-mile routes take me west on Seven Hills Road and east over by Cull Canyon. Also, I can run when I want; I don't worry about the opening and closing hours of facilities. It's not like using a court or gymnasium and being kicked out at ten o'clock, and I can run with or without daylight. Nor do I need to carry around lots of heavy equipment or paraphernalia—you know, clubs, balls, bats, and the like.   *Instances / Illustration / Instances*

So, my physical fitness returns are high with low cost; I can take part when and where I want, and to top it off, I get a psychological bonus. This "bonus" is sometimes the biggest motivation. It's the case of the body gracefully doing what it was built to do, while freeing the psyche to function at its highest level—mind and body working together.

The feeling of getting out and running free is wonderful. I find joy in gradually increasing my distance, for example, from one half of a mile a day to one mile, then later to two miles, and so on. As my high school coach used to say on the feeling of accomplishment, "In a good running program, before long your mountains become molehills." Also, bettering my time is satisfying. Over the years I have gone from a rate of over eleven minutes a mile to under eight. I want to add that running helps me to realign my mind. By "realign," I mean that it provides conditions for clearing my head of distractions and separating significant thoughts from those not worth holding. It has helped me to counter depression. One day about a year ago I was really down psychologically. I had made an error at work, rather inconsequential really, and allowed this fact, coupled with a minor car accident, to drag me down and mess up my interpersonal relations (what a grouch!) and professional life (don't go near him this week!). So one morning, under the influence of crisp, clean air, I talked to myself about it as I ran, and in twenty minutes I put the matter in proper perspective. I had similar therapeutic success when the expected salary increase didn't come through and when a good friend died. Out there I've solved numerous nagging problems: how to schedule the many events of a given day, when to take the annual vacation, how to say "no" to a person who's pressuring for a "yes."

Arriving back from a good run, I have a personal sense of well-being, of feeling "up" for the day. These are my reasons for choosing running: I get excellent bodily benefits from what I expend; everything is handy and easy; the emotional and mental lift is a plus.

Also, it's reassuring to know that experts agree with me. Dr. Frederick D. Harper, writer on running, or jogging, says, "A commitment to a jogging program is about the best thing that can happen to improve the all-around quality of a person's life."

I believe it!

Instances

Quotation

Statistics

Illustration

Instances

Instances

Quotation

Model Speech Outline 2 (In sentence form, with developmental materials indicated in brackets outside the outline)

Sacrifices of Parenthood

Though not written out, the examples are full, and actual, cases of parents and children. Indicated statistics and quotations are taken mainly from magazines and newspaper articles.

Introduction
   I.   Children are the true victims of our time.
        A.   Pity the crack babies.
        B.   Then there are the latchkey kids.
        C.   Abused children are all around us.
        D.   Homicide and suicide are increasing. [statistics]
        E.   Substance abuse is a serious problem.
        F.   Teenage pregnancy is prevalent.
   II. We do not do right by our children in this country.
   III. Clearly, a great many parents do not, or cannot, provide properly
        for their children.

Thesis

Men and women who aren't ready or able to make the sacrifice
shouldn't have children.

Body
   I.   To grow well, children need all the love that parents can give.
        A.   Dysfunctional parents cannot meet that need.
             1.   Self-absorbed persons are caught up in their *own*
                  interests.
                  a.   Professional interests are all-consuming to some.
                       [instances]
                  b.   For others, social interests have first priority.
                       [instances]
             2.   Psychological problems can interfere with lovingness.
                  a.   Depression is a major factor. [instances]
                  b.   Substance dependency contributes. [instances]
                  c.   Other hindering forces are at work. [instances]
        B.   Significant numbers of parents are unable to provide their
             children with this "irrational emotional attachment," call it
             real love. [quotation, Urie Bronfenbrenner]
             1.   Without it, self-esteem suffers.
             2.   Without it, learning suffers.
             3.   Without it, citizenship suffers.
        C.   We all know of actual cases. [illustration and instances]
   II. It takes lots of willingly given parental time to raise children
        properly.
        A.   It takes time to be there for them when they need support.
             [quotation, Bronfenbrenner]
             1.   One parent may be absent altogether. [illustration and
                  instances]
             2.   Consequently, the second parent has too great a
                  demand.
        B.   It takes time to help them with their learning.
             1.   Being supportive in their school work is one part of it.
                  [instances]

2. Relating to their teachers and to parents of classmates is another part. [instances]
C. It takes time to plan and carry out constructive family activities. [instances]
III. Much money is required in the rearing of children.
A. In this nation, millions of families live in poverty. [statistics]
1. Adequate housing may be beyond reach.
a. An extra room means higher payments.
b. A house in a secure environment costs more. [illustration and instances]
2. Clothing costs are high. [statistics]
3. Food costs are high. [statistics]
4. Dental and medical care can be very expensive. [statistics]
5. Assorted expenditures add up fast.
a. Children want and deserve toys and bicycles, etc. [statistics]
b. There are athletic uniforms to buy.
c. School supplies are among endless needs.
B. Government support is decreasing. [quotation, Geneva B. Johnson]

Conclusion
I. If you're not ready to provide adequately, don't procreate.
A. Children need parents who really want them and can love them.
B. It takes time in daily living to give children what they need from parents.
C. Ample amounts of money are required in doing it right.
II. If you can't give these, the role of parent is not yours.
III. It's simple logic! [quotation, William Raspberry]

Model Speech Outline 3 (In sentence form, with developmental material not indicated)

Notice that the two arguments of the body are completely bare of supporting material. What kinds of evidence would give adequate backing to those reasons supporting the thesis? Can you provide some specific examples, illustrations, instances? Your examples may arise from your own knowledge of the subject or from acquaintance with others whose experience is relevant. Where would you place such examples? Feel free to add subheadings if you think it necessary in developing one or both main heads.

What statistical data and testimony of authority would be needed? Where would you place them?

What specialized sources of material might be consulted? Where are they available?

Educational Opportunity

Introduction

I. Frequently we hear stories about possible increases in tuition.

    A. The proponents' side usually gets most attention.

    B. Consequently, few seem to understand the other side.

II. This critical question affects everyone.

Thesis

Tuition rates should be kept low.

Body

I. Higher tuition rates would deprive many students of an educational opportunity.

    A. The economically disadvantaged would be the hardest hit.

        1. Increases in costs force people to drop out.

        2. A significant number of these dropouts never return.

    B. Even the less disadvantaged would have to work longer hours at jobs to meet higher rates.

        1. Those students with heavy work schedules have less opportunity to learn.

        2. Time spent on the job also limits periods of leisure and recreation, necessary companions to quality learning.

II. Higher tuition rates would deprive the community of the opportunity for betterment.

    A. A community's general character is determined in part by the education of its people.

    B. A community's economic vitality is determined in part by the education of its people.

    C. A community's level of civic participation is determined in part by the education of its people.

Conclusion

I. Increases in tuition would limit learning and community improvement.

II. A great nation provides educational opportunity for all the people.

NOTES

1. C. Ray Penn, "A Choice of Words is a Choice of Worlds," *Vital Speeches of the Day,* LVII (December 1, 1991): 116.

2. Mary Hatwood Futrell, "Education, A Capital Investment," *Vital Speeches of the Day,* L (June 1, 1984): 505.

3. Andrew B. Wilson, "Developing Business Savvy," *Vital Speeches of the Day,* LVII (May 5, 1991): 475.

4. In Rosalyn Wiggins Berne, "Keeping Our Balance in the 90's," *Vital Speeches of the Day,* LVI (November 1, 1990): 57.

5. Eddie N. Williams, "The Future of Black Politics," *Vital Speeches of the Day,* LVII (March 15, 1991): 348–49.

6. Geneva B. Johnson, "The Changing Family," *Vital Speeches of the Day,* LVII (April 15, 1991): 395.

7. George S. Mitrovich, "Public Funding of Elections," *Vital Speeches of the Day,* LVII (May 1, 1991): 437.

8. Louis W. Sullivan, "Creating a National Culture of Character," *Vital Speeches of the Day,* LVII (January 15, 1991): 204.

9. Gale E. Klappa, "Journalism and the Anti-Media Backlash," *Vital Speeches of the Day,* LI (April 1, 1985): 378.

UNDERSTANDING
USES OF PERSUASION

8

★ **LOOKING AHEAD** ★

1. What is persuasion, and who are the persuaders?

2. Where does persuasion occur?

3. What is the connection of persuasion to democracy?

4. What is the connection of sociability to persuasion?

5. What are the principal modes of proof and appeal?

6. What patterns of organization are available to persuaders?

7. What language serves a speaker best?

8. What guidelines on delivery should be studied?

9. What are functions of the "good audience" in persuasion? What specifically should a speaker know about an audience?

10. What is responsible persuasion, and how should one go about answering persuasive speeches?

CHAPTER 8

UNDERSTANDING
USES OF PERSUASION

The dialogue that follows is what I hope my students might be saying to each other when we get to the part of the course dealing with persuasion.

He:	The way I get it, persuasion is influencing others to do something. Isn't that right?
She:	Right. That's a way of saying it.
He:	Then, when someone points a gun at me and says, "Give me your money," that's persuasion, right?
She:	Not right.
He:	Not right? But, you just said . . .
She:	You're not right because in persuasion you use *words,* not physical force.
He:	So, in persuasion I'm not *forced* to say yes, right?
She:	RIGHT! In persuasion, you've got a *choice.*

I like the way that the dialogue unfolded; those two arrived at a big truth. Violence is not persuasion, effective though use of physical force can be. No, persuasion involves use of *symbolic* means of influence: use of language, verbal and nonverbal. Whether pursued with vigor or rather quietly, **persuasion is a civil and respectable source of communicative power**, available to anyone who seeks to have effect on the thinking or behavior of others. And that includes *all* of us.

PERSUASION IN OUR LIVES

No act is more characteristic of human behavior than persuasion, the study of ways in which people affect the thinking, feeling, and behavior of others. Persuasion is normal, everyday behavior. In our relationships with others, you and I use our verbal and nonverbal powers to influence others. That's the way we are. **In a very real sense, we live by persuasion,** affecting others and being affected by them.

Functionally, persuasion is *identifying with people* because positively affecting others involves finding ways to relate to them, ways to *be with* them, whether in belief, feeling, or attitude, to *share* an idea. Virtually every instance of one person interacting with another can be understood in this sense. In all interpersonal exchanges, a person's purpose is to affect others in some way. Everybody wants to be influential. We seek gratifying responses, including acceptance of our ideas, plans, and values. Why is it so satisfying to observe that you have been understood? Isn't it from the realization that you and your views *count for something,* that you can have an *effect on someone?* Yes, I think so. When you know that you've been listened to, and your speech really heard, you know that you are *somebody,* a person with ideas of worth and significance.

Every social act can be viewed as persuasive in intent.[1] People speak to obtain a response from others, not merely to utter words without purpose.

> *Wherever there is meaning there is persuasion.*
>
> *Marie Hochmuth Nichols, professor of rhetoric*

An Ordinary Act

Thus it follows that the most common occasions of persuasive interaction are ordinary and informal daily relations: conversation with family or friends, talking with an instructor after class, a discussion with a group in the cafeteria. On the other end of the spectrum are the more unusual and formal occasions: reporting to the board of directors, courtroom speaking, or election campaigning. The purposes of persuasion are as numerous and varied as the intents of people in communicative interaction. They range from wanting Lisa to close the door, Ron to stay the night, and Dave to take your side instead of Jack's, to a politician wanting votes in Congress and a professor seeking tenure. But regardless of differences in purpose, occasion, and formality, the dynamics of persuasion are fundamentally quite similar. As you read the chapter and complete the class activities, you'll be able to visualize applications to ordinary interactions.

THREE ASSUMPTIONS ON PERSUASION

Adding to the point that persuasion typifies our interpersonal lives, this chapter rests on three assumptions:

1. Democracy cannot function without persuasion.
2. Speakers succeed in persuasion as they come to a meeting of minds with their listeners.
3. Listeners are affected by any and all features of the total communicative situation.

Let's discuss each assumption.

1. Our society needs speaking. The United States was built by talk. It was built by people hammering out decisions through debate and discussion and agitation. It was built from the humane resolution of controversy through persuasive acts of dissent. We Americans have a rich heritage. One of the precepts of the general culture is that citizens in a

One could write a short essay on contrasting communicative dynamics shown here. What title shall we use?

democracy have a "persuasive obligation" in relating to one another, to speak out and act as social commentators. The story of America is one of people taking stands, making their views known, and answering challenges. As noted in Chapter One, it's the story of those courageous people who came here from Asia, Europe, Africa, and all the Americas, and who learned to make their views known. It's a story of social checks and balances through free and willing speech.

Further, it's a story of taking risks, of daring to make a statement or offer a new plan, of exposing self to conflict. It's believing enough in one's ideas to make a bold presentation to others. It's welcoming communicative interaction and rebuttal.

And the talk must go on. **Preservation of the system and our way of life requires that people continue to function as originators and critics of ideas.** Such is the good citizen's role, regardless of background: to reveal his or her opinions to others and get a hearing. Out of the dialogue will emerge something that is just and of value to society. This is speaking in America. Such is the democratic faith.

Matters of Ethics

We should recognize, of course, that some speakers do rely on unethical means to sway others; furthermore, people will occasionally use this fact as an excuse for a blanket condemnation of the process of persuasion.

That's a short-sighted view. Let's answer that kind of cynicism with the position that cases of unethical behavior should offer a challenge to responsible citizens, not despair. **Ethical persuasion is never needed more than when unethical persuasion is used.** It's an error to blame the process of persuasion when a speaker insincerely plays on the sorrows of the downtrodden or oppressed. Instead, judge the one who is speaking, and do your part to prevent that person from being effective. Basic to being humane is genuine sensitivity to the well-being of others. We must trust, but we must be socially vigilant as well.

A society needs persuasion and counterpersuasion for promoting and testing ideas, for the collective good. No better process has been found to serve us in the pursuit of justice and truth.

2. People reach and influence listeners in a meeting of minds. You are aware that starting with Chapter One and continuing throughout I have stressed *common* understanding as a fundamental goal in communication. From this view, we come to an obvious conclusion: A person must know about audiences, that is, about people. Only when you're aware of where your listeners stand, of their feelings about a given topic, cultural perspectives, and beliefs, will you be able to bridge the gap between your proposal for them and "where they are" regarding it. What are their interests, wishes, and attitudes? It's the *gaps* and the *separateness* with which we have got to be especially concerned: our individualism keeps us apart.

President John F. Kennedy's 1963 Berlin speech.

Bridging the Gaps

In varying degrees, listeners necessarily are caught up in their own lives and patterns of habit and thought, in their private "provinces of being." Anyone who would communicate with others must recognize their "provincial" nature and meet them in their own province. That is, speakers must start from where listeners stand and make use of common elements from their own and their listeners' provinces of thinking and experience. Moreover, to communicate, speakers in some way should reveal this kinship to the audience. **Good communication—persuasion—is based on a transaction between speaker and audience, featuring means by which the parties involved can cooperate.** That's a truth in human interaction. Thus does the process of identification provide the theoretical grounding for this chapter and the entire book. Successful speakers first discern where they and their audiences are divided. Then they discover ways to act together, ways toward unity—grounds of agreement and mutual benefit. These grounds are found in the same places as the grounds of disagreement: in concepts, methods, attitudes, words, and customs, and values.

A speech by President John F. Kennedy illustrates the process of discovering similarities and shared sympathies among listeners. Though you may never find yourself in exactly the same situation, you will have many occasions in life in which you will want to follow the same principle. He delivered the speech in the last year of his life, at Rudolphe Wilde Platz in West Berlin, when the city was divided. There, with thousands of cheering Berliners, he found a great bond. Imagine the feeling in having your city linked to the glory of Rome. Here are some of his opening words:

I am proud to come to this city as a guest of your distinguished mayor, who has symbolized throughout the world the fighting spirit of West Berlin. And I am proud to visit the Federal Republic with your distinguished Chancellor who for so many years has committed Germany to democracy and freedom and progress. . . . Two thousand years ago the proudest boast was "civis Romanus sum." Today in the world of freedom, the proudest boast is "Ich bin ein Berliner."

Thus, the president of the United States of America declared himself to be *one of them,* a Berliner. And *he was accepted as one of them.* That's *identification!*

In December of 1941, Winston Churchill came to the United States to speak before a joint session of the Congress. It was December, very soon after the attack on Pearl Harbor, and the English Prime Minister wanted to tighten the ties of friendship with the United States so as to ensure continuation of American support for the war against Germany and Italy in Europe. A significant part of his strategy was to show his personal connection to the United States. In that regard, recall that Churchill's mother had been an American and that he had long served in the English legislature, the House of Commons. Among his remarks in the introduction to his speech was this passage: "I cannot help for reflecting, that if my father had been American—and my mother British—instead of the other way around, I might have got here on my own." Thus, he demonstrated his brotherhood as politician while creating something of a bond of blood with Americans, members of Congress. Such brilliance helps to explain Churchill's status as one of the greatest speakers on the international scene in the past 100 years. His "magic" lay in sensing a common spirit, in identifying his ideas and purpose with the souls of others.

Identification with the listener is everyone's constant aim in speaking: discarding a certain word for a more precise one, choosing this example instead of that, or altering the sequence of ideas from that originally planned. These are decisions to enhance effectiveness and to increase opportunities of securing favorable responses and unity with listeners.

3. All features of the speaking situation influence listeners' responses. Audiences are affected by the speaker's ideas, but they are also affected by the words used to convey ideas and by the speaker's personal bearing, mode of organization, delivery, and any other perceived attribute or act. **Even nonverbal symbols are persuasive.** To scowl is to threaten or criticize. To touch someone on the shoulder may be to give a "statement" of encouragement. To take off a jacket or loosen a tie may be to say "Let's be informal." Thus, people use many avenues for relating to listeners' thinking and expectations.

Often speakers strike the right chord with their audiences without consciously thinking about method. They seem to have a special sense of what's right. This is no surprise, surely. **Speech is a social act,** and socially responsive people have a feeling about getting along with others and addressing them. In other words, part of communicating a message to listeners involves nothing more than rhetorical sociability, being accommodative and gracious. Looking at the listener while you speak, talking at the listener's level and not above or below, showing respect and concern for the listener's comfort, acknowledging the listener's personal or professional identity through direct and thoughtful reference ("I know that as college graduates you have interests in . . ."), noting common feelings and beliefs about conditions of life experienced by all ("none of us enjoys being cheated."), attempting to fit the message to the listener's pattern of thinking—all of these acts and many more arise from social consciousness. They are common practices, and they facilitate a meeting of minds.

Let's turn now to a discussion of four specific areas of the process of persuasion in which speakers find bases for communicating persuasively: modes of proof or appeal, patterns of organization, language, and delivery.

PERSUASION: BASES IN MODES OF PROOF

Beginning with Aristotle and continuing to authorities in our own day, many writers on speechmaking have discussed the basic means of persuasion under three headings: logical proof *(logos),* psychological proof *(pathos),* and personal proof *(ethos).*

Logical Proof: Working with Ideas

The logical appeal of a speech is demonstrated by the audience's response to the speaker's ideas, supporting evidence, and reasoning. To neglect any part of the quality of thought, in selection or development, is to risk rejection of the thesis and entire case. At the minimum, a speaker needs the attention of the audience, something of a commitment or willingness to hear what's being said. Evidence and reasoning contribute to receiving a hearing and to the force of all ideas presented throughout the speech. Ordinarily, the presentation of bare assertions or untreated thoughts are not enough. In meeting an audience, it's necessary to *work with ideas,* making them cogent, appealing, and reasonable to the ear. The process starts with a mature view of audiences.

The Good Audience
During a speech class I sometimes ask my students for their opinion of the character of a typical audience. For example, do most audiences want and expect sound reasoning from a speaker? Or are they willing to let speakers get away with unsubstantiated opinion? Most answers to these kinds of general questions are quite positive in

view. That is, students think of audiences as sensible and rational; yes, listeners have feelings, but they aren't fools who are easily deceived.

From these discussions with students, I have a recommendation to make, a basic rule of communication: *The speaker who anticipates a clear-headed and watchful audience has a greater chance for success in communication.* Now, occasionally one may have good cause to be cynical, assuming the average listener to be oblivious to shaky reasoning. But observation tells me that the reasoning of speakers is usually better, and their speaking more effective, when they visualize their listeners as a "good audience." **A *good audience* is a self-assured and alert group of people with expectations and interests that must be met.** They look for clear, consistent thinking and logical conclusions. As they make themselves available to speakers, they expect premises that ring true and inferences that make sense. Not responsive to fallacy, a good audience can be reached and influenced only with well-conceived, supported thought and adequate reasoning. In the speech class and on other occasions as well, you will benefit by anticipating such an audience. There's no better way to find a good audience than by expecting one to be there. In this sense, speakers have a hand in creating their audiences. Thus, one of the first steps in persuasion is to "create" your audience.

A good audience responds to logic, but what does that mean? Being logical does not mean that a speaker must show an idea to be absolutely foolproof. Nor does it mean that a speaker's line of reasoning necessarily leads to an inevitable or absolutely final conclusion. Only rarely in our communications do we find ourselves in areas of absolute truth or inevitability. Most of the important and frequently discussed ideas are still unresolved and open for consideration. They are matters in dispute: labor–management problems, government aid programs, meeting a nation's health needs, choosing a profession, admission standards for colleges, reducing highway accidents, making a successful marriage, or providing for recreation. Whose arguments in any of these areas are final and indisputable? Usually the best judgment any of us can make about an idea is that its value is "highly probable" or that it "seems quite reasonable" or "suggests a strong likelihood." Thus, **logically acceptable means that an audience, a "good audience," would find the speaker's thoughts reasonable or convincing.** Therefore, *prepare for the good audience.*

Ideas and Proposals
Providing logical appeal should be a consideration from the very first in planning the persuasive speech. As you start putting ideas on scratch paper and begin to see the direction you might take, check the status of your thinking. For example, what kind of proposal and main ideas do you have in mind? What purpose have you conceived? What will you be asking of your audience? Do you have a certain *policy* that you want them to agree to or act on? Will you want them to recognize the *value* of an idea, or to accept something as *fact*? These are three common types of proposals made by speakers in persuasion and

> *Communication involves the use of verbal symbols for purposes of appeal.*
>
> *Kenneth Burke, writer on rhetoric*

argumentation. Let's discuss each individually, noting the kinds of structures inherent in each.

Policy. A thesis relating to policy calls for a change of system or plan. For example, proposals to restructure the divisions of baseball's National League or to change registration procedures at school are matters of policy. The speaker may want to demonstrate the need for a change, offer a workable plan to replace the existing one, and show that resulting benefits will outweigh current ones. I'll discuss structural options later in the chapter.

Value. Theses relating to value deal with questions of desirability and worth or goodness, for example, that cars made by General Motors are better than those made by Chrysler. In this value analysis, the speaker would need to decide which specific models to use as a basis for the case, what criteria to use in evaluating the products, what methods of evaluation to use, and so forth.

Fact. Theses relating to fact assert that something did happen, does exist, is true, and so on. For instance, a speaker may hold that lower enrollment at the school is the result of increased tuition. Here the task is to show the *probability* of a direct connection between two known pieces of information, low enrollment and increased tuition. The speaker will need to determine how best to measure the economic impact on students, to discover the economic status of students most affected, and to analyze various patterns of enrollment and influences on students' decision making.

Careful attention should be given to determining the kind of topic one has in hand, understanding relevant issues, and shaping a specific thesis. The result of such effort will be a logical substructure for the speech, *a reliable base for settling on main ideas and building a reasonable case.* That's the goal at this point.

Supporting Evidence   Once the thesis and structure are conceived and main points determined, the persuasive speaker will select supporting evidence. Use of evidence, developmental materials, is discussed fully in Chapters Six and Seven, but here the application is to persuasion. Although it's true that visual and audio aids can be very useful in influencing others, the basic types of support are verbal: examples, statistics, and quotations. A speaker planning to advocate restructuring baseball's National League will need illustrations and instances of inadequacies in the current system (the status quo), compelling statistics on conditions like attendance patterns in league franchises and lack of balance in team performance, authoritative opinion of league officials and the commissioner of baseball, market analyses, and so forth. Again, remembering the appeal of *logos,* the speaker will apply the standard tests to the supporting material for each point. First, does the evidence allow adequate and reasonable development of the point? Is it relevant? Is it sufficient in quantity? Does it allow adaptation to the audience's thinking on the topic? These are tests not only of soundness and clarity but also of accommodation to listeners' rational perspectives, taking into account their points of view and beliefs. Is the audience likely to find the evidence acceptable? What is expected by a good audience and what will appeal to their thinking?

Another important question relates to availability of evidence. **Can needed supporting materials be found?** If so, where? These questions must be answered as early as possible in the speech-building process. For help in this regard, consult Appendix B, "Doing Research on a Topic."

Drawing Conclusions   The final phase in establishing a logical structure for the persuasive speech is to complete the process of reasoning by relating the evidence to main ideas and drawing conclusions. This might be called the "therefore" step. For example, note this evidence and conclusions drawn from it.

> *In two representative and independent studies of causes for students not returning to campus this fall, 38 percent of those polled in one study and 42 percent in another gave increased tuition as their primary reason.* Therefore, *since 38–42 percent is a large number giving that reason, one can conclude that the tuition increase does affect enrollment negatively and significantly.*

This is a promising pattern of reasoning, very likely deserving use at some important point in the speech, probably in the development of a main head. Let's examine another sample of reasoning.

> *Finding that the quality of steering mechanisms is one important and relevant standard by which to judge cars, the speaker decides to include that point as an argument, main head, in a persuasive speech. As evidence, the speaker has opinions from respected car critics and results of reliable driving tests, showing that the steering mechanism in cars of Manufacturer A are definitely superior to those of Manufacturer B.* Therefore, *concludes the speaker, regarding this particular feature, Manufacturer A's cars are better.*

This is not the speaker's entire case; there is more, of course. But it's a good glimpse of one phase in the process of drawing conclusions and developing lines of reasoning. The speaker is off to a good start.

Thus, speakers proceed, building a trustworthy foundation from specifying and weighing ideas, collecting credible evidence, and coming to reasonable, logically appealing conclusions. For a more complete discussion of processes and patterns in reasoning, see Chapter Nine, "Thinking Critically."

Psychological Proof: Emotional Appeal

Next, let's take up psychological appeal. This mode includes elements with definite emotional character: appeals to human motivations, to feelings and values. Actually, **logical and psychological appeals can never**

be completely separated. They usually overlap, not existing in isolation. Any member of any audience is a *whole* person, one who responds to a point with both "head and heart" at the same time. Consequently, motivating an audience to share your view of your thesis often requires reasoning, yes, but more. Listener responses to a proposal will be influenced by both *logos* and *pathos.* Psychological self-interest is a critical factor to take into account when analyzing the makeup of an audience. In this regard, key issues in preparation for persuasion are personal status, acceptance of self, pride, recognition by others, and so forth.

Before deciding to accept a given policy, listeners want to know how it will affect them. Could it mean some kind of loss for them? "Will this proposal to change the company's scheduling of vacations disrupt my family plans?" the accounts manager asks. "Why wasn't my name mentioned when the new system of deciding prize winners came up at the meeting?" a student body officer silently asks. "What good will it get me to vote for Smith, a Democrat?" asks Jones, a Republican. People want to know how they personally will be affected, how they will be helped or hindered.

Motivation: Maslow's Theory Abraham H. Maslow's highly regarded theory of motivation has added to our understanding of how people act on one another.[2] Maslow developed a hierarchy of five human needs, finding that a basic need must be satisfied before the next one up the ladder will be effective in motivation (see Figure 8-1).

Physiological needs, for food, water, shelter, and the like, are the most basic and the strongest. Then come needs for *safety,* for protection, security, and tranquility, for example. Needs for *belongingness and love* are social: the need to be involved with others, to have relationships with family and friends. Needs for *esteem* have to do with status, personal adequacy, and power—the need to count for something. At the top in the hierarchy is the need for *self-actualization.* It might be thought of as the "purest," from which spring certain creative impulses, the quest to reach the highest level of personal growth and to live fully and productively in chosen areas of involvement, and so forth.

In the extreme, **an individual's most basic needs must be met, or met well enough, before he or she will be responsive to higher needs.** When fundamental requirements of food and drink are satisfied, a person's most basic need then is for safety. Next, with safety established sufficiently, the need for belongingness and love may be manifest. But until a lower need is met, a higher one is limited in force: a starving person seeks food before personal security. From this, you can see how Maslow's theory helps explain why some people are successful in their appeals and why others fail. A group of employees unsure of its status in an organization and with unmet needs for esteem probably will not be moved by a supervisor's request that they produce up to capability. They will not be responsive to the supervisor's notion of self-actualization until they feel respected. The lesson to you as a speaker is to **acquaint your-**

Figure 8-1

Maslow's ranking of human needs.

Self-
Actualization
Needs

Esteem Needs

Belongingness and
Love Needs

Safety Needs

Physiological Needs

self with your audience and determine their needs and level of satisfaction; then use that knowledge, approaching them at the optimal point.

Motivation: Common Needs, Possessions, Behavior
Now, let's extend the discussion of motivation to other categories and to more specific human attributes. I once asked groups of college freshmen and sophomores to think back on their own observations and experiences and list common human characteristics of which they thought speakers should be aware. Their suggestions were excellent and quite useful to students of communication. I have classified them into three areas: what most people, or all, *want and need,* what they *share,* and what they *do.* In this compilation, you'll notice some overlapping with elements in Maslow's theory, perhaps attesting to the soundness of both perspectives.

People want and need:
To be accepted, to be loved, to be needed, to be respected.
To be competent socially, to get along well with others.
To communicate with others, to relate to others.
To see justice done.
To acquire material goods and "wealth".
To succeed and be "prosperous" at work, home, school.
Security: economic, personal, and family—"a place to settle down."
Knowledge and education.

Longevity.

Good health.

The "good life," as variously viewed.

Peace: personal, community, national, international.

Happiness.

Friendship and companionship.

People share or possess:

Natural interest in other people: their natures, customs, habits, tragedies, joys, ideals, common problems.

Interest in the arts and other creative expressions: visual arts, music, literature, or dance.

Interest in matters relating to sex, dating, and marriage.

Emotional "stores," for example, love, hate, anger, fear, jealousy, pride, hope.

Common biological origin.

Sense of immortality.

Interest in children: hopes for, love for, desire to procreate.

Interest in pets and other animals.

Interest in the weather.

Loyalties and pride of citizenship in a nation, region, community.

Belief in democracy and various rights and freedoms.

Feelings of mutuality with people of the same sex, religion, culture, age group, and racial group; with people who have common problems, socioeconomic backgrounds, education, and beliefs.

Strong feelings for home and family: love, security of, security in, and so forth.

People do:

Manifest needs, beliefs, and expressions of religion, varied though the manifestations are.

Appreciate humor.

Carry on certain activities of daily living: eating, working, sleeping, wearing clothes, being in a dwelling.

Make mistakes.

Feel sadness and mental strife.

Respond to beauty: of nature, of the human body, in manufactured objects.

Enjoy sports, games, puzzles, and other such forms of leisure and recreation.

Respond to reason, to intelligent discourse, to logic.

If you allow yourself to be guided by the knowledge represented in this list, you'll be better understood by others and more influential with them. The items listed are bases for appealing to people and therefore useful to you in creating audience interest in your ideas. Many are universal in application. With thought and sensitivity, you can find ways to accomplish identification, making your ideas reasonably compatible with those of your listeners. That's **the ultimate in persuasion, the discovery that you and others can be brought together in thought.** As you listen to effective speakers and read speeches, such as those found in Appendix A, notice how they adapt to common attitudes and feelings of people.

Motivation: Practical Application

Among the successful speakers who can serve as a model for us was Hubert H. Humphrey, political leader from Minnesota and master of the art of communication. He had a very practical and moral view of persuasion, believing that it required conviction, hard work, and knowledge. His aim as a speaker was to cause others to understand and learn, and to challenge them to think deeply about important topics. To build a speech, said Humphrey, you need "a full and detailed understanding of the facts," a "thorough understanding of the particular audience to be addressed," and a "deep and thorough belief" in what you are saying.[3]

I accept Humphrey's philosophy and derive from it five points on motivating an audience to respond to a message. Consider them as you prepare your next speech.

1. **Acquire specific information about your audience.** One practical approach is to **visualize your prospective audience assembled before you and then figuratively** *place yourself among them* as you start your planning. As you mentally mingle with them, "take notes" on their backgrounds, knowledge of your subject, attitudes toward your subject, and attitudes toward you. Soon you'll be entering into an interpersonal relationship with them. Therefore, make no decision in preparation without "consulting" them, without giving high priority to their inclinations and requirements. Let's look closer at this.

Backgrounds. What is the predominant age level and gender? Your approach to a group of teenagers would vary greatly from your approach to middle-aged people; what might be pertinent at a men's club meeting might not stir an assembly of women.

What should you know about their political leanings? What of their educational, economic, and religious backgrounds? Awareness of ethnic backgrounds and features of varied identities is essential in communication. **In our pluralistic culture, a sense of audience pluralism is required, a recognition by communicators of diversity among listeners.** From such sensitivity, a speaker will be able to adapt, to achieve identification with them. I recall an occasion when a young man speaking to an audience composed largely of people born in Asia "came on too strong." He didn't know his audience well, and in his outspoken way,

albeit sincere, he applied too much pressure with his proposal. Consequently, the listeners felt somewhat "assaulted" by his directness. A less forward, more adaptive presentation would have helped him to meet his audience on their ground.

Knowledge of the subject. Determine the extent of the audience's familiarity with the subject and whether the acquaintance derives from formal study or direct experience. If they know something about nutrition, is the knowledge based on classroom training or practical experience or both? Such an analysis will help you enter into the life of your listeners at the proper point, and the point to which their learning has advanced.

Values and attitudes relating to the subject. **What do your listeners hold to be *good*?** What principles, programs, practices? Held values are primary bases of action, what people cherish, stand for, and want to defend. Among them are values—conceptions of the good—relating to family, progress, work, education, homeland, freedom, efficiency, economy, and health. Incidentally, many of those human wants, sharings, and behaviors listed on pp. 179–180 reflect values, some personal, others social and moral. As you pursue your purpose in speaking, you'd be well-advised to recognize audience values. ***To reject values of listeners is to ask for rejection of your thesis.***

Also keep in mind relevant attitudes and related feelings, emotional attributes, ways of thinking, and ways of looking at things. Though many such ways are universal, specific distinctions do exist. The key is to find means of accommodating audience predispositions and perceptions, while holding to your purpose and position.

As you prepare to get a hearing for your thesis, remember that *an alienated person cannot be a listener.* Values and attitudes provide grounds for coming together.

Attitudes toward you. Learn how much they are likely to know about you and what their opinion is of you. This information will tell you how much time should be spent in getting acquainted and in establishing good will and credibility. **Listeners who respect you will tend to respect your ideas.** Do they know and trust you? What is your reputation with them? Will you need to work at building ethos? These are important questions to consider.

About your relationship. Are they people with whom you can be "sociable"? Can you relate easily with them and be free to adapt to them? Or do you have some reserve or rigidity regarding them? Are there potential risks in the relationship, such as points at which you or they might become defensive? Do you have any hostility toward them? These very important questions must be answered. A working relationship is essential for adapting your thoughts to your listeners' thinking and motivations. Are you willing to be open? Do you really want to speak to this audience? If the answer is no, you face a problem of adjusting your attitude, your subject, or some other condition. The best solution may lie in further assessment of the total situation, and from that in finding some good reason for welcoming the chance to speak with them. **Intelligent and sincere human beings are capable of discovering workable answers to most communicative problems.**

2. **From audience appreciation will come grounds of inherent appeal.** Information on the listeners will suggest a foundation on which you can communicate with them. For help in this regard, refer back to Maslow's theory and also the listing of common needs, possessions, and behaviors. For instance, your listeners doubtless desire a long life. Does that realization help you in your planning? Are they especially aware of the benefits of sound health? The answers to such questions will indicate the kinds of emphases to give your message. Try to single out areas of motivation that seem dominant. Some success may arise from knowing the general nature of people, the "average." But without real effort to learn what the immediate and unique audience requires and expects, you may not reach them.

3. **Relate the grounds of appeal directly to the thesis and main ideas.** For example, if you plan to promote use of public transportation, show it be a *bargain* or a *fast* way of traveling or a *safe* way. If your purpose is to persuade people to attend a campus play put on by the drama department, could you link your goal to their desire for *cultural enrichment*? What about *loyalty to the school*? Or perhaps a desire *to have a good time with others*? And tickets are *inexpensive*!

Where exactly should you place motivational elements in your message? Almost anywhere, is the answer. You can add appeal to your thoughts in the introduction, in the words of the thesis, in wording the main heads, in pieces of evidence to support main heads, and in the concluding remarks, anywhere to serve your purpose. Also, **allow your knowledge of your listeners' needs and behavioral patterns to help you determine the structure of your speech,** for example, in placing a comparatively threatening main head in third position rather than first. The same counsel would apply to the selection and placement of examples, quotations, and other supporting materials, as well as language usage and preparations for delivery.

4. **Make plans to secure and hold your listeners' attention.** Practice using appealing language, and incorporate material to keep their minds on your message. Among the qualities of content that hold attention are concreteness, familiarity, color, variety, drama, and humor. Some of these will improve any speech.

Concreteness. Include particular data in your illustrative material, such as the season, time of day, descriptions of facial expressions, weather conditions, ages of people, and other relevant conditions. Instead of supporting a point with an abstract instance, give details. To illustrate, which of these two examples is better, and why?

> *Yolanda came from Cuba ten years ago.*
>
> or
>
> *Yolanda, a 28-year-old mother of two small girls, came from Cuba ten years ago, after her father, a newspaper editor, lost political favor with the government.*

Familiarity. Perhaps the heading here should be "Familiarity vs. Exoticness" because there is attractiveness in both attributes. Faraway places with strange-sounding names do appeal to some audiences, but the well-known things of life have welcome meaning and provide certain satisfactions. If, for instance, you're looking for an analogy to describe the richness of the Van Gogh art exhibit, you might say that your three-hour experience in absorbing those marvelous paintings was like gorging on a sumptuous feast, except that it was all dessert, a full and luscious treat of massive gobs of delight. In that analogy, one finds both the familiar and the exotic.

Color and variety. Be lively. **Paint full word pictures,** and vary your strategies. People respond to vibrancy and movement. The Van Gogh dessert analogy has color and life, though one could enhance it by mentioning the "well-fed" looks on the faces of the other "diners" and reporting on some of the things they say as they take in more and more. Use your creativity as you introduce color and variety to bring life to ideas.

Narration. Give yourself the expressive freedom to introduce dramatic elements into your speech, possibly through a compelling narrative. An interesting story that bears on a point in your message may help to draw listeners into your presentation and stimulate curiosity. **People love to hear about events in others' lives that touch on their own and possibly reflect their own backgrounds or cultural values.** A relevant narrative can make associations, reminding others of times and experiences that are vital parts of their lives. This is the way to communicate.

Humor. An occasional short funny story or quip that seems appropriate could put your listeners in a receptive mood and relieve any tensions that may exist. Though you may have an intense and serious desire to persuade, you should realize that **humor may help you to reach your goal.** You might even find something funny to include in a speech on a Van Gogh exhibit. In any event, choose humor that is suitable to your audience and valuable in achieving your purpose.

5. Lead the audience to a response. Here I want to stress *completion* of the appeal, perhaps the most difficult and most neglected phase in persuasion. Of course you should be alert all through the speech for opportunities to attract listeners, to connect your proposal to their needs, to make your thesis *inviting,* and to make it *easy for them to respond,* offering a thesis that they can accept or act upon readily. But remember that it's in the concluding part or "action phase" that you will win or lose your cause. So go all the way with your proposal. It's not enough to assume that people will respond without specific direction and urging; you must give definite guidance. In the interest of certainty and clarity, be sure to provide all the information they will need in following through. If, for example, you want your audience to attend the festival of cultures to be held in Athenian Park, tell them where it is and exactly how to get there, in words like these:

> *Athenian Park is located on the east side of Bradley Boulevard, just over the Viaduct and at the tall flag pole on the right. Events are scheduled for the entire week of May 19—all seven days, from 10 in the morning to 10 at night. If you don't have a car, you can take the 103 bus from the campus or anywhere along College Avenue. Here, let me write the hours and the address on the board.*

Whether urging your listeners to do something or to be convinced of something, you must "take them there," making their response easy and convenient.

Motivation: Two Opposing Views

One often hears two conflicting views regarding audiences of persuasive speeches and the use of emotional appeals. The first might be stated like this: "People are gullible, easy to fool or flatter. If you find their weak spots, you can lead them around by the nose." Are we such "easy marks"? This cynical outlook reflects a rather dismal picture of human beings in general. In contrast, we have the second point of view: "People can be moved when they are offered satisfaction of their needs and given answers that meet their expectations; they can be led to better their opinions and improve their ways of doing things."

What is the essential difference between these two views? Both agree that motivational persuasion is *effective,* but the second statement suggests that it can and should be *responsible* also—and *humane.* Persuasive

> *I speak straight and do not wish to be deceived.*
>
> *Cochise of the Apaches*

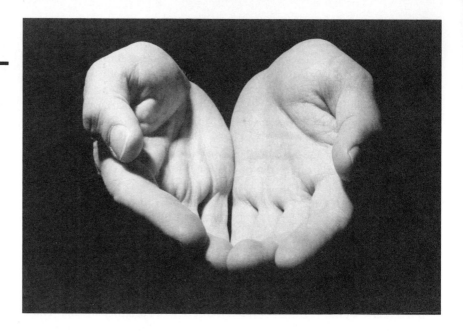

speaking is responsible and humane, if the listener is respected as a dignified human being and treated honestly and fairly. Conversely, persuasive speaking is irresponsible if the listener is shown the disrespect of being subjected to deceit or heartless, crude, or unprincipled appeals.

In responsible speaking, the emphasis is not on manipulation of people. **The most responsible and ultimately most effective persuasion is that which finds greatest *mutual* benefit.**

Personal Proof: Credibility

The third mode of proof, called *ethos* by the ancient Greeks, may be the most potent force in persuasion. Ethos is personal appeal, the reputation and manner of the speaker as an influence on audiences. It's the character, intelligence, and goodwill of the speaker, as perceived in listeners' minds. It can be positive or negative.

There's no denying that your reputation, appearance, personality, and behavior affect an audience and influence their analysis of your ideas. If they are favorably impressed by you, they will give you and your ideas a fair hearing. If they suspect or fear you, you'll have to work harder at creating an attitude of trust and friendliness. Behavior that's strongly authoritarian, "too clever," condescending, indifferent, or deceptive, ordinarily is counterproductive. You can take it as a general rule of thumb that when an audience is kindly disposed toward you, it will be kindly disposed toward listening to your message, willing to take a chance.

In a real sense, the personal element in speaking represents "content" because **the speaker's "self," as seen and heard, conveys a particular message and says something to the audience.** In other words, it carries substance. Successful speakers are able to show that their substance, what they stand for, is akin to their listeners' substance. The outcome of the exchange between speaker and audience will depend to a great extent on the audience's acceptance of the speaker's way of dealing with them, on the speaker's ability to identify with them, in showing a kinship in ideas or spirit.

Effective speeches contain language showing speakers' strategies in identifying themselves with their audiences. Let's examine some examples.

Speaking at Seton Hill College graduation, business leader Cecile M. Springer reminded her audience that she once sat where they sat. Note the personal content.

> *How well I remember sitting with my graduating class, almost overwhelmed with contrasting feelings of joy and sorrow. I was happy, sad, scared, and determined—all at the same time. Happy to be finished with four years of hard labor; happy to leave. . . . Sad to leave. . . .* [4]

Following is an excerpt from a speech of a West Coast college student running for a campus political office. Note the positive ethos, especially as reflected in the speaker's sense of humor, humility, indications of readiness and confidence, successful experience, and optimism. Consider ways to incorporate such personal appeal in your speaking, in your own way.

> *You read in the* Cougar *that I'm running for student body president. It's not because of the great salary [laughter] or benefits. It's mainly because I enjoy taking on a big job and like working with others to make things better, if we can. Most people agree that the Reform Committee brought about some real improvements last year, and I appreciated the opportunity to chair that committee. I'm hopeful that we can do even more. . . .*

Developing Credibility   No one disagrees that **credibility is an all-important element in persuasion, in all communication!** But how does a speaker develop it? First, it must be said that there's no magic key to success in this. Actually, the work of refining the many components that make up personal proof is a lifetime project for all of us. It's something that we attend to as we live and relate. Here are five specific recommendations, each of which is very important.

1.   Know the value of a good reputation. What people think of you affects their reception of everything you say. A known and respected person has fewer obstacles arising from an audience's indifference or negativity. A good name is an enviable asset in communication.

2.   Consider how you appear to listeners. Face it, dress and appearance are factors in persuasion. But what is appropriate? Certainly no universally endorsed prescription is available. Expectations differ. For

Ethos "may almost be called the most effective means of persuasion."

Aristotle, Greek writer on rhetoric

example, a style of dress that is acceptable on a given occasion may be unacceptable in other scenes. Really, it's a matter of communication. Dress, hair styles, and manner convey messages. If such messages arouse suspicion or act as barriers to the building of trust, your potential for relating effectively is greatly diminished. If this seems unfair to you, you'll empathize with the job-hunting students whom you occasionally see on campus all dressed up for an employment interview.

3. Discover ways to identify with your audience. If you study the audience beforehand, you can avoid such poor practices as speaking down to them, talking over their heads, or being tactless. Show respect for your listeners by accepting them as partners in the interaction.

Follow the lead of speakers who are effective in relating to others. It may not be too extreme to say that any person before any audience can discover shared interests, experiences, problems, or goals. **A common ground can be found in most instances,** if it be nothing more specific than a shared hope for peace or economic betterment or insistence on fair play.

4. Let listeners know you. Give evidence of your personal qualifications. Is it exceedingly vain to mention your relevant strengths or accomplishments? Not necessarily. **Remember that communication depends in large part on people knowing you.** Modestly work into your message an occasional remark referring to your background and achievements. Show that you are open to others and deserve their trust. Along with other commendable characteristics, you might show that you have a sense of humor, self-confidence, good character, and knowledge of your material. A student once gave a talk in class urging listeners to consider a career in the computer industry. He began by offering his credentials, so to speak:

> *I've worked for Computers Unlimited for three years and now am in charge of training new employees. While in this job, at the main plant and at the four satellite branches, I've been able to become fully acquainted with the entire operation, from beginning to end.*

Another student, speaking on skydiving, was very successful in building credibility:

> *I don't know why, but some people are surprised that women do skydiving as a hobby. Well, here I am. I'm one of them. Yet I don't want you to think that I'm any great authority on the subject. I've made 19 jumps so far, just enough probably to say something regarding the excitement of the sport.*

PERSUASION: BASES IN ORGANIZATION

With a solid foundation of logical, psychological, and personal proof, the persuasive speaker turns next to strategic arrangement. Organization, too, can facilitate a hearing for ideas. And it, too, can be viewed as substantial;

patterns carry messages. **Clear organization bespeaks clear thinking and concern for the audience's welfare.** Poor arrangement may tell of the speaker's confused thinking or lack of real interest. In giving clarity to your speech and in showing respect for listeners' needs, good organization is persuasive. These are only two of the benefits.

In organizing ideas for persuasive speaking, you should take into account criteria of both logic and psychology. Understand that you need to develop your thoughts in a sequence that is logically sound *and* psychologically advantageous. It's folly to cast ideas aimlessly in all directions; an orderly manner and well-conceived plan are vital.

Direct Patterns

A direct pattern of speech organization was discussed fully in Chapter Four: the introduction-thesis-body-conclusion formula with which you are familiar. The essential characteristic of the direct plan, as opposed to the indirect discussed in the next section, is that it involves development in a general-to-specific pattern. The speaker presents general points before backing up with specific supporting details (for example, main-head statements would come before evidence).

The direct pattern is practical, certainly logical, and it's easy to handle. It's excellent for achieving clarity and directness in expression. As with any system, however, care should be taken to make it work right. The thesis and main heads must be laid out with a particular audience in mind. To illustrate, here is a poorly worded proposal: "I will convince you that people who don't vote, do not know the meaning of democracy." In some speech situations this would be a threatening statement and could make people uneasy, if not hostile. Instead, one might say, "Let's consider advantages of voting in elections," or "I'd like to discuss with you why everyone eligible should vote." Most audiences cannot be forced to accept a proposal, but they can be encouraged to give it a hearing.

Some Forms Persuasive speeches on the four-part plan may assume various forms. When dealing with a social problem, such as juvenile crime, you can set up main heads in a causal pattern (the first one treating causes and another effects, or vice versa). For another speech, a climactic structuring may be best for achieving your goal (beginning with the least important main head and ending with the most important). Perhaps your purpose can be achieved with a series of questions as main heads: (I) What is CPR?, (II) Who should learn it?, (III) Where can one take the course? Or, if you're advocating a change of some sort, for example, the campus parking policy, you could develop two main heads as the body of your speech: (I) The current policy, and (II) A new policy. This kind of ordering would allow for side-by-side contrast, a method with considerable promise. One of the most common and effective patterns calls for wording the thesis as a statement of belief or position on a question, and wording every main head as a reason for the contention. Main heads are "because" statements. Here's an example:

Thesis
Our football team will be a contender in the coming season.

Body
  I.   [because] The quarterback is versatile.
  II. [because] The running backs are outstanding.
  III. [because] The defensive line is the best in the league.

To refresh your memory on the reason order of development, turn back to the discussion in Chapter Four.

Use your imagination in analysis, and let your total assessment of the job at hand indicate a promising structure.

Indirect Patterns

There are times, when dealing with certain persuasive speeches that an indirect plan will be psychologically more effective than the direct. The indirect is an upside-down system of arrangement, in which the thesis is placed near the end of the speech with the conclusion. The speaker presents a brief opening, develops the main heads, and finally unveils the thesis. Development of each individual main head may be handled directly in a deductive pattern, the way most familiar to you, or it may be done indirectly. If accomplished indirectly, the speaker presents all supporting material for a given main head *before* stating the main head. The main head comes as a conclusion to the gathered evidence.

The indirect approach, since it allows the speaker to withhold the statement of objective until the last minute, makes two accommodations to listener behavior: (1) It minimizes buildup of negative feelings against the proposal, and (2) it adds suspense to the speech. The following outline is for such a speech, one designed to create interest prior to the naming of a specific proposal. It asks people to give up, or cut down on, certain things.

  A. Our environment is cluttered with sound.
      1. A typical day offers hundreds of hisses, clicks, hums, rumbles, pops, bangs, and thuds. [instances]
      2. Measured in decibels, the intensity of environmental sound is often great. [definition]
          a. The reading for one food blender is 93 decibels. [illustration]
          b. For a loud power mower it is 107. [instance]
          c. A rock band produced a reading of 122 decibels. [instance]
          d. A full crowd in the Kingdome in Seattle can produce a level of 110 decibels. [instance]

3. Other sources of loud noise are television sets, tape players, jet skis, and motorcycles. [instances]

B. A federal study estimates that noise pollution doubled from last year's level. [statistics]

Main Head I. Therefore, whether you are aware of it or not, you are a consumer and producer of lots of noise.

A. Noise and hearing loss are related.
    1. "There is incriminating evidence that community noise levels are causing hearing loss." [quotation of a public health physician]
        a. Medical authorities believe that "excessive exposure to noise can cause nerve deafness." [instance and quotation]
        b. Many of the 15 million Americans with hearing losses (4 million of them are children) can blame noise as a causal factor. [statistics]
    2. The fact that continuous exposure to sounds of 85 decibels or more can cause permanent damage is ample evidence to alert us.

B. Noise and mental health are related.
    1. Psychiatrist Bruce L. Welch reports that stimuli overloading can cause a breakdown of mental health. [quotation]
        a. Noise causes irritability, which leads to reduced efficiency and impairment of sociability. [illustration]
        b. Noise can trigger major emotional outbreaks. [instance]
        c. Noise causes lack of sleep, which leads to poor mental states. [instances]
        d. Noise may contribute to development of personality problems. [quotation]
    2. Part of the problem stems from the normal function of noise in alerting the body to danger.

Main Head II. Therefore it's easy to see that too much noise can adversely affect your health.

Thesis–Conclusion: Because you are hearing too much noise and because it's adversely affecting your health, you must do your part to keep the volume down.

A. Do it now.
    1. Turn down your radio, record player, and television set.
    2. Refuse to purchase noisy power equipment such as mowers, mixers, and unmuffled motorcycles.
    3. Support ordinances to lower city noise.
    4. Wear earplugs if you work at a noisy job.

B. I hope you'll be able to hear me the next time we talk.

While having certain uses, **the indirect plan should be selected only after careful consideration.** You know, it can be hazardous to speak to an audience without benefit of a stated thesis. People need guidance and direction. Do the values of nondisclosure—suspense and receptivity—outweigh the possible buildup of confusion concerning purpose and goal? Sometimes, but it's a gamble. An extra touch of artistry is required in handling the indirect method.

Combined Pattern: Direct and Indirect

On some occasions you might find that a combination of direct and indirect organization will serve best in achieving your purpose. Patterns A and B illustrate two of the possible variants.

Pattern A

Introduction

Thesis

Body, with main heads developed indirectly, that is, with supporting material preceding the statement of each main head

Conclusion

Pattern B

Introduction

Body, with main heads developed directly

Thesis–Conclusion

You may have good reason to use a combined pattern. As a fresh approach, it can enhance listeners' interest or stimulate curiosity. Possibly, while preparing your speech, you'll find that your ideas and materials seem to fall into place better when allowed to conform to a combined pattern.

Monroe's Motivated Sequence Pattern

One option for structuring persuasive speeches on a four-part direct plan includes only two main heads: Problem and Solution. You may recall that pattern from the discussion in Chapter Four. A strategic elaboration of the problem–solution plan is one called "motivated sequence," which was developed by the late Professor Alan H. Monroe of Purdue University. Comprised of five parts—Attention, Need, Satisfaction, Visualization, and Action—**the motivated sequence tends to impel the listener to move along with the speaker from one step to the next,** from first awareness of a problem to a course of action. In a process of identification the listener is inclined, rather "naturally," to relate to the sequence of thought as one section of the speech flows on to the next. Presumably, the plan attains its psychological effect by paralleling listeners' typical patterns of response in dealing with problems. If listeners agree with the speaker during the presentation of the first and second steps, they'll be moved to go with the speaker to the next step, and so forth. Thus, its appeal is both logical and psychological.

Note that there are essential tasks to accomplish in each of the five parts.

1. **Attention**

   Handle this first step as you would an introduction. Stimulate interest, identify with the audience, and suggest the existence of a problem. The message to convey: **"Listen, here's an important topic that affects all of us, and we must look into it."**

2. **Need or Problem**

   Lay out the problem, under main heads as aspects of the problem, for example, the social, political, economic, and so forth. Another pattern of main heads could be the extent of the problem, the causes, the effects, and so on. The message to convey: **"Here's the kind of problem we have."**

3. **Satisfaction or Solution**

   Present a solution to the problem, perhaps after you have examined and dismissed several possible solutions. The message to convey: **"We could approach the problem in a number of ways, but this is the best way to meet it."**

4. **Visualization**

   Envision results of your chosen solution. See it in effect, and/or visualize the consequences of *not* adopting it, of letting things go on as they are. A strong contrast can be very effective here, the good that is likely to result from the adopted solution alongside the bad that will continue if the solution is not adopted. The message to convey: **"This is what it will be like if the solution is adopted"** or that plus **"This is what it will be like if the solution is not adopted."**

5. **Action**

   Motivate the listeners to take a specific and practical course of action. The message to convey: **"Now here is what we must do and how we can do it."**

I have one additional suggestion on using the motivated sequence plan: **Have adequate knowledge of the problem.** Some persuasive speeches break down because the speaker really does not understand the problem under consideration. Study it fully, and be sure to know the history, causes, effects, and relevant ramifications. For a model of the motivated sequence speech, see "The Other 99% of the Population" that is printed in Appendix A.

PERSUASION: BASES IN LANGUAGE

The language used in persuasion can contribute greatly to achievement of your purpose. Well-chosen words and phrases promote interest and help to identify speaker and listener, that is, to achieve unity in belief and feeling.

Useful language is clear, lively, varied, and acceptable. Actually, we can cluster all these criteria of usage under one term, *rhetorical value.* It's a matter of function. Whenever you consciously check yourself on style and usage, you must eventually ask one question, "Will this word or particular way of expressing my thought help me gain the desired response from this audience on this occasion?" Said another way, the question is **"Will this word, or particular way of putting the idea, help me unite my purpose with my listeners' interests and aims?"**

Ideas in a persuasive message are dependent on the language used to convey them. You will find a full discussion of the four criteria of usage in Chapter Eleven, but let me briefly review them here and introduce passages of a modern speech to illustrate. The speech is "The Power of Art," given by Isabel Allende to the Congress of the Arts that met in California.[5] Ms. Allende, a writer and native of South America, has been devoting much energy in recent years in advocacy of freedom in the world. She has a particular interest in freedom as it relates to artistic expression. She speaks in a bold and direct style that holds attention.

Clarity

Highly effective in establishing positive identification with listeners, Allende is unmistakably clear, as you see in this passage.

> *The tremendous power of art lies precisely in this unique faculty to represent and interpret us. This power cannot be easily measured at the moment when the work of art is created. It takes awhile, often years and sometimes centuries, to appreciate it. Art transcends and therefore only time can determine artistic value. . . . Most human beings are born with some degree of imagination, but few have a chance to expand it and only some chosen ones are able to produce a memorable work of art.*

Liveliness

I use the word *liveliness* to cover a discussion of sense-appealing and figurative language. **Appeals to the senses and figures of speech do add liveliness to thought, and more.** They are of great value in crossing over to listeners' provinces of belief and interest and in finding common ground for communication. Note, for example, the compelling dream metaphor in the following passage from Allende's speech.

> *Art is to humankind what dreams are to individuals. In dreams we wander in a no-man's land, where all rules are abolished. Dreams*

unclog the mind of the fog and the noise of the world, they clear our thoughts and, if we learn to pay attention, they teach us about ourselves. They speak to us with those inner voices that cannot be silenced, mingling the facts of our daily lives with their images in the psyche.

Variety

All audiences like variety. They are impatient with cliché and redundancy (for example, overused word patterns and repetitive sentence structure). Ms. Allende seems to know well people's nature and expectations. Accordingly, she diversifies her language and finds fresh ways of verbalizing an idea. She stimulates her audiences with varied word choice and sentence length. She switches from balanced to periodic sentences, always alert to achieving emphasis and force. These and other methods serve to heighten interest and motivate listeners to go along with her. Here is a sample.

When nothing else remains, when the spoils of war, the treasures of kings, the walls of mighty cities have been reduced to ashes, sometimes a work of art survives. In spite of the cataclysms that turn the earth upside down, the systematic destruction by innumerable generations of warriors, the whims of the weather, and the consequences of oblivion, a work of art reaches us intact, bringing us a gift from the past. These messages tell us about ourselves and our journey through history; they reveal the struggles, fears, and hopes, the deities, and ways of life of the people who created art.

Acceptability

Occasions make requirements on speakers in a number of ways, including use of language. As speaker, you should **observe the nature of the occasion as you choose your ways of expressing yourself.** Propriety is a concern yes, but the dominant need is *audience identification with the message.* Audiences, having certain images of themselves, tend to resent and reject usages that do not fit their images. The self-image of college students differs, of course, from the image that the Downtown Merchants Association has of them. On a specific occasion, what level of formality is indicated? What attitude? What are the expectations of the group that you will face? Can you get away with a bit of slang, or will the occasion's formality forbid it? Can you use the same modes of expression that you'd use with your close friends, or would the audience reject them?

And regarding events of the day, how critical of conditions and behaviors can you be? Allende was highly critical of certain tendencies of military leaders, politicians, and others who were inclined to repress artistic expression. But she appeared to know that artists, often in conflict with bureaucrats and censors, may be taken as malcontents, and she wanted to avoid that designation. Though seeming to believe that a natural conflict exists between the artist and elements of the establishment, Allende remained hopeful and optimistic in outlook. Thus, she had her say, *and* she received an enthusiastic response from the audience. She satisfied herself *and* the occasion. Note the tenor of this passage near the end of her speech.

> *I am sure that I will see the improvements in my life-time. Yes, we will not destroy the planet with a nuclear cataclysm, we will not disappear in sidereal ashes [ashes of the stars]. On the contrary, we will probably reach an agreement not only for peace, but also to defeat poverty. We are witnessing the beginning of a new era, a time when the deities of power and war will be replaced by benevolent and nurturing gods. . . . The time has come for artists and for all the people with the gift of imagination and intuition. Their mission is to invent the future. . . . The creation of the future is the great adventure of our lives.*

Thus, one successful speaker presented herself and her ideas. Though outspoken and sometimes sharp in judgments, she found language to convey an obvious sincerity, intelligence, and good nature.

PERSUASION: BASES IN DELIVERY

The presentation of a speech contributes to accomplishment of purpose. To speak before others is to involve oneself in a give-and-take of ideas. **The true spirit of communication is speaker-audience *interaction.*** As "leader" of the interaction, the speaker willingly engages the audience, motivated by an interest in achieving a purpose. The consequence is vocal and bodily expression; sounds of the voice and movements of the body work together to relay the message. That act, coming after all the preparation, is what we call "delivery," or "giving the speech."

In our time, **the standard of delivery is good conversation. It is represented by the purposes and best attributes of speakers in a one-to-one communicative relationship**. Recall our mentioning this topic in discussion of extemporaneous speaking in an early chapter. But conversation can be achieved even in the most formal of occasions— when the speaker enters into the exchange of ideas, intent upon reaching the listeners and *talking with* them. Effective public speakers have learned to incorporate into their presentations essential qualities of conversation, like directness, ease, and openness.

For a more complete exploration of the delivery phase of oral communication, see Chapter Twelve, "Giving the Speech."

ANSWERING PERSUASIVE MESSAGES

It's a truism that society needs persuasion, and it's also true that it needs *counterpersuasion*. **Democratic interaction requires that positions be challenged**, at times directly and at other times in one's own mind. This is the function of the "good audience," the alert and self-respecting person or group that in its own interest operates as a positive influence on the speaker, by formulating a reaction to the speech. Such an audience expects sound reasoning, fairness, and adequate supporting evidence. When direct and overt, the act of response is called *refutation.* In a real sense, all the principles discussed in this chapter on persuasion apply to refutation because a response to a message is surely as persuasive in intent as the original message. But to add to the theory, I suggest implementation of two basic steps in refuting persuasive messages: listen to the message and present a response.

> *Hear the other side.*
>
> *St. Augustine,*
> *Roman writer*

Step 1: Listen to the Speaker's Message

What's the speaker's thesis? What are the main premises of the speaker's message? Are supporting data adequate? Note the kind and quality of the lines of reasoning, modes of appeal, and developmental material. The following three tasks represent the scope of your work as you prepare a speech in response to a persuasive speech.

Grasp the Reasoning
Listen to determine the soundness of the speaker's fundamental premises. Do you spot a weak or dubious premise? Do the premises relate to one another? Are they parts of a cohesive pattern of thought? Which, if any, do not belong? Are the conclusions relevant to the premises from which they are drawn? Is the solution sufficient to meet the problem presented?

Note the Appeals
Would you judge the message to be fair and respectful of opposed positions? Is the speaker unduly self-serving in purpose? Is the speaker ethical and considerate in the use of motivational appeals? Do you find examples of unjustified emotional appeal? Does the speaker seem to take unfair advantage of persons who might not be able to defend themselves, for example, very old people, children, or groups with limited political or social power? Is the speaker's message free of objectionable stereotypes, name-calling, and derogatory code words?

Evaluate the Support
Are the speaker's chosen materials—supporting evidence—relevant to the points developed? Is the evidence sufficient to justify conclusions? Are the speaker's "facts" consistent with known facts? **Do the speaker's opinions seem well-founded?** Does the

speaker rely on qualified authorities? Are the speaker's terms acceptably defined? Are the statistics reliable?

Step 2: Present Your Refutation

When you have made a thorough check of reasoning, appeals, and supporting evidence and put together a response, present your points of refutation in a confident and logical, well-organized manner.

State the Matter at Issue
First, in a clear and fair statement, raise the matter at issue. Identify the specific weakness, whether it be faulty reasoning, unacceptable appeal, or inadequate supporting material.

Present Your Response to the Inadequacy
Present a constructive counterstatement in answer to the speaker's weakness in particular thought or material, precisely meeting its questionable character with an explicit interpretation.

Conclude Convincingly
Draw the appropriate, logical conclusions(s) to clinch your counterargument. Your statement should be a speech that establishes the strength of your view and shows the significance of your point(s) to other points at issue. Further, you may ask the speaker to clarify a point, warn about dangers in treating such a subject unthoughtfully, and urge listeners to continue their study of the topic, and so on.

As you can see, knowledge and preparation provide the foundations of effectiveness in refutation—as in all persuasive speaking.

LOOKING BACK

Such, then, is persuasion: **the process of people verbally and nonverbally establishing identification of self and idea with their audiences.** In this process of finding means of influence with others, we should keep in mind these points:

1. Persuasion has a significant place in the lives of all of us.
2. Without persuasion no democracy can last.
3. Bases of persuasion are to be found in modes of proof, organization, choices in language, and delivery of the message.
4. The good audience plays a central and important part in persuasive interaction.
5. Though many elements in motivation are universal, speakers should remain sensitive to specific differences among listeners.
6. Strategies are available for answering persuasive speaking.

It may be true that any group of people can be unified on some ground. "But what is that ground?" the speaker asks. "Where 'are they coming from,' and what do they want? Where do their ideas and mine coincide? How can I reach them?" And the big question: "How can I reconcile the differences that separate us?" These very practical questions have highly significant ramifications.

Persuasion does have to do with reconciliation of differences, a truth that we ought to put in the context of the racial, ethnic, and national differences that characterize the human family in this nation and across the world. **We can discover how to communicate with others, different others, if we are willing to work at it.** In this regard, a wise philosopher named Reinhold Niebuhr once said that people, setting themselves apart in classes, races, and nations as they do, have only one way to "achieve a tolerable harmony" with others and that is to settle "their competitions by standards of . . . justice, or by stratagems that would discover the point of concurrence between the more parochial and the more universal interests." That's how we get along, by acting justly and discovering *common* ground. No challenge of living and relating in this diverse nation and world is greater or more important.

Persuasion, a study of the means of locating points of mutual interest and thereby bringing people together, can serve in that great cause. Wouldn't you agree?

SUBJECTS AND TOPICS FOR PERSUASIVE SPEECHES

Skin cancer
Beaches for nude bathing
Protecting wildlife
Getting "guzzlers" off the road
Forest fires
Ozone depletion
AIDS and HIV testing
Television and public needs
My hero, José Rizal
Being a woman today
Child abuse
Tipping in restaurants
Immigration
Intelligence tests
Religious instruction and the public schools
Head Start programs
Clean beaches
Among the disabled

Organized labor
Credit cards
Recycling
Returning home
Clear-cutting of timber
Do you know Miguel de Unamuno?
Advertising
Lotteries
Sexual orientations
Professional opportunities
Daniel Webster
Responsibilities of scientists
Going to a rodeo
A compact disc player
Carlos Fuentes
Civil rights
Peace in the Middle East
Water resources

Investing in real estate
Sun Yat-Sen
Local government
Fashion trends
Mental illness
Participation in athletics
Lucy Stone
The jury system
The local art gallery
Ethnicity
A liberal education
The stock market
Sojourner Truth
The grading system in college
Animal protection
Water safety

"Know thyself"
Equal opportunity
Weight reduction
The police and the community
Fallacies in reasoning
Going away to college
The greatest baseball player of
 all time
Participating in politics
A third political party
Poetry reading
Peaceful coexistence of nations
Studying a foreign language
Wasting time
Economic good times

SAMPLE ANALYSES

Let's take three of the above ideas for speeches and work up sample analyses of each, demonstrating three different frameworks for persuasive speeches.

1. Reason Analysis (with "because" main heads)

Many of the subjects or topics above will yield theses that could be analyzed with *reasons* as main heads. For example, a speaker might formulate this thesis from the topic of mental illness, "Mental illness is an extremely serious problem in this country." Three possible main heads are:

I.   [because] It ruins the lives of the afflicted.
II. [because] It puts an unbearable burden on family members.
III. [because] It drastically curtails the nation's productivity.

Another speaker could argue the thesis that problems of mental illness are more serious than those of physical illness. What three or four main heads—reasons—could the speaker set up from that thesis?

2. Causes–Effects

With this structure, it's obvious what two main heads would come out of any thesis. What topic or subject on the list would you choose to analyze this way? If I were to choose "equal opportunity," the first thing I would do is narrow it, for example, to equal *employment* opportunity. Then I would face the task of shaping a thesis from that. This is a possibility: "I'd like to show you what lies behind the inequality in job opportunity that exists in America." In the first main head I would explore *causes*, why it exists, and in the second I would show *effects,* such as the results as seen in people's lives and social conditions. Incidentally, very likely the introduction of this speech would make some general reference to the problem. After that, the thesis would fall into place.

3. Problem–Solution

This is another structure calling for two main heads. The problem–solution pattern will serve in almost every instance in which a speaker wants to discuss a bad condition and offer a remedy. Assume that a speaker selects the subject "The police and the community." Again, narrowing will be a necessary first step, for example, to "overaggressive behavior of police officers." Let's say that the thesis is "Consider with me the question of aggressiveness in law enforcement by police officers." In the first main head, the speaker will lay out the problem of overaggression as he or she perceives it, perhaps with specific types of behavior as subheads, and of course with ample supporting materials: examples, statistics, and testimony. The second main head will present a solution. The subheads, very likely, would detail aspects of the solution and steps to take in implementing it.

MODEL SPEECH OUTLINES

Model Speech Outline 1 (The motivated sequence plan in sentence form)

Cultural Awareness

I. Attention
    A. The United States is a nation of various cultures.
        1. Some of these cultures are old and well-established. [examples]
        2. Others are new, coming with recent waves of immigration. [examples]
    B. Problems relating to cultural differences do exist.
        1. They occur across the country. [examples]
        2. They occur on this campus.
II. Need
    A. Campus insensitivity to cultural differences is apparent.
        1. It's seen as lack of knowledge. [examples]
        2. It's seen as indifference. [examples]
    B. Cultural conflict is a consequence.
        1. Members of minority cultures feel threatened.
        2. "Hard feelings" develop. [examples]
        3. Status struggles develop. [definition, examples]
    C. From conflict arise unsatisfactory conditions.
        1. The costs are high.
        2. They assume various forms.
            a. They may be interpersonal. [example]

        b.   Some are educational. [example]

        c.   Some are financial. [example]

    3.   They show up in the quality of campus life. [examples]

    4.   Recovery is a very slow process. [examples]

III.   Satisfaction

    A.   Possible solutions have been mentioned.

        1.   Publish informational articles on cultural diversity in the school newspaper.

        2.   Sponsor a film series on multicultural issues.

        3.   Require for graduation a course in cultural appreciation.

        4.   Form a student body commission to investigate conditions and mount a campaign of awareness on cultural diversity.

    B.   I propose adoption of this last solution.

        1.   Members of the Commission would be appointed by the student council.

        2.   In its campaign, the Commission could incorporate some of the other specific remedies.

IV.   Visualization

    A.   Now, we have the choice of continuing to deny the pain or take action.

        1.   We can let the sore fester and throb.

        2.   We can let the infection spread through the system.

    B.   Or we can create health.

        1.   We can know the joy of being healers.

        2.   We can live in a healthy campus environment again.

V.   Action

    A.   Our course of action seems clear.

        1.   Let's establish a planning committee before leaving today.

        2.   Then, we can start working on a proposal.

        3.   From there, we'll take all necessary steps to get action.

    B.   I urge you to lend a hand in this.

        1.   Solving problems is something we Americans know how to do well. [examples]

        2.   Let's all be leaders in improving campus life.

        3.   As President Kennedy once said, with a small change in wording, "Ask not what your campus can do for you, but what you can do for your campus." [quotation]

    C.   Give me a show of hands on your interest in this!

Model Speech Outline 2 (Indirect structure in sentence form)

Talking to a Professional

    A.   Teresa wasn't able to talk herself out of feeling as though she had to please everyone. [illustration]

B. William tried to use "good sense" in fighting his serious depression. [illustration]

C. Decisions to "get better" are often useless. [illustration]

Main Head I. Therefore, willpower alone doesn't work in handling a mental disturbance.

A. Well-meaning family members may worsen conditions. [hypothetical illustration]

B. Friends who try to help become frustrated. [illustration]

C. And as the Mexican *dicho* reminds us, "If you cannot do better yourself, how can you advise another?" [quotation]

Main Head II. The advice of others does little to help with serious emotional problems.

A. Some troubled people try do-it-yourself psychology magazines. [quotations]

B. Lots of advice is out there in books, pages upon pages of popular psychology. [illustration and statistics]

Main Head III. To those with real problems, articles and books often are not very useful.

Thesis

Since self-help is not enough, and the assistance of friends goes only so far, and books and magazines have limited value, the answer to emotional problems lies in professional therapy.

Conclusion

A. So, take the step.
   1. Consult a psychologist, psychiatrist, licensed social worker, or other qualified therapist. [definitions]
   2. Therapy does work. [illustration and instances]
   3. Fees may be reasonable. [statistics]

B. Get names of qualified therapists.
   1. Call the university or college counseling office.
   2. Or call Family Service.
   3. Or call the Health Department.
   4. Or call medical, psychological, or other mental health associations.

C. Now is the time to do it.

NOTES

1. For a more complete development of the view that all communication is persuasive in intent, in other words, that it is to achieve identification, see Phillip K. Tompkins, *Communication as Action: An Introduction to Rhetoric and Communication* (Belmont: Wadsworth, 1982), 43–45.

2. Abraham H. Maslow, *Motivation and Personality,* 2d ed. (New York: Harper and Row, 1970).

3. Ben Padrow, "Hubert H. Humphrey: The Glandular Zephyr," *Today's Speech,* XII (September 1964): 2–3.

4. Cecile M. Springer, "It's Time to Win with Women," *Vital Speeches of the Day,* L (July 15, 1984): 591.

5. Isabel Allende, "The Power of Art," *Representative American Speeches, 1989–1990,* ed. Owen Peterson (New York: H. W. Wilson, 1991), 71–82.

COMPLEMENTAL FOUNDATIONS

THINKING CRITICALLY

9

Here's a portion of a conversation that occurred on my campus recently.

She:	So, you think that the tenure system should be abolished?
He:	Yes, that's what I think. Absolutely! Why should all instructors be guaranteed a job for life? There's no tenure where my dad works.
She:	You think fairness is the issue, then?
He:	Yes, and competence. I had an instructor once who never showed up for office hours. Think of that!

Analysis of the Dialogue

What's going on in this dialogue? Note that both persons use the word "think" in every statement. That suggests that they're *thinking* together. At least, they *think* they are. But what *is* thinking? A dictionary defines thinking as an operation of the mind: conceiving something, forming judgments or opinions, holding views, making inferences, reflecting and imagining. The person who objected to the tenure system held an opinion or view; he reflected and judged. But did he do so critically? **To think critically is to apply tests to thinking processes, our own and others': to evaluate premises and ideas, conceptions, judgments, opinions, evidence, inferences, reflections and imaginings, and assorted data.**

Return to the dialogue above and check the opinions and judgments expressed. Are they sound and accurate? What tests would you apply? What weaknesses do you find?

SPEAKING AND LISTENING: THINKING TOGETHER

Here's another relevant case to consider. Let's say that on your way home from school one day you begin thinking about your job—*critically thinking* this time. Although you have accepted the fact that the salary is low, you now begin to think that it's really minimal! And it's not likely to improve, given company policy and general conditions. "Face it," you tell yourself, "commuting is too expensive, and it's time-consuming, too." So you do some heavy thinking with this evidence, all the while remembering important basic ideas; for example, you do need an adequate income, time for study, and time for social events and recreation. Ultimately, your critical thinking takes you to a conclusion that you decide to follow.

In Interaction

Later, when discussing the job with a friend or relative, you may hear yourself using the same line of reasoning with them, testing it and seeking their reaction. Alone or in communication with others, your thinking goes on during every waking moment, sometimes critically, sometimes not. Because communication is our constant focus, the exploration of critical thinking in this chapter will keep in mind the actions of two parties: both speaker and listener, you and the others. Indeed, communication depends on the quality of thinking by both; therefore, the two primary purposes of the chapter are (1) to help speakers use critical thinking to solve problems in preparing messages and in relating to audiences (listeners) and (2) to help audiences use critical thinking to listen better and respond effectively to speakers' messages.

With this double perspective, you can see that the emphasis here will be on speaker and listeners *thinking together,* with each asking the best of the other in communicative interaction. **Though often done silently, critical thinking usually has a *social* dimension, that is, it's carried on in reference to the thinking or actions of another.** To think critically is to ask questions, yes, and at times to present a challenge, but it's most productive when done with a *communicative spirit,* in cooperation with others, even when in disagreement with them.

Before taking up the specific ideas on thinking and functions of speakers and listeners as thinkers, we need to put down two foundation stones, those related to certainty versus probability and the nature of issues. Included in the latter topic will be a discussion of objectivity versus subjectivity and an explanation of false issues.

CERTAINTY VS. PROBABILITY

It isn't often that people, whether teachers, lawyers, students, business people, or politicians, are able to reason together about certainties. For example, the following are virtually unattainable: the *certainty* of solving the school dropout problem; the *positive fact* of jealousy as the cause of a certain murder; the *infallibility* of memorization as a method of study for an examination; the *absolute assurance* of a coming boom in business; the *inevitability* of a political party's defeat. Regardless of how confident we may appear, we usually find ourselves reasoning about possibilities and probabilities and likelihoods. For example, believing that rehearsing a speech adds to effectiveness in delivery, you advise a friend to practice his speech aloud a few times. Rehearsal is not certain to increase chances for success, but it *probably* will. **Though searching for the happiness that certainty provides, we rarely get it.**

What should listeners expect of speakers in regard to certainty in thinking or judging? In a class speech, a student explained that a certain plan for bilingual education would help elementary school children learn better and improve their use of English as well. What is sufficient proof in this instance? Should we expect complete assurance that all children under this plan will learn more and speak better? Should we expect full demonstration that every child will make significant progress? What should we expect of any proposed plan to meet any existing condition, whether in education, public health, highway safety, or any other area? In answer to that, it seems realistic to ask of most solutions that they offer *reasonable* promise of meeting the need. None will be perfect. None will be foolproof. None will satisfy the requirements of each and every involved person or apparent need. The best solution is the one that comes closest to meeting group or community needs. Ordinarily, a high degree of satisfaction is the best that we can expect when dealing with the recurring problems of life. **Probability provides the guideline for critical thinking, both in receiving and sending messages.**

ISSUES

Any discussion of critical thinking eventually comes to the topic of *issues.* Recall that I defined that word back in Chapter Four. **An issue is a point on which people differ.** Issues generate arguments for debate; **if there are no issues, there's no debate.** An issue may be broad like the stock issue of *need:* Is it necessary to impose a tariff to protect the American industry from foreign competition? Is there a real *need?* That's a big issue. To raise the level of student achievement, do we need a national high school examination for all graduating seniors? There are many other common issues, most of which are narrower than need, for example, money, time, competence, age, gender, political control, and so on. These sorts of issues apply to a great variety of problems.

Take the position that the federal government should give greater support to the arts. What are the issues, the points that are to be argued? Creativity is one (Will it be encouraged? Will it be stifled?). Money is one (Will a new tax be imposed? Will other programs be threatened?). Favoritism is another (Will federal involvement lead to politically friendly artists being favored?). Can you think of other distinct issues? When John Fitzgerald Kennedy ran for the United States presidency in 1960, his religion was made an issue: Should a Catholic be elected to the presidency? Can a Catholic president's first loyalty be to the country? Since then, most Americans, it seems, have come to discount religion as a dominant issue in national political campaigns. Or have they? If we have made progress

in our thinking about religion as a qualification of elected officials, have we done the same in regard to race, gender, and age? Do they remain as issues in the minds of the electorate? Yes, it seems that they do at times, notwithstanding American values to the contrary.

Though not always identified as such, *self-interest* is one of the most primary of issues. Take the case of whether to reorganize a company. Financial expense is an issue, as are timing, customer relations, and other factors. But the question asked by many in the company is "How will the plan affect me, my status, my salary?" When meetings are held on the topic, those who speak and those who listen may find personal issues coming into their thinking quite often.

THE SELF AS ISSUE: OBJECTIVITY VS. SUBJECTIVITY

The issue of self-interest brings up the question of objectivity vs. subjectivity. **To be objective is to tend toward viewing an event, act, idea, and so forth, apart from self-bias or needs of self.** Objectivity is learned behavior that allows us to remain detached from a given event or unprejudiced in perception of someone's action. And sometimes it's beneficial to be able to prevent self-interest from having full sway in making judgments.

All humans have a self which they invest in things and happenings. **To be subjective is to be unable to separate oneself or one's feelings from things and happenings.** For instance, it's natural for parents to have strong self-interest in their children's welfare and accomplishments. It's difficult for parents to be objective about their children.

What of your subjectivity? If you have a favorite athletic team or musical group, you make a certain investment of self in their activity. And in comparing yours with the favorite of someone else, you will reveal your personal interest, your subjectivity. Can you be objective in speaking or listening when the following subjects come up? Which ones bring out personal emotional reaction? Which do you find threatening in some way?

Gun control versus positions of the National Rifle Association

Abortion—"Right to life" versus "Pro-choice"

Welfare—dependence and needs of families

Health care—private systems versus a national system

American-made products and foreign-made

We all experience subjective pressures; we have our tastes and make our personal choices. But **it's the narcissistic extremes that we need to recognize, the bent toward viewing all phenomena as they affect the self.** A persistent narcissistic perspective precludes the use of a reliable gauge of measurement. It's an orientation based on the premise of self-meaning, beginning every time with a silent or stated phrase like *"For me, the truth is . . ."* or *"The way I see it is . . . ."*

Can personal concern be removed entirely from any expression of thought or any moment in listening? Probably not. Nor should it be, for in our communicating we need both forces. Feelings can be of real value, even in critical thinking. It's excessiveness that must concern us, when at the wrong moments "narcissistic mental operations conflict with objective reality, producing unreliable images and faulty judgments."[1]

False Issues

That brings us to the topic of false issues. Consider *time* as an issue. For example, have you ever named time as the issue in deciding on whether to go to a ball game or party, when the real issue was the extent of your interest in the event? You said, "I don't have *time* to go," but really it was your lack of interest that decided the matter. Often we make money an issue, when it isn't. "I'd go to Washington with you, if I had the money." Maybe! Other cases are more serious. For example, in this democracy, isn't a presidential candidate's religion a false issue? **Are not ethnic identity and gender false issues in deliberation on political, educational, and social questions?** When we see them as non-issues, not the real questions of debate, we can then turn to the genuine issues. For example, don't you agree that we should vote for a president on the basis of his or her knowledge of domestic and foreign affairs, leadership experience, philosophy of government, and positions on trade, national defense, environmental needs, human resources, and administrative expertise? Those are *real* issues! The candidate's college, marital status, or gender are not.

Two Selves: The Objective and the Subjective

In their speaking and listening, it can be said that people have two powerful selves: one that pulls them toward acceptance of the idea of probability as a guide to thinking, an awareness of the real issues in any given situation, and a mature balancing of objectivity and subjectivity. A second self pulls people toward involvement in the vain search for certainty, perfection, and absolute security. This second part, controlled by subjectivity, stresses extraneous and personal issues. In the following mental dialogue, a silent exchange that occurred inside one person's mind, we see the interaction of these two selves.

One:	Where should we invest the money that Aunt Mary left us?
Two:	That's easy. Let's put it in something that'll be sure to return 10 or 12 percent and has no chance of failing.
One:	But with that terrific interest rate, we've got to expect some risk. Before jumping in, don't you think we should get expert advice?
Two:	Naw, we don't need it; anyway, we've got to act now. There's no time to spend on visits to some so-called expert's office.
One:	Wait! Isn't it worth giving up a couple of hours? After all, we're talking about several thousand dollars.
Two:	Listen, you can't trust someone you don't know. Personally, off the top of my head, I've got a gut reaction on this one, man. I'll know a perfect investment for us when I see it. In my heart, I feel . . .

In this intrapersonal dialogue, I must admit to being on the side of the first self, and I hope that the more realistic and intelligent position shown by that side ultimately prevails. But I'm not sure it will in every conversation of theirs. Given pressures, conditions, temptations, predispositions, and lack of training—all forces at work against critical thinking—one can't be sure.

FORMS OF REASONING

To offset that absolutist and heavily subjective kind of thinking, the second self will need a lesson in reasoning, in formalities of thinking. Let's provide that now, stressing *cognitive* elements. Five of the most common forms of reasoning are generalization, causation, analogy, sign, and principle. Though the discussion here will consider each form separately, it should be noted that in actual practice we often let one form overlap another. For example, while reasoning about the *cause* of a couple's divorce we might use an *analogy* to see similarities between their case and another case.

Generalization

To generalize is to reach a conclusion through the examination of a sampling of closely related data. It's the process of noting something common in a collection of evidence and determining what it means, that is, coming to a conclusion. If you have to wait in a long check-out line every time that you shop at Bradshaw's Grocery, you may find yourself generalizing that Bradshaw's is not the place to shop when you're in a hurry. You have a lot of evidence to support your generalization. Here is another example:

Barnard Park is a clean, attractive place in which to relax and play.

Jesse Owens Park has a variety of playground equipment that children enjoy immensely.

Rivera Trails is a fine spot for hiking and picnicking.

Jefferson Park is big enough to accommodate all outdoor activities.

Conclusion: This city has a good park system.

Is this sound reasoning? To check the validity of the process of generalization you should ask yourself three questions:

1. Do I have a sufficient number of instances (enough evidence)? In the preceding example, have I included a fair number of parks? How would I determine a fair number in such a case?

2. Are my instances typical and representative? Are the parks that I include reasonably similar to, representative of, most of the others in the system?

3. If any contradictory instances exist, can they be explained? How do I account for exceptions to the rule? How can I explain the fact that one park in the city, Oak Grove, is dusty, treeless, and poorly equipped?

Causation

Causal reasoning, a pattern commonly used in communication, has three subtypes:

1. Reasoning from cause to effect, or *this will cause that.* Excessive cutting of timber on that plot of land (cause) will lead to soil erosion (effect).

2. Reasoning from effect to cause, or *this was caused by that.* Traffic on 19th Avenue was backed up for blocks (effect), a result of the accident at the Midway intersection (cause).

3. Reasoning from effect to effect, or *that caused that which caused this.* The government's anti-inflation measures (cause) produced increased unemployment (effect), which led to heavy withdrawals from personal savings accounts (effect of the effect).

To check the accuracy of a conclusion reached by causal reasoning, you should ask yourself the following questions:

1. Is there more than a chance relationship between cause and effect? Coincidences do occur, don't they. Poor wiring may have had nothing to do with starting the fire that occurred downtown yesterday.

2. Was the cause sufficient to produce the effect? Was it Senator Alcott's age alone that led to her defeat in the election?

3. Have I considered other possible contributing causes? **More often than not, the cause is multiple.** Was high speed the only cause of that car accident? What about those bad brakes? Or the driver's fatigue?

In 1896, William Jennings Bryan, one of America's greatest orators, was nominated for the presidency after giving his memorable "Cross of Gold" speech, in which he excited his audience by blaming bankers and "big-city" interests for the nation's economic depression. He drew upon causal reasoning, at times with great flourish, as you see in this excerpt. By the way, note also Bryan's dramatic use of contrast in this sampling of his causal reasoning:

> *You come to us and tell us that the great cities are in favor of the gold standard. We reply that the great cities rest upon our broad and fertile prairies. Burn down your cities and leave our farms, and your cities will spring up again as if by magic. But destroy our farms, and the grass will grow in the streets of every city in the country.*

Such was one famous speaker's attempt to make a point with cause-to-effect reasoning. Clearly, the majority of Bryan's audience was in agreement. Economist David Reed, a speaker of our day, illustrates quite common causal reasoning, as he warns an audience in the city of Phoenix that the United States' economy is becoming "electricity-intensive." Why? Because we're

> *moving away from basic industry. We're moving toward more technologically advanced products and processes. And building those products and using those processes, in general, requires a lot more electricity than the old ways of making steel or even building autos.[2]*

Analogy

To reason by analogy is to use similarities to make logical connection of the known to the unknown or to the undetermined. The reasoner attempts to make a point by *comparing* phenomena or events. When you observe on a certain weekday that the post office and banks are closed, and conclude therefore that the public schools will be closed as well, you reason by analogy. You draw the conclusion from some feature shared by the school and the other institutions. What is the similarity between schools and the post office? In attempting to reach their audiences on complex economic topics, some speakers like to compare national spending with household budgets. They will say, "A country is no different from a family. The money comes in and goes out. The country, too, has its bills to pay, and it, too, should not spend more than it earns . . . ." Of course, a nation is not a family, and the success of the analogy depends on the willingness of the audience to accept the comparison for what it's intended to show.

Because most things have inherent differences, because they cannot be compared precisely, **reasoning by analogy is risky** and not a reliable aid to critical thinking. Yet when dealing with closely related elements, analogy can be helpful, especially in clarification. You may want to review this topic, as covered in Chapter Seven.

Test the usefulness and validity of an analogy with these questions:

1. Are the compared elements sufficiently similar in all vital aspects? If it's too far-fetched to compare a family with a nation, perhaps the speaker can draw an analogy between the nation and another nation. That kind of comparison would provide a more literal connection.

2. Can dissimilarities be explained or dismissed? An audience may be reluctant to accept a comparison between an animal lending service and a public library. ("You don't have to feed a book," they note.) The speaker may have to add a word of explanation.

Professor David F. Linowes, at the Smithsonian Institution, used a number of analogies in his speech on computers. Here are two that added clarity to his thought.

> *It is always difficult to grasp and convey the significance of a technological trend which is progressing at an exponential rate and which shows no signs of letting up. An analogy with a more familiar technological development might help. If the internal combustion engine had developed as rapidly as the central processing unit of the modern computer since 1945, a Rolls Royce would now have 45,000-horse power, cost $4, and do 3 million miles to the gallon.*
>
> *In aviation, if jet travel technology had developed at the same rate as the computer has in the past 25 years, we would be traveling to Europe in seven minutes at a cost of two cents and the airplane would be the size of a shoe box.*
>
> *This same technology is giving computers the capacity to learn, thus enabling them to enlarge the human mind's horizons, or even to displace the mind in many tasks. Just as the machine had become the extension of a person's limbs and muscles, so is the computer becoming the extension of one's mind and memory.*[3]

Carlos P. Romulo

Sign

To reason by sign is to use indicators or symptoms, signs of something, to come to a conclusion. Something observed is taken as a sign of something else. A fever is a sign of infection. Geese flying south is a sign that it's time to get out snow tires. Recently the newspaper carried a story about the prospects of a weakening national economy, a conclusion that experts drew from signs. In this case the signs were what are called "leading economic indicators," such items as new building permits, stock prices, money supply, claims for unemployment, and new orders for consumer goods. Signs are the bases of much daily reasoning. Imagine the kinds of signs used by farmers in deciding when to bring the cows down from the summer pasture, by a physician diagnosing illness, by a teacher finding meaning in examination scores, by a baseball pitcher analyzing the foot movements of the runner at first base, or by a baby pondering its mother's scowl. The reading of signs is essential in critical thinking.

These are some questions to ask when checking on the strength of any reasoning from sign:

1. Are the indicators reliable? The fact that the coach sent the punter into the game is not a sure sign that the team will kick the ball.

2. Are enough indicators available? Unable to explain the low midterm examination scores, the teacher may need to give another test before reaching a judgment on the students' progress.

3. Are other signs in agreement? The baby who now hears his mother humming—the scowl is gone—may change his reasoning about Mom's state of mind.

Carlos P. Romulo, one of the finest statespersons and orators in Filipino history, spoke eloquently at the historically significant Asian-African Conference that was held in Bandung, Indonesia. In urging participating nations to adopt a democratic course, he used reasoning from sign to unite his audience.

We in this room are, for our brief moment, a part of this history. How do we see it? How do we understand it? To begin with, the very fact that we have come together here in this manner illustrates the great new fact that these issues of freedom, equality, and growth are no longer merely national problems but world problems. Indeed the United Nations was created as an attempt to grapple with this great new fact. In one sense this Conference suggests that for the peoples of Asia and Africa the United Nations has inadequately met the need for establishing common ground for peoples seeking peaceful change and development.

Later in the address, Romulo again reasoned from sign, this time concerning human behavior.

I think that over the generations the deepest source of our own confidence in ourselves had to come from the deeply rooted knowledge that the white man was wrong, that in proclaiming the superiority of his race, qua race, he stamped himself with his own weakness and confirmed all the rest of us in our dogged conviction that we could reassert ourselves as men.[4]

Principle

To reason from principle is to begin with a premise. By premise I mean an idea, a point of view or principle, perhaps a "truth" of some sort, applied as a standard by which to judge some specific act or case. All of us have a very large stock of general premises, our "learnings" from living. We accumulate premises over the years and employ them in reasoning and deciding. For example, assume that you have come to believe that children should be taught good table manners (premise). That premise will influence your reasoning as you meet situations in life. Holding that view, you may, therefore, not think well of the Turners, who allow little Teresa Turner to play with her food (case). It's a "matter of principle," you say. This form of reasoning, often called deduction, is used in declaring something right or wrong, fair or unfair, workable or unworkable, pretty or unpretty, successful or a failure, and so forth. Some people contribute to the United Fund; others do not, and their reasoning about whether to contribute is likely to depend on held premises. An individual's reasoning may follow from the principle of being or not being my brother's keeper or from a view on the meaning of self-reliance or social responsibility.

Syllogism. In formal logic, deductive reasoning is structured as a *syllogism.* Note the following types of syllogisms and accompanying examples, each containing a *major premise* (as it's called in logic), a specific case (called *minor premise*), and a *conclusion.*

1. Categorical Syllogism
   Major Premise: All automobiles are subject to mechanical failure.
   Minor Premise: The Rolls Royce is an automobile.
   Conclusion: Therefore, the Rolls Royce is subject to mechanical failure.

2. Hypothetical Syllogism
   Major Premise: If Judy is ill, we must find a temporary replacement for her.
   Minor Premise: Judy is ill.
   Conclusion: Therefore, we must find a temporary replacement for her.

3. Disjunctive Syllogism
   Major Premise: That man in uniform is either a police officer or a firefighter.
   Minor Premise: That man in uniform is not a firefighter.
   Conclusion: That man in uniform is a police officer.

Only rarely are formal three-part syllogisms used in speaking; however, they can serve as skeletal plans to be expanded in developing ideas. They can serve, also, as tests to check on critical thinking.

Verifying the soundness of a syllogism depends on the type of syllogism, and I won't discuss the technical details here. Nonetheless, three questions apply to all methods of reasoning from principle.

1. Is the basic premise sound? In a speech, it's a main idea or assertion; in a syllogism, it's the major premise.

2. Is the specific case relevant to the major premise? In a syllogism, the specific case is the minor premise.

3. From the premises offered, does the conclusion logically follow?

Enthymeme. Much more common in speaking is **the *enthymeme*** (pronounced EN-thuh-meem). This is **a kind of syllogism that typifies our usual thinking and characterizes almost all our daily deliberations.** Aristotle called the enthymeme a *rhetorical* syllogism, a practical form of deductive reasoning used in speaking. **The enthymeme has two marks that distinguish it from the syllogism: (1) it deals in probabilities, and (2) usually it's stated with fewer than three premises.**

Whereas the syllogism is used to reason about certainties, or absolutes, the enthymeme is used to reason about probabilities. Let's take a practical example, overheard at a meeting of the Art Club. Because it's likely that the weather will be fair on June 6, a member of the club suggests that the club hold its annual art sale outdoors. But the members can't be *sure* of

fair weather, can they? You'll notice that the reasoning to hold the art show outdoors is based on a probability, and that it leaves out a step in the chain of reasoning. That is, it doesn't deal with a certainty, nor does it show all three parts. The enthymeme can be formally construed this way:

Major Premise [assumed but not stated]: An art show should be held outdoors only in fair weather.

Minor Premise: On the date of our show, June 6, the weather will be fair.

Conclusion: We should plan to hold the art show outdoors on June 6.

In this instance, the premise assumed and supplied by the listeners is the major premise. It wasn't necessary for the speaker to state it because the listeners held that view already. In other words, why use full syllogistic form and risk boring or appearing to condescend to the listener? The speaker's success may depend on saying enough to allow for the listeners' participation in the line of thought, but not too much.

Thus, people in their speaking rarely talk in absolute terms or use fully constructed syllogisms. Instead, they unfold their thinking with enthymemes, patterns of thought based on probabilities and designed for an audience's acceptance. Besides having to do with probability, an enthymeme is usually "open" at some point; that is, it's incomplete, as I have mentioned. There's a gap in the reasoning. **If speaker and listener are thinking together, the speaker doesn't have to delineate every step because the participating listener will fill in the gaps.**

Consider this example. A book salesperson talking to a group of history teachers probably should not say, as in full syllogistic form, "All history teachers want to use the best books; you are history teachers; you want to use the best books." That would seem foolish. But the salesperson might reason informally with this type of enthymeme: "As history teachers, you want to use the best books, right?" The audience realizes and accepts, perhaps subconsciously, the omitted step.

Analyze the following enthymeme from the famous "Call to Arms" speech of Patrick Henry, the American patriot. He presented it to his fellow Virginians in 1775, as the British were threatening the colonies. Did Henry include all three steps as he reasoned to a conclusion? No, he didn't. What idea or premise was the audience expected to bring to the argument? Was Henry's thinking compatible to his listeners, do you imagine? **Listeners' identification with a speaker depends on their having a chance to help complete the reasoning.**

> *If we wish to be free, if we mean to preserve inviolate these inestimable privileges for which we have been so long contending, if we mean not basely to abandon the noble struggle in which we have been so long engaged, and which we have pledged ourselves never to abandon until the glorious object of our contest shall be obtained, we must fight!*

Thus, Henry involved his audience, successful in securing the response he sought.

A woman, in a classroom speech, presented the following brief argument, worded as an enthymeme. What premise is omitted? Why did she omit it? Laid out with three syllogistic premises, what is the full statement of her thinking as you might have perceived it as a listener? Do you imagine that most people in the audience shared her perception?

> *In the past, whenever there's been a strike of bus drivers, it's been impossible to find a parking space on campus after 9 in the morning. Well, you've heard the news; the drivers are going on strike at six tonight.*

Do you imagine that they responded favorably to her reasoning? Yes, they did—enthusiastically.

ANOTHER PERSPECTIVE IN REASONING

A different system for understanding reasoning was developed by Stephen Toulmin, an English logician. His system may be useful for preparing reasoned arguments to use in your own speeches, in improving listening, and for studying the communication of others. It enables one to examine more microscopically and operationally the elements in a line of reasoning and to identify strengths and weaknesses. To see how the system works, let's analyze an excerpt from a student's speech to his class:

> *We read a lot these days about the great number of children abused by their parents. Unfortunately, this means that among the next*

generation of children there quite likely will be even more abused children, since children who have been abused themselves become abusers. Many studies show that.

Using the Toulmin method and its terms—*grounds* (observation, general information, or other such data), *claim* (conclusion), and *warrant* (a premise allowing the connection of *grounds* and *claim*)—we might structure the reasoning with this diagram.

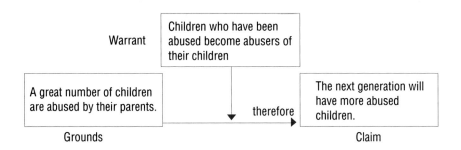

The main thrust of the reasoning is that the current high incidence of child abuse foretells an even greater incidence in the next generation. Such are the *grounds* and the *claim,* but note the *warrant,* the pivotal point that permits the *claim* to be drawn. The *warrant* allows the conclusion.

Now look more closely at the wording in the original paragraph and observe two more elements, the *backing* and a *qualifier.* The backing of "many studies" (evidence) supports and strengthens the *warrant.* The *qualifier,* the phrase "quite likely," realistically restricts the *claim* to a degree of probability: Who can say anything for certain about human behavior in the future? Here, then, is a more complete diagram of the reasoning. Start with *grounds* and go through the *warrant* and its *backing* to the qualified *claim.*

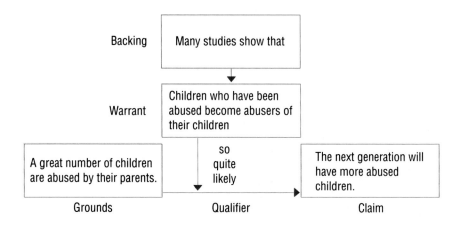

A *reservation* or *rebuttal* could be added if the speaker had included exceptions for specific limitations to the *claim*. For instance, the speaker might have modified the *claim,* saying, "Yes, the next generation quite likely will have even more abused children, *unless* society can find ways to intervene with better education or therapy to alter patterns of behavior." On the diagram, a *reservation* to a conclusion is placed below the *claim*.

Reservation | Unless we have intervention of effective education or therapy.

Another student in the speech class developed this line of reasoning on world population.

> *Experts testify that the problem of population in the world is reaching dangerous proportions, as technology has so reduced death rates that we face a tripling of the population in the next 50 years. Many countries, with too many mouths to feed and facing misery and hunger among their peoples, are helpless in meeting the problem. Numerous countries in Africa, with millions of destitute people, are examples. Since individual nations are not solving the problem, the United Nations is probably the only agency with sufficient strength to be effective in meeting the crisis. Yet we must recognize that in dealing with peoples of varying beliefs and customs, an outside agency like the U.N. may find its efforts resisted or thwarted.*

How would you begin to examine or analyze this reasoning? Try using the Toulmin model. Your completed diagram may provide increased understanding of the developed thought. For instance, you'll be able to observe the position of the *warrant*—the premise that individual nations are not solving the problem. Although diagramming elements in reasoning is sometimes hard work, it may help you as listener to perceive others' reasoning patterns and strengthen your own reasoning capability.

Incidentally, another perspective on reasoning is found in this book. John Dewey's pattern of reflective thinking offers useful processes for sharpening critical thinking. You'll find it laid out in Chapter Thirteen, as it applies to structuring small group discussion.

OBSTACLES TO CRITICAL THINKING

Errors in thinking can be classified into two general types: those with *cognitive* bases and those with *affective* or emotional bases. The first type relates to inadequate use of mental resources and powers of reasoning. Critical thinkers have advantageous cognitive power available to them, but application is another matter. That's where the challenge lies. The second kind of obstacle relates to psychological interference, particularly the intrusion of needs of self: unfavorable narcissistic influence that may affect any of us.

Cognitive Bases

1.   Lack of information. If speaking on the failure of rehabilitation systems in federal prisons, how much should one know about existing programs? The answer is that one should have enough information to provide material for credible arguments and to allow for the confidence that comes from having a solid understanding of the topic. Speakers who make claims and offer premises—all of us do—and want listeners to listen and think along with them, need data, such as good ideas and evidence to support them. Of course, the most fundamental advice is "speak on a subject on which you have some knowledge." That's the best first step toward sound thinking.

As critical thinkers, listeners expect speakers to be sufficiently knowledgeable in their chosen subjects. Information is basic to establishment of credibility, a precious asset, and to the building of all messages.

2.   Ambiguity. As with insufficient data, **one's purpose has a limited chance of receiving a hearing if ideas are not made clear.** The likelihood of clarity is greater if the immediate aim is clear, if the speech is well-structured, and if premises are reinforced with carefully chosen primary processes. Further, speakers should attempt to make their thoughts cohesive, logically related and connected in a meaningful pattern. At this point, you might want to review Chapter Five on use of primary processes.

Note below an ambiguous excerpt from a speech. As a listener and critical thinker, how would you rate it? What main fault(s) do you observe? What suggestions for correction would you make?

> *Why are the white fir trees in the Sierra Nevada dying in such great numbers? If you travel to those mountains, you can't help noticing that many conifers have been blighted. I believe that something should be done about the bark beetle. Twenty-five percent of all trees are gone now. Why must this continue? Also, they put salt on the roads in the winter months.*

3.   Faulty generalizing. In the process of concluding from a body of collected data, speakers do make errors occasionally. One problem lies in taking into account too few instances. That mistake leads to *hasty generalizations:* "Last night on Main Street I saw a driver go through a red light, another one going 70 down Front Street, and yet another illegally parked across from the southend bus station. This city is full of bad drivers." Drawn from a small sample, the conclusion is erroneous, as listeners who think critically will observe.

Another kind of flaw in generalization will result if the communicator includes a *nonrepresentative instance,* one that does not fit with other instances. For example, in talking about efficiency in large organizations, one probably should place government organizations and private organizations in separate categories. Very likely it would be fallacious to put the U.S. Department of Agriculture with a group of business organizations and generalize about the whole. The two represent vastly differing systems and have contrasting purposes and characteristics. They don't belong together, and conclusions drawn from associating them would be unsound.

4.   Faulty thinking on causation. One error in making causal connections arises from *projecting with insufficient data,* when trying to show that something is likely to cause something else. We may speculate, for example, that Paul's irregular study habits will result in bad grades. But other factors, unobserved by us, may be working in Paul's favor—high motivation or use of special aids, for instance. He may have ways to compensate for poor habits.

Another kind of fallacy in causation occurs if a communicator overlooks *contributing causes.* In thinking about what caused something, we should always be aware of the likelihood of *multiple* causation and ask, "Could any additional causes be at work here?" Often the answer is yes. A boating accident may have been caused by a wind storm, in part, but what about the boat's bad condition and the inexperienced sailor? What caused the company's bankruptcy? Very likely it was more than any single factor. It was not the national economic condition alone. What about management efficiency, labor costs, the timing of new ventures, and the obsolete accounting system?

Can you think of a happening or event that people mistakenly believe had only one cause?

5.   False analogy. When things are compared, especially unlike things, *false analogy* may result. Is it sound reasoning to view the human body as a machine? Some people have called this a false analogy, believing that not all bodily processes are explainable in mechanical terms. And just because New York and Seattle are cities with important harbors does not mean that labor relations on their docks are similar. Respective conditions in the two cities may not be sufficiently analogous to make that line of reasoning convincing. The same error can be made in discussing human behavior, without taking cultural variables into account. From one group to another, cultural beliefs and habits may be dissimilar, or not comparable. Among most Asian-Pacific people, for example, elders are respected unconditionally. Not so in the larger American culture. Audiences often notice the false analogies that speakers themselves miss in their own speeches.

6.   Faulty sign reasoning. Diplomats and politicians who look for meaningful signs in the behavior of their counterparts in other countries occasionally *misread the signs* or *fail to notice significant signs.* A foreign country's decision to withdraw troops from certain occupied territory is not necessarily a sign that leaders of that country have changed their policy on expansion. Thus, speakers and listeners should ask more questions, think more critically.

The baseball announcer who declares that a hitter's stance is a sure indication of his intention to "pull" the ball may be guilty of a fallacy in interpreting signs, particularly if the hitter is skilled in giving false signs and fooling the opposition.

Cultural variables offer many examples of error in interpretation of signs. When she smiled at him, he should have thought about possible cultural differences between them, before responding in his usual way. Take another case. People of Asian-Pacific backgrounds tend to value silence more than those of the general American culture. Thus, a person of the general culture may interpret erroneously a period of silence from an Asian: "Have I said something wrong to Mr. Matsumoto?" or "What's Chan's problem, anyway?" It's just that most Americans typically feel a greater need to "keep up the talk."

7.   Dubious premise. Oftentimes, **problems in thinking arise when conclusions are based on unsound premises or false principles.** If one starts from a false premise, the resulting conclusion or judgment will be false. This is an error of deduction, of the type seen in enthymemes that are built from a questionable major premise. Consider the case of the physician who was denied use of a certain hospital because she openly favored a national program of health benefits for the poor. The hospital administration contended that this philosophy amounted to "welfare medicine" and consequently was "un-American." A review board, finding that contention to be fallacious, concluded that it's not un-American to advocate health benefits for all poor people.

The *either-or* fallacy involves reasoning from a false premise. For example, it may be fallacious to say, "Either we levy a sales tax or endure our present financial crisis." Perhaps other alternatives are possible and ought to be examined.

To *beg the question* is to begin a line of reasoning with a dubious assumption, one that makes false all that follows: "Now we all know that war is inevitable, don't we! So let's take it from there and get this thing over with." Aristotle had the answer to this fallacy: If one thing is possible, so is its opposite. If war is possible, so is peace.

Another type of faulty deduction is the *allness* fallacy. Whenever a communicator holds fast to the use of terms like *every, all, never,* or *without exception,* it's time to think critically. What is your response to each of the following assertions?

All alcoholics have problems in relationships.

It's never proper to kiss in public.

In life, when one guy wins, some other guy loses, somewhere, somehow.

Face it, every individual has his or her price.

Stereotypes are a particularly pernicious kind of allness error, even when only suggested, as in these statements:

"Talk to a corporation executive, and you can bet that you'll be talking to a Republican."

"Of course, you know that Hispanics are Catholic."

"Hey, I read the sports pages all the time, enough to know that Brazilian soccer fans can't control their emotions at the stadium."

"Conduct a law practice honestly? Get outta here!"

"If he's a member of the National Rifle Association, you can rest assured he's got no compassion for kids killed by guns."

This is **a good rule of thumb for critical thinkers: locate the key premise; if it doesn't hold up, none of the rest will.** Remember also to check for lack of information, ambiguity, errors in generalizing, errors in causation, false analogy, and errors in sign reasoning.

Emotional Bases

The second major type of weakness of communicators in concluding, judging, interpreting, and so forth, is emotional. Let's look into this.

1. Self-preoccupation. Intruding self-concern is a serious source of failure in efforts to think critically. When one is unsure of oneself, personal attention goes to protection of self. For example, when in a situation where one feels vulnerable, fear often rules out use of mental resources. Such situations are not uncommon in this life. The very act of standing to speak before an audience is a relevant instance. To be able "to think on one's feet," as it's sometimes put, requires considerable security. Insecurity is the arch enemy of clear thinking. Psychologist Abraham Maslow probably would agree, for if a speaker is preoccupied with the dangers of self-exposure and audience judgment, he or she may experience significant reduction in "higher-level" powers, such as, thinking critically.[5]

Other prominent examples of threatening situations, those challenging competence in thinking, are the job interview, the call to the boss's office, or any occasion involving talking to an authority figure or individual in the position of judging one's personal performance. There are innumerable less obvious occurrences, some of them as common as having to return unacceptable merchandise to a store, responding to a high-pressure telephone solicitation, and talking to a professor about a disappointing test score.

She's alone now, but when speaking to others, she must give them priority.

Self-preoccupation works against good thinking in another sense. In communication, *thinking together* is essential. Communication requires a giving of self, one's thinking self and one's feeling self. Such generosity involves running the risk of disclosing one's feelings, ideas, *and* thought processes. Only in a climate of reciprocity, of give-and-take and trust, can distance between listener and speaker be reduced and premises of the mind shared.

2. Insensitivity to Others. Self-preoccupation often leads to insensitivity to others and their states of being. Only through caring about and being responsive to others' thoughts and feelings can ideas be shared.

We've already talked about behaviors like stereotypes, which are expressions of insensitivity. Often they are traceable to early experiences in learning, but they can arise also from personal insecurity.

Related insensitive behaviors are those that include the condition called "centrism," or the feeling that one's own group or point of view is superior to all others, for example, one's ethnicity ("ethnocentrism"), religion, politics, language, socio-economic status, and so forth.

Insensitivity to variations in human behavior, such as those related to a person's race, sex, age, and culture, is another condition that negatively affects thinking and communicating. Though this deficiency at times may be attributed to lack of knowledge, fear is not to be excluded as a basis for it.

3. Narcissistic Perception. In taking up disturbances in perception, I'll focus on problems in thinking and perceiving that bear on such major acts as selecting material for use in communication, grasping meaning of ideas, and being aware of others' needs. The treatment here relates principally to psychological obstacles to effectiveness in communication. It's an "I" orientation that distorts the view. **The distortion occurs when a person's outlook is so heavily influenced by personal need or concern about self that he or she can't see the real issues, or when a dominating preoccupation with personal status rules out simple respect for the other.** It may be expressed as a right, an entitlement, as when the "I-deserve-special-treatment" premise is obvious. It may be seen as rigidity or reflective of the uniqueness premise: "I am one-of-kind, and everybody should be impressed." In a word, the problem, the threat to critical thinking, is *individualism.* Now, individualism differs from individuality, and one's individuality is not at issue. Each of us is different, and advantageously so. No, individualism, as attitude and basis of prejudice, is a kind of extremism, an exaltation of the self that precludes reciprocity and fairness in interaction with others. It diverts the mind from effective choices in discovery of promising material and productive perception in communicating. It sabotages the process of thinking together. No matter how learned a person may be or how well-schooled in the rules of formal logic, if he or she is constrained to perceive the personal self as privileged and apart from others, thus disposed to resist a meeting of minds, thinking and communicating will suffer. Losses can be great.

4. Mental Dampening. This category of emotional forces working against critical thinking is suggested by words like indifference, apathy, ennui, and lassitude. All refer to mental unassertiveness, a holding back or dampening of mental powers. The result is a waste of vital resources. With some, peer pressures may be at the root of under-utilized capacity. With others, the problem seems to stem from lack of purpose.

> Why do some persons let others do their thinking?
>
> Why are some unable to decide what's best for them?
>
> Why are some people easy targets of high-pressure pitches?
>
> Why do some say "So what!" when the government announces plans to change the income tax system or the farm policy?

The attitude or emotional predisposition running through these hypothetical questions is passivity or listlessness, the opposite of mental engagement—of making contact and putting forward one's critically thinking self. Though I have known quite a number who would deny it about themselves, my experience tells me that very few college students are limited by inadequacy in their "thinking equipment." But the *failure to use it* can be another matter, and it's a psychological question, frequently. Self-esteem is often the real issue. Those who know and accept

> *No member of a crew is praised for the individuality of his rowing.*
>
> *Ralph Waldo Emerson, essayist*

their abilities are able to make use of them; those who do not, cannot. **Said another way, people who do not identify themselves as potentially good thinkers, fulfill that evaluation. Believing that they "are not," they "cannot."** That's what we call a self-fulfilling prophecy: *They will believe themselves into being dependent rather than assertive.* "Know thyself," advised Socrates. As a promoter of critical thinking, he knew that self-knowledge is basic to the process.

5. Defensiveness in Thinking. In a discussion of emotional explanations of weakness in thinking, all elements, self-preoccupation, insensitivity to others, narcissistic perception, and mental dampening, can be put together as defensiveness in thinking. Basically, these patterns are self-protective; they are kinds of strategies designed to avoid injury to self or to conceal felt self-deficiency.[6] **When unsure of ourselves, we are not at our thinking best. Insecurity leads to the inability to put promising personal resources to work. Thus defensiveness backfires.** Usually, it's self-defeating strategy.

STRENGTHENING CRITICAL THINKING IN COMMUNICATION

Given the cognitive and emotional bases of critical thinking and the kinds of errors into which we humans can fall, how can you strengthen your speaking and listening?

Awareness and Assessment

To begin the program, make an assessment. In this, you might make use of the two parts of yourself that we introduced earlier. Remember the dialogue involving those two? One part is characterized by maturity, sensibility, and good judgment. Your second side is something of an absolutist, is excessively subjective, and is rather undiscerning on issues. As I see it, the first one is your personal and internal *good audience.* You may recall from discussion elsewhere in the book that a prime role of the good audience is as critical thinker. As such, the good audience is a confident, self-respecting, and mature communicator. Whether in responding to messages and practices of others or to those of *oneself,* **the good audience** is an active, trustworthy participant, one who **appreciates sound reasoning, does not accept fallacy, and, while aware of diversity among participants in communication, remains a seeker of unity.** A big "secret" to success in communication lies in enlisting the powerful services of *your* good audience. Keep that in mind—hold to that as a goal—as you go over the following questions about you. In making your assessment, you may have occasional need to refer to prior sections of the chapter.

Primarily Cognitive Questions

1. Do I identify myself as a critical thinker? As potentially one?

2. What are my strengths in reasoning?

3. Where is improvement needed? In generalizing? In use of analogy? Or sign? In spotting dubious premises?

4. Am I able to apply the tests of reasoning to each form of reasoning?

5. Do I have a good grasp of the workings of the enthymeme, as opposed to the formal syllogism?

6. Can I make use of the Toulmin system for diagramming thinking patterns?

7. What are my thoughts on the matter of certainty vs. probability? Though questing for "the best," for perfection in thinking and for indisputable premises, am I able to accept the realities of life in this world, in which infallibility and inevitability are very rarely known?

8. Do I know an issue when I see or hear one?

9. Can I identify a false issue? In my deliberations, can I sense when I have made self-interest the prime issue?

10. Do I appreciate the need of objectivity in thinking? When is objectivity called for in communication? Am I able to be reasonably objective, when that attitude of mind is needed?

Primarily Emotional Questions

1. To what extent does self-preoccupation intrude upon my thinking when I speak and listen?

2. To what extent, if any, does insensitivity, for example, to the cultural backgrounds of my listeners, intrude upon my thinking when I speak and listen?

3. To what extent, if any, does narcissistic perception intrude upon my thinking when I speak and listen?

4. To what extent, if any, does mental dampening intrude upon my thinking when I speak and listen?

5. To what extent, if any, does defensiveness intrude upon my thinking when I speak and listen?

Finally

1. What is a recent instance of my "letting down" in critical thinking? In the future, can I sometimes prevent such a result?

2. In what circumstances am I tempted to give up on critical thinking?

3. What can I do *right now* to be more successful in thinking critically?

Application

A personal assessment of strengths and weaknesses in critical thinking will help you to improve this vital faculty. Additionally, it's suggested that you make a compact with yourself to apply critical-thinking principles as you enter into every assignment and activity in this class. **Check yourself as you put together a speech or take part in class discussions. If you begin to suspect that a piece of your reasoning is faulty, apply proper tests to determine its soundness.**

Then take this same useful checking discipline to your other classes, when preparing papers and reports of any kind. Eventually, you may discover that you've adopted an *attitude of monitoring your thinking.* What a happy achievement! With that accomplishment, you're on your way to better communication.

LOOKING BACK

The conclusions of critical thinkers are based on a high degree of probability. Critical thinkers are able to distinguish between real and false issues. They strive for objectivity. They understand the various forms and systems of reasoning. Bent on self-improvement, they work to avoid errors in thinking, both the cognitively based and the emotional.

Critical thinkers have an edge in communication.

NOTES

1. Harold Barrett, *Rhetoric and Civility: Human Development, Narcissism, and the Good Audience* (Albany: State University of New York Press, 1991), 50.

2. David Reed, "Electricity Supply Shortage," *Vital Speeches of the Day,* LVII (April 5, 1991): 399–400.

3. "Computers and the Learning Environment," *Vital Speeches of the Day,* L (May 1, 1984): 439.

4. In Lionel Crocker, *Rhetorical Analysis of Speeches* (Boston: Allyn and Bacon, 1967), 146–54.

5. Abraham Maslow, *Motivation and Personality,* 2d ed. (New York: Harper and Row, 1970).

6. Harold Barrett, *Rhetoric and Civility: Human Development, Narcissism, and the Good Audience* (New York: State University of New York Press, 1991), Chapter 3.

LISTENING

10

★ LOOKING AHEAD ★

1. What are the differences between the roles of hearer and listener?
2. What are the goals of listening?
3. When does listening malfunction?
4. How can listening be improved?
5. What's the role of the "good audience?"

A ROLE CHOICE: TO BE OR NOT TO BE

Writings regarding communication tell us that people spend a very high percentage of their daily lives in oral communication—as much as 75 percent.[1] That would seem to mean that we're listening most of the time, but that's not true. It *is* true that people act as *hearers* a lot, **but much less often as real *listeners*.** Though reasons vary, hearing is decidedly more prevalent than listening. It's one of our role choices, to be a listener or a hearer.

TO BE A LISTENER

Hearing is a physiological function; to hear is to act as a receiver of sound waves that have been generated by the vocal apparatus of another person or other source. Any animal can hear. But listening, when it occurs, is something quite special. True listening is not an every-moment event. **To listen is not only to *hear the symbols*, but also to *find meaning, to interpret and comprehend*, and to *respond accordingly*.** Moreover, retaining can be part of the process.

Further, listening is more than hearing and dealing with *words*. It's also comprehending *nonverbal* acts and symbols of the message senders: body language, vocal symbols, and other relevant symbolic phenomena. Besides the standard symbols of a language, a listener perceives nonverbal behavior, such as clicks of the tongue or whistling, eye movements, movements of the body, posture, the speaker's clothing and other adornment, facial expressions, visual aids, and vocal characteristics such as pitch level. These are just some of the general forms of nonverbal cues of message content. See Chapter Twelve for a more complete discussion of this topic.

Perhaps that wise man was not being facetious when he advised, **"When people are speaking to you, listen to what they say with their eyes."** As people listen, their perceptions are affected by the bodily movement and vocal behavior they observe. Again, in face-to-face communication people rarely present all the thoughts of a message in words. They use bodily action and vocal nuances to complete the structure of an idea. Imagine, if you can, the incompleteness of this thought, expressed in words alone: "I just saw a huge St. Bernard dog run across the freeway," Patti said. Her words carry a message, but a rather bland one. Next, add the following perception to your image: Patti's voice is extremely high-pitched, and its rate is rapid. When uttering the word *huge,* Patti raises and

balloons her arms, while her eyes bulge and her mouth twists. She gives heavy stress to the final word, *freeway.* Now what's the message? Obviously she's greatly impressed by the inordinate size of the animal and is probably fearful for its safety. The full thought could not be communicated with words only. Understanding Patti's full message involves *seeing* and *comprehending what is seen.* **To listen is to perceive and grasp *all* relevant stimuli constituting a message.**

Engaging Cooperatively

Thus, to understand the act of listening is to take it as a mental process involving both verbal and nonverbal modes of communication. Actually, there are two mental processes to be understood. Listening is part of a two-way act between the one who originates the message and the one for whom it is intended. To have real communication, speaker and listener must work in concert; that is, as has been stressed in this book, the participants in the exchange must mentally *engage* one another in shaping the message. Together and cooperatively they build thought and meaning. If the listener invests nothing, there is limited interaction and therefore limited effectiveness. As in many other events of life, active involvement is necessary for success.

Oral messages are elliptical. They are only partially developed, with some parts omitted. Therefore, listeners must cooperate by filling in the gaps with their understanding and experience. For example, if a speaker says without explanation, "Darwin's *Origin of Species* changed the course of thinking in the biological sciences," the responsive listener immediately "helps" the speaker by bringing to bear his or her personal knowledge of evolution and specific topics such as natural selection and the struggle for survival. If aware of the speaker's purpose, the listener can supply the necessary data for adequate completion of thought and creation of understanding. Thus, the speaker's aim of evoking appropriate responses from the listener is achieved. To be sure, the speaker has a part to play in the accomplishment of listening. ***Communication is working together. There's no other way.***

An Art, A Discipline

Another important dimension is courtesy, being civil with others. For whatever motivation, listeners have a major responsibility in a communicative exchange, one relating to cooperation and respect. You see, speakers and listeners enter into a kind of unwritten "contract": **"You do your part and I'll do mine."** Of course the contract can be broken; a member of the audience can get up and leave, for example. Thus, to be a listener is to make an appropriate decision on how to be with others and what to do. **Achievement in the art of listening comes by way of maturity, training, and commitment.** It's a hard-won discipline, but one that's well worth the effort that it takes to master it.

Rewards

Among the benefits of speaker-listener cooperation, besides the obvious, is effectiveness in deciding on the value of the message. How can you distinguish between useful and useless ideas other than by careful listening? How otherwise can you intelligently decide between the proposals of Speaker X and Speaker Y? How can you begin to understand what someone is really trying to say? How can you tell which one to believe when two experts disagree?

Rewards can be great in improving the general quality of life. **Effective listening helps us get along well with others, have satisfying relationships, and learn.** Good listeners are popular people; good listeners do better in school than those who are not. Getting the most out of our leisure hours requires adequate listening habits. Receiving maximum benefits from watching television, plays, and movies becomes important because we spend so much time with these media. Then, too, raising a family, taking part in community events, and being successful in almost every interpersonal activity demand good listening.

The proven economic importance of listening is seen in the attention given to it by American business. The Sperry Corporation, for example, spends many thousands of dollars on television and magazine messages promoting good listening. They also prepare instructional materials and conduct listening classes for their employees. They recognize the connection between good listening and good business. They believe that knowing how to listen can double business efficiency.[2] The Sperry Corporation has found that listening adds to profits, for as they acknowledge in their advertisements, "It pays to listen." And in the words of a former president of the United States, "Nobody ever listened himself out of a job." **Financial gain and listening skillfully are linked.**

GOALS OF LISTENING

Yes, oral communication is a joint enterprise. And because, as speakers and listeners, we act together reciprocally—whether in a public speaking situation, in a group discussion, or in ordinary conversation—it's logical to assume that listeners' purposes are determined by those of speakers. In an important sense that's true. For the moment, we'll look at the relationship that way. The speaker initiates the interaction, and the responsive and cooperating listener adjusts accordingly. Though we as speakers and listeners have multiple and overlapping general goals, let's single out three main ones.

Listening Primarily for Enjoyment

Most people take delight in listening to jokes, stories, comedians' speeches, selected television programs, poetry readings, or dramatic programs. We listen to be entertained. The usual attitude we assume in such a situation might be called one of attentive appreciation. Our listening behavior is guided by our tastes, by what we as individuals like and enjoy.

Listening Primarily for Understanding

To comprehend—to grasp an idea, to know—is a basic and essential listening goal. But to understand is not to accept a message, not necessarily. First, it's to perceive meaning. We listen to understand sermons, class speeches and lectures, newscasts, and debates, discussions, and conversations. **Listening is basic to satisfactory participation in the democratic process**. It's a function of our heritage and our way of life as members of society. We may want to remember someone's ideas, either to use or refute, but first we must understand them.

Listening Primarily for Evaluation

Next consider evaluative listening and its uses. Note the saturation of our lives with messages designed to alter our behavior. Everybody wants to influence us: "Spend the weekend with me," suggests a friend. "Read this new novel," someone recommends, or "Don't take Professor Albert's class." From the broadcast and print media come other types of messages: "Buy this," "Vote for me," "Join us now." Whenever someone involves me in any sort of "Do-this" or "Stop-that" message, I try to listen hard, for I know that someone intends to affect my life and being. In a way, I'm on the spot, and I'll have to evaluate the message and make a choice on how to react. Since this takes us into the area of persuasion, you may want to refer to Chapter Eight, "Understanding Uses of Persuasion," and relate that theory to the function of listening.

WHEN LISTENING MALFUNCTIONS

If the restaurant waiter brings the wrong dish to your table, the error may be traceable to faulty listening. And so it may be when a student turns in the wrong assignment or when one listener shows up at 11:00 to attend a meeting that was announced for 10:00. In life, we note these mishaps daily.

Many studies have been made in recent years to find out how well people listen. The results indicate that there's much room for the improvement of listening skills. **People do not listen as well as they should, or as well as they think they do.** Tests show that at best people retain only a fraction of what they hear, and after a lapse of time, retention scores drop drastically. There are several critical factors to be analyzed here. The difficulty may be traced to the speaker, to the physical environment, to the listener, or to a combination of these elements. If unprepared or uncaring, the speaker cannot expect the audience to listen. When there are extraneous noises and other environmental conditions competing with the listener and speaker, a breakdown in the listening process is likely to happen. Finally, the fault can rest primarily with the listener. If communication is to occur, the listener must do more than occupy a seat. Building a relationship of trust and meaning is a two-way process, not the speaker's burden alone. **Both parties, or all parties, must be willing to accept active roles.**

Listening Problems

My observations reveal a number of problems in listening. Probably you've also noticed them. Among the principal ones are the following six. You'll see that I haven't put them in order of frequency or significance. Though they apply to formal speechmaking, related problems can be observed in all sorts of speech-communication situations—even in speech classes.

Is he listening, really?

1. **Lack of design.** Members of an audience who do not know what they should listen for or who do not know their function, profit little. This is lack of design, a kind of behavior that might be represented by the person's silent testimony, "Here I am, but I'm not sure why." A functioning listener will work to understand the speaker's purpose, to visualize the structure of thought, to perceive relationships or comparative values of ideas, and to determine the meaning represented by words as well as nonverbal cues. **The good listener participates *purposefully* and *by design*.**

2. **Impatience.** Sometimes people in an audience are anxious or in too great a hurry. They get fidgety and become bothered by the speaker's labored pace or rambling manner in saying things; they're unwilling to hear the speaker out. Admittedly, some speakers have problems in "getting on with it" and in focusing their thinking; yet, shouldn't listeners be willing on occasion to indulge a sincere speaker's habits? I think so. With hope that the speaker eventually will make major speech improvements, the best response for the moment may be patience.

One of the most bothersome forms of impatience is seen in the behavior of people who just cannot wait to "reply." Over-anxious, they seem to give full attention to preparation of a rebuttal but not to real listening. Such eagerness can disturb the communication process, for the person's mind is only on getting ready to transmit, not to receive.

3. **Hypercritical outlook. Faultfinding attitudes and behaviors can be as destructive as impatience.** Would you be willing to join me, and the rest of humanity, in admitting that you've allowed your listening to be weakened by giving undue attention to faults? For example, we may be critical of aspects of the occasion: "Why do we have to hear all this

anyway?'' or ''Why did they decide to hold the meeting at this hour?'' We may find ourselves taking issue with the speaker's grammar, even minor examples. We may unfairly criticize the speaker's dress or shirt, hair style, voice, or posture. Needless to say, at moments when we're distracted by petty features, we can't focus on the intended message.

4. **Indifference.** In the case of indifference, the listener is inactive or apathetic. Listeners do have choices, and the indifferent person, lacking genuine interest, *chooses* to remain uninvolved, to offer nothing in response. Though the choice may be to stay there physically and possibly to be a hearer, it's not to be a listener. **A nonparticipating member of an audience neither gives nor receives.** Why does indifference occur? At times it comes from a ''show me'' attitude. And, in fairness, let's acknowledge that some occasions are boring; sometimes we may be able to justify a ''ho-hum'' response. But don't we have something of an obligation to go at least halfway? I think so.

A species of indifference that's much harder to excuse is excessive individualism. As said before, oral communication requires giving up a measure of self. Speaker and listener must choose to approach each other, to join in the interactive process and share something of their selves, creating a degree of intimacy and engaging willingly. Holding the self back, resisting partnership and close involvement in a cooperative activity, defeats goals of communication. If an audience member takes the position of ''I'm here; you come to me,'' speaker and listener remain apart. And when apart, they can't achieve identification, the condition on which communication depends.

5. **Self-absorption.** ''I didn't really listen,'' Christy confessed. ''My mind was a thousand miles away.'' Powerful forces are at work among audiences. Competing for attention with the speaker's message are emotional pressures and a variety of demands imposed by self needs, manifested at the moment. What can you do in a listening situation when you feel rotten and can't get into the role of listener? Maybe you're sad or depressed right then. What can you do when you're preoccupied with an unsolved personal problem, or when you can't free your mind of that horrible mid-term exam coming up? Or, on a happier note, when you eagerly anticipate and dream about the trip planned for next weekend? The problem is self-absorption—the inability to make oneself mentally available for interaction. The condition is certainly not uncommon, and the losses are quite obvious.

6. **Insecurity.** This topic extends the discussion of self-absorption, taking it to another level. The emphasis here is on preoccupation with personal status, being unsure of self and consequently feeling vulnerable and threatened. Too often the response is unfavorable defensiveness. No state is more counter-productive in oral communication, whether experienced by speaker or listener.[3]

While related to indifference, impatience, and hypercritical attitude, the problem has to do with wasteful self-protectiveness. **When sensing** that their identity or intelligence or values are being challenged or repudiated, some people either pull themselves in and withhold participation or strike back in one way or another. On these occasions, sensitive people will evade issues, let old grudges flare up anew, or resist new ideas. For instance, a person may be defensive and hard-pressed to listen well when the speaker makes a comment that seems to deny personal status or dismiss a cherished belief. The response is to shut out the thought and condemn the speaker.

Sometimes the problem appears as a kind of selective perception, reflecting an attitude that one's own view of reality is the only legitimate view. Thus, the mind opens only to topics that confirm his or her personal orientation.

It's at times when one is not really sure of oneself that one's worst characteristics emerge. And communicative failures show it. The would-be listener may become overwhelmed with resentment. Intolerance and prejudice rush to take over, appearing as racial animosity or bias regarding gender, differences in culture, sexual orientation, or religion. Fears from a perceived threat trigger antipathy toward people and ideas, especially those who seem to be different, hence alien, and with which a defensive person can't identify.

Fundamentally, the problem of defensiveness is limitation in self-esteem, feelings of inadequacy that motivate activity enforcing separation of listener and speaker. No aspect of listening pathology is more serious or more difficult to meet by oneself. But is there any solution to this large problem? Yes, there is. In a word, it's movement toward maturity, toward enhancement of self-worth. Feeling positive about ourselves leads to feeling positive in responding to others' ideas. **How we feel about ourselves affects relations with others, including our effectiveness in assuming the role of listener.**

> *We see things not as they are, but as we are.*
>
> *H.M. Tomlinson, writer*

IMPROVING LISTENING

At this point, you might refer to the communication model and discussion of the process of communication in Chapter Two, noting especially the variables that enter in:

Knowledge

Experience

Values

Feelings

Ethnic or cultural backgrounds

Communicative skills

All of these affect both the encoding and decoding of messages—the sending, receiving, speaking, and listening. People with relevant knowledge and experience have a basis for understanding one another. Shared values and mutual appreciation of ethnic and cultural attributes provide grounds for relating well. Positive feelings associated with a message further the process. And of course, communicative skill in both speaking and listening is fundamental to success. These are all to the good, but remember that every variable has a reverse side, representing a deficiency. If any one of them should have a negative value, for example, when knowledge of speaker or listener is insufficient or respect is not shared, there can be trouble in communication.

Shortly, we'll go to a discussion of listening improvement that involves the listener directly, but first let's remind ourselves of the speaker's role and look briefly at environmental conditions that affect the outcome of an interaction.

Role of the Speaker

The speaker must assume a big share of the responsibility for establishing communication. We know about the well-established criteria that speakers adhere to in preparing and delivering a talk, and we need not review them at length. In general, though, a speaker has three basic obligations:

1. To choose ideas wisely

2. To use proven methods of composition and delivery

3. And in all phases of planning and presenting, to discover means of joining with the audience: identifying, seeking unity of self, message, and listener

Environment and Atmosphere

In the best circumstances, the physical environment will have a positive effect on listening. We know how important it is to have a fitting atmosphere accompanying any important activity. Somehow, food eaten by candlelight, with soft music playing in the background, tastes better than it would if it were served in a brightly illuminated and noisy setting. **Atmosphere makes a difference.** The people who are responsible for speaking occasions have an obligation to set up and maintain an atmosphere that allows people to hear and listen well.

Assume that at some time this becomes your responsibility. What do you do? First, plan carefully. Think through all of the details relating to the arrangement of the setting. Be sure to have an understanding with all the people involved. For example, be sure to have clearance from those in charge regarding your access to the room, the availability and use of facilities, the length of time for your use, and so forth. If a band is scheduled to play outside during your meeting, determine what you can do about it. In short, do all in your power to prepare for everyone's "listening comfort." Specifically, you can increase the possibility of success in communication by:

1. Controlling distracting noises
2. Providing ample ventilation
3. Controlling the temperature of the room
4. Providing comfortable and properly arranged seating
5. Providing a speaker's stand
6. Providing for the unobtrusive entrance of latecomers
7. Making the environment attractive

A MODEL: THE "GOOD AUDIENCE"

It's time now to ask you to face up to your abilities as listener. How well do you fill that role, as opposed to being just a hearer? What are your competencies, habits, and weaknesses in listening? One way to start evaluating your listening strengths and shortcomings is to use the general standard or model of the "good audience," a concept introduced in Chapter Eight on persuasion. What is a good audience? First, this audience can be thought of either as an individual or a group. What does this person or group of persons do? Since communication depends on listeners cooperating with the speaker and contributing time and attention, we can say that one mark of a good audience is being accommodative to speakers, being more than hearers, by listening diligently and adjusting to speakers' behaviors. In this, a good audience is guided by principles such as fair play, equality, reciprocity, and openness. The good audience is willing to meet the speaker on the speaker's ground.

Realistically, however, there's a limit to the extent an audience might be expected to adjust. That is, the good audience will say "no" when necessary. For example, it's unreasonable to expect listeners to suppress personal values and interests. Indeed, a good audience does contribute support and help things along, but in so doing, maintains self-respect and personal dignity. When listeners deny their own integrity, for example, when they let a speaker get away with fallacy or questionable statistics, they not only diminish themselves and their listening power but also mislead the speaker on the nature of the interpersonal dynamics that are at work. Communication will be negatively affected by unreliable feedback from the listener. **A responding listener as good audience gives the speaker information on acceptability of ideas as well as the status of the entire exchange.**

Listening intelligently and maturely, the good audience knows that his or her doubt is sometimes justified, that raising questions is permitted—in fact, needed!—in a democratic society, and that in the final analysis, ideas or material which are personally unwelcome can be rejected. Good audiences know their obligation to others and to themselves. The ideal audience member is a secure and self-confident person, one whom we all should aspire to be in our communicative lives. Discussion of the following questions, directed to you, will be reminders of several particular listening attributes.

Questions for You

1. **What's your overall rating as listener?** What are your abilities and habits? Have you ever made a list of your good and bad habits? Are you usually more of a listener than a mere hearer? Many of your ways of conducting yourself as listener probably work very well for you. But, you may be aware of certain bad habits that you'd like to break. What behaviors would appear on your "Need to Improve" list? For example, are you one of those who occasionally lets your mind wander off the topic of the speech or sometimes finds yourself impassive—just occupying a seat in the audience and that's all? In this regard, do you sometimes fake attention, wanting the speaker to believe that you are really listening? Are you ever guilty of minor faultfinding, for example, of a speaker's appearance or use of language?

The Maturing Self. As you know, **the key factor in listening is the *self of the listener,* the personal element that affects responses to others' messages.** Are you willing to give of your mind to the speaker? Usually, are you able to keep a focus on the speaker's topic, avoiding self-absorption? We know that when confident in ourselves we are better listeners, and when feeling attacked or shown disrespect, our listening productivity diminishes drastically. In this sense, how is it with you in most speaking situations? Are you able to hear the speaker out, without reacting defensively? Growing personally—coming to know self-confidence and strength of self—is one product of a course in speech communication. Other support is available, particularly from friends, family, and professional counselors. There are numerous approaches to becoming a better listener, most tied to overall self-growth.

Now for some specific questions.

2. **Do you choose an appropriate seat?** Do you usually select a seat or standing place that will allow you to see and hear comfortably? Other needs also influence this choice. For instance, if you are one of the 4 to 6 percent of the population with a serious hearing loss, you probably place yourself close to the speaker. Good audiences make themselves available to the speaker, offering their physical selves and making eye contact.

3. **How do you handle "noise" or distractions?** Some distractions are unavoidable, whereas others can be eliminated. If the construction

crew down the corridor can't be asked to stop, perhaps the best solution
is to "listen louder than they're pounding." Whisperers, however, can be
given courteous suggestions to be quiet; doors and windows can be
opened or closed depending on need; and the lights can be turned on.
**The good audience helps handle distracting physical elements and
ignores those that are beyond anyone's immediate control. Discipline is the key.**

How Listeners Feel. Intrapersonal noise that's emotional in nature may
be even more bothersome than the physical. A listener brings to the occasion complex feelings. For example, on Monday, James may be confident
and secure, but on Wednesday he may arrive with certain anxieties and
preoccupation with himself. How can he put aside his personal disturbances and pay attention to the speaker? The answer is not a simple one,
nor do I presume that he or anyone will solve the problem by reading a
chapter on listening. Nonetheless, there are some possible starting
points. First, some people find that they can sidestep their own feelings
by plunging wholeheartedly into a speaker's speech, by silently challenging themselves to give keen attention to the speech and transcend intrusions of the moment. Such discipline is commendable, and I admire it.
Other persons achieve success by self-analysis. They try to determine why
they feel defensive or why their personal problems are more pressing
than the speaker's ideas. **When a listener's competing feelings
become an obstacle to communication, some means of handling
the "noise" is urgently needed.**

Speakers' Personal Characteristics. Are you able to avoid being distracted by a speaker's personal characteristics or mannerisms? All of us *are* individuals; each of us *is* different. That's good *and* bad, both boon and bane, as some say. It's in the nature of humans to develop distinct voices, physical appearances, habits, personality characteristics, and all the rest. It's said that a new acquaintance "takes getting used to." So it is with speakers. And that's the solution to differences among communicators. **The good audience soon moves beyond differences and concentrates on the essences of the prepared message.** Again, discipline is a key.

Listening in a World of Difference and Diversity. How do you handle **the noise of insensitivity**? I refer to **a speaker's misguided comment, sometimes out of ignorance or habit, to conditions of gender, physical attributes, ethnicity, sexual orientation, religion, age, and so forth.** Speakers who make reference to "a man and his wife," to "*that* part of town," to "fags," or to "older employees who always need help" may not know that they're putting noise into the circuits of communication. And eventually, for their growth as people and communicators, they should come to know about the "slips" and insults that can hurt listeners and disrupt the communicative process. But what's to be done at the moment? Truly, only a special kind of good audience can hear the speaker out when experiencing a statement that irritates. Upon occasion, such magnanimity may be worth trying. I think so. Of course, in the speech class, an instructional situation, we can deal with those occurrences directly and learn from them.

4. Do you know and appreciate your purpose as listener? Do you have a clear, acceptable reason for being there as a listener? What do you want from the experience? Would you rather be elsewhere? If attendance is not your free choice, what can you do? Since you are there, can you find sufficient reason for making the effort to listen? **The good audience always operates with purpose**, perhaps to gain specific information, to see another's perspective on a topic, to discover the issues of a question, or merely to learn more about human behavior. What are some of your general purposes?

5. How do you analyze a speech? Effective listening involves use of skill in analysis. Follow these suggestions.

During the speech, make an overall running analysis. First, be alert and grasp the speaker's purpose. Remember that it may be stated directly or merely implied. Continually ask, especially on controversial subjects, "What's the speaker saying, *really*?" "What does the speaker want, *really*?" Listen to determine the speaker's intent and what is sought from you, whether it be your vote or support, or merely your interest in some innocent idea.

Then, as you perceive the speaker's purpose, mentally outline the points and subpoints that are set down in its development. To help reconstruct the broad structure of the speech, notice little cues that indicate movement from thought to thought. Such transitional aids may be verbal, but often they are helped by vocal inflection or bodily movements.

Because seeing is a part of listening, facial expressions and gestures can assist you in following the flow of ideas. **Be aware of all possible sources of meaning, including nonverbal signs and nuances.**

After the conclusion, analyze the speech further. Think about the speaker's approach, the reasoning used, and the conclusions drawn. Ask yourself some key questions. Was the appeal basically emotional or did the speaker reinforce the talk with reasoning? Was there enough evidence to support the generalizations? What motivated the speaker? Did he or she have an "ax to grind"? What of the person's character? What of credibility? All speeches should be subjected to this type of post-mortem examination, but especially those that are intended to change our beliefs and influence our actions.

6. **Can you listen with empathy? Empathic listening, another mark of the good audience, is of great value in discovering a speaker's full message and in staying focused.** Such listening may be thought of as part of analysis, and yet it goes deeper. It occurs when we're able to project our personality into another's and thus have a genuine understanding of the other person's point of view and feelings. To be empathic is to be occupied with speaker and speech and less with self. A lot is required of listeners.

The Power of Empathy. Though empathic listening requires very special sensitivity and is not easily achieved, it's well worth cultivating. It involves development of the kind of listening maturity that checks hasty evaluation, for example, of unfamiliar or threatening ideas. **To listen empathically is to listen from the speaker's perspective, patiently and reasonably allowing the speaker fair time to present the message.** Besides concentrating on the speaker's thoughts and being aware of the speaker's related feelings and attitudes, **empathic listening calls for self-confidence, even courage**, because to be receptive to another's communication is to chance being influenced by it. **It's "daring to listen."** That's a choice to be commended.

Empathic listening, in any degree to which you are able to develop it, is a personal resource of inestimable worth.

7. **Do you participate actively?** Do you allow yourself to act on your analysis and empathy, to become involved with the speaker? The speaker needs you and very likely will have a worthwhile message to offer in return for your participation. You may find something of value in a speech, if you're willing to open yourself actively to it and work hard to check your selective perceptions.

Listeners as "Speakers." Overriding any personal indifference and responding fully, the good audience actively works along with the speaker and thereby facilitates communication. It's a truth in speech communication that **active listeners stimulate speakers, who, in turn, stimulate listeners.** And so goes the exchange, this act of reciprocity. There's a necessary interdependency in that circular process. In a real sense, **good audiences are speakers, too, because with the force of**

> *A person is a person through other persons.*
>
> *Desmond Tutu, political and religious leader*

their responsive mental and physical being they "talk back," non-verbally and dynamically.

Yes, *both* speaker and audience are equipped with methods and ideas; communication is the result of their saying things together in their respective ways. A fully functioning, confident listener who finds a message unclear will be able, through feedback, to "tell" the speaker about it, during or following the exchange. This active listener will spot significant omissions of information, check questionable reasoning, disallow unfair advantage—and commend good sense. **Straightforward and positive feedback helps speakers to know their listeners' needs and expectations,** and thus to maintain realistic perspectives.

The good audience, then, is watchful and reasonable, giving the speaker the benefit of a discerning, and balancing, presence. The resulting effect is influential in encouragement, support, guidance, and correction. That's the productive power of good feedback.

LOOKING BACK

It's probably true that sleeping is the only activity taking up more of our time than listening. What a waste of resources when the frequent and vital function of listening is neglected! How much we miss in our lives when we let ourselves get by as mere hearers! Although it's impossible to measure the losses of inefficiency and lapses, it's not too late to do something about it.

1. Remember that in communication, listening is every bit as important as speaking, if, indeed, we can separate the roles.

2. Cooperation and reciprocity, with speaker and audience working together, are hallmarks of the communicative relationship.

3. The products of a good communicative relationship are mutually beneficial.

4. Noise does intrude, but conscientious participants can take corrective measures.

5. The art of the "good audience" can be developed.

In a word, **effective listening doesn't just happen. People must care and make a commitment to work at it, actively and with empathy, all the time.**

NOTES

1. See, for example, Florence I. Wolff et al., *Perceptive Listening* (New York: Holt, Rinehart and Winston, 1983), 3–4.

2. Sperry, Inc., "Knowing How to Listen Could Double the Efficiency of American Business: Did You Hear That?" (New York: Sperry Corporation, 1980).

3. Harold Barrett, *Rhetoric and Civility: Human Development, Narcissism, and the Good Audience* (Albany: State University of New York Press, 1991).

PUTTING IDEAS INTO WORDS

11

★ **LOOKING AHEAD** ★

1. How should language vary with purpose?

2. What does it mean to say that "words are only symbols"?

3. What does it mean to say that "meanings are in the minds of people"?

4. In what sense is language a "social agreement"? How do the following usages relate to that agreement: standard versus substandard language, formal versus informal language, and respectful versus disrespectful language? What's the connection of "functional value" to the agreement?

5. How do we distinguish between denotation and connotation?

6. How are common ground in language use and "good language" related?

7. How is identification facilitated by language choice? What parts do clarity, liveliness, variety, and acceptability play in this?

8. What's the meaning of the suggestion, "Use *your* language"?

9. What are the four major actions to take that will lead to improvement in language use?

CHAPTER 11

PUTTING IDEAS INTO WORDS

Imagine the following telephone conversation.

He: I'm really glad you're home—I got this funny note from Pam, and I need a translation.

She: Let me hear it.

He: Okay, I'll read it: "Are you still upset about the other night? If I could I'd like to explain that I was just kidding when I told you I really didn't mean what I said about changing my mind on whether or not to reconsider my decision. These are my honest, sincere thoughts."

She: What's she trying to say?

He: I guess she thinks I know the code.

Yes, you have to know the code. Pam does know English, but there seems to be another code in use in that note. It can be said that all of us have developed individual ways of saying things, but **in communication with others, we need to make an accommodation to others and their understanding of chosen words, phrasings, and figures of speech.** That's the focus of this chapter.

LANGUAGE AND PURPOSE

Whether presenting information, arguing a case, or attempting to persuade, effective speakers are in a constant state of deciding on use of language. In this, their purposes direct them. Let's see some examples. Neal E. Cutler, political science professor speaking on the American political system, had in his audience a number of people visiting from Europe. Knowing that many listeners did not understand our political structures, he wanted to be very clear in his explanation. Notice his skill in selection of words.

In our Constitution, adopted in the year 1789, Federal *means a division between State and National government—specifically that only a few and specified powers are granted to the central*

*government, and others, including those not specified, are then
retained by the State and the State governments. We are, as I said at
the beginning, a Nation of States.*

Of course, this concept of Federalism—*this balance between the
Federal Government and the State governments—is not a stagnant
one; it is very dynamic. Think of this in terms of a pendulum slowly
swinging back and forth between the view that the States should
have more power and responsibility, and the view that the national
government should have more power and responsibility.*[1]

Thus did one speaker make his choices in use of language, as he
addressed his audience. The listeners, though mature and intelligent,
required basic instruction, but without disrespect for their lack of knowledge or understanding. You might want to read Cutler's entire speech;
it's a model of expert handling of abstract concepts that are unfamiliar to
an audience. As you consider that model or any others, recall times when
you, too, wanted to be just right in conveying a certain message to a person or group and were very careful with your words.

Contrast Cutler's language to inform with the following persuasive
words of Edward R. Roybal, an elected politician who spoke to his colleagues in the United States House of Representatives. Though he obviously has a point of view, he shaped his strong message as an explanation.

*. . . the search for unity is more than a search for symbolic cultural
solidarity. It is more than a dream—more than mere defense against
continuing inequities committed against the Spanish-speaking
people. It is the strong human desire for self preservation, a desire
that compels us to seek a united strategy to overcome the many
problems which weigh most heavily on us.*[2]

Susan B. Anthony spoke for women's rights. In the speech excerpt
below, she showed unmistakably the legal and fair ground of her cause.
Her language was clear, precise, and powerful; it was intended to
convince.

*It was we, the people; not we, the white male citizens; but we, the
whole people, who formed the Union. And we formed it, not to give
the blessings of liberty, but to secure them; not to the half of ourselves
and the half to our posterity, but to the whole people—women as well
as men. And it is a downright mockery to talk to women of their
enjoyment of the blessings of liberty while they are denied the use of
the only means of securing them provided by this . . . government—
the ballot.*[3]

Abolitionist Frederick Douglass, in 1850 in Rochester, talked with the
ethos of a man who had known slavery. His persuasive authority is apparent in his words.

*But how is it with the American slave? Where may he assemble?
. . . . Where are his newspapers? Where is his right of petition? Where is*

his freedom of speech? his liberty of the press? and his right of locomotion? He is said to be happy; happy men can speak. But ask the slave—what is his condition?—what his state of mind?—what he thinks of his enslavement? and you had as well address your inquiries to the silent dead. There comes no voice from the enslaved, we are left to gather his feelings by imagining what ours would be, were our souls in his soul's stead.[4]

Seeking independence for his people, Mohandas K. Gandhi, Indian leader, found language to represent his purpose. His words "ordeal of fire" are in reference to his adopted method of nonviolent civil disobedience.

I shall hope against hope, I shall strain every nerve to achieve an honorable settlement for my country, if I can do so without having to put the millions of my countrymen and countrywomen, and even children, through this ordeal of fire. It can be a matter of no joy and comfort to me to lead them again to a fight of that character, but, if a further ordeal of fire has to be our lot, I shall approach that with the greatest joy.[5]

LANGUAGE SYMBOLS

Whether for momentous or ordinary occasions, we use words and combinations of words to *stand for* or *refer to* the thoughts and things about which we want others to hear and make responses. But **a word is a word.** ***Its effectiveness and power is in the meaning it can stir up in others' minds.*** This truth of communication applies to the speaking of Frederick Douglass and Susan B. Anthony, as well as to that of any one of us living and speaking in these times. This is the first important lesson on language use. The second is equally important and tied necessarily to the first: *Meanings are in the minds of people, not inherent in the words themselves.* Any word is just a word. The word *tree* is not a growing thing with a trunk, branches, and leaves. The word *tree* is a symbol composed of four letters of the English alphabet and put together into a pattern that is intelligible to those who read English, or when spoken, to those who understand spoken English.

On the surface, words are innocent, but their users, we humans, are not innocent. We all have aims and purposes, and we use symbols to suit our purposes as we communicate with one another. **Thus words carry great power, but only if they have meaning to an audience.** A "dirty" joke is neither repulsive nor amusing to someone who does not know the language in which it was told. The words of the joke symbolize nothing; they have no meaning. Therefore there's no joke, nothing to which to react.

"The map is not the territory," say general semanticists. The map is only a graphic depiction, markings on paper. Words are not the things to which they refer. To illustrate this, take the alphabetical symbols A, E, K, N, and S. How do you feel about those letters? Put them into a pattern and you get KANES, an old word meaning goods exchanged in bartering. Do you have any feeling about that? No? Then, put them into this pattern: SNAKE. Now, some people *will* have a feeling. But why the negative response to five letters of the alphabet? As spoken, the word "snake" is only an arrangement of sounds, not a slithering creature that may or may not be threatening. Conceivably, some person exists somewhere who is afraid even to utter the word snake because he or she confuses the idea with the word. For that person, the word and thing have become the same. Some snakes are harmful, whereas others are quite useful. And though that short word is in itself harmless, as a representation of an object it can arouse great anxiety.

It's true that words are only symbols. Yet they must be respected for what we can do with them as we interact with others; however, it's not enough to recognize the power of language in awakening unpleasant feelings. We can dwell on that part of the story and continue to ask, "What's the matter with people? Why do they let mere words disturb or hurt them?" But in perceiving the force of language as something to be overcome, we go in the wrong direction. While knowing that words can hurt, let's look at the other side: the power of language as the enabler of communication. **Without language, there can be no identification of speaker, listener, and message.** The very predisposition that facilitates a response to the word "snake" makes possible appeals to peace, profit, justice, and more. From that predisposition, good causes have been furthered and civilization advanced. Humans as communicators, by nature and nurture, are responsive to symbols comprising messages. That statement gets to the essence of our being, of our *being together.* It's through such acting on one another that meaning is generated. And, yes, it's an enterprise of great risks and rewards.

As communicating creatures, wanting to understand and be understood, we rely on a great variety of symbolic forms. **The symbols used in communication are significant only to the degree that others are able to find a common meaning.** Of course, in understanding others we must take into account nonverbal as well as verbal cues, for meaning is also found in bodily action, eye movement, and vocal intonations. Behavior of the total person is representative of the person's message. It would help to maintain this broad perspective as we isolate and discuss verbal symbols in language use.

> *[By]* consent of the people . . . certain sounds come to be appropriate to certain things as their signs.
>
> *George Campbell, writer on rhetoric*

A SOCIAL AGREEMENT

Language systems are rooted in convention; they are organized and based on mutual agreement. In this sense, *agreement* means the acceptance and use of language by people in a "community" (area, nation, or cultural group). Of course, people born into a language do not individually make the agreement, not in a strict sense. But a culture over the years adopts and "agrees on" a language as a code for communication. Language and language patterns are necessarily founded on social agreements. **If a word has no meaning to others, it's socially useless to a communicator.** Yet it's true that some cohesive groups use terms not agreed on by the larger society, and for a time these expressions are acceptable only in the smaller communities. Not too long ago, for example, terms like "bummer" and "bummed out," "dude," "ripoff," "spaced out," and "into" (meaning "involved in") were useful for communication among members of discrete communities. But when they were adopted by the general society, they lost force in the smaller communities. Language agreements are continually renegotiated. Can you think of a term that once was "in" but is now losing currency?

We see then that language usage is constantly changing. Words fall by the wayside, as do also language conventions of all types. For example, the splitting of infinitives and ending sentences with prepositions now seem to be acceptable informal oral usages to the ears of most people. These are only two instances of change in recent times.

Standard-Substandard

The people who use a language make other agreements. They conclude, for example, that certain usages are *standard* (representative of the usual language choices of educated people) and that others are *substandard* (of persons with a limited range of choice). The following are substandard expressions as generally agreed upon by society.

There's twenty people in this class.

He hits the ball good.

The runner was throwed out.

The baby should have drank her milk.

Pass me them pliers.

It's just like I said.

Formal-Informal

Furthermore, language use often varies with the social situation in which it's used. It will be *formal* or *informal,* depending on a speaker's perception of the situation. All four of the following expressions are standard. But notice the greater degree of informality of those on the right.

They shall do no more.	They won't do any more.
Thank you for providing the drink of water.	Thanks for the water.
I reside in an apartment.	I live in an apartment.
We met on the corner of Twelfth and Grove streets.	We met at Twelfth and Grove.

Respectful-Disrespectful Appropriate language use is tied to interpersonal sensitivity, to being thoughtful of others as we go about choosing the words of our messages. Respectfulness rests on our awareness of
the meaning of our language as sensed by our audience. Respectfulness
is being mindful of others' perceptions and feelings. This means that **the
sensitive communicator tries to be empathic in selection of symbols.** I want to believe that among college students, maturity and intelligence will provide the civility that's necessary for respectful interaction
with listeners in the classroom—most of the time. But lapses do occur.
There are times, and we all know of them, when a speaker portrays
another group's values or societal roles disparagingly or when bias or stereotyping enter in. Because this is true, it wouldn't hurt right now to
remind ourselves of some "rights and wrongs." In our communications,
we should:

    1.   Avoid disrespectful stereotypes of all kinds: those relating to
race, sexual orientation, gender, national origin, age, religion, physical or
mental condition, and so forth. For example, a speaker's portrayal of the
flustered, unmechanical female homemaker or of the woman who gets
upset while a male correspondingly gets *angry;* references to a salesman
instead of a salesperson, chairman instead of a chairperson or chair, post-
man instead of postal worker; saying "A good nurse is worth her weight
in gold; be kind to her" instead of "Good nurses are worth their weight
in gold; be kind to them." Other hurtful stereotyping relates to insensitive

characterizations of behaviors or attitudes of racial and ethnic groups and of those perceived as "different," for example, disabled persons.

2. Avoid unnecessary ethnic, racial, and other associations relating to identity, particularly those that link the identity to negative situations or personality traits. For example, African American airline pilot, male kindergarten teacher, and capable handicapped person.

3. As one worthy source advises, **be aware of "the positive contributions of minorities, women, and others to the development of society.** Prejudice can be expressed through emphasis on any one group, through lack of recognition of achievement or leading role of a group, by omission of certain persons as role models, and by assignment of certain roles to specific individuals."[6]

4. Be knowledgeable about current and acceptable names for groups, for example, African Americans and Asian-Pacific peoples. In general reference to some groups, it's proper to say "people of color."

Functional Values Along with standards, levels of formality, and respectfulness, language has *functional values*. In terms of practical usage, functional values in language include standards, levels of formality, and decency, but they are more basic. Functional values have to do with an audience's acceptance and response, with the effect that language has on the listener. **Good language,** functionally, is suitable and adaptive in a given speaking situation. It **helps achieve a meeting of minds with listeners and does not detract from the thought.** It means "talking the listener's language." Overly formal or substandard language will detract on most occasions. And fair-minded people consider malicious stereotyping wrong. Language that is pedantic or highly complex, unfamiliar, or ungrammatical, or threatening may prevent identification of speaker and audience and therefore block intended communication. In this regard, the key is the situation and the speaker's strategies in responding to the situation. In sum, sometimes effective language choice is a matter of right and wrong, or of what is useful, or both.

DENOTATION AND CONNOTATION

Words and terms have two kinds of meanings: denotative and connotative.

Denotation. Denotative meaning is the logical, explicit, dictionary meaning. This is the objective meaning, that on which most people would agree. For example, *home* denotes a dwelling or residence in which one or a number of people live. A *police officer* is a member of a police force.

Connotation. The connotation is the emotional, subjective, personal meaning. This is the meaning that an individual finds in the word. Your personal meaning—connotation—of *home* and *police officer* will differ from mine. The more abstract the term, the more it's open to connotation because the more varied are people's reactions to it. Contrast your meaning of the word *wealth* with another person's meaning. Do the same with

such words as *education, conservative, happiness,* and *faithful.* Probably you have heard that "beauty is in the eye of the beholder." It means that each person has a different connotation of the word beauty. *America* may be the United States of America or the United States along with Canada, the United States of Mexico, and all countries to the tip of South America. But beyond geographical denotation, what does the word *America* mean to you personally? What does it *connote?* Don't expect your connotation to be exactly like any other person's. As speakers and listeners, we find highly personal meanings in most words, as we use and hear them. Given that fact, should we wonder about the prevalence of communication problems?

A COMMON GROUND IN USAGE

In about every chapter of the book, you'll read that communication depends on communicators' willingness and ability to address others on their own ground or, better, on a *common* ground. This is the meaning of *identifying.* One might say that speakers meet listeners "as they find them." That is, people are not all the same. And they're not always ready to understand a person speaking to them, regardless of the value of the message. Some listen fairly well while others do not. Some may be prepared to grasp the ideas of a given speech while others may not. Some in an audience, but not all, may have certain experiences similar to the speaker's and share the speaker's connotations, to some degree. In any event, we must realize that words can further the separation of speaker and listener, or they can bring them closer together and thereby improve the chances of communication. Communication involves use of appropriate symbols in the identification of people and their beliefs, feelings, and values. Thus, **good language is language that serves to unify speaker, message, and audience.**

Although communication requires exactness and clarity, absolute precision is impossible. Moreover, even if it were possible, who would want to listen to mechanically perfect language for very long? Speech should be clear, but it should also be *appealing*. It ought to have some kind of human interest and be adapted to a feeling as well as thinking audience. **People respond best when the language of a message is engaging.**

The following passage is from a speech given by Professor Porter Crow to an industrial association in South Carolina. Notice the combination of subjective and objective elements that allows the speaker to offer a solid message and make it attractive. Notice also the brevity of clauses, their variety in form, and their sharpness. There's nothing fuzzy in the language. And notice the use of questions to promote audience response. The content could be rather heavy, but Mr. Crow lightens it for his listeners, while remaining faithful to his ideas.

> *But what is the "mind"? Is it the brain? The nervous system? Or some secret combination? Today's most relevant questions are being asked about the mind and its activity and creativity. Your wonder, your awe, your interest in the mind should never stop. Because that's where you live.*
>
> *Perception is the foundation of the mind, and perceptions fuel the basic activity of thinking. And that's the activity that makes us human. To sharpen our thinking, to stimulate creativity should be our constant goal.*
>
> *Creative thinking, as a result of such stimulation, originates in the lobes of our brain. Now, here's where all of this gets fascinating because you have two lobes, a Right and a Left, and they work differently.*[7]

The speaker appeals to the rational sense *and* to the feelings of his audience. His basic information seems sound and verifiable. But his spirited language is subjective and stimulating, likely to bring about the audience's close involvement. His expressiveness enriches the discourse and adds interest. In sum, he has a reasonable point and probably communicated it to a highly interested audience.

In choosing language, you, the speaker, must consider the four familiar elements of speaking: yourself, your speech, your audience, and the occasion. When preparing and rehearsing your speeches, ask this question about your choice of language: "Is this word or phrase suitable for me to use in communicating this thought to this audience on this occasion? Will it help my listener and me to understand each other, to bring our worlds closer together?"

Effectiveness in communication is built from choices of language that identify people with one another. Four bases for facilitating identification are clarity, liveliness, variety, and acceptability.

FACILITATING IDENTIFICATION

Clarity

1. Use simple, straightforward language. If the message is complex, find words to simplify it. Communication suffers if the terminology is too technical, if a speaker uses "big words" for their own sake and lets the language become overly complicated. The use of too many words or ornate or pretentious words may detract from ideas and violate criteria of clarity in speaking. **Those criteria are directness, economy, and aptness.**

To be successful in communication, you must make your words "smaller than your ideas," said Ralph Waldo Emerson, the great speaker and writer. The language found in John F. Kennedy's best speeches exemplifies a style that was highly effective in communicating his ideas. He, and those who helped him phrase his thoughts, knew the importance of simplicity and straightforwardness in expression. This passage from his Inaugural Address is an example:

> To those people in the huts and villages across the globe struggling to break the bonds of mass misery, we pledge our best efforts to help them help themselves, for whatever period is required . . . not because we seek their votes, but because it is right. If a free society cannot help the many who are poor, it cannot save the few who are rich.

As President Kennedy's speeches illustrate, very often the simplest language is the most profound and practical. The opposite style, seen in lush and fancy expression, bothers listeners and causes them to resist contact with the speaker. The same lesson applies to choosing short and simple phrasing; lengthy expressions become cumbersome and hard to manage. **When an audience becomes concerned with *how* something is being said instead of with *what* is being said, communication suffers.** Style should serve the thought and be congruent with it.

It's usually better to say:	Instead of:
lie	prevarication
choices	available avenues for action
bright, fair, or mild	halcyon
I have to go now.	I must take my leave.

By all means give your thoughts significance and meaning, but in so doing be guided by ancient wisdom: "A profound thought is a clear thought."

2. Use precise language. We all recognize that the human organism is not a precision instrument. We make mistakes. We waste motion. We're often quite inefficient.

Though we are able to create mutual understanding, it's impossible, even for the greatest of speakers, to convey to others the fullness of an

> *A good style must first of all be clear.*
>
> *Aristotle, writer on rhetoric*

idea. We are able to communicate only a fraction of any thought or feeling. Therefore, recognizing the certainty of inefficiency and error in communication, we ought to be as exact and precise as our words will allow.

It's often better to say:	*Instead of:*
apartment, mobile home, mansion, farmhouse, cottage, etc.	house
valid, useful, commendable, choice, valuable, etc.	good
exclaimed, shouted, noted, answered, stated, etc.	said
novel, anthology, pamphlet, text, encyclopedia, etc.	book
intriguing, exciting, appealing, attractive, provocative, etc.	interesting

Especially troublesome are vague words such as *very* and *nice.* To find more specific substitutes for these and other hazy terms, consult your dictionary or a good thesaurus. In his quaint way, Mark Twain reminds us of the need for being exact: "The difference between the right word and the almost right word is the difference between lightning and the lightning bug."

Euphemisms, or roundabout words or expressions, are special problems. Speakers occasionally use a euphemism when they want to avoid being blunt or frank. This form of soft-pedaling an idea may be justified now and then, for example, in trying to avoid a defensive reaction or unnecessary emotional reaction. On the other hand, if the use of euphemisms is extensive, or if they are used to deceive, audiences will come to question the speaker's ideas or intent. Wishing to avoid undesirable connotations of words like *death* or *dead,* speakers often refer to "his passing," "the departed," or being "called away" or "laid to eternal rest." Soldiers in the Vietnam war talked of "wasting" an enemy soldier. The cautious parent who finally works up enough courage to discuss the "facts of life" (a euphemism itself) with a son or daughter may rely heavily on euphemisms. Army generals may say that their troops made a "strategic withdrawal," instead of a "retreat." A politician, not wanting to arouse voter hostility regarding a controversial tax bill, may say, "The overall impact on the economy will not be inconsiderable."

Though audiences and purposes vary:

It might be better to say:	*Instead of:*
Laura failed the examination.	Laura's score on the examination fell to a point below the passing level.
The company fired Bill.	The company terminated Bill's employment.
I like your idea *or* I do not like your idea.	I am not unsympathetic to your idea.

| Paul is overweight. | The number of pounds that Paul is carrying amounts to considerably more than the table specifies for one of his height. |

Check your precision in language usage. Realistically, **euphemisms may be called for in some situations, but when excessive or unwarranted, they result in flabby expression.** They can raise doubts about your purpose or sincerity, thus turning off the listener.

Liveliness

1. Use language that appeals to the senses. Paint word pictures that help listeners visualize form, texture, and color. Put life into your speaking, and use words that contribute to achievement of your purpose. In his Inaugural Address, President Kennedy used language that appealed to the senses of his listeners and thereby influenced them to believe in his ideas, to identify with them. Note, in the following selected portion of that speech, the specific appeals to movement, to light, to texture, and to taste. The result is an uplifting and exciting statement of resolve. It's strong and youthful; it invites identification.

We dare not forget today that we are the heirs of that first revolution. Let the word go forth from this time and place, to friend and foe alike, that the torch has been passed to a new generation of Americans—born in this century, tempered by war, disciplined by a hard and bitter peace, proud of our ancient heritage—and unwilling to witness or permit the slow undoing of those human rights to which this nation has always been committed, and to which we are committed today at home and around the world.

Infuse your ideas with life and spirit; release your verbal powers. You may be quite pleased with the way listeners respond to your expressiveness.

It might be better to say:	*Instead of:*
The red Cessna pierced a puffy cumulus cloud at 4,000 feet above the Rio Grande.	The plane went into a cloud.
Crusty but kind, poor but rich in spirit, the old man was a fixture on Sixth Street.	The old man was a fixture on Sixth Street.

2. Use apt figurative language. It's impossible to talk without using some kind of figurative language. Samples are found in any speech or conversation. A figure of speech can animate an abstract idea and draw listeners to a message. Although many types of figurative language are available to speakers, simile, metaphor, personification, irony, synecdoche, and hyperbole are especially useful.

A *simile* is a short comparison introduced with *like* or *as*.

It might be better to say:	Instead of:
Like an annoying wind on a March day, her presence put everyone on edge.	Her presence put everyone on edge.
Rowing furiously, as if under penalty of death, Larry put his boat across the finish line.	Rowing furiously, Larry put his boat across the finish line.

A *metaphor* is an implied comparison in which something is spoken of as being something else. The words like and as are not used. The following excerpt is from African American activist Malcolm X's speech called "Message to the Grass Roots." Given in 1963, a time of great struggle over rights and freedoms in the United States, it contains a graphic metaphor. It's a figure designed to penetrate listener consciousness and inspire change in an accepted attitude.

> *This is the way it is with the white man in America.* He's a wolf—and you're sheep. *Any time a shepherd, a pastor, teaches you and me not to run from the white man and, at the same time, teaches us not to fight the white man, he's a traitor to you and me.*[8]

When inaugurated as mayor of New York, David N. Dinkins used this metaphor to identify with his diverse audience:

> *We are all footsoldiers on the march to freedom, here and everywhere; we all belong to the America that Lincoln called "the last best hope of the earth."*[9]

It might be better to say:	Instead of:
Experience is a key to many of life's locked doors.	Experience is helpful in life.
Wow, he's got a short fuse.	He's very defensive.
"The torch has been passed to a new generation."	A new generation is to lead.

Personification gives human qualities to inanimate objects.

It might be better to say:	Instead of:
The creek gurgled and giggled as it flowed along.	The creek made interesting sounds as it flowed along.
Law speaks for everyone.	Law represents everyone.

Irony is a figure of speech in which the intended meaning is opposite to that indicated by the words used. Often it's sarcastic in tone.

It might be better to say:	Instead of:
Brutus is an honorable man.	Brutus' honor is questionable.
Children just hate to play in the water!	Children love to play in the water!

Synecdoche is a kind of figure that names part of something to stand for the whole (or more rarely, the whole to stand for the part). In his Inaugural Address, President Kennedy could have said, "The direction of our country is up to you, my fellow citizens, more than to me." Instead, he said, "In your hands, my fellow citizens, more than mine, will rest the final success or failure of our course." *Hands,* as representative of the total power of the people, is an instance of synecdoche. Another speaker might say, "Your *voice* is needed in this campaign," intending that voice represent the individual's total persuasive power.

Synecdoche must be used carefully. It's a type of language usage that can detract from the message unless expressed skillfully and chosen to fit the particular thought, as well as the audience and occasion.

Occasionally it might be better to say:	*Instead of:*
In the movie, he played a hired gun.	In the movie, he played a professional killer.
The company wanted her brain, and they paid well for it.	Because she was smart, they gave her a big salary.
Friends, Romans, countrymen, lend me your ears.	Friends, Romans, countrymen, listen to me.

Hyperbole is an inventive and obvious exaggeration that if presented well will be accepted by the audience and responded to favorably. President Kennedy's speech offers a model. In the following excerpt, note his five uses of the word *any.* Did he mean *any,* literally? Or were his words to be taken for their *spirit?*

Let every nation know, whether it wishes us well or ill, that we shall pay any price, bear any burden, meet any hardship, support any friend, oppose any foe, in order to assure the survival and success of liberty.

Occasionally it may be better to say:	*Instead of:*
Determined to win the race, he spent every last ounce of energy he had.	Determined to win the race, he ran very, very hard.
We all worked day and night for a whole week.	We all worked exceedingly hard for a whole week.
I was in heaven for the entire time in Jamaica.	My time in Jamaica was thoroughly enjoyable.

Recently a student included this bit of hyperbole in a speech: "When we got home, we were absolutely dead." She made her point.

One caution: As with any kind of expression, excessive use or awkward handling of figurative language can alienate the listeners. **Develop a modest number of figures, those that are both easy for you to use and for your audience to accept.**

Variety

1. Use diversified language. People like variety. As poet William Cowper once observed, "Variety's the very spice of life, that gives it all its flavour." People change the interior colors of their apartments and houses, their choice of weekend trips, their wearing apparel, and other interests. Why not allow language to follow a similar course? When people give listeners the experience of a wide range of personal expressiveness, mutual understanding may have a greater chance to occur. **Diversified language is attractive and appealing.** It reflects an enthusiastic, responsive attitude and can promote a positive relationship with others.

How can you achieve more variety? Try varying the shape of your oral sentences. If you characteristically speak in long and loosely constructed clauses, it would be well for you to break the habit. If your habit is to begin with the subject, you can add variety by occasionally introducing periodic construction—that which withholds the important thought until the end.

In the following excerpt, taken from student Maggie Hooper's speech in Appendix A, notice the varied sentence structure. One sentence has two independent clauses that are linked smoothly, another asks a provocative question, and a third with two clauses derives force from the impact of one against the other. This kind of diversification contributes interest and force and heightens the meaning of the message.

This is a political society, and you must have a broad knowledge of the natural environment to function effectively in such a society. How will you vote on issues related to the President's current energy plan, in which he proposes to eliminate many environmental safeguard laws, when you have no idea what the elimination of these safeguards will do to the environment? This issue is serious; it might even mean great danger to your health.

Occasionally it might be better to say:	*Instead of:*
Since Maria was born in Mexico and went to school there for ten years, she speaks Spanish fluently. (periodic construction)	Maria speaks Spanish fluently, for she was born in Mexico and went to school there for ten years.
While everyone was at the dance, Penelope gave birth to a litter of five pups. (periodic)	Penelope gave birth to a litter of five pups while everyone was at the dance.
Unless the members cooperate better, the weather becomes more favorable, the park is available to us, and the beverage workers' strike is settled, there's no way we can hold our annual picnic. (periodic)	There's no way we can hold our annual picnic unless members cooperate better, the weather becomes more favorable, the park is available to us, and the beverage workers' strike is settled.

Have you ever thought of occasionally trying different forms for expressing your ideas? There are ways to do that. Among the choices are climax, parallelism, alliteration, and the rhetorical question. With purpose and patience, you can become sensitive to them and learn to use them well without being self-conscious about it.

Climax is a form of building interest within a passage in accordance with listeners' expectations and motivations. The speaker structures words and phrases to achieve force and effectiveness with a strong ending and thereby increases the listeners' attention to the thought. The final sentence in this portion of President Kennedy's Inaugural Address is the climactic statement.

I do not believe that any of us would exchange places with any other people or any other generation. The energy, the faith, the devotion which we bring to this endeavor will light our country and all who serve it, and the glow from that fire will truly light the world. And so, my fellow Americans, ask not what your country can do for you, ask what you can do for your country. My fellow citizens of the world, ask not what America can do for you, but what together we can do for the freedom of man.

Parallelism sets one phrase or clause against another in a balanced relationship. In form, each element is equal to the other. The symmetry appeals to listeners' sense of proportion and basic desire for balance. Remember the balanced clauses of Julius Caesar's report of victory: "I came, I saw, I conquered." In President Kennedy's passage above are two samples of parallel structure, a favorite language usage of his. They're the clauses beginning with "ask not." Here are two more from his inaugural.

> *If a free society cannot help the many who are poor, it cannot save the few who are rich.*

> *United there is little we cannot do in a host of cooperative ventures. Divided, there is little we can do.*

Alliteration is the artful reuse of sounds in a passage. It, too, adds variety and is designed to heighten the force of an idea. One who wants forcibly to say, "The community, shocked by disaster, attempted to regain its normal operations," might communicate the thought more effectively by saying, "The community, torn by tension and terror, attempted to right itself."

A *rhetorical question* is one to which no immediate answer is sought or anticipated. Speakers use a rhetorical question to put variety into their language and to draw listeners into their messages, to involve them in the thought. President Kennedy wanted silent "yes" answers—and commitment—from his audiences around the world when he asked:

> *Can we forge against these enemies* [*tyranny, poverty, disease, and war*] *a grand and global alliance, north and south, east and west, that will assure a more fruitful life for all mankind? Will you join in that historic effort?*

Try using climax, parallelism, alliteration, and rhetorical questions in your speaking. With practice, such language forms can become valuable resources for expressing ideas.

  2. **Use fresh language.** You can also vary your use of individual words and phrases. In most speaking situations, it's appropriate to vary usage by including contractions and other useful colloquialisms. Unfortunately, some clichés and older slang expressions that seem to serve people well on certain occasions create listening blocks on others. Many words that once were attractive are now worn out and useless before most audiences. Take the word *groovy,* for example. A 15-year survey of my students shows clearly that for them this is one of the most repellent words in the English language.

  Seek attractive variety through new and current language, and try to avoid distracting expressions. Remember always the realities of audience taste, which brings up the topic of acceptability.

Acceptability

  1. **Use language appropriate to the occasion.** The nature of the occasion, whether formal or informal, in the classroom or school gymnasium, at a banquet, in a religious setting, or elsewhere, will make certain language forms more acceptable than others. Again, remember social agreements on usage, that is, what's expected. When speakers are overly formal or overly informal, listeners have a tendency to become distracted,

to forget the message and focus on expressions. **Communicative purpose is lost if people's minds are not on the message.**

Depending on the kind of occasion,

It might be better to say:	Instead of:
you people	you guys
ranked	prioritized
You're right!	You got that right!
Where are you going?	Where are you going to?
I'm not related to him.	He's no kin of mine.
He must go alone.	No one shall accompany him.

2. Use standard language. As I mentioned earlier in the chapter, linguists often classify language as standard or substandard. Education provides one with choices in language use, and standard language is usually the better choice. Very likely it's the language you'll find most useful in your life. Substandard expression can be a real hindrance in communication. A listener hearing "we was" or "they is" often is critical of both the idea and the person delivering it, and the message never gets a fair hearing. That's a real loss.

It's always appropriate to say:	Instead of:
He gave it to Jan and me.	He gave it to Jan and I.
All persons should park their cars in the lot or Park your car in the lot, everyone.	Everyone should park their cars in the lot.
I'll go, regardless.	I'll go, irregardless.
The lamp is broken.	The lamp is busted.
I can't do it.	I can't hardly do it.
He did it.	He done it.
I'm going to lie down.	I'm going to lay down.

USE YOUR LANGUAGE

Make choices in language that will help you get a hearing for your ideas. Use clear, vivid, and undistracting language, but also use *your* language. And use your *oral* language. Remember that in speaking, the verbal message is "for the ear rather than the eye," as one of my colleagues puts it. Speeches are not essays; they are to be heard, not read. In one sense, reaching people aurally (by ear) is more difficult than writing for them. It's a challenge to cause the "ear to see." And therein lies a major value of the language skills discussed in this chapter. In another sense, speaking (addressing the ear) is easier because you have greater freedom. As you interact with the audience before you, you're expected to be open and rather free, for example in the use of contractions and fragments. *Appropriately less formal* may be the way to characterize the norm for speaking.

Improve your use of English, but start from the foundation you have been laying these past years and continue your program of self-improvement. Instead of trying a major overhaul in language usage, work gradually and steadily for increased effectiveness. A radical change in style could make your behavior incongruent and not easy for others to accept. Instead, occasionally substitute new words, improved phrasing, and more appropriate forms for weaker and less effective modes of expression. Work in new ways of saying things. In this way of maturing as a communicator, you'll be able to do away with a common fear: "If I don't speak the same old way, if I change my speaking habits, I won't be able to relate to friends." Growth and personal appeal need not be incompatible. Move ahead, step by step.

The Adaptable You

As you reflect on the nature of *your* language, remember, that *you have more than one language in your repertoire.* Think of it this way: **As your audience and occasions vary, you'll be motivated accordingly to make use of the various dimensions of your available language resources.** The setting and the backgrounds of one group of listeners, varied in age, level of sophistication, and so forth, will encourage your use of certain personal language patterns which at another time and with another audience might not be fitting. On both occasions, the language will be *yours,* yours *as adapted.* As emphasized throughout this chapter, adaptability is a prime virtue in putting ideas into words and identifying with audiences.

ARE YOU READY TO WORK AT IT?

Now for a final word on working at self-improvement, on exploiting all available strategies in developing your verbal power. If you're ready to take action, there are four proven ways.

Listen   Make an effort to listen to yourself, to your language patterns and habits. Listen also to the users of standard English. Compare your language with theirs, and weed out words and forms of expression that do not serve you well. Listen to learn about yourself, to check yourself with the standard, and to decide on acceptability in features of your style of speaking as it has taken shape over time.

Read   Read as widely and as avidly as your time and interests allow. Read speeches and essays, newspapers and magazines, novels and poetry. Read without consciously thinking about language development. *Just read.* While enjoying the material, you'll incidentally acquaint yourself with varied and useful forms of expression and increase your appreciation of each person's unique way of putting ideas into words. What a happy way to become stronger!

Write   Here's some hard work, if you're ready. Almost any kind of writing is beneficial in developing communicative skill and in sharpening sensitivity to language use. Whether your choice is an essay, letter, or poem, it makes no difference. Just write, write, write! The practice of putting a sentence on paper and then recasting it, and recasting it once more, is an invaluable builder of the discipline of shaping ideas in language. The transfer value in strengthening your speaking may be well worth the required rigor and dedication.

Speak   I hope you'll take advantage of every opportunity to speak. True, it may take a lot of courage. But **why not try that word "Yes" when asked to chair a meeting, conduct a forum, or make an announcement?** Experience will add to your ability to cope with situations that require competence in thinking and putting ideas into effective language. You see, language is tied to thinking processes and therefore to your ability to think in front of people. **Each appearance before an audience is a chance to learn and to gain in personal effectiveness.**

LOOKING BACK

Speech communication requires the use of symbols that members of a community have adopted. Assuming that you are committed to improving your language use, where do you start? First, make an accounting of your strengths and weaknesses. Become conscious of your habits and gradually replace the less reliable words and phrases, finding grounds of identification with your audience.

1. For clarity, use simple and precise language.
2. For liveliness, use sense-appealing and figurative language.
3. For variety, use diversified and fresh language.
4. For acceptability, use standard language and language appropriate for the occasion.
5. Use *your* language.
6. And you have to work at it.

Remember above all that the thought is supreme; it's the thought that you want to "protect," to communicate well. Your choices of words, figures of speech, and phrasing influence the meaning of the message and facilitate identification with the audience. Language is substantially bound up with ideas and with the thought processes and responses of listeners. It can't be viewed as a cosmetic, added on to "pretty up" ideas.

Because communication of ideas necessarily depends on good choices in language, improvement deserves a full share of your daily attention.

NOTES

1. Neal E. Cutler, quoted from Harold Barrett, *Practical Uses of Speech Communication,* 6th ed. (New York: Holt, Rinehart and Winston, 1987), 291–296.

2. Edward Roybal, quoted from John C. Hammerback and Richard J. Jensen, *A War of Words: Chicano Protest in the 1960s and 1970s* (Westport: Greenwood, 1985), 113.

3. Susan B. Anthony, quoted from James Andrews and David Zarefsky, *American Voices: Significant Speeches in American History, 1640–1945* (New York: Longman, 1989), 300–301.

4. Frederick Douglass, quoted from James Andrews and David Zarefsky, *American Voices: Significant Speeches in American History, 1640–1945* (New York: Longman, 1989), 174.

5. Mohandas K. Gandhi, quoted from Paul D. Brandes, *The Rhetoric of Revolt* (Englewood Cliffs: Prentice-Hall, 1971), 113.

6. *Holt, Rinehart and Winston, Inc., et al, Author's Guide* (New York: Holt, Rinehart and Winston, 1987), 27–29. This source has supported the writing of the entire section on respectfulness in language use.

7. Porter Crow, "Waking Up the Right Lobe," *Vital Speeches of the Day,* L (July 15, 1984): 600.

8. Malcolm X, "Message to the Grass Roots," *Malcolm X Speaks,* ed. George Breitman (New York: Grove Press, 1965), 13.

9. David N. Dinkins, "Mayor of All the People," *Representative American Speeches, 1989–1990,* ed. Owen Peterson (New York: H. W. Wilson, 1991), 149.

GIVING THE SPEECH

12

"GIVING" A SPEECH: THE LAST STEP IN COMPOSITION

The word "delivery" usually appears in the title of a chapter on the presentation of a speech. But the idea of "giving" is much better to have in the title because it suggests *generosity,* the spirit of offering something of yourself to others. **Giving and sharing are at the heart of successful communication.** Indeed, among the words under *communicating,* a good thesaurus lists both *giving* and *sharing,* not to mention others quite similar.

After making all the basic preparations for speaking, there's the giving. And that phase, the last in the process, involves the making of choices. In extemporaneous speaking, the final composition takes place as you stand before the audience. Rehearsal has given you options and confidence, and speaking extemporaneously, you are free to choose words that seem most fitting at the moment. In this sense, content and presentation are not separated. They are "of a piece," parts of the total message. *How you say it* is integral to *what you say.* **The whole, the full message, is everything perceived by the audience through all channels of sight and sound.** Keep this unitary concept in mind as the chapter unfolds.

IDENTIFYING

As a start in tying presentation to other parts of the process of oral communication and explaining its function, consider the concept of adapting. To adapt, according to *Webster's Collegiate Dictionary,* means "to make suitable; to fit, or suit; to adjust." You are successful to the extent that you are able to adapt to your audience. But communication goes deeper than that. As I have noted throughout the book, the aim is to achieve *identification.*

In the predelivery stages of preparing a talk, you make major steps toward identifying your message with listeners' lives and interests by planning and composing intelligently. Included are the following acts:

Choosing a suitable subject

Thoughtfully wording a purpose

Analyzing and arranging your thoughts carefully

Strengthening your thoughts with primary processes and supporting the thoughts

Preparing to use effective language

Finally, you step before your audience with your prepared thoughts, to begin the exchange with them. While planning the message, your involvement is largely *intrapersonal*—with yourself—as you make choices and decisions dependent on your purpose, reasoning, values, attitudes, and so forth. In presentation, the process becomes directly *interpersonal*—with others and the varying beliefs and feelings that others bring. Thus **the act evolves into a face-to-face, dynamic relationship—and of the moment. It's in this phase that you shape the "final draft" of your message, *giving* it in close interaction with your audience.**

Reciprocity is the ideal condition, as the speaker, ever mindful of audience response, is able to make use of feedback. This closeness, this connection with the audience, occurs as an experience in the recreation of ideas "at the moment of utterance,"[1] causing listeners to feel involved in the process. Thus is identification established in extemporaneous speaking. If you need a reminder, refer back to Chapter Three for clarification on the differences among extemporaneous speaking, verbatim memorization, and speaking from a manuscript.

Speak conversationally, recreating "the thought at the moment of delivery."

James Albert Winans, pioneer in speech communication

YOUR SELF

In oral communication, you have one instrument to use in relating your thoughts and feelings, and that is *you, yourself,* the sum total of your physical, mental, and emotional characteristics, those patterns of behavior, interests, temperaments, stores of knowledge, attitudes, values, and motives that distinguish you from others.

Knowing Your Self

All attributes of the self play roles in oral communication. What are specific features of *your* self? What are *your* distinguishing characteristics of body, mind, and emotions? What is your identity? Are you an outgoing person who enters into many social activities, or does your temperament lead you to minimize your social life? Are you generally liberal or rather conservative? Are you ambitious or easygoing? Optimistic, idealistic, realistic? In communicating, are your ideas and bodily actions congruent; that is, are they consistent with each other and compatible? Whatever your personal qualities, it's important for you to recognize them, to continue learning about yourself. **Self-improvement is based on self-knowledge.**

Accepting Your Self

Beyond knowing yourself, effectiveness in speaking requires your accepting yourself. Now, acceptance doesn't mean neglecting personal growth. Certainly you want self-improvement and progress in coming to terms with yourself. To grow is to be alive and to make things better. No one, however, should refuse to recognize and accept basic and important personal assets. Too many people have the habit of being overly dissatisfied with themselves. Negative self-criticism restricts efficiency in speaking—indeed, in any social situation. When you are apologetic and otherwise give the impression that what you have to say is not worthwhile, the audience just might believe you. If this happens, both you and the others lose. Related is the condition of defensiveness, a common indicator of reduced self-esteem. Often it draws attention to speaking behavior and thus competes with speaking purpose. **Self-acceptance is basic to effective speaking.**

We quite naturally feel a certain reluctance in opening up and revealing a portion of ourselves. Truly, one of the most difficult choices to make is to drop social defenses and put ourselves in front of an audience. No matter how normal or conscientious we are, the motivation to protect ourselves is strong. We don't want to be hurt, to suffer a loss of status or dignity. That's why we become apprehensive. Very few people feel fully adequate in all situations, yet realizing the rewards of personal growth and effectiveness with others, we stand up and speak. How we handle ourselves may depend on the situation and how we feel at the moment. **With courage, we gain a little more each time we take the chance.** Experience is a great teacher.

YOUR BODY AND VOICE: NONVERBAL BEHAVIOR

The body and voice of a communicating person send vital messages to an audience through nonverbal language. **Any gesture, movement, or vocal sound may be perceived by others as a part of what's being said.** When President Eisenhower talked to the nation on television, he occasionally would remove his glasses and lean toward the camera, saying, in effect, "Your president is close to you on this question of mutual concern." The feeling of physical closeness can serve to relate speaker and message with the audience. An instructor's brisk underlining of a statement on the blackboard may say, "Remember this point!" Another example of the union of purpose and delivery is seen in the soft voice and unhurried rate of speech that may come from the feeling of a speaker who wishes to communicate a message of friendliness and warmth.

Of course, most vocal and bodily behavior is not premeditated or planned. Ordinarily, people give very little conscious thought to the way they walk, raise their voices, move their arms, direct their eyes, stretch out their words, or tilt their heads. These actions happen spontaneously and are the result of learning, habits, and various other influences such as their beliefs on relevant issues. Nonverbal expressions are outward signs of how people feel at the moment, their view of themselves, their attitude toward a given idea, their needs, and so forth.

General Functions

Recall that nonverbal actions are tied to words of the speech and thereby serve as partners in forming a message. In various ways they add punctuation and emphasis and meaning to verbal expression. **Nonverbal action is powerful.** A sigh may tell more about a person's point of view than any number of words. In particular contexts, a clenched fist, an abrupt toss of the head, or vibrancy in one's voice will send messages more unmistakably than any other means.

As one general function, nonverbal actions can serve as *repeaters* of verbal statements, for example, giving reassuring words to a child and then patting the child's head. Also, nonverbal messages can be used as *substitutes* for the verbal, for example, in the case of the smile that by itself indicates gratification, saying silently, "I'm happy." Some nonverbal expressions are *regulators* of the message. A good example is the act of a speaker looking over to a chart that he or she has put up and thereby directing audience attention to it. *Complementors* add meaning to a verbal message. Examples of these are bodily movements or vocal changes that reinforce what's being said: a broad grin, giggle, gasp, a wave of the hand, and variations in vocal pitch or loudness.[2]

Other Functions

Many other kinds of behavior or stimuli also communicate messages. Some of the more obvious are uniforms and insignia, clothing, cosmetics, scents and smells, posture, the way a speaker uses the rostrum, jewelry, and so forth. The physical distance maintained between speaker and listener may say something significant, as well as the way a speaker stands or makes eye contact with an audience. And silence or stillness, forms of "nonbehavior," also convey messages.

Receiving Information Nonverbally

Throughout any exchange, the speaker who sends nonverbal messages is also a *receiver* of nonverbal messages. With the language of smiles, facial and vocal expressions, eye movements, and posture changes, an audience feeds back its reactions. For example, an instructor can tell when an audience of students objects to an assignment. They will probably frown, grimace, or moan. A speaker's ability to process these messages, to interpret accurately and use this feedback, is one of the best signs of maturity in speaking. Again, experience in speaking before audiences is the path to development of the invaluable ability to "read" the messages sent back.

Whenever two human beings with the power of sight or hearing face one another, it's certain that they'll communicate *something*, even without the use of words—just by being there.

USING NONVERBAL STRATEGIES

Bodily and vocal behavior have many practical applications in speaking. Consequently, speakers should be aware of the uses of nonverbal strategies in communication.

Six Strategies

Of the many possible nonverbal "statements," here are six that make frequent and obvious appearances in support of communication.

1. "Now hear this!" Nonverbal behavior can give emphasis to a point. It may say, in effect, "You better believe it!" or "Listen carefully!" The statement may be expressed vocally by a dramatic increase in loudness. It may be the physical statement of a speaker who is moved to shake a warning finger or step closer to an audience and seize them with tight eye contact. The end result is focus, emphasis, or accent on a key thought.

"Now hear this!" is a useful message, yet some speakers are reluctant to use it. When unable or unwilling to assert themselves with this kind of request, it may be because they feel uncomfortable—too bold, possibly. But in getting a hearing for a good idea, is it too assertive to reveal one's feelings through use of a strong voice? What is *your* typical nonverbal behavior when an idea needs to be stressed? Are you free to allow your voice and body to help emphasize a point in communication?

2. "This is my feeling about it." Speakers have nonverbal ways of revealing their inclinations and attitudes. Consider, for example, a frown appearing across the forehead, showing worry or reservation of some kind; the indistinctness of voice that may show indifference; an active, loose body that seems to indicate a good and happy feeling; a speaker's late arrival, which reveals a particular personal attitude about the event; the speaker spending twice as long on main head A as on B and thereby saying something about their comparative significance.

In speaking to others, people make many nonverbal "side statements" along the way. Revealing the speakers' attitudes, these statements are parts of the total message. Do you allow yourself freedom to communicate what you feel about your topics? What personal characteristics tell audiences how you feel about topics that you discuss?

3. "Let me direct you." As I've noted, nonverbal action can guide listeners during the unfolding of the message. Without such direction, it's easy for listeners to get lost. When a speaker takes a step to the left or right, usually without conscious thought, it can show a change of idea, with the stepping providing a transition. Also, a change from one idea to another may be indicated by sharply turning the body to one side or by using certain kinds of vocal intonation. Speakers also manage transitions with hand

movements, gestures that seem to say, "On my right hand was this point, and now we turn to another, on my left."

Numbering points in a message, with one finger, then two fingers, and so forth, gives direction to an audience. Arms raised halfway, with palms open and pushed out to an audience, can say, "Hold it; don't come too fast to that conclusion." A speaker's eyes traveling to a spot on the ceiling will lead listeners' eyes in the same direction. Speakers constantly give orders to listeners, much of the time without conscious thought. In turn, listeners usually are quite responsive. Directions that are congruent with verbal content assist communication because people need guidance. They welcome it. But when directions are not consistent with the verbal message or when they detract, communication suffers, for example, when a speaker inadvertently glances at a latecomer entering the room. Listeners' eyes will follow the speaker's eyes, as will their minds.

4. "It's nice to be with you." How do speakers tell audiences that they like being with them? Certainly they can indicate their good feelings with words, but other actions may be even more appropriate and effective. People express their liking by being open, expressive, and honest. Physical signs reveal this feeling: free movement; extension of the limbs ("laying the self out," so to speak); vocal expressiveness and responsiveness; and physical closeness to the audience. Giving one's time is revealing, too. Physical restriction, distance, and short, "stingy" expressions very likely will communicate the opposite message.

What modes of behavior that show liking have you observed? What modes show the opposite?

5. **"You can trust me on this."** The topic at this point is the speaker's ethos or credibility. Statements of trust relate to liking; yet giving them a separate category here acknowledges their distinct importance in communication. What kinds of behavior seem to show trustworthiness? Expansive behavior—large movements and wide gestures—is one. A generous manner is another, a giving of the self through voice and motion, making the self available by placing the body near the audience. A calm manner is another. Frankness, too, may say, "You can trust me." A candid statement may be expressed with full, open eyes or eye movement in coordination with relevant facial expression, or a certain tilting of the head.

6. **"This is what I mean."** This statement can be conveyed in a visual aid or a specific vocal or bodily action that gives new meaning or in some way adds clarity. Included are not only the photograph that actually lets people see snowcapped Mount Fuji and the blackboard sketch of plant-cell structure but also voice changes and hand movements that help describe the shape of a winding mountain road. Included is a particular kick of a foot to indicate a move in a playground game and the rocking of folded arms to stress a point on the importance of holding and loving babies.

These, then, are six of the ways that nonverbal behavior contributes to message content. More strategies could be added to the list. You may want to do that, as you think about your nonverbal expressiveness. **Speakers who are sensitive to listeners' needs and are willing to express themselves with all available resources have an advantage.** They allow their various modes of nonverbal behavior to augment their communicative power.

It should be repeated that all of these modes of expression are not "techniques" to be applied. No, it's not like pulling tricks out of a box. These useful nonverbal actions are *communicative responses,* arising out of the speaker's feelings and thoughts on all essential features of the communicative event, on personal purpose, the speech as prepared, the feelings and beliefs of the audience, and so forth. The ideal basis for a successful presentation has two parts, discipline *and* freedom: (1) full preparation of a speech one is committed to, *and,* (2) the freedom to engage the audience in a sincere and mutually satisfying interaction of reciprocal trust.

WHAT'S RIGHT FOR YOU?

From each individual self come individual expressions of physical and vocal activity. Some people are extremely active and seem to move constantly, whereas others exhibit a minimum of action. The postures of people vary, as do head movements and styles of dress and speaking rates. What's right for you may not be for another person. The right pattern for you is the one that is a reflection of your self. It's vocal and bodily action that's consistent with who you are and the ideas you're communicating. For example, if you're one whose physical movements are extensive, you'll probably use arm gestures and other movements automatically when communicating a strong point.

There's no formula for nonverbal action that can be applied to all people. If you have a deep desire to communicate and if you feel free in speaking and are prepared and sure of your thoughts, usually the rest of you will respond naturally. One of America's outstanding speakers of the last century, Robert G. Ingersoll, said, "If you really understand what you say, emphasis, tone and gesture will take care of themselves. All these should come from inside."[3] That's sound advice. Real understanding of the message, and a desire to convey it, are indispensable in allowing the appropriate nonverbal processes to function satisfactorily.

Nonetheless, a degree of control may be called for at times. Remember that **nothing in the presentation should bring attention to itself,** since delivery is important only insofar as it assists in reaching the desired end—*communication.* Therefore, one should avoid wasteful pacing, shifting the weight from one foot to another, uncomfortable stances, window gazing, "waltzing" with the speakers' stand, toying with a pencil, anxiously attempting to conceal notes, and slouchy posture, because these types of movements send messages that conflict with the main one. They're out of sync. Some of the more common competitors in vocal behavior are speaking rates that are too rapid to be understood, voices not loud enough to be heard by all, and indistinctness in voice and articulation.

Distracting also, is action that is incongruent or incompatible with the verbal symbols. Once, some years ago, there was a dean at a California college who had a terribly annoying nonverbal habit. While sternly admonishing students and instructors for violating this rule or that, he would maintain a big wide smile. Needless to say, people did not know what he intended with his two messages, one of which contradicted the other. If nonverbal actions "drown out" words or are at odds with them, confusion probably will result.

EYE CONTACT

Eye contact performs extremely significant functions in speechmaking. **Looking at your listeners is part of talking with them.** It's a mode of address that audiences expect. Audiences anticipate eye contact and are bothered when speakers do not look at them regularly. As with humans in other situations, audiences want attention. They expect a speaker to recognize their presence, not by mechanically fixing the eyes at some point over their heads. Genuine eye contact can be accomplished only when a speaker *really wants* visual interaction.

Listeners like it when your eyes find theirs and, moreover, in the process you get information on how your message is being received. By signs like smiles, physical movements, and postures, audiences will indicate their responses to your speech. You can learn to use the information of this nonverbal feedback in adjusting your message. It may tell you that a point needs more explanation, that you are laboring a point, or that you have pleased the audience with an idea. If face-to-face communication is more effective than communication by radio or television, it's primarily because of the presence of live, reacting people who are sending messages back to speakers as they send out theirs. Able speakers react to listeners' messages by making adjustments along the way, thereby strengthening the total effort. **Learning how to use feedback should be a prime goal of all speakers.**

A word should be said on eye contact and the use of speaking notes. Excessive reliance on notes can be an obstacle to communication, because of the resulting neglect of the audience. Ample practice, along with other special effort, will help you escape this pitfall. Your notes should be brief, and for some speeches, recorded only in your head. Whenever you can get by without notes, you'll have removed one more source of potential distraction. For a reminder of suggestions on the use of notes, I urge you to turn to the Model Speaking Notes and explanation of their use in Chapter Four.

VOICE, ARTICULATION, AND PRONUNCIATION

From our overview of nonverbal elements and strategies in communication, let's go now to some relevant technical aspects: vocal characteristics, articulation, and pronunciation. This section, with its particular focus on specific functions, may be helpful in suggesting areas to deal with in a program of personal improvement in presentation of ideas. As you read along, keep in mind that *communication* is *always* the topic. In the final analysis, the goal of a speaker is to maximize efforts toward positive audience response and minimize distraction from that purpose.

Vocal Characteristics

One's voice can be analyzed from four characteristics: *pitch, volume, duration,* and *quality.*

Pitch, or frequency, as it's sometimes called, is the characteristic of a sound as it relates to the musical scale. Pitch is determined by the vibration that occurs when air is forced up from the lungs through the tightened vocal folds of the larynx (the folds are sometimes called vocal chords). The greater the number of vibrations, the higher the pitch. If you press a finger on your Adam's apple (the front point of the larynx) and say a deep "ah," you can feel a slight vibration.

Each person's voice has a certain pitch level that may be considered high, low, or medium. The pitch level depends on the *tension, length,* and *weight* of the vocal folds. It's because of differences in these three features that women's voices differ from men's. On the average, women's vocal folds are about a half-inch in length, whereas those of men average three-fourths of an inch. Then, too, female folds are stretched more tightly and weigh less.

Basically, three pitch conditions can call attention to one's speaking and interfere with communication:

1. When it's too high
2. When it's too low
3. When it lacks variety and is monotonous

Volume, or loudness, is another factor that characterizes a voice. Volume depends on the amount of a person's *breath power* and the *degree of amplification given* when the sound is resonated in the mouth, throat, and nasal chamber. Three conditions of volume give speakers difficulty:

1. When it's too great (not adjusted to room size, for example)
2. When it's too weak (especially at the ends of words or thoughts)
3. When it lacks variety

Duration is the product of two variables: (1) how long a sound lasts and (2) the length of time intervals between words, phrases, and sentences. The influence of the first variable is seen graphically in the production of vowel sounds. Extending or prolonging the vowels results in a drawn-out speech characteristic, commonly called a *drawl.* Omitting or cropping vowels results in a rapid or possibly staccato speech pattern. The overall rate of speech may reflect the speaker's personality and mood, the kind of content and the speaker's feeling for it, the speaker's emphasis (shown by pauses), the speaker's hesitations, and so forth. The three chief problems are:

1. Overlengthening of vowels
2. Eliminating or shortening of vowels
3. Inappropriate timing of intervals between words, phrases, and sentences

Quality is difficult to explain in a few words. One source defines it as "that element of voice which makes one voice recognizably different from another or which makes it possible for us, upon hearing a voice, to say to whom it belongs."[4] Quality is that vocal characteristic most like a fingerprint; no two people have identical voice quality.

Quality is determined by the nature of the sound waves produced. Some sound waves have more noise elements, and some have more harmonious or musical elements. The greater the degree of harmony, the "better" the quality, it is said. Of course, judgments on voice quality, as with other human creations, may be subjective. Five common faults are:

1. Nasality (too much resonance in the nasal passages)
2. Denasality (too little nasal resonance, for example, when one has a cold)
3. Harshness
4. Hoarseness
5. Breathiness

Articulation and Pronunciation

Articulation is the phase of speech production during which speech sounds are formed and combined. The chief articulators are the tongue, lips, teeth, and palate (roof of the mouth). In a way, they have a function similar to that of a football quarterback. The quarterback decides how to advance the ball; the articulators call the signals for controlling and directing the breath stream. For the *t* sound, the tongue tip is placed against the upper gum ridge; for an *m*, the lips are put together momentarily. One inconsistency in the football analogy is that the articulators call many more plays in a minute of speaking than a quarterback calls during an entire game, and then some! The average college student delivering a speech utters about 150 to 160 words per minute, and the average word is made up of four or five sounds. Therefore, the articulators must handle at least 600 sound units in a minute. Knowing the complexities of the articulatory process, it's easy to understand why it may break down under fatigue, emotional stress, or other influences.

Misarticulation is different from *mispronunciation*. Misarticulation is a malfunction in producing and joining sounds. It results from the inability to make particular sounds distinctly or to blend them appropriately with other sounds. Mispronunciation, however, results from the selection of the wrong sound or emphasis. It's mispronunciation when a person may be able to articulate satisfactorily but makes the wrong choice from lack of knowledge on pronunciation. By "wrong" I mean as judged by standards of acceptability of a community or region or dictionary. Therefore, a person who pronounces the word "mischievous" as "mis-*chee*-ve-us" instead of "*mis*-chuh-vus" mispronounces the word (does not have the correct pronunciation). When a person says "ny-stays" for United States, the problem is misarticulation, for the correct pronunciation is well known.

Standards and customs concerning articulation may vary. Acceptable articulation in one region or social environment may be unacceptable elsewhere. Usually, an occasion marked by a high level of formality calls for more careful articulation. Successful speakers accommodate their behavior to the character of the environment, often automatically and without conscious control. Just as speakers adapt their ideas to audiences and occasions, they want also to adapt their behavior and their modes of utterance. They seek unity or identification with listeners where they find them. **Responding to situations, effective**

speakers make whatever adjustments personal standards and codes, predispositions, and collected habits will allow.

The convention of "sociability in speaking" is applicable here. Most effective speakers are *sociable,* that is, willing to make some kind of adaptation to an occasion's demands. A young person moving from Iowa to Texas probably doesn't plan on learning to say "y'all," but after a period of living in Texas among Texans, he or she very likely will do so. A person changes speech to fit in, to adjust to surroundings. Perhaps you would never pronounce *horse* "hoss" or *iron* "*eye*un," but if you lived in certain parts of the East or South for a time, you just might adopt these pronunciations. *The NBC Handbook of Pronunciation* recognizes varying standards: "Americans have never consented to have 'correct' pronunciation laid down for them by a government academy, as is done in several other nations." The handbook's advice to broadcasters, suggesting variation according to audience, is well taken for all who are likely to find themselves as speakers before different types of audiences, not broadcasters alone.

> *The pronunciation is best which is most readily understood, and that pronunciation is most readily understood which is used by most people. Thus a standard of pronunciation for the American radio and television broadcaster is reasonably based upon the speech heard and used by the audience that the broadcaster reaches. This means that the broadcaster would use the pronunciation that is spoken by the educated people of the area served by the station. If the station is a local one, the broadcaster would do well to pronounce*

words as the educated people of his community pronounce them. Otherwise he might be difficult to comprehend and might even alienate a part of his audience.[5]

Again, this is the concept of sociability, people finding ways to interact successfully. It's good advice for communicators in all situations.

Be true to yourself and to your personal standards, yet at the same time, accept and profit from your tendency to be "sociable" with your various audiences.

Particular Problems

For most of us, good pronunciation and articulation require conscious attention. Knowing that, we who have grown up using English can appreciate the great undertaking of non-native speakers to be clear and correct in their daily use of this challenging language, and listeners should be patient with them.

Among common reasons for articulation and pronunciation problems are early learning, habit, carelessness, lack of knowledge, and occasionally, indifference. People become accustomed to using certain patterns and forms, frequently without being aware of it. Children learn to speak by listening to others. As they adopt available usages and fuse them with their personalities, they develop personal patterns of expression. These patterns may have few faults, or they may be sprinkled with unacceptable practices.

When one says *nucular* for *nuclear, reconize* for *recognize, aks* for *ask,* or *fer* for *for,* a distraction is likely to occur in many situations, with a probable loss in communication. Since such usages are prevalent, it's possible that there are sounds or words of yours that distract some audiences. If so, can you identify them? Here are some specific questions.

1.   In given situations, do you ever create a possible distraction by *substituting* one sound for another?

d for *th*	*dat* for *that, da* for *the, dis* for *this*
d for *t*	*liddle* for *little, starded* for *started*
u for *aw*	*yur* for *your*
uh for *oo*	*tuhday* for *today, ought tuh* for *ought to, yuh* for *you*
uh for *o*	*winduh* for *window, yelluh* for *yellow*
eh for *a*	*pel* for *pail*
ih for *uh*	*jist* for *just*
ih for *eh*	*git* for *get*
in for *ing*	*runnin* for *running*

2.   Do you ever *insert* extra sounds?

ath-*uh*-lete *(athlete)*	barbar-*i*-ous *(barbarous)*
Ap-*uh*-ril *(April)*	across*t* *(across)*
fil-*uh*m *(film)*	e*k*scape *(escape)*

3. Do you ever *omit* certain sounds?

em *(them)*	er *(her)*
hep *(help)*	kep *(kept)*
slep *(slept)*	libary *(library)*
pitcher *(picture)*	guvment *(government)*
cross *(across)*	thurly *(thoroughly)*
prolly *(probably)*	worl *(world)*
plitical *(political)*	acshly *(actually)*

4. Do you ever *misplace* an accent?

the-*a*-ter (*the*-a-ter)	pre-*fer*-able (*pref*-er-a-ble)
im-*pie*-ous (*im*-pi-ous)	com-*pair*-a-ble (*com*-par-a-ble)
re-*spite* (*res*-pit)	*ho*tel (ho-*tel*)

5. Are you ever *indistinct* as you express sentences? Indistinctness of articulation and incorrectness are more apparent when observed in continuous speaking. Perhaps you've heard expressions similar to the following. Do you find any such patterns in your speech?

Jeet?	Did you eat?
Wutchadoonigh?	What are you doing tonight?
Ahm gunna cuz ah hafta.	I am going to because I have to.

6. Have you ever made a formal analysis of your pronunciation and articulation? Do you have speaking habits (other than those that require specialized attention, such as stuttering) that call attention to themselves? This may be the time to try an analysis. Besides helping you to spot and correct problems, an analysis can increase your awareness of your patterns in articulation and pronunciation. Start by tape-recording a paragraph from a magazine or newspaper. As you play it back, write down any words or phrases needing improvement or correction. Then make specific suggestions for improvement under the headings of *Voice* and *Articulation-Pronunciation.* Here's a sample:

Voice

1. Needs more variety, should bring out the full color of my ideas
2. In too much of a hurry, should take time to express the meaning

Articulation–Pronunciation

1. Substitutions: *jist* (just), *lenth* (length), *yer* (your), *becuz* (because)
2. Additions: *acrosst* (across)
3. Omission: *kep* (kept), *probly* (probably)
4. Misplaced accents: luh-*ment*-uh-ble (*lam*-en-tuh-ble)

7. Would you like to practice refining your pronunciation? What about the words in the following list? Do you pronounce all of them correctly? Are there troublesome words that you would add to the list? You might try writing sentences in which you include the words most difficult for you to pronounce. With the use of a dictionary, spell them according to sound. Review the exercise daily, and be ready to read it, should the instructor call on you.

acquiesce	hiccough
adversary	human
agile	infamous
alacrity	inference
arduous	insurance
ascetic	integral
ask	irrevocable
bade	Italian
baptize	library
cello	maintenance
cement	municipal
chaste	naive
chic	novice
copious	nuptial
corps	orgy
dearth	propitious
decadent	recess
defense	rendezvous
detail	repertoire
discretion	saga
docile	salmon
efficacy	schizophrenia
emaciate	scion
epitome	servile
et cetera	solace
exquisite	subtle
gala	suite
genuine	superfluous
gesture	tyrannical
grievous	vehement
gross	wane
hearth	wreak
height	zoology

8. Would you like to practice sharpening your articulation? Each of the following sentences contains a selected consonant sound in all three possible positions, at the beginning of the word (initial position), in the middle of a word (medial position), and at the end of a word (final position). Use the sentences for practice in improvement of your speaking, giving special attention to careful articulation of the consonants.

1. Paul prepared to clip the paper tape.
2. The drab ebony board was burned above the neighbor's lab.
3. Lemons make Tom remember many moments of gloom.
4. One never knows how many cannons are necessary.
5. Running ink I think is instinctive.
6. Peter takes teeter-tottering too tensely to get fun out of it.
7. Heed Dora's words, Edward, and do not demand the guarded hoard.
8. An unthoughtful but enthusiastic thinker in math gave baby Thelma a bath.
9. The boy could not bathe because his father put the leather there.
10. Fifty-five and one-half fifes filled Phil's safe.
11. "Very lovely voice," averred Ev from above.
12. Kirkwood carried the cake quickly and cackled at the cook.
13. Glenna's toes wiggled as she giggled at the whirligig.
14. Save all excess sassafras, sister.
15. Because of Zeb's raising pigs, the zebra was lazy.
16. Should a ration of sugar, hash, or shoe polish be assured?
17. Jean and Jacques (who pronounce their names the French way) had a vision of the treasure of rouge put in the garage by a beige measurer.
18. Chimpanzees lurched in bunches by the church but did not chortle much.
19. George jumped over Roger to juggle the gauge.
20. Which whippersnapper shall I whip somewhere on the pinwheel?
21. Walter, overweight but unworried, ate Wilma's sandwich willfully.
22. Yes, you can make W's brilliantly.
23. The terrible rapids passed the bar very readily.
24. Lazy Lola laughed and trilled on the hill and in the dale.
25. The high-handed hermit heaved the headhunter uphill.

A PROGRAM OF IMPROVEMENT

What should you do if a study of your vocal and articulation–pronunciation patterns indicates serious faults? First consult your speech instructor, who may have suggestions. What you consider faults really may not interfere with your communication. On the other hand, if your problem needs attention, perhaps a program of correction can be set up for you, or you can take a special course in vocal improvement. **Should you seek appropriate guidance and follow it earnestly, your chances for improvement are great.**

Above all, the main question to ask about bodily and vocal action in speech communication has to do with utility: What kind of contribution do my voice and body make as I interact with others? Do they add positively to message content? Are they supportive of verbal expression? As you continue to develop awareness of your vocal characteristics, check on congruence to thought. For example, overly soft vocal expression may contradict a verbal statement intended to describe the noise and clamor of a political convention. Or a jerky speech pattern may conflict with an explanation of rhythm in lyric poetry. **If there's any secret ingredient in delivery, it's the freedom to express yourself in accordance with your thoughts, your purpose, and the interpersonal conditions of the occasion.**

What Do You Want for Yourself?

Let's take the long-range view for a minute and think ahead a few years. Faulty expression, from carelessness, bad habits, or indifference, may not be a detriment to communication in the early years of one's life, when the guiding standard is that of a limited group, when others don't judge all that much. But then one moves on to other groups, those of college and new social scenes. And ahead lies a career, more training, and the association of new people. It's at this time that good speech starts to make a real difference. **In the majority of occupations, advancement depends considerably on skill in oral communication.** At a certain rung on the ladder of life, one begins to realize the importance of speaking more appropriately and clearly. It may happen to you when you apply for a job, when you're up for a promotion, or when you're selected to represent your employer in some important way.

Ask the big question: What do you want for yourself? What do you want to accomplish? You may be able to accomplish more than you presently realize, and it's time to make preparations for the future. **In addition to preparing yourself in your major field, whatever your choice, also check your speech habits.** Now is the time to start.

REHEARSAL

Let's get back to your work in the speech class and your next extemporaneous speaking experience there. After thoroughly preparing the basic content of the speech and the outline, make definite preparations for the moment of presentation by following these steps in rehearsal.

1.   **Read the outline aloud several times, fixing the main ideas in your head.** Read it through each time without stopping. Your immediate purpose is to grasp the whole speech, the main ideas and their relationships. You might be astonished to know the number of people who give speeches without really appreciating the full meaning of their thoughts.

2.   **Find a vacant classroom and practice the entire speech with the aid of the outline, consulting it as frequently as necessary.** Once again, go right through and do not stop. Repeat the process at least twice. Your purpose at this point is to fix the ideas in your mind and become acquainted with words and other modes of expression that may be useful in the final delivery.

3.   **After sufficient practice with the full outline, prepare speaking notes, using a three-by-five-inch card or small piece of paper.** See Chapter Four on preparation of these notes. At this point, give the speech two or three times with the support of speaking notes only (see Chapter Four). At the end of each rehearsal, check the full outline to see if you have omitted any significant details. Perhaps a friend will be willing to listen to a rehearsal and give reactions.

4.   **Put the outline away; then practice with or without notes to the point of being able to give the speech freely and effectively.**

Right now it would be a good idea for you to review the section in Chapter Three on using the extemporaneous mode. As you do that, recall that conversational ease depends on mastery of ideas *and* form. The guiding philosophy is like that of Bill Evans, the great jazz pianist who attributed success in music to a creative combination of "discipline and freedom."

And when it's your turn to speak, move to the front of the room confidently, in a manner that fits the occasion and your purpose in speaking. Remember that your message begins the moment you leave your seat. As you find your position before the audience, take a second or two to get set, and begin talking with self-assurance.

MATURITY AS A COMMUNICATOR

Finally, let's tie idea, attitude, and personal choice to the act of presenting a speech. It's in giving the speech that integration of all relevant elements occurs. Because speech communication involves the total self, it follows that **what a speaker is and what a speaker does help determine effectiveness in delivering the message.** What should *you* be and what should *you* do to be successful? Much may depend on your thoughts, commitment, and manner—on your maturity as a communicator.

Anyone who is able eventually to answer yes to the following four questions is approaching maturity in speaking to others.

1.   Can you give the welfare of your audience first priority? Think of what they need from you. First, they need a chance to know you. Be open with them and sociable, in your unique way. Your interest in them will generate interest in your ideas and bring about identification of the audience with you and your message. Honesty, sincerity, and respect for others are elements of good delivery. In the process of achieving identification, audiences need to be attended to and shown that you have a real interest in creating meaning with them.

In a way, a speaker is like a guide taking people on a tour of ideas. Effective vocal and physical action can help a speaker be the good guide who escorts a group over the course of thought. The welfare of the people "on the tour" should be a speaker's primary consideration.

2.   Do you have something you want to say? Ideas coupled with a desire to convey them are essential to good delivery. The famous speaker Booker T. Washington expressed strong conviction on this point.

I do not believe that one should speak unless, down deep in his heart, he feels convinced that he has a message to deliver. When one feels, from the bottom of his feet to the top of his head, that he has something to say that is going to help some individual or some cause, then let him say it.[6]

Your subject matter and how you feel about it will influence the manner in which you express it. Good delivery is a natural response to a yearning to communicate ideas. Content and delivery are "of one cloth."

3.   Are you willing to make a personal investment? Will you let personality, body, and voice speak for you? Can you allow yourself to relate conversationally to the audience? You may be amazed at how effective you can be when you're able to free yourself. One who gives gets something in return; **your willingness to invest yourself in the speaking situation can bring truly satisfying rewards.**

On the act of making a personal investment, Booker T. Washington wrote, "I always make it a rule to make especial preparation for each separate audience. No two audiences are exactly alike. It is my aim to reach and talk to the heart of each individual audience, taking it into my confidence very much as I would a person."[7] Yes, talk as you would to a person. Have trust. Give of yourself.

4. Can you center your efforts on the task of communication? At the moment of delivery, your attention should be on accomplishing your purpose, not correcting your speech problems. Your preparation and practice are over for now. Up to this point in the process, your involvement has been a *private,* largely *intra*personal experience. Now begins the *public,* directly *inter*personal phase. Facing the audience, your program of self-improvement in speaking is suspended for the time being. Your purpose now is *communication.* Work on your problems, whatever they may be, at other times and during rehearsals, for they are your problems, not your listeners'. So put them aside for the duration of the talk, while you direct your energy toward getting a hearing for your ideas.

LOOKING BACK

Giving the speech is the final phase in identifying with an audience. Self-knowledge and self-acceptance are basic to effective use of vocal and bodily behaviors in this process. These behaviors, adding significantly to the message, vary in mode from person to person.

1. Numerous kinds of nonverbal statements of the voice and body contribute to communication.

2. Eye contact is vital to success in speech communication.

3. Attributes of the voice and body that function in communication, along with articulation and pronunciation, can be improved.

4. Effectiveness in giving speeches relates to maturity and involves keeping audience welfare uppermost in mind, having something that you want to say, making a personal investment, and maintaining one's focus on the task of communication.

The advice, then, is to start with a body of well-conceived thought, carefully selected, organized, and developed. Then extend yourself to communicate it with interpersonal awareness, allowing your ideas, words, body, and voice to work naturally and harmoniously together.

NOTES

1. See James Albert Winans, *Public Speaking,* rev. ed. (New York: Century, 1923), 31.

2. See Ronald B. Adler, Lawrence B. Rosenfeld, and Neil Towne, *Interplay: The Process of Interpersonal Communication,* 5th ed. (Fort Worth: Harcourt Brace Jovanovich, 1992).

3. C. P. Farrell, ed., *The Works of Robert G. Ingersoll,* Dresden ed. (New York: Dresden, 1900), 594.

4. Roy C. McCall and Herman Cohen, *Fundamentals of Speech,* 2d ed. (New York: Macmillan, 1963), 182.

5. Thomas Lee Crowell, Jr., *The NBC Handbook of Pronunciation,* 2d ed. (New York: Crowell, 1963), ix.

6. Booker T. Washington, *Up From Slavery: An Autobiography* (New York: A. L. Burt, 1901), 243.

7. Ibid., 214.

APPLICATIONS IV

DISCUSSING IN SMALL GROUPS

13

CHAPTER 13

DISCUSSING
IN SMALL GROUPS

Some matters require group communication. That's what these two people found.

He: What should we do about Tabby? At fourteen years, she's about lived all her nine lives.

She: Yes, she's barely able to walk, but we can't just put her to sleep.

He: Maybe we should.

She: But others in the family wouldn't agree to that.

He: Then we'd better all get together and discuss it.

She: Yes, we should.

Thus another discussion group is formed, from a need to hear the views of all concerned. That's what this chapter is about: **people seeking answers or solutions in small group interaction.**

TALKING TOGETHER

Most groups are casual and seem to form without planning: Some students sit around a table in the Student Union and talk; two or three professors drop by a colleague's office to say hello and ask how the book is coming along. We are social animals. We need and enjoy the interaction provided by groups and, it seems, can't get along without it.

Other groups are planned and scheduled for a definite purpose: a nursery school board, a student council, a therapy group, a panel for a class project, and innumerable kinds of committees.

Our society could not function without people talking together. That's a main theme of this book, and it applies to discussion as well as public speaking. Group communication is about one of the necessary interactions of people. It's the process of discussion that's often used to discover answers to people's problems.

A group of people acting together and pooling their mental resources and feelings frequently can accomplish goals that are impossible to attain by individual action. Their decision may be superior to an individual's. Moreover, when directly involved, people are more likely to accept and carry out a decision.

Discussion allows for the expression of multiple points of view. A group working together rather than as individuals may be able to discover intelligent and creative answers to needs, and may do better in distinguishing between reliable and unreliable options.

The general goals of small group discussion are the same as those of other forms of speech communication: (1) to further personal and social growth and (2) to get things done. The balance of this chapter explains the process of group discussion, with an understanding of both the interpersonal and the problem-solving dimensions. The purpose is to increase your effectiveness in small groups.

> *Sometimes the best way to solve a problem is to talk it over with others.*
>
> *Heard at a gathering of club leaders*

GOAL: PERSONAL AND SOCIAL GROWTH

Starting at birth, we become involved with many clusters of people. In relating to them, we grow and learn. Most interaction in these groups is informal and spontaneous, without plan or preparation. The family is the primary group, of course, but also included are school friends, neighbors, children who come to play, and many others. Through these associations in the formative years, we develop a self. **We shape a personal identity by relating to others and experiencing reflections of our behavior and being.** Others act as mirrors, feeding back information that we use in self-development. Growing is a process of selecting and maintaining ways of being and refining roles that seem useful and congruent to us in our cultural environment. There is much trial and error in the process. Relationships in all these casual groups are influential in the development of our character, outlooks on life, codes of ethics, values, a sense of curiosity, courage, a scholarly attitude, personal charm, wit, and scores of other individual attributes; some are strengths; some need improvement. All are parts of an identity.

In the growth process, we also develop attributes in the social art of relating interpersonally. These are the social strategies of pleasing others, hiding fears, getting sympathy, praising and accepting praise, showing affection, fighting back or retreating when threatened, playing, and so forth. For most people, lessons of social interaction are primarily positive and promote constructive personal and social ends. They facilitate our getting along in this world of people and their great diversity. But of course, all of us can list personal weaknesses and blind spots in interpersonal dealings, some of which we know too well. For example, we can learn how to be unkind—to hurt by withholding love and attention, to condemn unfairly, to be prejudiced, to torment, and to suppress or reject. Fortunately, however, it's never too late to open our minds and grow. Others help in this. Constructive interaction provides an opportunity for personal and social growth, finding security and maturity in relating.

GOAL: TO GET THINGS DONE

While enhancing personal and social development, **small group discussion also provides a practical means of doing a job.** A problem needs solving, and people put their heads together to see what they can do about it. Or they need to decide among alternatives. Discussion remains vital in our society, despite the occasional overreliance on authoritarian judgment or advice created by computers. Thus, all over the country groups may be found discussing social issues in classrooms, sales campaigns in business offices, forest preservation on television, family vacation plans in kitchens or living rooms, nurses' problems in hospital conference rooms, tax measures in legislative committee chambers, and so forth. On and on the discussion goes. And it works!

THE SUBJECT

Obviously, in day-to-day affairs, the selection of problems for discussion poses no difficulty, for problems pop up continually. But in a training situation, such as this class, in which there may be no immediate or pressing concern to motivate a meeting, a subject must be sought. In class, subject selection will be one of the first steps in planning, along with choosing a person to lead the group.

Selecting a Subject

How do groups in a speech class decide on a subject for discussion? Most of them start by talking about it, bringing up one subject after the other. Of course they need to keep in mind their interests, time constraints, and the expectations of their audience, if they will be discussing before an audience. Some groups have success with brainstorming.

Brainstorming   Using this method to turn up subjects requires much open-mindedness from the participants. In the brainstorming process, group members are encouraged to come forth with all possible subjects—*any and all*—offering them freely and without another's saying, "Oh, no, that's a bad one!" The more subjects named, the better. A volunteer will write down every subject named. The idea is to get a great variety "on the table," before imposing judgment on any. Often, from such innovative freedom and uncritical attitude come new and promising ideas.

Criteria for Subject Selection   Regardless of the method of discovery employed, the moment comes when the final selection of one subject must be made. Then criteria must be applied. These are questions to be asked.

1. **Is the subject meaningful and interesting to all group participants?** Is it sufficiently relevant and significant to involve the people in your group? Even though the class is a training situation, try to maintain

real-life conditions by choosing a subject that has immediacy to all members, an area that touches their lives. If you plan to conduct your discussion before an audience, you'll want to consider them, too, as you decide on a subject. What of importance is happening in the school, community, state, nation, or world at this time? Is there a question of contemporary interest that's worthy of investigation and consideration? What problems now face people in the class, the student body, or the city? Is there a national matter of special significance to you?

2. Is the subject one with which you can increase your familiarity? Can you learn more about it? To insure a worthwhile discussion, it's necessary to investigate, to find new information; it therefore is essential also to know if new information is available. You should survey possible sources of material before settling on your subject. What library material can you count on? Are other resources available?

3. Is the subject one with which you can become sufficiently knowledgeable in a limited time? Ordinarily you don't have a long period of time in which to prepare for a discussion. In class, a group will have only a few days to get ready. If you find that certain needed materials on your subject will not be available for at least two weeks, your only alternative is to choose another subject. Or if adequate exploration seems likely to take too long and cause last-minute pressure in preparation, a change of subject seems necessary.

4. Is the subject appropriate for the occasion? In class, the setting usually remains the same unless a hypothetical situation is set up. If you plan a discussion for presentation in another setting, you will be expected to adhere to the demands of that occasion, just as you would for any oral presentation. Find out what is expected of you, exactly how much time your group has, and all pertinent details about the purpose and plans for the meeting, including how the group's part relates to other scheduled events.

Narrowing the Subject to a Topic

Take a close look at your subject and decide if it's too broad to be treated in the available time. How much time has been allowed for your group's discussion? Do you have the full period, or has the instructor reserved a few minutes at the end of the hour for evaluation? Has the instructor planned for a second discussion group to precede or follow yours? Scale your scope according to time available. You may find that you need to select a portion or division of a subject as your area for consideration. If necessary, review Chapter Three at this time, for reminders on narrowing subjects.

WORDING THE QUESTION

The group should word the discussion question to indicate the scope of the discussion and suggest a purpose.

Criteria for Wording the Question

1. Will the question, as worded, help get the discussion off to a good start? Something like a speech thesis, the question should contain one idea and be brief and clear. Unlike many theses, it's usually stated in the form of a question. A question suggests that the matter is up for discussion and unsolved at the present time; it's open for consideration.

2. Is the question stated fairly, without prejudice or bias for a particular point of view? An unfair question implies that the group already has decided on the answer or solution. With such a question, members cannot talk impartially, for they're prejudiced from the beginning. This violates the basic characteristic of much small group discussion: an open-minded, intelligent search for an answer or solution to an important problem. The italicized words in the following question seem prejudiced:

> How can teenage mothers be taught *to provide better care for their babies?*

Could a group in your class carry on an impartial search for a solution to this problem? Not likely. "Better" than what? The question makes a biased assumption, and a full hour could be spent in debate over the words at issue. These questions also are not worded fairly:

> Should the *useless* system of giving final examinations be abolished?

> What can be done to improve our *inadequate* immigration policy?

3. Is the question stated in a way to avoid unnecessary debate? You should word the question in a way that will avoid setting up sides. If a discussion results in one side upholding the *con* and another side the *pro,* you're in debate, not discussion: The fault often lies in the wording of the question. Notice how these sentences promote debate rather than cooperative problem solving:

> Should the national government provide health care for all citizens?

> Should all students be taxed to support the programs of student government?

> Should speech communication be a required course?

Instead of discarding them, let's restate each question in a way to encourage more cooperative discussion.

> How can the nation's health-care needs be met?

> What are the students' responsibilities in funding student government programs?

> What can be done to insure competence in oral communication for all students?

4. Would the question best be worded as an inquiry into fact, value, or policy? Depending on the nature of the subject and the group's goals, questions are worded ordinarily to set up discussions that seek factual information, assessment of value, or determination of policy. Discussion problems can thus be classified as questions of *fact, value,* or *policy.* The first type involves a search for information regarding present conditions, actual accomplishments, historical facts, definitions, requirements, and so forth. The second evaluates a condition, program, idea, or course of action, asking if something is good, beneficial, or effective. The third, policy, is perhaps the most commonly used in speech communication classes. With this type of question, the purpose is to work out a suitable policy or plan for solving the problem at hand. In these three classifications, you will notice a similarity to the types of theses in persuasion, as examined in Chapter Eight.

The following questions illustrate the three types of discussion questions.

Fact

1. What is the meaning of the term *postmodernism?*
2. Are successful group leaders necessarily authoritarian?
3. What kinds of financial aid are available to students on this campus?

Value

1. What are advantages of the semester system over other systems?
2. How important are sales taxes in the economy of our state?
3. What are benefits of trust in communication?

Policy

1. Can a practical and fair alternative to the jury system be found?
2. How should the competence of teachers in public schools be measured?
3. How can a person handle fear in a speaking situation?

You'll notice from these examples that discussion questions ordinarily deal with one of two areas of concern. First is the one that primarily seems to be personal and social, as in the question on trust in communication. This area focuses on topics of self and interpersonal relationships. The second bears on broader community issues, such as student affairs, poverty, pollution, civil rights, and crime; examples of these are the questions on sales taxes and teachers' competence. Because both types of questions can lead to useful discussion, the choice will depend on your interests, the instructor's guidelines, audience interests, available time, and the nature of the occasion.

In summary, these are the marks of a good discussion question.

1. Centered on one idea
2. Brief

3. Worded clearly
4. Usually worded in the form of a question
5. Worded fairly
6. Designed to encourage discussion
7. Focused on an inquiry into fact, value, or policy

The Case Method

Another way to motivate discussion is through use of the case method. It's sometimes superior to the question method because participants are able immediately to involve themselves in a realistic narrative that somehow bears on their present concerns. The case may be prepared by students or the instructor, by anyone who has particular skill in setting up a problem in a short narrative. This is an example:

> *Weston College, where Joe is a sophomore, follows the honor system. Upon entry, students sign a pledge that they will not cheat on examinations or in the preparation of any assignment and that they will report all observed violations to a student board. Students judged by the board to be nonobservant of the code may be recommended to the Dean for dismissal from school.*
>
> *On Wednesday, during a history examination, Joe saw Sue use notes, a practice disallowed in this examination. The violation was clear and certain. Joe recalls signing the honor pledge, and thinks of Sue's predicament: Sue is on academic probation, and without a high grade in history, she will flunk out of school. That she knows. Should she be unsuccessful at Weston, her father has vowed to cut off any further support for her education.*
>
> *Joe is also under parental pressure to succeed at Weston.*
> *What kind of problem does Joe face? What should he do about it?*

ORGANIZING THE DISCUSSION

How does a discussion unfold? What system or order should be followed? For questions of *value* or *fact,* the organization should be quite simple. What order does good sense prescribe? To illustrate, in discussing the question "What are advantages of the semester system over other systems?" the following six questions might provide the needed structure:

1. How are we to define "semester"?
2. What are other options?
3. Are there educational advantages to the semester system?
4. Are there economic advantages?
5. Are there advantages of convenience to persons involved?
6. Are there other advantages?

A conclusion would follow, including a summary and appropriate final comments, perhaps suggestions for further study or plans of action.

The Dewey Pattern

The handling of *policy* questions requires an explicit design, such as the practical system developed from philosopher John Dewey's pattern for reflective thinking. Following is an interpretation of that system, showing its use in organizing a small group discussion.

   1.   Recognition of a problem. Under capable leadership, to be discussed later, a group will begin by acknowledging the existence of a condition or question that requires attention, a remedy or answer. The members will recognize that problem facing them, determining why it ought to be addressed.

   2.   Analysis of the problem. Next the group will examine essential aspects of the problem that they've chosen to explore. They'll define basic and relevant terms. They'll discuss the extent of the problem, citing pertinent ramifications, for example, economic, educational, social, and practical issues. Also, they'll acknowledge limitations on the scope of their concern; for example, in discussing child abuse, they would limit their discussion to an agreed-upon age group. Two additional aspects ordinarily included in the analysis are causes and effects of the problem.

   3.   Naming of possible solutions. At this point, often over halfway through the discussion, the group will begin to name ways to meet the condition under consideration. This is another chore that may call for brainstorming. To the extent that time allows, the **group members ought to encourage each other's freedom and creativity** in bringing forth numerous solutions, and to withhold criticism for the moment.

   4.   Selection of a satisfactory solution. Then the time comes to propose a workable and promising solution, the *one that seems capable of meeting the need as members have laid it out.* Drawing from those put forth earlier, they may select a solution as is, or they may choose to combine two or more of those named. In the process of coming to the best solution, the membership will use agreed-upon criteria for determining the solution, standards or tests that a solution must meet. Setting up criteria for a solution is like saying, "These are the standards of merit—the values, we agree to use in weighing any proposed solution." For example, a group might decide that any solution to population control must be (1) economically feasible, (2) trustworthy, (3) safe to use, and so on. Criteria are used to judge the acceptability of proposed solutions.

   5.   Implementation of the solution. The job isn't done until the group has devised a specific plan and schedule for putting their chosen solution into effect. "What action shall we take?" is the question to answer. The action taken will depend on the locus of the problem, where it's centered: on campus? downtown? in Washington, D.C.?

   Although implementation of a well-conceived solution should not be curbed in any way, a group must face up to possible limitations. Costs may limit implementation of some solutions. Too, power may be a factor, that is, the extent of the group's influence. Any group of people can only do so much. That's realistic, and yet, they can try, if a fair chance of success seems to exist.

Adapting Dewey to the Four-Part Method

You can accommodate the Dewey discussion pattern to the familiar four-part method for speaking, the one detailed in Chapters Three through Seven. That is, the public speaking outline will work as an organizer for small group discussion. The following outline is an adaptation of Dewey's steps for reflective thinking to the standard speaking formula.

Introduction
(Often presented by the leader)

 I. The need
 II. General background

The Specific Question
(statement of the problem as presently visualized)
Body

 I. Analysis of the problem
  A. Defining, determining the extent of the problem, limiting
  B. Citing causes and effects
 II. Naming of possible solutions

Conclusion

 I. Selection of a satisfactory solution
  A. Testing proposals with criteria
  B. Determining a single solution
 II. Implementation of the solution

A framework of some sort is needed to ensure adequate discussion, but it should be *flexible* and a *general* guide only. **Room for creative thinking and spontaneity must be provided.** Actually, a general outline of steps to take in treating a question, when used intelligently, can *add* to freedom of thought. A group of people who are confident in knowing "where they are" and how to get back should they wander, can feel free to explore a bit.

An Alternate Form

One alternative to Dewey's framework is the Ideal Solution Form, a design tested successfully by discussion researcher Carl E. Larson.[1] If such a system seems more fitting for your needs, you might try it. It's based on questions:

 1. Are we all agreed on the nature of the problem?
 2. What would be the ideal solution from the point of view of all parties involved in the problem?

3. What conditions within the problem could be changed so that the ideal solution might be achieved?

4. Of the solutions available to us, which one best approximates the ideal solution?

The Ideal Solution Form seems especially suited to the discussion of a problem posed by a case study. As you read the following case (an actual experience) visualize using this method.

> *About two-thirds of the way through the summer quarter, on August 23, a speech class decided that it would suit their personal schedules best if their final exam were held on the last regular day of class, September 3, instead of on Friday, September 10, the last day of finals' week. The change in schedule would give most people at least two more days for needed rest and relaxation before registration for the fall quarter on September 27. Some people had other problems, too, which would be solved by the change.*
>
> *Thus, the group decided on the change, and individuals arranged their work and vacation plans accordingly. To compensate for loss of class time, the class met an extra five or ten minutes on several regular class days.*
>
> *But on September 1, the Dean sent a strong memorandum to all faculty, announcing that all final exams were to be held as scheduled, in accordance with college policy, and that he did not anticipate making exceptions.*
>
> *At this stage, whose problem is it—the instructor's or the entire group's? Should the Dean's order be challenged? What should be done?*

DETERMINING THE STRATEGIC FORMAT

Here I use the terms "format" or "discussion plan" to distinguish specific variations from the general frameworks or systems that I have been explaining. A variety of formats is available to discussion groups. Some are rather formal, while others are less structured. Some demand much of the leader, while others give the members a greater burden. Some require a "guest expert," while others depend solely on the original group. The format you use should provide the best opportunity for achieving group goals.

A number of informal formats are used frequently by leaders of businesses, churches, and clubs to solve internal problems of their organizations or to seek enlightenment on a topic. These are *private* discussions because the officers or executives deliberate among themselves, without an audience. Different names are often attached to these: conferences, roundtables, committee meetings, councils, or simply meetings.

Three very useful formats for *public* discussion, before audiences, are the panel, the symposium, and the lecture-panel.

The Panel

The panel is probably what most people have in mind when they think of public group discussion. The participants assemble before an audience, in positions that will allow visual and oral contact with the audience and among the group. This may be accomplished by arranging the chairs in a semicircle or halfway around a table. The leader sits in a central position in view of the audience and panel members.

The panel is usually composed of four to seven persons, who under the guidance of a leader, discuss a question in an orderly fashion. There are no set speeches with this format. Each person taking part has studied the question carefully and may make contributions freely, based on adequate preparation. This is not to say that a person may talk of anything at any time. For the benefit of all concerned, remarks should be pertinent to what's being discussed at a given moment. To help the group stay on the point, the leader has an outline as a constant reminder of their overall plan. The outline, prepared in prediscussion consultation with all members of the group, is a layout of the probable movement of the discussion. It's based on the Dewey pattern, the standard four-part formula, the Ideal Solution Form, or some other system.

A word of advice may be helpful here. Remember that the outline should be an assistant, not a dictator. Use it; let it help you, but don't allow it to handcuff you. You know how an outline functions in individual speaking. Occasionally you change some part of the speech as you are speaking. You omit a certain example or add one. You think of a good statistic on the spur of the moment and decide to include it. You make adjustments because the situation seems to demand changes. Fresh thinking increases effectiveness. Considerably more freedom is found in group discussion. **Effective participants follow a basic structure but permit promising modifications along the way.**

A Model Panel Discussion

Let's illustrate one panel's experience. It was the spring term, and the 9:00 speech communication class was involved in setting up panels for group discussion. One group was comprised of Anne, James, Julie, Jennifer, and Rick. As luck would have it, they were to be the first to present their discussion before the class—and in just eight days. At their first meeting, the group considered possible topics and the matter of leadership. After a brainstorming session, three subjects emerged: safety in air travel, drug rehabilitation, and campus attitudes. Eventually, they arrived at the decision to focus on a local topic. The one that they liked very much had to do with what they perceived as a kind of individualism on campus, a lack of community spirit. They named it "Campus Narcissism." Jennifer, who had shown great interest in the topic, as well as considerable knowledge of it, was chosen as leader.

At this point, Julie and Rick declared that they had to go to work. But before breaking up, the members assigned themselves the task of exploring the topic on their own for a couple of days. They would meet again

on Wednesday. They did meet on Wednesday, at which time they shared observations and findings, drafted a loose tentative structure for the discussion, and developed plans for conducting research on the topic. For the next few days, the members observed campus behavior in various settings; interviewed students, faculty, and administrators; read selected college and university newspapers as well as the campus paper; made telephone calls to people on other college campuses; and read available library material on the topic and related issues. A day before their scheduled presentation, they held a long session to make final plans. At the end of that meeting, they felt ready. They were confident in their knowledge of relevant material, had a clear sense of purpose and a workable, flexible outline that would allow for useful spontaneity and creativity, to keep the exchange fresh and real.

As indicated on the left in the following layout, the group chose the Dewey pattern of problem solving. On the right is a sketch of the discussion, an abstract of the way it unfolded before the class. Many nuances of the interaction are omitted, as well as finer points of Jennifer's leadership.

I.   Recognition of a problem
     A.   The need

Jennifer introduced members and told how her group had come to the topic. Observations had shown them that the campus lacked a sense of community.

B. General background

The problem was quite serious, as they saw it. The student body was a population of groups and cliques, with very distinct demographic separations, Jennifer reported. Anne agreed, citing an example. Rick added an example. James and Julie told of how the condition created an unpleasant and somewhat depressive campus climate.

C. The specific question

"So here's the question we're faced with," announced Jennifer. "What can be done to create a community here?"

II. Analysis of the problem
    A. Definition

"Do we have an understanding of what we mean by 'community'?" Jennifer asked. The panel concluded that to them community referred to a group of people with a certain amount of advantageous cohesion, people with common interests and respect for individual members.

    B. Extent of the problem

Jennifer then asked members of the group for more specific information on the extent of the problem. Anne suggested that some students cluster together in continuation of high school relationships. "Why not see what the rest of the world looks like?" she asked. "Also, we are a commuter school," Julie noted. "People zoom into the parking lot, go to a class or two, and then get in the car and take off. They're missing something." James agreed and then brought up the point about racial or ethnic groups that have a tendency to stay apart from others. "Go into the cafeteria and look around. The Asians are over in the area by the piano, the African Americans cluster at the South end, and the whites hang

hang out in other sections." He said that as an African American himself, he was especially concerned about this. James' point prompted the support of Rick, who was Hispanic. He, too, had seen this segregation with people of his culture, and he wanted to have conditions change. "Those tight little units," as he called them, "have to go!" Others mentioned the same tendency among Asian students. "And what about the jocks?" asked Julie. Others brought up the formation of cliques that often worked against campus unity. "Even the students from the Disabled Students Center could mix in more, I'd say," proclaimed Anne, "and the older people!"

C. Limiting the problem

The members agreed that they were not so much worried about people of the same major who tended to group together because they had educational reasons for doing so. Too, members of the forensics squad and those from the theater might be exempt from criticism. Maybe. But shouldn't everyone make a real effort to look beyond his or her "cozy circle"?

D. Causes of the problem

"What are causes of the problem?" asked Jennifer. Rich, a sociology student, had to admit that there was a natural tendency of people to be drawn to others with similar backgrounds. "As they say, 'birds of a feather flock together.'" James brought up the fact that the school was large and that people felt more secure with others like them—and more welcome. "And those who are like us understand us better," added Julie. After members discussed

E.   Effects of the problem

these and similar reasons at some length, Jennifer said, "We haven't heard from you on this, Anne. Do you have anything on your mind?" Anne responded that just about all of the causes had been named, she thought. Jennifer then gave a summary of the discussion as it had unfolded to that point. "Well, we've determined that we have a problem of importance here. Also, we have limited it and cited a number of causes. Now what are effects of the problem?" Anne, feeling the need to make a comment, jumped in. "For one thing, these students who stay apart, both as individuals *and as groups, make it difficult to conduct successful campus activities. They don't support events. You can believe me on this." James wasn't so sure of that: "Often the reason for poor support is because people have other things to do." "That's just what I mean," returned Anne. "They've got their* individual *things to do!" Julie, who was in agreement with Anne, sharpened the point to show that when students aren't willing at any time to look beyond self interest, a campus community will eventually find itself not functioning, and in that event, everybody loses something of real value. "That's a great argument," Rich declared. "Bravo! And, you know, one of the specific losses is in the opportunity to get to know one another and learn how to communicate with one another." James thought that the worst effect was a general feeling of apathy around the school, a kind of "Who cares?" attitude. "I care,"* be said, *"and I want others to care. That's what's wrong with this apartness." "Right!" said Julie. "It really is campus narcissism, isn't it. A kind of 'me-ism'." All agreed.*

III. Consideration of possible solutions

"What are we going to do about this," Jennifer asked. Then she led the group in a brainstorming activity that turned up seven or eight solutions. Finally Jennifer asked, "What criteria should be used to help us decide on the best solution?"

A. Criteria for solutions

"Given the financial situation these days, we have to keep costs down," declared James. "That's right," said Julie. "Also, any solution must be respectful of all persons and groups. No one should be embarrassed in all this." Anne couldn't see that any person would be embarrassed, but she did want to say that the group's decision should be agreeable to the administration. "We can dream all we want and use a lot of high-sounding words, but they always have the final say." James agreed that it was no use "fighting city hall," as he put it. Rick didn't like that attitude. "Being practical is OK," he said, "but I want our solution to touch everyone's soul and to transcend lines of race, native language, professional interest, commuter or campus residency, sexual orientation, and so forth. Individualism goes only so far!" James and Julie applauded Rick's inspiring statement. After much discussion, with agreements and disagreements, the panel settled on financial feasibility, respectfulness, and breadth of appeal as criteria for their solution.

Solution 1

Solution 2

Solution 3

Julie, with the criteria in mind, came back with the proposal she had made during the brainstorming: to publish a campus magazine featuring essays, poems, and so forth, on topics cutting across all backgrounds and interests. This time, her offering was barraged with objections. "Costs will be too high." "Who reads those things, really?" "Those magazines die after two or three issues." Rather miffed, Julie withdrew her idea, but she wasn'tconvinced of its weakness. Then Rick reminded everyone of his idea. "Let's devote two weeks every year to a fair or some sort of celebration of our diversity and our unity. We'll have music, dancing, food, booths of various kinds, readings of literature that reflect our differences as well as our universal human identity, forums on male–female, ethnic, and age issues. And a lot more. We'll call it something like 'All Together Now.' It'll become a tradition!" James was excited. "Fine," he said. "Perhaps the instructors will cooperate and make related class assignments, like relevant literary works, pertinent historical accounts, sociological studies, and all that." Anne replied, "I think most people on campus would really go for it. It'll take a lot of time and energy, but costs could be kept down." Then Jennifer asked Anne to explain the suggestion that she had made in the brainstorming. "Well," said Anne, "what if we have a contest each term in which students create something on the theme of unity in diversity, for example, a

IV. Selection of a satisfactory solution

V. Implementation of the solution

song, painting, or dance number. We'll give prizes. It'll bring people out, won't it?" All responded that it sounded good, yet some believed that few students would feel qualified to write a song or poem. They dropped it, at least for the moment.

"Where are we then?" Jennifer asked. "Everybody seems to like this idea of celebrating our unity," James noted. "Yes, but why not extend it to include the contest—to widen the appeal?" questioned Rick. "Why not!" proclaimed Julie, "but two weeks is too long for any celebration, even of unity!" After agreeing to limit the duration to one week, several gave affirming views on how well the solution seemed to meet the problem of campus narcissism. At one point, Julie interrupted and insisted that the group reconsider the rejection of her proposal of a campus magazine. James answered with some figures on costs and results of a survey of expenses incurred at other campuses. All, even Julie now, appeared to be convinced of the financial infeasibility. "Now," requested Jennifer, "let's put together an outline of features of our event, estimate probable expenditures and money available, and pick up on all other details." Everyone got involved in that task.

"Well, we've got a great solution," Jennifer declared proudly. "Next we've got to put it into action, right?" Most members thought that the administration should be consulted, as well as other student body leaders. "But

the next big step will be to convince the Student Events Committee," suggested Jennifer. "I'll arrange for a meeting with them, and all of us must attend and be ready to make a great case. Agreed?" "We'll be there," everyone replied.

This is only a summary of a hypothetical panel discussion. Just the highlights were presented; you can fill in the details mentally. I didn't repeat all the examples, statistics, quotations, definitions, and other information that might have been used. I didn't go into the finer points of leadership that Jennifer might have employed.

And I didn't suggest how much time elapsed during the discussion. Timing depends on the peculiarities of the problem. **In some cases it may take the majority of your allotted minutes just to develop the problem.** Others require a longer consideration of solutions. Assuming that the preceding discussion lasted 30 minutes, the following is a *possible* distribution of time:

Recognition of a problem	3 minutes
Analysis of the problem	9 minutes
Consideration of possible solutions	11 minutes
Selecting a satisfactory solution	5 minutes
Implementation of the solution	2 minutes

The Symposium

The symposium follows the same general pattern of organization as the panel but differs greatly in other ways. **The panel is characterized by free exchange of ideas within the pattern, whereas the symposium is composed mainly of prepared speeches on parts of the whole.** With the exception of the conclusion, a symposium is made up of a series of ordinary speeches similar to the ones discussed in the first chapters of this book.

If we assigned Jennifer, Julie, Rick, Anne, and James to a 30-minute symposium, their parts might be distributed as follows:

Recognition of a problem	Jennifer (leader or moderator): 2 minutes
Analysis of the problem	James: prepared speech, 8 minutes
First solution	Julie: prepared speech, 4 minutes
Second solution	Rick: prepared speech, 4 minutes
Third solution	Anne: prepared speech, 4 minutes
Selecting a satisfactory solution and implementation	Entire membership: panel discussion, 8 minutes

Besides introducing the problem and guiding the concluding discussion, Jennifer has the responsibility of tying parts together with effective transitions. For example, following James' speech, she might summarize very briefly and introduce Julie, who would offer the first solution.

The Lecture–Panel

The lecture–panel calls for a speaker to deliver a prepared speech. That person should be well versed in the subject to be discussed.

After the leader, or moderator, as one in that role may be called, introduces the problem and the speaker, the speaker analyzes the nature of the problem and presents possible solutions. During the panel discussion that follows, the members may ask questions of the speaker, make comments of their own, and discuss any aspect of the matter among themselves. They may accept, reject, or modify any of the offered solutions. Finally, with the solution in mind, the members will work out a plan for putting the solution into practice.

The nature of the problem will dictate the selection of a speaker. That person may be from outside the class or a class member who is well-informed on the topic. Outside people often invited are civic leaders, recreation experts, radio and television figures, government representatives, teachers, lawyers, business people, agriculturists, and newspaper personnel.

If an outside person is not available, probably someone in your class can be encouraged to assume the role of speaker. That individual will have to be well-prepared to handle the topic, but of course, everyone will need to prepare. Here's a sample time distribution plan for a 30-minute lecture–panel.

Recognition of a problem and introduction of the speaker	Leader or moderator: 3 minutes
Analysis of the problem and possible solutions	Speaker: 12–15 minutes
Questions, comments, selection of a solution; plan for implementation	Members' discussion: 12–15 minutes

Incidentally, one common variation is the lecture–panel forum, in which full audience participation is added or substituted for the panel. Weigh the possible usefulness of this form as you consider audience participation.

Audience Participation

An explanation of public discussion forms should not leave out the audience. **Listeners participate also, to the extent that their personal interest influences them to follow the course of the discussion and identify with the remarks made.** Thus motivated, they too make an effort to understand, interpret, and evaluate while the small group explores the topic.

Public discussion forms allow oral audience participation after the group has concluded. This part of the program is called a *forum*. The forum in ancient Rome was the marketplace, a large public square where public or private affairs were discussed, speeches delivered, and courts of law held. Today the word is used to name an occasion at which everyone has an opportunity to express ideas. Actually, when the audience is allowed to become involved following a discussion, the entire program is called a forum. Thus we have the panel forum, the symposium forum, the lecture–panel forum, and others that groups may devise.

In the forum phase, audience members may ask questions of specific speakers or of the group as a whole. They may refer to any relevant aspect of the topic and make statements of their own. A question from the audience should be directed to the leader, who in turn submits it to the group for response—or to a certain member.

GATHERING MATERIAL

One of the certainties in human interaction is that a group discussion cannot succeed without a well-informed membership. Gathering useful material is everyone's task. But where are data to be found?

1. Your store of personal experience. Perhaps you've had immediate contact with the subject. A summer job might have introduced you to labor–management relations. Babysitting could have given you insights on the behavior of children. What possible connection might you have with the subject? What have you seen that pertains to it? What have you heard knowledgeable people say about it?

2.   Scenes of action related to the topic. One of the best ways to become well informed is to make firsthand observations. If you plan to discuss "Community Recreation," visit the playgrounds, the pools, and other facilities. Make the field trip worthwhile by planning carefully and by keeping your purpose uppermost in your mind.

Schedule an interview with an authority. The head of the city recreation department, for example, might be able to assist. Arrange for an appointment, and prepare your questions in advance.

3.   Library services. Besides all the books, periodicals, and other reference aids available, some libraries have special files on timely topics. Also, librarians often are well versed in topics that students frequently investigate. The advice: *ask questions.*

For a more complete explanation on gathering materials, see Appendix B, "Doing Research on a Topic."

MAKING A POINT IN DISCUSSION

Although it's true that some people seem to be naturally gifted in group interaction, numbers of others lack the basic skills for expressing points of view, sharing ideas and opinions, giving pieces of information, building reasons, laying out plans, detailing solutions, and the like. That is, *many do not know how to make a point in a discussion.* Among the key questions are the following:

What do you say in discussion?

How do you say it?

How do you get the "right-of-way" to say something?

How do you make the point count?

What to Say

There are moments of surprise in small group discussion, and no one can anticipate every turn in the road. Therefore the question of what to say depends on events in the discussion. But when prepared, you have a store of knowledge from which to draw as you involve yourself in the discussion. **As you perceive the movement of the discussion, what do you feel *needs* to be said? How can you help the group?** Do you have information that would benefit the discussion? Possibly you're aware that the group is overlooking a vital topic. If so, bring it out. Or you may see that one area is being emphasized to the neglect of others; or the discussion is digressing, as you view it, and you can bring it back on course. The many contingencies and circumstances that occur in small group discussion provide reasons for making contributions. They also suggest what to say—for the good of the group's purpose.

When to Say It

How do you determine when your point is needed and relevant? Again, be aware of the flow of discussion, where it's going, and be ready to offer your contributions when they seem timely and fitting. Timing is important. Even in informal discussion, the people involved find themselves adhering to a sequential structure of some kind. There are steps in almost every process. Members sense a developing order, and they respond in accordance with it. The advice, then, is to be aware of the overall pattern, to be sensitive to moments along the way as they relate to the whole, and to determine the suitability of your resources to the moments.

Entering the Discussion

Depending on the level of formality established by the group, you can either ease your point in without recognition or you can address the moderator or leader, or other appropriate person, with eye contact or raised hand, indicating that you have something to say. In informal procedure, people devise all sorts of ways to tell others that they want to speak. Have you noticed these? Wide, expectant eyes seem to be the strategy of some. Others request "right-of-way" with an opened mouth, a forward body lean, a tap on another's arm or shoulder, and so on. Many have learned to take advantage of pauses that provide opportunity to have a say.

Remember that verbal interruptions are proper if group norms seem to allow them. But acceptability may depend on how one does it. Don't you envy the one who has mastered the art of interrupting graciously?

Making the Point Count

Assuming that you've been listening well—certainly nothing is more essential to useful discussion—and that you have found the right time to make your point, you'll then choose the appropriate mode. You can reinforce another person's point, ask a question, introduce a new perspective, or do whatever is indicated at the time. You can address the point to a certain member, to a number of members, or to one in a leadership role.

You can handle the point in any number of ways: express a view and be satisfied that you were heard; express a view, and after another person has intervened with a comment, come back with a revision or additional view; ask a question, get a response, and follow up with a conclusion; and so on.

It's in the handling of the point that it'll be made or lost. These suggestions are fundamental in making a point count.

1. **Connect your point to the specific point under discussion.** By specific point, I mean the point of the moment. **Show how your point fits in.** Sometimes, perhaps quite often, you'll find it useful to restate the specific point under discussion as you introduce your relating point. For example, the italicized words in these two excerpts from a hypothetical discussion are restatements of points under discussion:

Since we seem to be looking for advantages in short-term loans, I know of one real benefit that I'd like to mention.

Jerry's idea is that the books be made available to all children, and I agree with him. But, I'd like to include teenagers and young adults, all young people, in the distribution plan.

Know the point of the moment, and tie your point to it, showing its relevance.

2.   Develop your point. Development may require only one sentence. A carefully phrased question, for instance, may be all that you need to get the desired response. On another occasion it may be necessary to provide a full 20-second development of a point. Such a construction might be thought of as a "mini" main head, a small package of thought comprising the point to be made and the support of a piece or two of material, such as an example and statistics or possibly some quoted material. A concluding statement would be added, to clinch the point or show its significance to the matter under discussion.

Reasoning with your material is an essential part of developing the point. The goal is to make good sense. "Is it reasonable?" is the question to ask of ideas or supporting material. It's not sufficient to offer an example of something or quotation of an authority without reasoning to reveal its practicability or meaning. The only purpose for introducing materials is to develop ideas and reach conclusions. Therefore you must put your mind to your data, showing their significance, and come to valid and acceptable conclusions. In other words, use processes of critical thinking to establish your ideas and relate them to the ideas of other participants. Consult Chapter Nine, "Thinking Critically," for a more complete explanation of reasoning and fallacies.

Making a point is the kind of spur-of-the-moment impromptu speaking that characterizes group deliberation, whether in panel discussions, seminars, committee meetings, or whatever. In summary, here's the formula:

1.   Refer and connect to a point of the discussion.

2.   Then state your point.

3.   Support your point with evidence and reasoning.

4.   Conclude.

The critical factors in making a point in discussion, then, are knowledge, timing and awareness of the status of the discussion, mastery of technique, and effective speaking.

INTERPERSONAL PROBLEMS IN GROUP INTERACTION

Up to now, emphasis has been on subjects, questions, structure, the content of discussion, and making a point. It's the last subject that reminds us that **people and their behavior with others are fundamental facts of all communicative interactions,** and therefore we turn now to the interpersonal dimension.

The most brilliantly conceived system will fail, unless the people involved are dedicated to making it work. Moreover, the ideal result is rarely achieved in any small group. So let's face up to counterproductive behavioral activity that can appear in real-life discussion. The following list of group predicaments reminds us of conditions to remedy or avoid. How many of these events have you observed?

"Mob Rule"

In this situation, members refuse to adopt even the semblance of order for fear of stifling free expression; no one is willing to offer leadership. But there's plenty of talk—about this and that and everything. In its confusion and extreme interpretation of good discussion, the group equates disorder with freedom.

"Following Orders!"

Directly opposite is behavior of the group that establishes a rigid and sanctified order of business and moves only "by the numbers," without the slightest deviation, as though working on an assembly line. The leader is infallible, directing the show and judging the fitness of all comments. Members accept the regimen and apparently feel entirely comfortable with it.

"Where're We Goin'?"

In this instance, one or more members forget the group's purpose. Perhaps they were not consulted in the planning. They seem disoriented and make frequent irrelevant comments or wander off from the others into hinterlands of unrelated thought.

"I Won't Play!"

This is the response of people who choose to sit on the sidelines. They seem unable to realize their personal purposes in participating. Their behavior is characterized by silence or brief and infrequent contributions. With no view of a possible reward for involvement, they elect not to invest themselves.

"Sounds of Different Drummers"

Occasionally a group of four or five highly individualistic persons will not be able to locate grounds for unity in spirit or objective. One person is concerned only about racial problems or the environment; another questions the usefulness of discussion in the first place; another insists on sitting around a table, whereas others demand different physical arrangements or show some similar disunity. Because of their extreme independence or single-mindedness or unwillingness to compromise, they never get the process of interaction underway.

"Who Am I, Anyway?"

Perhaps because of a "following-orders" atmosphere, reduced self-esteem, or some other influence, one sees now and again the frustration of people who seem unable to find parts to play. They make attempts but feel unsure of themselves and ineffective. They are uncertain of their status, not convinced that they belong there. Momentarily at least, they have trouble accepting themselves as competent contributors.

"Don't Ask Me!"

This is the problem of the uninformed members lacking the information necessary for taking part. Possibly their experience is limited, or their study of the topic has not been adequate.

"Flying Blind!"

BLIND is an acronym, a term made from the first letters of words naming a collection of problems in interpersonal communication. Most of the problems named come from faulty perception, from a kind of *blindness.* Truly, interpersonal blindness can imperil the flight of any group discussion that otherwise might have real promise. *B* is for the *blocking* of free and spontaneous interaction by any act or influence that suppresses useful expression. *L* is for *limiting* a discussion to one's own special interests, problems, or understanding, an unwillingness to relate beyond a personal sphere. *I* is for *indicting* others, stressing the negative rather than accepting, being hypercritical or penalizing, verbally or nonverbally. *N* is for *neglecting* the contributions of co-participants, for ignoring and not recognizing relevance or utility of contributions or not helping to fit ideas into the discussion, for being insensitive to feelings and unaware of needs. *D* is for *debating* rather than discussing, for playing the part of adversary rather than cooperator, for stressing difference and conflict.

SUCCESSFUL GROUP INTERACTION: TEN QUALITIES

There are antidotes to weaknesses in discussion. Through study and experience, we have learned much in recent years about success and failure in discussion and interactions of people in small groups. Here are ten qualities of successful groups that you can seek to establish in your small group discussions.

1. Cohesiveness. Whether it's called group spirit, esprit de corps, interdependency, identity, or some other term, a sense of working together in unity toward a common end is a vital factor in discussion. Cohesiveness comprises and fosters an array of conditions conducive to productive group interaction: mutual trust and security, free expression and spontaneity, involvement, loyalty, diligence, and many others. Indeed, in certain group situations, for example, a training or therapy session in interpersonal relations, cohesiveness may be the *goal* of discussion as well as the dominant force in the *process* of discussion. In a sense, all the other nine qualities are subsumed in this large and important topic because all contribute significantly as bases of cohesiveness.

It's important, then, that you **recognize the need for a cooperative spirit in achieving a successful discussion.** Though you may not always agree with the ideas of others, perhaps it's possible to muster tolerance and willingness to understand all points of view. Thus, free expression is encouraged. Acknowledge your prejudices. Anyone may have a prejudice; most of us do, but not everyone has the special kind of courage it takes to admit it and do something about it. An aware person examines personal opinions and attempts to weed out those that are based on bias. Group cohesiveness, a *vital* condition, may depend on it.

2. Clear group purpose. All participants should know the group's goal, the direction of its movement, its object for being. People need to know the aim of the activity in which they may be involving themselves. Since the purpose should be mutually acceptable, all should participate in reaching it.

Find a way to commit yourself to the group's purpose. Remember that the occasion is not one for long, time-consuming speeches. Contributions should be short, clear, and relevant. Since discussion is a group effort, no member should take up an unreasonable share of time. The good member nevertheless avoids the opposite extreme, too little participation.

When in doubt about what to do in a discussion, try asking yourself, "What can I do for the good of the discussion?" If you are undecided about expressing a given thought, ask yourself, "Will it help further the progress of the discussion?" In all cases, be guided by your knowledge of purpose and your desire to make the group's efforts successful.

3. Democratic spirit. People have rights, and that's one good reason for fostering democracy in small group work. Also, to produce a worthy product and lasting good effects in discussion, it's advisable to establish a climate that encourages freedom of participation for all members. People who have a say in early phases of deliberation are more likely to be useful contributors in final stages, for example, in implementation of the solution. They will support a decision best when they have had a hand in making it. And let's not forget that **groups need the ideas of everyone, all points of view.**

4.   **Well-conceived role of the individual.** While working harmoniously in a group, individuals may differ in personal role or objective. And they should be aware of reasons for their particular involvement. Better participation usually results from visualizing possible personal return, for example, fulfillment of a need to interact with others in a worthy cause or a desire for acceptance by a group.

Central to role is usefulness. **Participants in a discussion seek to determine functions that they can serve, useful parts to play.** Acceptance in a role is vital to them. They need to realize that they can be influential and have some social effectiveness or control, and that others will honor their established function.

People are most productive when able to maintain their identity, to assume a role that is congruent to the self. An example is success in resisting social pressure toward adoption of a view that is personally unacceptable. As in all communication, harmony of self-concept and behavior, matched with awareness, is essential to the realization of one's potential and finding satisfactory personal involvement.

In regard to function, one important way to serve the group is to act as "participant–observer." As defined by John K. Brilhart and Gloria J. Galanes, this is the important role of the one who is "an active participant in a small group who is at the same time observing and evaluating its processes and procedures."[2] Such intelligent and constructive dual-mindedness represents the best in small group interaction, the person that you want in your group.

5.   **Acceptable procedures and level of formality.** The group should reach consensus on methods of operation: rules, organization and format, time schedule, and other formalities. Such decisions ought to be made on the basis of the group's needs. Some groups require a loose and informal atmosphere and find their ends thwarted by imposition of a tight frame. Others may profit from greater formality, even going so far as addressing each other as Mr. or Ms. and adhering closely to an agenda, as well as to specified times for opening and adjourning a session.

6.   **Limited size.** Research and experience show that **the ideal size for a group is from four to seven members.** A group usually needs at least four members to avoid such possibilities as a two-against-one relationship, proven to be a real threat to harmony in human interaction. Moreover, groups benefit from the breadth of view and variety of experience and talent offered by a number of members. But the group should be small enough to allow development of cohesiveness, to give participants opportunities to know each other and relate with sensitivity and to explore new ideas and solutions.

7.   **Good leadership. Groups need guidance,** whether a leader is appointed or elected, whether leadership is shared, or whether leadership emerges in the process of discussion. If you have ever been in a

group in which no one was willing to give direction, you know the problems. Of course, opposite extremes, such as letting a leader do everything and accepting authoritarian leadership, are seldom called for. What is called for in most situations is a balance, providing for necessary guidance that avoids the counterproductive results of either anarchy or dictatorship. The group may choose the leader or moderator, and that is the typical procedure, but still be free and willing to allow incidental sharing of the leadership role so that at a given moment, on a given topic, one who is especially knowledgeable or aware can step in to guide. This kind of adaptation can be made gracefully and may prove to be highly beneficial.

Recognize the value of leadership, and remember the importance of orderly progression of thought for which the leader and members are responsible. Assist the leader or moderator and refrain from getting ahead of the discussion. For example, you shouldn't insist on discussing solutions when the group doesn't seem to have finished considering the problem.

8. Positive interpersonal climate. This is one of those qualities necessarily overlapping all others on the list, but here I refer to specific conditions, such as openness, trusting and relating without anxiety or fear of penalty, and sufficient permissiveness. With these conditions, the promise of positive interpersonal relationships is high.

Moreover, interpersonal relationships are strengthened when participants are willing to relate; when they respect and understand others, for example, members of different cultural background or experience or age; when they are sensitive to others' feelings and aware of their needs; when they look for positive qualities in others and are able to ignore the seemingly negative; when they recognize the usefulness of others' contributions; when they are willing to search for grounds of cohesion, even though some participants may clash strongly in personality or ideas.

At points of conflict, it may help to remind yourself to center on *ideas* **rather than personalities.** You need not accept or endorse all ideas, but certainly it's not giving too much to accept the person and the right of expression. Further, what do we lose in overlooking minor instances of annoying behavior? Tact and civility go a long way in working with people in small group discussion.

Another recommendation is to **avoid needless debate.** This is not to say that a person should refrain from supporting personal convictions. It merely means that the good discussion speaker knows that extended debate can generate strong feelings and perhaps cause the discussion to bog down. Persistent debating forces people to take sides. It can thwart open-mindedness and objectivity. The advice, then, is to know when to stop, when to yield for the sake of the discussion as a whole. Discussion needs open and inquiring minds that are not adamantly committed to sides. In avoiding unnecessary debate, you need not become a conformist—one who too easily yields to group pressures. Easy conformity is as counterproductive as heavy debate.

One solid contribution to the establishment of a positive interpersonal climate is capable listening. Be conscientious in following the flow of discussion and attempt to understand and interpret comments before referring to them. **The considerate participant ignores emotional and physical distractions and listens intelligently.**

9. **Sufficient preparation and relevant information.** Being informed, though mentioned earlier, is mentioned here to stress the general and collective good as opposed to individual accomplishment. Groups that have an inadequate supply of available data cannot be successful. To accomplish most goals, people need information. The two principal sources of information are direct personal experience and formal study. Though both may be useful in most groups, the priority of one over the other will depend on the group's function and immediate purpose.

Some people have the false notion that preparation means thinking a little about the subject and getting ready to offer an opinion here and there in the discussion. No view is more ridiculous or more revealing of lack of training in the process of group problem solving. **Not until members have analyzed the problem rationally, organized their thoughts, and gathered substantial materials are they ready to contribute constructively to the group effort.**

To be informed and ready is to show respect for other discussion members. It's a very substantial way to show interest in the group purpose and to contribute toward building a trusting relationship.

10. Appropriate language. Communication among the members is based on clear, lively, varied, acceptable language. Vague and abstract thoughts usually mean very little to others. The good member adapts ideas to the lives and experiences of listeners. You may want to refer to Chapter Eleven for additional suggestions on language usage.

THE LEADER

Clearly, discussion is a collective effort, and each member makes contributions to its development. But the special contribution of leadership deserves particular mention because it provides guidance in making the activity purposeful and productive. Ordinarily, the primary leadership function is vested in one person. How does a group choose a leader? Answers range from the adoption of formal nomination and voting procedures to reliance on the informal emergence of a leader, someone who shows ability and willingness to be the guide and who says "OK" when group consensus points to him or her. The need for leadership usually is seen from the beginning of the planning period. The leader can help the group go about selecting and narrowing the subject, wording the question, determining the form, and preparing an outline of the main points to be discussed. Of course, any member may offer leadership when needed at points during either planning or discussion.

What are the particular requirements that groups place on their leaders? What are they expected to do?

1. Prepare thoroughly. If selected as a leader, you should have substantial overall knowledge of the subject. You'll have the primary responsibility for developing the discussion. A captain must know the whole ship in order to coordinate the work of various officers. Also, sound preparation serves to inspire confidence and trust in the leader. **The leader's specific preparation should be at least as extensive as that of any other member.**

2. Promote group spirit. You ought to have real respect for the discussion process, as well as an awareness of the cooperative nature of discussion and the value of cohesiveness. As you work together toward the solution of the problem, give members as much responsibility and freedom as they can assume. By all means avoid being an overlord, yet be firm when necessary. Use your intelligence, tactfulness, and sense of humor. Be impartial and foster an open and positive interpersonal atmosphere. Have an attitude that will enable the group to have confidence in you. Remember that you are the leader and not a member. As such, you probably will be more effective if you don't enter the discussion with personal views or positions on issues of the topic.

3. Provide an appropriate beginning. Open the discussion in much the same way you would start any speech. You might use an example or possibly a quotation or a statistic. Work in an explanation of the question's importance along with background information. Introduce the individual participants and announce the procedure agreed on by the group.

4. Guide the group. This is your main job. It's your duty to insure progress toward the final goal. You may clarify or ask for definitions and restatements. You should summarize whenever the group needs to be reminded of what it has accomplished. Occasionally ask questions to keep the discussion moving or to bring out key points. Recognize those and see that they are sufficiently emphasized. For example, **if a member makes a significant contribution, acknowledge it.**

Be sensitive to positions and attitudes of others and encourage all members to participate. Help the quiet member bring out ideas. Everyone has something to share, and will, if the risk is not too high. When Terry has not spoken for a time, you may need to say, "We haven't heard your thinking in this area, Terry." On the other hand, be ready to deal firmly but respectfully with the overtalkative member. Be friendly and maintain a balanced discussion, ever aware of the group's goal and feelings.

5. Provide an appropriate ending. Include a summary of results or findings, along with other remarks designed to round out and complete the discussion. If the audience is to take part, remind them that they may ask questions of individual speakers, or of the group as a body, and that they may make comments of their own. Guide the forum period and bring the program to a smooth conclusion.

LOOKING BACK

In addition to serving as a medium for personal and social growth, small group discussion is an indispensable method for use in solving problems and finding answers to important questions. It's to be found in all realms of life: at school, at work, in business, in government, in church activity, in political affairs, everywhere. **Whenever practical and democratic group action is called for, small group discussion is useful.** It can be a trusted form of communication, if it's appreciated and used wisely. But good discussions rarely just happen. They are built from:

1. Well-chosen and appropriately limited subjects
2. Carefully worded questions or cases
3. Purposeful organization
4. Appropriate formats
5. Ample and relevant material
6. Well-made points
7. Interpersonally sensitive group interaction
8. Sound leadership

The ideal group is a cohesive, secure, democratic, hard-working, well-informed gathering of four to seven people, guided by a clear purpose and a set of procedures selected and accepted by all. Further, all participants know their purposes and roles, are ready to assume leadership if indicated, and are willing and able to do their part in providing a positive interpersonal atmosphere.

QUESTIONS AND IDEAS

The following may suggest appropriate kinds of discussion questions:

How can a person develop self-confidence?

How can automobile accidents be reduced?

What are the values of public education?

What can be done to foster appreciation of cultural diversity in America?

How can more people be provided with the opportunity for a college education?

What can be done to make more part-time jobs available to students?

What standards should guide a person in choosing a career?

How can the number of unhappy marriages be reduced?

Can problems of noise pollution be solved?

What policies should guide the use of intelligence tests in school?

How can more community housing be made available to students?

Some of the following ideas may be shaped into acceptable discussion questions:

Questionable advertising methods

Abuse of natural resources

Roles of women in industry

Defining disability

National defense

The United Nations as a world force

Child abuse

Film ratings

Drug use

Rearing children effectively

Urbanization and the family

Medical transplants

More leisure time for Americans

Neighborhood improvement

Electric cars

The Third World

Increased world population

Home entertainment

Funding higher education

Violence in athletics

NOTES

1. Carl E. Larson, "Forms of Analysis in Small Group Problem Solving," *Speech Monographs,* XXXVI (November 1969): 452–455.

2. John K. Brilhart and Gloria J. Galanes, *Effective Group Discussion,* 6th ed. (Dubuque: William C. Brown, 1989), 23.

PREPARING FOR
SPECIAL OCCASIONS

14

★ **LOOKING AHEAD** ★

1. What is meant by the suggestion "Know the demands of the occasion"?

2. How is impromptu speaking like the type of speaking discussed in early chapters of this book? How is it different?

3. How is the announcement like the type of speaking discussed in early chapters of this book? How is it different?

4. What should be included in a speech of introduction?

5. What are the peculiarities of an after-dinner speech?

6. How does one prepare a nominating speech?

7. What are the particular requirements of presentation speeches?

8. What is expected in the speech to accept a presentation?

9. What are the particular requirements of welcoming speeches?

10. What is required in speech to respond to a welcome?

CHAPTER 14

PREPARING FOR
SPECIAL OCCASIONS

DEMANDS OF THE OCCASION

Fundamentally, all types of speeches are similar. All require thoughtful consideration of the subject, formulation of a definite thesis, sound organization, adequate development of ideas, and effective delivery.

But **certain occasions demand more than the application of fundamental principles.** The final shaping of any speech will be determined by the speaker's view of the specific situation. In effect, **the question to ask oneself is, "What kind of talk should I make to this audience on this occasion?"** For example, if you are called on to speak at some gathering without benefit of extensive preparation, it'll be necessary for you to gather your thoughts immediately. Special speaking events such as making an announcement, presenting a guest speaker to your club, nominating a candidate for office, giving a speech to honor someone who is leaving the community, accepting an award for service to your school, or speaking as official host to a visiting delegation have peculiarities to which you must adapt. At some time during your life, you'll probably have occasion to deliver one of these speeches—maybe more than once.

THE IMPROMPTU SPEECH

The impromptu speech is a short talk given on the spur of the moment. Does this kind of situation frighten you? Actually, the main difference between the requirements of impromptu speaking and other types of speech making is the amount of preparation time. I can't say that this difference is insignificant, yet every speech that you've made can be thought of as a training experience for making future impromptu speeches. In all your speaking, in this class and elsewhere, you've been getting ready to give such speeches. Because much of the groundwork has been laid, the job now is to carry over to that specific occasion what you have learned about composition and delivery. You'll find this less difficult than you now think.

The following instructions will help you to be successful in the impromptu situation.

1. Give thought to your subject. In some situations you may be allowed to choose your own subject, whereas at other times someone will name a subject. When the choice is yours, choose an appropriate subject.

Speak about the occasion, its purposes, high points, or humorous aspects. Speak about the people assembled, their success, future plans, or other group interests. Current events can offer impromptu topics, such as popular fads or recent happenings in the community. Don't attempt to cover a wide area; **limit your scope.**

2. Plan your course. Immediately after getting the subject, decide on your thesis or theme and select two or three main heads for developing it. The thesis might suggest that the main heads be topical, spatial, or chronological; or it may be that a pattern of reasons or a problem–solution pattern is suggested. Pairs of opposites are frequently quite handy structures, for example, east and west, ups and downs, right and wrong, advantages and disadvantages, or past and future.

The following situation is not unusual. You're at a formal meeting or dinner of your club, and the chair, knowing of your long-time membership and service, asks you to "say a few words." You could comment on current club problems or new legislation that will impact the group. But on this happy occasion, you decide to be upbeat and briefly review (in no more than two minutes) chief accomplishments of the organization in the past year. You select three: the fund-raiser, success in increasing membership, and the dance that everyone enjoyed. Such a speaking role may fall to you.

3. Select materials as you speak. During the time it takes you to push back your chair and assume your speaking position, you can be gathering together a few introductory words. Make no apologies about "being unaccustomed to giving impromptu speeches." At a banquet you can refer to the beautiful table decorations, to a timely conversation that you had a minute ago, or possibly to the committee's excellent work in arranging the program, or you can tell an appropriate story.

After leading to your thesis, state it. Present your first main idea; elaborate on it with a story or example, some statistics, or a quotation, if one should come to you at the time. Available visual aids might be used as a means of development. Look around. Benjamin Franklin, who had the last word at the happy signing of the new American Constitution in Philadelphia in 1787, found a useful visual aid. This is the way James Madison reported on the signing and Franklin's speech:

> *Whilst the last members were signing it Dr. Franklin looking towards the President's Chair, at the back of which a rising sun happened to be painted, observed to a few members near him, that Painters had found it difficult to distinguish in their art a rising sun from a setting sun. I have, said he, often and often in the course of the Session, and the vicissitudes of my hopes and fears as to its issue, looked at that behind the President without being able to tell whether it was rising or setting: But now at length I have the happiness to know that it is a rising and not a setting sun.*

Use your imagination; capitalize on the tone of the occasion and factors related to it.

You cannot speak of ice to a summer insect—the creature of a narrower sphere.

Old Chinese saying

Speaking occasions vary.

Before sitting down, perhaps you should summarize and then clinch your purpose. In speaking before an organization, it's often appropriate to close with comments relevant to the group's goals and aspirations, the challenges faced, its future gatherings, or the noteworthy efforts of its officers and members.

4.   Guard against speciousness. Specious speaking is hollow, without substance. I refer here to a danger that may present itself to a person who has had enough impromptu speaking experience to gain a feeling of overconfidence but not enough to motivate preparation of a substantial message. **Glibness and smoothness do not necessarily indicate effectiveness.** Impromptu speakers who have worthwhile messages and present them sincerely will avoid becoming "inebriated with the exuberance of their own verbosity," to use words applied by the statesman Benjamin Disraeli to a political enemy.

Another kind of impromptu speaking is found in the interactions of participants in group discussion. See the section in Chapter Thirteen called Making a Point in Discussion.

THE ANNOUNCEMENT

Whether given in an impromptu fashion or after advance notice, the announcement speech is often poorly made, probably because it's not thought of as a "speech." Some people seem to think that only formal public addresses require organization and other careful preparation.

What are the rules for making announcements?

1.   Plan your talk.

2.   Open with an attention-getting sentence.

3. Relate all the essential information succinctly and clearly: who, what, when, where, and how much.

4. Be enthusiastic; make the subject inviting; emphasize its importance.

5. Repeat the essential information briefly.

6. Be seated!

The following is a sample outline for an announcement speech.

Introduction
    I. Don't save your money.
    II. Bring it with you next Wednesday, and throw it away.

Thesis
    Throw it away at the Jester Club's Annual Candy Sale, to be held all day Wednesday along the arcade.

Body
    I. Throw it away on creamy homemade fudge.
    II. Throw it away on tantalizing taffy.
    III. Throw it away on mouth-watering peanut brittle.

Conclusion
    I. Each generously filled bag of fudge, taffy, or peanut brittle will cost you only $1.50.
    II. Remember that Wednesday is Candy Day along the arcade.

THE SPEECH OF INTRODUCTION

If you have ever had the uncomfortable experience of being thrown into a group of strangers without an introduction, for example, at a party, you will know why guest speakers deserve appropriate speeches of introduction. The loneliest and most anxious time in a speaker's experience can be that period of waiting to become acquainted with the audience. Mentally, the speaker may ask, "What have they heard about me? What do they think of me?" "Have they heard of me at all?" There may be other thoughts of concern: "Will my ideas be accepted? Can I get across to them? I wish I were better acquainted with them."

Clearly, speeches of introduction are important. They help to reduce anxiety and create a friendly relationship between the speaker and audience. Vital though they are, such talks occasionally are mishandled. When you have the opportunity to introduce a speaker to an audience and help set up a good interpersonal climate, follow these suggestions.

1. Know your function. You're to make a talk; however, **you're not the *main* speaker.** Like the waiter in a restaurant, you provide a service, but like the waiter again, what you introduce is the more important element. Subordinate yourself on this occasion, and be the good host, giving the main speaker the rightful position of prominence. Rarely would you be justified in speaking longer than two or three minutes. In fact, the introduction of a very well-known person might be accomplished in a few seconds with "Friends, our president, Dr. Wagner."

2.   Learn about the speaker. Study the person's background by consulting printed sources and people who have relevant information. If possible, arrange to have a personal talk with the speaker—and well ahead of time.

Be certain that all your information is accurate, including, of course, the proper title and correct pronunciation of the speaker's name.

3.   Include appropriate data. Remember again that *the person you introduce* is the one with the message that people want to hear. Avoid trespassing very far into the speaker's subject area. General comments that show how the subject relates to the occasion or that summarize the speaker's work in the field are appropriate. Your knowledge or personal philosophy of the subject normally would not be needed.

Specifically, what information is to be presented? Though occasions vary, usually you would summarize the speaker's qualifications and tell why everyone anticipates the speech. Capitalize on background data that are especially meaningful to the audience.

Point out the primary accomplishments of the speaker, yet do not overburden your introduction with many statistics and facts. Use humor if you wish, but with care and good taste. Build the speaker up, yet not to an embarrassing extent. You can sympathize, certainly, with a person who is introduced as "the greatest speaker in Ohio." You may envy the announced reputation, but you wouldn't want to be in the position of having to live up to it.

On the other hand, if the speaker is your second choice, you shouldn't cause embarrassment by revealing that fact. It would be most uncomplimentary to say, for instance, that the group had tried to get Ms. Wilson to come but that Mr. Rogers, here, will surely give a good speech.

4.   Organize your remarks. Like any other oral presentation, the speech of introduction should be properly arranged. Many people choose a kind of indirect plan or one that combines direct and indirect structures, like the following. As you see, it has a brief opening to get attention and interest, develops two or three main heads, and finishes with a joined thesis–conclusion.

Introduction
    I.   As you know, communication within organizations has become a topic of great interest in recent years.
    II.   Organizations are hotbeds of messages going every which way.
    III.   The dynamics of organizational message-sending is the special interest of the woman who is to speak to us today.

Body
    I.   Her most recent experience is 11 years with the Triton Corporation.

A. She started out with them as publications editor in the Eastern Division.
B. Then she moved up to be Editor-in-Chief for all their publications.
C. After giving her extended experience in other capacities, they created a position titled Facilitator of Intracorporation Communications, her present post.

II. Our speaker believes that internal communications are every bit as critical as public communications.
A. She has proven this to the industry.
B. Today we'll hear the latest.

Thesis–Conclusion
Members of the Communications Club, I present, speaking on the topic "Talking Inside," Sue Brach of the Triton Corporation.

Use of indirect and combined patterns of organization, illustrated in this outline, are discussed at greater length in Chapter Eight.

5.   Present the speaker. As indicated in the sample outline, at the end of your introduction you should make an appropriate statement to let the speaker know that the time to speak has arrived. Sometimes there's a moment of embarrassing hesitancy because the introducer fails to *present* the speaker properly to the audience. **At the end of your introduction, turn toward the speaker and lead the applause.**

When Mary Robinson, President of the Republic of Ireland, spoke at the University of California in 1991, she was introduced by the chancellor of the university, Chang-Lin Tien.[1] Dr. Tien began with these words: "One hundred thousand welcomes—as they say in Ireland. And one hundred thousand welcomes to our distinguished guest: Mary Robinson, the first woman in history to serve as President of Ireland. The University of California at Berkeley is deeply honored by your visit." He reminded the listeners that "Berkeley's ties with Ireland run deep" and that the name comes from Bishop George Berkeley of Ireland. Tien made additional references to connections of his university to Ireland, including the fact that Berkeley is one of the few American universities to offer a major in Celtic studies, including Irish traditions. Speaking on, he said,

I can imagine no greater honor than welcoming Mary Robinson to Berkeley today, the first woman to win the presidency of Ireland. Making history is nothing new to President Robinson; she has blazed new trails all her life.

At the age of 24, President Robinson joined the faculty of the prestigious Trinity College at Dublin. This appointment in 1969 made her the youngest professor in the college's history. But breaking this age barrier was not enough for President Robinson. Later that year, the determined young woman set her sights on the Irish Senate. She believed it was unjust for only elderly male professors to represent Trinity College in the Senate. . . . No one as young as this new professor had ever won a Senate election. No Roman Catholic had ever represented Trinity College. But Mary Robinson ran—and Mary Robinson won.

Chancellor Tien then told of specific issues on which Ms. Robinson had taken strong stands, for example, gay rights, women's rights, and the legalization of the sale of contraceptives in Ireland. Acknowledging her election as president, Tien brought her to the rostrum with these words: "That was a great, great day for Ireland. And this is a great, great day for Berkeley. It gives me great pleasure to introduce President Mary Robinson."

THE AFTER-DINNER SPEECH

Unlike some banquet speeches which may be quite serious in purpose and development, the traditional after-dinner speech is humorous. It's a special kind of talk, presented to give pleasure following a dinner. But **along with the fun and beneath the laughter, the audience usually expects to find a message of some sort.** A theme ought to run through the speech, carrying a significant idea.

One of America's most celebrated after-dinner speakers was Mark Twain. Perhaps you have read his "A 'Litery Episode," in which he poked fun at the literary works of Emerson, Longfellow, and Oliver Wendell Holmes—with all the authors present. His "New England Weather" and "The Babies" are also famous samples of his after-dinner wit.

Once a student in Oregon had occasion at a dinner gathering to speak on the topic "South of the Border." He found his humor in subtopics related to Oregon's neighbor, California: the terrible smog, the stress of driving the freeways, crazy Hollywood, crowded classrooms, and so forth. He concluded with a tribute to California for efforts to solve its growth problems.

On another occasion, a teacher of 20 years recalled funny experiences in classrooms of prior days as she developed a theme on the special challenges of students wanting to learn in this day. At a forensics award banquet, a speaker humorously characterized varying types of student debaters: the "fast-talking lawyer type"; the "frowner," always grim and deeply serious, believing the world is coming to an end; and the lion, who paces as though in a cage, thus wearing out a pair of shoes at each speech tournament. Accompanying the speaker's humor was an acknowledgment of the values of debating experience.

After-dinner speakers use all types of humor. Stories are favored by some. Among the more universally enjoyed topics of humor are fashions, climate, animals, the generations, car drivers, children, marriage, commuting, college life, professors' lectures, politicians' promises, love and relationships, habits and idiosyncrasies, family affairs, sports, life's ironies, money, and music.

The fabricated personal-experience story sometimes fits in very well. This is the sort of narrative that often begins with "A funny thing happened to me on the way to the banquet this evening" or "When I was in Washington last week, I happened to run into the President waiting for a bus. . . ." After the opening, the speaker fabricates some fantastic story to fit the purpose of the moment. Speaking at a dinner honoring past presidents of a college, a professor reported, "The other day on campus, I ran across President Beltran mowing the lawn in front of the theater." The speaker then went on in gentle ridicule of college administrators who, wanting to prove that they're needed, turn conspicuously to doing various campus chores, like gardening and delivering mail from department to department. After having his fun, the speaker got to an expression of gratitude for the commendable leadership given by past presidents. You might try this sort of approach sometime.

Puns and other plays on words may be useful. Among the other types of comic material are humorous verse, witty descriptions and illustrations, entertaining allusions to famous persons and events, and clever references to local persons and topics, not to mention endless other varieties of jokes, epigrams, one-liners, and funny anecdotes. You may want to consult "treasuries" of wit and wisdom or books of jokes and other humorous material. Most libraries have these, as well as collections of model after-dinner speeches.

Free your imaginative spirit, and all kinds of possibilities for raising a laugh will come to mind.

In addition to following proven practices of speech preparation, consider the following suggestions when preparing the after-dinner speech:

1. Choose a theme that's suitable to the audience and the occasion.

2. Plan carefully and follow the selected theme; avoid irrelevant detail.

3. Develop the theme with appropriate material, being careful to eliminate any that may offend or otherwise distract the listeners.

4. Give special attention to transitions—devices that connect and give coherence to ideas and materials.

5. Use only *your* kind of story or piece of humor, the type that's easy for *you* to handle.

6. Be brief, especially if in doubt about the amount of allotted time.

THE NOMINATING SPEECH

Most of the recommendations for speeches of introduction apply to speeches designed to nominate a candidate for office. However, you should pay special attention to the following points:

1. Mention requirements of the office and how your candidate is qualified to meet them.

2. Be positive in your approach; avoid sarcasm and ridicule if you must refer to the other candidates running for the same office.

3. Consider using an indirect pattern of organization, one allowing you to lead up to the naming of your nominee. See Chapter Eight.

4. You might include a memory point—a catchy phrase or slogan that the voters will be likely to remember. The famous "I like Ike" was enormously helpful to Dwight D. Eisenhower during his first campaign for the presidency.

5. Let your conviction and enthusiasm facilitate the delivery of your thoughts.

THE PRESENTATION SPEECH

Some organizations, communities, and companies present symbols of acknowledgment to praiseworthy persons or groups. An award or gift is made in recognition of long or exemplary service, scholastic or athletic accomplishment, or the commemoration of an event.

To the people involved it's an important occasion, and the accompanying speech should be given in the proper spirit. If this speaking opportunity ever arises for you, what should you do?

1. Discuss reasons for the presentation and what the symbol being offered represents.

2. Discuss the characteristics and qualifications of the recipient.

3. Find a basis for being sincere in expressing the genuine pleasure felt by those giving the award or gift.

4. Avoid making embarrassing exaggerations, while maintaining the proper spirit of bestowing the honor.

In a public ceremony on February 23, 1962, President John F. Kennedy presented Colonel John H. Glenn, Jr., with a medal for his accomplishment as the first American to fly a spacecraft in orbit around the earth. The speech is printed here in full.

Now Colonel Glenn, will you step forward.

Seventeen years ago today, a group of marines put the American flag on Mount Surabachi, so it's very appropriate that today we decorate Colonel Glenn of the United States Marine Corps and also realize that in the not too distant future a marine or a naval man or an Air Force man will put the American flag on the moon.

I present this citation:

"The President of the United States takes pleasure in awarding the National Aeronautics and Space Administration's Distinguished Service Medal to Lieutenant Colonel John H. Glenn, Jr., United States Marine Corps, for services set forth in the following:

"For exceptionally meritorious service to the Government of the United States in a duty of great responsibility as the first American astronaut to perform orbital flight.

"Lieutenant Colonel Glenn's orbital flight on February 20, 1962, made an outstanding contribution to the advancement of human knowledge, of space technology, and in demonstration of man's capabilities in space flight.

"His performance was marked by his great professional skill, his skill as a test pilot, his unflinching courage, and his extraordinary ability to perform most difficult tasks under conditions of great physical stress and personal danger.

"His performance in fulfillment of this most dangerous assignment reflects the highest credit upon himself and the United States."

Colonel, we appreciate what you've done.[2]

Another model of a presentation speech is that of University of California Chancellor Chang-Lin Tien, made as he bestowed the Berkeley Medal upon Mary Robinson, President of Ireland, after she addressed the audience at the Berkeley campus. Since he had already given her an introduction before she spoke, as mentioned above, his presentation was brief.

Today you have honored us by sharing your insight and your inspiration. Before you leave, I have the pleasure of making a special presentation. In your campaign for president, you told the people of Ireland, and I quote: "You have a voice, I will make it heard."

And that is what you have done. You are a champion of women's rights. You are a fighter for saving the environment. You are an ardent proponent for a lasting peace in Northern Ireland. President Robinson, you are making the voice of Ireland heard round the world and we salute you.

As a token of our great admiration and esteem, President Robinson, I am honored to present to you our highest honor—the Berkeley Medal.

THE ACCEPTANCE SPEECH

A speech given to accept an award or gift may be an impromptu effort. Even if the recipient has advance notice of the honor and is ready with a response, some remark in the presentation may require special acknowledgment. The nature of the occasion, the type of symbol offered, and the preceding formalities will influence the response. However, there are general guideposts that apply to most speeches of acceptance:

1. Speak briefly, unless you know that a long speech is expected.
2. Discuss the importance of the award to you; show your appreciation.
3. Modestly discuss significant and relevant facts that led to the honor being paid to you. Discuss the roles played by other persons.
4. Pay tribute to those responsible for the presentation.

Notice how Colonel Glenn follows all four of the guideposts in his response to President Kennedy's presentation. His first five words are in acknowledgment of the extended applause.

All right. Fine. Thank you.

Sit down, please.

I can't express my appreciation adequately to be here in accepting this when I know how many thousand people all over the country were involved in helping accomplish what we did last Tuesday and knowing how—particularly this group here at the Cape and many of the groups here on the platform, our own group of astronauts who were scattered all around the world and who performed their functions here at the Cape—also we all acted literally and figuratively as a team and it was a real team effort all the way.

We have stressed the team effort in Project Mercury. It goes across the board, I think, sort of a crosscut of Americana of industry and military and Civil Service, Governmental workers, contractors, the—almost a crosscut of American effort in the technical field, I think. It wasn't specialized by any one particular group.

It was headed up by NASA, of course, but thousands and thousands of people have contributed certainly as much or more than I have to the project.

I would like to consider that I was sort of a figurehead for this whole big tremendous effort and I'm very proud of the medal I have on my lapel here for all of us—you included—because I think it represents all of our efforts, not just mine.

Thank you very much and thank you, Mr. President.[3]

In response to Chancellor Tien's presentation of the Berkeley Medal, President Robinson said,

It is an enormous pleasure that I should come to Berkeley today to receive the great honour of your Berkeley Medal. The name Berkeley connects us across two countries and an ocean. Bishop Berkeley was, after all, a Fellow of Trinity College, my own University, and his name is attached both to your University and to this medal which I am honoured to receive.

THE WELCOMING SPEECH

Noted groups or individuals who visit your school, community, church gathering, or club may be accorded the courtesy of a welcoming speech, as might new members of a professional or social organization to which you might belong. These suggestions may be helpful to you in handling this type of speaking role:

1. Comment on the nature of the occasion.
2. Comment on praiseworthy and interesting traits or characteristics of your visitor(s) or new member(s).
3. Mention pertinent features of the welcoming group (your group).
4. Be a genial and cordial ambassador of good will; put out the welcome mat.

When President Miguel de la Madrid of Mexico came to Washington, D.C., to discuss topics of concern to his country and the United States, he was welcomed by President Ronald Reagan. In his cordial speech, Mr. Reagan stressed mutual interests of the two countries.

Mexico is now the third largest trading partner of the United States. We, on the other hand, are the world's largest market for Mexican goods. The prosperity and happiness of our peoples is inexorably linked by these bonds of commerce and friendship. . . .

The United States and Mexico have a common border and a common "American" heritage as well. The people of our countries— Spanish- and English-speaking alike—represent the values and culture of the New World, a bond shared by 650 million Americans from the north slope of Alaska to the tip of Tierra del Fuego.

After a number of references to serious economic and political problems in the Americas, he concluded,

Let me reaffirm today that the United States will do what it can. It will go the extra mile to find peaceful solutions and to protect democracy and independence in the hemisphere.

Cooperation and respect between the United States and Mexico will do much in our efforts to promote peace and improve the standard of living of our people. As adversaries, our horizons would be limited. As friends, equal in each other's eyes and drawing from each other's strength, a universe of opportunity awaits.

Mr. President, I speak for all the citizens of my country when I say your friends welcome you to the United States.[4]

Think back to Chancellor Chang-Lin Tien's introduction to Irish President Robinson. Though one of his purposes was to introduce her as speaker, another was to welcome her to his campus. Thus, his speech serves also as model of a welcoming speech.

THE RESPONSE TO A WELCOMING SPEECH

When welcomed, you may be expected to respond briefly. If so, consider the following recommendations:

1. Graciously acknowledge the host's courtesy.
2. Bring greetings from the group that you represent (if you are a representative) and point up common bonds.
3. Sincerely praise the welcoming organization.

President de la Madrid graciously responded to President Reagan's remarks, including the following comments:

It is with great pleasure that I transmit to you warm greetings from the people of Mexico to the great people of the United States of America. We Mexicans wish to continue building not only peaceful and dignified neighborly relations, but also a fruitful and positive friendship. Our two countries are reliable neighbors and friends, and we know how to conduct our relations in mutual respect for our independence and our cultural and political concepts.

We have learned to solve our problems with serenity and realism. Two peoples with different histories and cultures with imbalances and disparities have found the path of dialogue and communication to be the basis for their understanding. The wide range and diversity of our bilateral relations highlight our dialogue.

Echoing President Reagan, President de la Madrid referred to conditions in Latin America needing the attention of the United States and Mexico. Then he concluded,

Mr. President, I have no doubt that in a climate of frankness and friendship our talks will enhance our understanding of these topics, and we will be able to find new solutions to the problems that concern us. Mr. President, I thank you very much for your warm welcome.

LOOKING BACK

When preparing for a special occasion, remember three governing principles:

1. Know the demands of the occasion.
2. Employ sound speaking fundamentals.
3. Adapt to the occasion.

These principles apply to all types of speaking, including those discussed in this chapter:

1. The impromptu speech
2. The announcement
3. The speech to introduce a speaker
4. The nomination speech

5. The after-dinner speech
6. Speeches of presentation and acceptance
7. The welcoming speech
8. The response to the welcoming speech

There's a type of speech for nearly every special occasion, and not all of them could be considered in this chapter. One form of specialized speaking not mentioned is *interviewing,* treated in Appendix B. Also, Chapter Thirteen discusses a major specific form: small group discussion.

NOTES

1. Texts of Ms. Robinson's and Chancellor Tien's remarks were supplied by the Public Information Office of the University of California, Berkeley.
2. *New York Times,* February 24, 1962, 16.
3. *New York Times,* February 24, 1962, 16.
4. *New York Times,* May 16, 1984, A4.

MODEL SPEECHES   APPENDIX A

THE TABLE OF SPEECHES

Making Lincoln Live by Howard W. Runkel
  A model of the four-part speech used to argue a case, with:
      Clear purpose
      Strong organization
      Full verbal development of ideas, including examples,
         statistics, and quotations
      Fitting language
      Logical and psychological appeals
      Helpful summary

Trumpet Mutes by Julie Taner
  A model of the four-part speech used to inform, with:
      Clear purpose
      Strong organization
      Development of ideas with visual and audio aids
      Effective transitions
      Fitting language
      Helpful summary

What Is an Average? by Patrick Manion
  A model of the four-part speech used to inform, with:
      Clear purpose
      Strong organization
      Development of ideas with visual aids
      Effective transitions
      Fitting language
      Helpful summary

The Other 99 Percent of the Population by Maggie Hooper
  A model of the motivated sequence pattern used to persuade, with:
      Clear purpose
      Strong organization
      Verbal development of ideas, including examples, quotations, and
         statistics
      Fitting language
      Logical, psychological, and personal appeals

Farewell Address by Chief Black Hawk

A model of the Native American final surrender speech, with:

Strong personal appeal

Deep emotional appeal

Vivid figurative language

Clear, direct, precise language

Parallel construction

Effective contrast

Useful repetition

Opportunities for Hispanic Women by Janice Payan

A model of persuasive speech relying on personal experience, with:

High positive ethos

Compelling argument that helped effect identification with the audience

Psychological appeal that helped effect identification with the audience

Fitting humor

Effective examples, including both illustrations and instances; much personal narrative

Persuasive explanations

Useful repetition

Clear, lively, and varied language

Racial and Ethnic Relations in American Higher Education

by Michael L. Williams

A model of the speech to convince, with:

Appealing logos

Well-chosen examples, including personal narrative

Extensive use of quotation and authority

Useful statistics

Effective contrast

Strong appeals to general American values

Clear and varied language

MAKING LINCOLN LIVE
Howard W. Runkel

*Howard W. Runkel, professor emeritus of speech, Willamette
University, has addressed hundreds of audiences throughout the
West. Usually he speaks at conventions, commencements, service
club meetings, and similar gatherings.*

*On February 12, 1957, he spoke before the Oregon State
Legislature, which convened in joint session to commemorate the
birth of Abraham Lincoln. The text, supplied by Dr. Runkel, is a
model of four-part speech composition.*

A few years ago 55 outstanding authorities in American history were
invited by Harvard University to rate the presidents of the United States in
five categories—great, near great, average, below average, and failure.
The only one to receive every vote for the top rank was Abraham Lincoln.

More than one writer has linked the American Civil War President with
Jesus and Socrates as the three transcendentally great figures of all time.
Russia's Count Tolstoy, whose tremendous volume *War and Peace*
immortalized its author, declared that "Lincoln aspired to be divine and
he was."

Abraham Lincoln has become the most written about human being in
history; more than 5,000 books have been written about his life. His letters, state papers, and speeches in print today total over 1,100,000 words,
more than are contained either in the Bible or the sum of Shakespeare's
works. At least two of Lincoln's speeches, the Address at Gettysburg and
the Second Inaugural, have been translated into nearly every known language and are recorded on monuments and plaques the world over. The
Lincoln Memorial in our nation's capital is year after year our most visited
shrine. Countless thoughtful legislators admit having derived inspiration
and guidance by standing in contemplation before that moving statue of
the Great Emancipator.

Lincoln's likeness appears on millions of coins and adorns the walls of
thousands of classrooms. The ethical quality of the name "Lincoln" has
given priceless impetus to numerous political campaigns, sales programs,
and philanthropic drives. It is no secret that if one can quote Lincoln on
behalf of his cause he is more nearly assured of success.

That this remarkable man should have been the product of our newly
freed soil; that he should have been nurtured in the budding institutions
of this infant nation has always been a matter of justifiable pride to us
Americans. It is only natural, therefore, that the anniversary of the birth of
Abraham Lincoln, sixteenth President of the United States, has traditionally become an occasion for redetermination on our part "that this nation,
under God, shall have a new birth of freedom."

Today, February 12, 1957, is the 148th anniversary of Lincoln's birth. Any eulogist is tempted once again to dwell upon those uniquely appealing qualities of this extraordinary personality—his integrity, his patriotism, his gentleness, his humor, his tact, his insight, his vision. However, were Lincoln alive he would, characteristically, be more impressed by tributes in the form of action, rather than diction. To this end, let us briefly note only three of his qualities which every one of us, regardless of party, color, creed, or tongue, might well exercise as he attempts to live worthily in these complex and perilous times.

Abraham Lincoln was, above all, humble of spirit. No tribute ought to omit reference to this, his most endearing quality. Few, if any, are the instances in which he succumbed to mankind's most fundamental failing—the inability to put self in proper perspective among people and issues.

Do you remember how Lincoln drove out of Washington after a wearying day behind the desk in the White House to confer with his subordinate, General McClellan? The arrogant McClellan, aware of his commander-in-chief's presence, loftily instructed his orderly to tell the President that no interview was possible any more that evening; that he had gone to bed and was not to be disturbed. A witness to the embarrassing scene indignantly besought Lincoln to "pull his rank." "Are you going to tolerate such insubordination?" he pleaded. That stooped and worn figure merely shrugged and answered: "I'd hold McClellan's horse if that would give us victories." History records that on that evening the immortal had waited upon the mortal.

Then there was the time that a high government official discovered Lincoln in the act of blacking his own boots. "Mr. President, gentlemen don't black their own boots," was the protest. Lincoln looked up and replied innocently: "No? Whose boots do they black?"

Almost touching was that priceless little autobiography Lincoln submitted upon request for a minor "Who's Who?" of his day. It is well worth reading again. Here is what this humble man wrote:

> *My parents were of "second families." I can read, write and cipher to the rule of three, but this is all. I was raised to farm work. I became postmaster at a very small post office. There is not much of this autobiography for the reason, I suppose, that there is not much of me.*

Such a man must inevitably recognize the omniscience of his Creator. Hence, when a lady pushed through to him at a public gathering and cried: "Oh, Mr. President, do you think God is on our side in this terrible war?" Lincoln could only reply gravely: "Madame, I'm more concerned with whether or not we are on God's side."

The living memory of him whom we commemorate here this morning teaches us, every one, the truth of the Beatitude: "Blessed are the meek, for they shall inherit the earth."

Abraham Lincoln was a man of rare understanding. Historians marvel at the discernment of this rough, unschooled frontiersman. It showed in his interpretation of a war as a struggle for the survival of the Union; it was evidenced by his saving of the border states for the North when one false move would have driven them to the Southern fold; it was seen in his timing of the Emancipation Proclamation which, by giving the war an antislavery twist, made all but impossible British intervention in behalf of the Confederacy. And it is clear in his familiar definition of democracy: "As I would not be a slave, so I would not be a master. This expresses my idea of democracy."

But more touchingly, Lincoln's understanding is manifest in his associations with individuals. In 1864 he wrote words of sympathy to a grieving mother in Boston. This is one of the most quoted personal letters in our language.

> *Dear Madam:*
>
> *I have been shown in the files of the War Department a statement of the Adjutant General of Massachusetts that you are the mother of five sons who have died gloriously on the field of battle. I feel how weak and fruitless must be any words of mine which should attempt to beguile you from the grief of a loss so overwhelming. But I cannot refrain from tendering to you the consolation that may be found in the thanks of the Republic they died to save. I pray that our Heavenly Father may assuage the anguish of your bereavement, and leave you only the cherished memory of the loved and lost, and the solemn pride that must be yours to have laid so costly a sacrifice upon the altar of freedom.*
>
> > *Yours very sincerely and respectfully,*
> > *Abraham Lincoln*

This letter, replete with humility and understanding, has become a part of the American bible. How it stands out as peculiarly symbolic of our democratic heritage is dramatically revealed in contrast to a letter written by Kaiser Wilhelm to a German mother whose loss was not five but ninefold! Written in the third person of royalty, the letter reads:

> *Madame:*
>
> *His Majesty the Kaiser hears that you have sacrificed nine sons in defense of the Fatherland in the present war. His Majesty is immensely gratified at the fact and in recognition is pleased to send you his photograph with silver frame and autograph signature.*
>
> > *Wilhelm II*

Lincoln's understanding of human nature was expressed, too, in a letter written to General Joseph Hooker. Hooker had distinguished himself more as an imprudent critic of the President than as a winner of battles. Lincoln had every right to accuse him of remarks smacking of disloyalty. But note the letter with its tactfully worded rebuke:

> *General:*
>
> *I have placed you at the head of the Army of the Potomac. Of course I have done this upon what appears to me to be sufficient*

reasons, and yet I think it best for you to know that there are some things in regard to which I am not quite satisfied with you. I believe you to be a brave and skillful soldier, which of course I like. I also believe you do not mix politics with your profession, in which you are right. You have confidence in yourself, which is a valuable if not an indispensable quality. You are ambitious, which, within reasonable bonds, does good rather than harm. . . .

I have heard, in such a way as to believe it, of your recently saying that both the army and the government needed a dictator. Of course it was not for this, but in spite of it, that I have given you the command. Only those generals who gain successes can set up dictators. What I now ask of you is military success, and I will risk the dictatorship. . . .

And now beware of rashness. Beware of rashness, but with energy and sleepless vigilance go forward and give us victories.

Note how Lincoln opens with a series of compliments, then administers his rebuke and concludes with a challenge. The General has been reprimanded but with that understanding that spares feelings. Can any of us today say he needs not more of his rare quality of understanding—in the home, at the workplace, in the classroom, yes, even in legislative chambers. The life of Abraham Lincoln gives new vitality to the words of the Old Testament: "Wisdom is the principal thing; therefore get wisdom; and with all thy getting get understanding."

Abraham Lincoln was a man of generous spirit. He was the President who commuted scores of death sentences for condemned soldiers. To critics of this policy he answered: "Must I shoot a simple-minded soldier boy who deserts, while I must not touch a hair of a wily agitator who induces him to desert?"

Lincoln was the President who, smarting under harsh criticism of the imperious but capable Edwin M. Stanton, nevertheless appointed him Secretary of War. The snobbish Salmon Chase treated the President with condescension and caused humiliation on more than one occasion. The big man in the White House did not let this blind him to Chase's qualifications and he made him Chief Justice of the United States.

Of course Abraham Lincoln's most imperishable expression of bigness of spirit is contained in his Second Inaugural Address, considered by scholars here and abroad to be one of the glories and treasures of mankind. On this occasion he spoke amid the drama of the war's climax. The victory of the North was clearly in sight. Already meaner spirits were calling for a vengeful peace. But Lincoln counseled his huge audience in words of the Sermon on the Mount: "Judge not that ye be not judged." Then he summed up his message:

With malice toward none; with charity for all; with firmness in the right, as God gives us to see the right; let us strive on to finish the work we are in; to bind up the nation's wounds; to care for him who shall have borne the battle and for his widow, and his orphan—to do all which may achieve and cherish a just and lasting peace among ourselves, and with all nations.

As a thoughtful boy in Indiana, Abraham Lincoln had spoken for himself; as a prairie lawyer in Illinois he had spoken for clients; as a politician–debater he had spoken for a faction; as a campaigner for the Presidency he spoke for the North; as a President he spoke for the Nation; now, at the Second Inaugural, he was speaking out for all humanity.

As Lincoln lay dying only six weeks later, one of his most severe critics who had come to appreciate the heroic qualities of this humble, discerning, and generous man, pointed at the figure on the bed and said: "There lies the most perfect ruler of men this world has ever seen."

My fellow citizens: Each of us has inherited the legacy of this great American ruler as he faces the tremendous public problems and perils of our day. God grant on this 148th anniversary of Abraham Lincoln's birth that we in his spirit may resolve to "take increased devotion to that cause for which he gave the last full measure of devotion." Then, and only then, will we have made Lincoln live in our time.

TRUMPET MUTES

Julie Taner

*Ms. Taner gave this four-minute speech as a student in one of my
classes in the principles of speech communication.*

This is a trumpet [holds up a trumpet], an instrument I have played for 10
years now, and I am still fascinated by the great variety of sounds which
can be produced by a trumpet. One of the main ways to change the sound
of a trumpet is to use things called mutes.

Today I would like to explain to you the differences among the three
most common kinds of trumpet mutes.

The most typical trumpet mute is a straight mute. As you can see [shows
mute], the sides of this mute are basically straight. A straight mute quiets,
or mutes, a trumpet. And it changes the tone to a slightly brassier, biting
tone. This is what the trumpet sounds like if it is open, or without a mute
[demonstration]. This is what it sounds like with a straight mute in [dem-
onstration].

If you take a straight mute and add a cup to it, you will have the next
most common mute, a cup mute. As with the straight mute, the cup mute
gets its name as a result of the shape of the mute. It has this cup on the
bottom of it [shows cup mute]. These mutes are very useful because they
soften the volume, but only slightly alter the tone of the trumpet. As a
reminder, this is what the trumpet sounds like without any mutes [dem-
onstration]. And this is what it sounds like with a cup mute in [demonstra-
tion].

While straight and cup mutes are used in all kinds of music, the next
most familiar trumpet mute, the harmon, or wa-wa mute, is used mostly
in jazz playing [shows harmon mute]. The harmon mute was named after
its inventor, but its nickname, the wa-wa mute, is a direct result of one of
the uses of this mute, which I will demonstrate a little later. For most purposes, the harmon mute is used without the added stem [pulls stem out
and holds up], and it produces a very distinctive sound [demonstration].
For a special effect, the stem can be put in, and with the use of your left
hand, a sound similar to "wa" can be produced. The trumpet can sound
almost as if it is speaking [demonstration].

Do you remember the name and sound that went with each mute? The
first mute [shows straight mute] was a straight mute and sounds like this
[demonstration]. The next mute was a cup mute [shows cup mute] and
sounds like this [demonstration]. The third mute was a harmon mute
[shows harmon mute] and can be played without the stem [demonstration]
or with the stem [demonstration]. The next time that you listen to the
radio or your favorite record or tape, listen carefully and you might be able
to recognize the sound of one of the mutes you heard demonstrated
today.

WHAT IS AN AVERAGE?
Patrick Manion

Mr. Manion gave this four-minute speech while a student in one of my recent classes in principles of speech communication. The outline for the speech is found in Chapter Six.

Often we are bombarded by statistics. We hear and read about the percentages of this or that event happening. Also, we are informed that he is an average student, the average price of houses in an area is X dollars, and so on.

Since the word average is a loose term, it is easy to be tricked when someone uses the term without qualification.

Today I would like to describe three ways of looking at "average."

The first and most common kind of average is the arithmetic mean. This is the measure that most people think of when they hear "average."

Finding the arithmetic mean involves two steps. First, sum up all the data points in the data set, and then divide by the number of things you counted.

Let's see what we get. A student's grade-point average is an example of an average computed using the arithmetic mean. Here, I'll show you on the blackboard [sketching]. First, you list all grades in all courses; then divide by the number of courses.

As another example, consider last year's earnings of my hypothetical siblings and myself. Let me put this on the board—with a little humor [sketching]. My eldest sister has her own business and earned $1,000,000. My twin sisters are also dynamos, and they each earned $200,000. As a student working part-time, I earned $10,000, while my three younger brothers, Daryl, Larry, and Harry, each earned just $2,000. By summing these amounts, we get $1,416,000. Now, dividing by the number of siblings (seven in this case), we have $202,285.71, and I claim that the average wage for my brothers and sisters and myself last year is over $200,000. Sounds pretty good, doesn't it! But how prosperous are Daryl, Larry, and Harry?

In addition to the mean, the median is another very common form of average.

The median is simply the middle point in a set of numerical data. Exactly half of the data points are above this middle element, and half are below.

Again, let's see what we get with some cases. The price of houses in an area is often described by a median price figure. For example, in the San Francisco Bay Area it is $239,000 [sketching]. Returning to the board and the example of my siblings' wages, you can see that my wage, $10,000, is in the middle of the group. My three sisters all earned more than I did, and my three brothers earned less than I [sketching]. The rationale then is that since exactly half of the people earned more than I did and half earned less, my wage must be average. It *is* average—a kind called median. I now claim that the average wage for my brothers and sisters and myself last year is $10,000. The word average *is* confusing, isn't it.

While the mean and the median are frequently used forms of average, the mode is a third and important notion of average.

The mode is simply the most frequently met-with number in a set of numeric data. To remember mode, think of *most.*

Again, let's see what we get. Returning to my family, you can see that my brothers each earned $2,000. If we look at this same set of data from the modal viewpoint—here, I'll put up the figures—three out of seven (or about 43 percent) earned the same amount [sketching]. Since "most" of the people earned $2,000, I now claim that the average wage for my brothers and sisters and myself last year is $2,000! And so it is, when mode is the kind of average found.

Can you see what I've done? I have packaged the same data to look differently, depending on whether I chose the mean, the median, or the mode. If we use the mean, the average is over $200,000 [reference to the sketching]. If we use the median, the average is $10,000 [reference to sketching]. If we use the mode, the average is just $2,000 [reference to sketching].

Finally, the next time your hear that something is considered "average," you will ask yourself whether that computed average is the mean, median, or the mode.

THE OTHER 99 PERCENT OF THE POPULATION

Maggie Hooper

Ms. Hooper prepared this speech while a student of Professor John E. Baird at California State University, Hayward. It's an excellent model of the motivated sequence method of organization.

Attention

Ten million different kinds of living things share this planet with us. Have you seen most of them? It's my guess that you haven't noticed more than a thousand different kinds of living things, which is one hundredth of one percent of the total number. Isn't it time you learned how some of the other 99.99999 percent live? In the age of the environmental movement it is amazing to me that people know very little about the planet on which they live or the other creatures on it.

It's no wonder they also do not know what will affect the environment negatively and what will affect it positively. For example, most of us know that the amount of phosphates added to detergents has been cut down to help stop pollution in our lakes and streams. But how many people know why phosphates cause these problems? Plants thrive on phosphates. What happens is that algae in the water grow and multiply so rapidly when phosphates (or other phosphorous compounds) are added to the water, and use up so much oxygen, that the fish and other creatures actually suffocate. On the other hand, some very effective fertilizers are made from mixtures of phosphorus and nitrous compounds. So phosphates may help some parts of the environment and devastate other parts. If you didn't know what phosphates did, how would you know in what parts of the environment to put them and in what parts to keep them out?

People do not know enough about the natural environment.

Need

This is the source of many serious problems. I'd like to talk today about two areas of problems caused by this ignorance regarding the natural environment: the political problems and the psychological problems, and how to solve these problems.

This is a political society, and you must have a broad knowledge of the natural environment to function effectively in such a society. How will you vote on issues related to the President's current energy plan, in which he proposes to eliminate many environmental safeguard laws, when you have no idea what the elimination of these safeguards will do to the environment? This issue is serious: it might mean great danger to your health. You cannot rely on the lawmakers or the government agencies to protect your rights for you. Even the people related to environmental projects sometimes cannot be trusted to watch out for your interests. Brook Evans, northwest representative of the Sierra Club, says, "I have never forgotten my first meeting nearly five years ago with the supervisor of the Willamette National Forest in Oregon. He put his feet up on his desk, leaned back and said, 'I don't like you people. I'm not going to let you lock up any more wilderness.' And he referred to the Oregon Cascades Wilderness as a 'forest slum.'" With such insensitivity from a protector of our resources, it becomes obvious that you must take the initiative yourself to find out more about the natural environment if you are to preserve, by political means, your water, your parks, and your planet.

In addition to political reasons, it is also necessary to take the initiative in increasing environmental knowledge for psychological reasons. My friend, Susanna, who lived all her young life in Chicago, had never seen a garden snail before. I had to show her one! We both worked in a medical research facility which used and sacrificed great numbers of animals in scientific experiments. After being exposed to the animals, Susanna realized that animals have personalities, too, and she started having problems with her conscience and with guilt. I had already had many pets and spent half my life at the creek, so the decision was easy for me: I refused to work with the animals from the start. Susanna could have saved herself a lot of heartache and guilt if she'd been exposed to animals earlier. Not being environmentally aware can also cause deeper and more widespread psychological problems. The late Alan W. Watts, noted philosopher and author, believed that modern Western society has a serious problem that stems from the fact that man has become a frustrated outsider in his own world, a world of the natural environment. Watts recommended development of a greater understanding of nature to alleviate this problem. There seem to be so many widespread psychological problems in our society now.

Hopefully your sanity will be preserved with the help of some basic study of the environment.

It becomes all too plain to me that studying the natural environment is more than an aesthetic pleasure; it is a necessity in our world, for political and psychological reasons. In the words of Edward Stainbrook, professor and chairman of the Department of Psychiatry at the U.S.C. Medical School, "We must urge a general insistent concern about the meaning and functions of the natural environment for reasons other than a romantic agony over the loss of natural man and of natural nature."

Satisfaction

The solutions to this problem of environmental ignorance are really quite simple, but the solution process must be a long-term commitment. An excellent way to learn about the biosphere around us is to look to mass media. In our University library alone there are more than 200 books on the environment with topics from thinking like a mountain, to ecology and the industrial society, to population genetics. There are over 15 periodicals solely dedicated to environmental issues and education, such as the *Journal of Environmental Education* and *American Naturalist.* The National Geographic Society and the Jacques Cousteau Society periodically broadcast television specials that are incredibly fascinating and informative ecologically. There is a National Geographic special on TV tomorrow night.

If you don't want to go to the library or watch TV, there are many classes being offered by community colleges, nature centers, and different organizations that could be invaluable. At Chabot College, here in Hayward, there are five day classes and two evening classes next quarter with titles such as "Man and the Environment," "Environmental Quality Control," "Backpacking," "Plant Identity," and "Oceanography." On the Valley campus of Chabot College there are also classes with titles like "Coastal Redwoods" and "Effects of Radiation Technology." And these classes aren't boring! Instead of memorizing biological data, as was done in the past, there is a trend toward some exciting new teaching methods. For example, in some cases, students are given contrived environmental predicaments for which they must make decisions and solve problems.

Although mass media can give you an excellent background, you must see the system in action for yourself. You must see real-life examples of nature.

A great way to become an amateur ecologist and have a great time, too, is to join a club. Join the Sierra Club, join Greenpeace, or volunteer for the State Parks Foundation. There are scores of other environmentally oriented clubs that provide lectures, hikes, and conferences to help you in your exploration of the environment. Parks are a good place to look for public activities. This weekend, Tilden Nature Area in Berkeley is featuring a wild-life hike through a redwood forest, a "Look-for-Bugs" nature walk, slideshows, and more. Coyote Hills Regional Park also has activities this weekend.

Thirty years ago very few people had heard of air pollution or water pollution. Today we have the Clean Air Act and the Clean Water Act as evidence that education through mass media and direct contact can help solve the problems. Five years ago we didn't have protection for our redwoods. Today we have the Redwoods National Park established through efforts to educate the public by concerned individuals and clubs. People who have joined these clubs, and spent some time with the other 99 percent, tell me they learned something about themselves and their position in the universe and that they have found places in which they can really relax.

The choice is really yours. In the future we can have a world of people confused and frustrated about themselves and the world around them, a world envisioned in Ray Bradbury's *Fahrenheit 451,* where a girl is thought insane because she is curious about the natural world around her, what there is left of it. A nuclear war isn't necessary to destroy our planet and our race. The destruction of our biosphere, including ourselves, has already begun, with pollution and the extinction of some species. If we let this go on, knowing how important this problem is, we will be committing mass suicide. Wouldn't you get involved if you could help prevent all this? We could create a world where all species are healthy and protected from extinction, where people understand their places in the universe and are happy. How much more like the Garden of Eden would this planet

Visualization

be if we were to understand our environment?

Go to the library, check out a book on the environment and read it, or join a club, or go out and get muddy looking for newts, or look for ways in which the plants at the beach adapt to constant wind and spray.

I have copies of a list of the addresses of different clubs, and information on how to join them, which I'd like to pass out now. This list includes the dates, times, and channels of those specials on TV I was telling you about. It also includes information about environmental classes at Chabot and how to sign up for them, and tells you of environmentally oriented events in the parks I mentioned.

The 99 percent of other living creatures invite you to learn about them.

Action

FAREWELL ADDRESS[1]

Chief Black Hawk

Black Hawk, chief of the Sauk tribe, was one of the most powerful and resolute of the Native American orators. But like most other great leaders of the tribes, he had no choice but to accept the reality of the white man's superior military force. His farewell speech, presumably given to authorities at Prairie du Chein when he surrendered in 1832, is a sample of his eloquence.

You have taken me prisoner with all my warriors. I am much grieved, for I expected, if I did not defeat you, to hold out much longer, and give you more trouble before I surrendered. I tried hard to bring you into ambush, but your last general understands Indian fighting. The first one was not so wise. When I saw that I could not beat you by Indian fighting, I determined to rush on you, and fight you face to face. I fought hard. But your guns were well aimed. The bullets flew like birds in the air, and whizzed by our ears like the wind through the trees in winter. My warriors fell around me; it began to look dismal. I saw my evil day at hand. The sun rose dim on us in the morning, and at night it sank in a dark cloud, and looked like a ball of fire. That was the last sun that shone on Black Hawk. His heart is dead, and no longer beats quick in his bosom. He is now a prisoner to the white men; they will do with him as they wish. But he can stand torture, and is not afraid of death. He is no coward. Black Hawk is an Indian.

He has done nothing for which an Indian ought to be ashamed. He has fought for his countrymen, the squaws and papooses, against white men, who came, year after year, to cheat them and take away their lands. You know the cause of our making war. It is known to all white men. They ought to be ashamed of it. The white men despise the Indians, and drive them from their homes. But the Indians are not deceitful. The white men speak bad of the Indian, and look at him spitefully. But the Indian does not tell lies; Indians do not steal.

An Indian who is as bad as the white men, could not live in our nation; he would be put to death, and eaten up by the wolves. The white men are bad schoolmasters; they carry false looks and deal in false actions; they smile in the face of the poor Indian to cheat him; they shake them by the hand to gain their confidence, to make them drunk, to deceive them, and ruin our wives. We told them to let us alone, and keep away from us; but they followed on and beset our paths, and they coiled themselves among us like the snake. They poisoned us by their touch. We were not safe. We lived in danger. We were becoming like them, hypocrites and liars, adulterers, lazy drones, all talkers, and no workers.

We looked up to the Great Spirit. We went to our great father. We were encouraged. His great council gave us fair words and big promises; but we got no satisfaction. Things were growing worse. There were no deer in the forest. The opossum and beaver were fled; the springs were drying up, and our squaws and papooses without victuals to keep them from starving; we called a great council and built a large fire. The spirit of our fathers arose and spoke to us to avenge our wrongs or die. We all spoke before the council fire. It was warm and pleasant. We set up the war-whoop, and dug up the tomahawk; our knives were ready, and the heart of Black Hawk swelled high in his bosom when he led his warriors to battle. He is satisfied. He will go to the world of spirits contented. He has done his duty. His father will meet him there, and commend him.

Black Hawk is a true Indian, and disdains to cry like a woman. He feels for his wife, his children and friends. But he does not care for himself. He cares for his nation and the Indians. They will suffer. He laments their fate. The white men do not scalp the head; but they do worse—they poison the heart; it is not pure with them. His countrymen will not be scalped, but they will, in a few years, become like white men, so that you can't trust them, and there must be, as in the white settlements, nearly as many officers as men, to take care of them and keep them in order.

Farewell, my nation! Black Hawk tried to save you, and avenge your wrongs. He drank the blood of some of the whites. He has been taken prisoner, and his plans are stopped. He can do no more. He is near his end. His sun is setting, and he will rise no more. Farewell to Black Hawk.

OPPORTUNITIES FOR HISPANIC WOMEN[2]

Janice Payan, an Hispanic woman and vice president of U.S. West Communications, delivered this stirring speech to the people attending the Adelante Mujer (Onward Women) Conference at Denver in 1990.

Thank you. I felt as if you were introducing someone else because my mind was racing back 10 years, when I was sitting out there in the audience at the Adelante Mujer conference. Anonymous. *Comfortable.* Trying hard to relate to our "successful" speaker, but mostly feeling like Janice Payan, working mother, *glad for a chance to sit down.*

I'll let you in on a little secret. I *still am* Janice Payan, working mother. The only difference is that I have a longer job title, and that I've made a few discoveries these past 10 years that I'm eager to share with you.

The first is that keynote speakers at conferences like this are *not* some sort of alien creatures. Nor were they born under a lucky star. They are ordinary *Hispanic Women* who have stumbled onto an extraordinary discovery.

And that is: *Society lied to us.* We *do* have something up here! We *can* have not only a happy family but also a fulfilling career. We *can* succeed in *school* and *work* and *community life,* because the key is not supernatural powers, it is *perseverance.* Also known as *hard work! And God knows Hispanic women can do hard work!!!* We've been working hard for centuries, from sun-up 'til daughter-down!

One of the biggest secrets around is that successful Anglos were not born under lucky stars, either. The chairman of my company, Jack MacAllister, grew up in a small town in eastern Iowa. His dad was a teacher; his mom was a mom. Jack worked, after school, sorting potatoes in the basement of a grocery store. Of course I realize, *he could have been hoeing them,* like our migrant workers. Nevertheless, Jack came from humble beginnings. And so did virtually every other corporate officer I work with. The major advantage they had was living in a culture that allowed them to *believe* they would get ahead. So more of them did.

It's time for *Hispanic women* to believe we can get ahead, *because we can.* And because *we must.* Our families and work-places and communities and nation need us to reach our full potential. There are jobs to be done, children to be raised, opportunities to be seized. We must look at those opportunities, choose the ones we will respond to, and *do something about them.* We must do so, for others. And we must do so, for ourselves. *Yes,* there are barriers. You're up against racism, sexism, and too much month at the end of the money. *But so was any role model you choose.*

Look at Patricia Diaz-Denis. Patricia was one of nine or ten children in a Mexican-American family that had low means, but high hopes. Her parents said Patricia should go to college. But they had no money. So, little by little, Patricia scraped up the money to send herself. Her boyfriend was going to be a lawyer. And he told Patricia, "You should be a lawyer, too, because *nobody can argue like you do!*" Well, Patricia didn't even know what a lawyer was, but she became one so successful that she eventually was appointed to the Federal Communications Commission in Washington, D.C.

Or look at Toni Pantcha, a Puerto Rican who grew up in a shack with dirt floors, no father, and often no food. But through looking and listening, she realized the power of *community*—the fact that people with very little, when working together, can create much. Dr. Pantcha has created several successful institutions in Puerto Rico, and to me, *she* is an institution. I can see the wisdom in her eyes, hear it in her voice, wisdom far beyond herself, like Mother Teresa.

Or look at Ada Kirby, a Cuban girl whose parents put her on a boat for Miami. Mom and Dad were to follow on the next boat, but they never arrived. So Ada grew up in an orphanage in Pueblo, and set some goals, and today is an executive director at U.S. WEST's research laboratories.

Each of these women was Hispanic, physically deprived, but *mentally awakened to the possibilities of building a better world,* both for others and for themselves. Virtually every Hispanic woman in America started with a similar slate. In fact, let's do a quick survey. If you were born into a home whose economic status was something *less than rich* . . . please raise your hand. It's a good thing I didn't ask the *rich* to raise their hands. I wouldn't have known if anyone was listening. All right. So you were not born rich. As Patricia, Toni, and Ada have shown us, it doesn't matter. It's the choices we make from there on, that make the difference.

If you're thinking, "that's easy for *you* to say, Payan," then I'm thinking: "little do you know. . . ." If you think I got where I am because I'm smarter than you, or have more energy than you, you're wrong. If I'm so smart, why can't I parallel park? If I'm so energetic, why do I still need eight hours of sleep a night? And I mean *need.* If I hadn't had my eight hours last night, you wouldn't even want to *hear* what I'd be saying this morning!

I am more like you and you are more like me than you would guess. I'm a third-generation Mexican-American . . . born into a lower middle-class family right here in Denver. My parents married young; she was pregnant. My father worked only about half the time during my growing-up years. He was short on education, skills, and confidence. There were drug and alcohol problems in the family. My parents finally sent my older brother to a Catholic high school, in hopes that would help him. They sent me to the same school, to *watch* him. That was okay.

In public school I never could choose between the "Greasers" and the "Soshes." I wanted desperately to feel that I "belonged." *But did not like feeling that I had to deny my past to have a future.* Anybody here ever feel that way?

Anyway, the more troubles my brother had, the more I vowed to avoid them. So, in a way, he was my inspiration. As Victor Frankl says, there is meaning in every life. By the way, that brother later died after returning from Vietnam.

I was raised with typical Hispanic female expectations. In other words: If you want to *do* well in life, you'd better . . . can any body finish that sentence? Right! *Marry well.* I liked the idea of loving and marrying someone, but I felt like he should be more than a "meal ticket." And I felt like *I* should be more than a leech. I didn't want to feel so dependent. So I set my goals on having a marriage, a family, *and* a career. I didn't talk too much about those goals, so nobody told me they bordered on *insanity* for a Hispanic woman in the 1960s.

At one point, I even planned to become a doctor. But Mom and Dad said "wait a minute. That takes something like 12 years of college." I had no idea how I was going to pay for *four* years of college, let alone *12.* But what scared me more than the cost was the *time:* In 12 years I'd be an *old woman.* Time certainly changes your perspective on that. My advice to you is, if you want to be a doctor, go for it! It doesn't take 12 years, anyway. If your dreams include a career that requires college . . . go for it! You may be several years older when you finish, but by that time you'd be several years older if you *don't* finish college, too.

For all my suffering in high school, I finished near the top of my graduating class. I dreamed of attending the University of Colorado at Boulder. You want to know what my counselor said? You already know. That I should go to a business college for secretaries, at most. But I went to the University of Colorado, anyway. I arranged my own financial aid: a small grant, a low paying job, and a *big* loan. I just thank God that this was the era when jeans and sweatshirts were getting popular. That was all I had!

I'm going to spare you any description of my class work, except to say that it was difficult—and worth every painful minute. What I want to share with you is three of my strongest memories—and strongest learning experiences—which have nothing to do with books.

One concerns a philosophy professor who, I was sure, was a genius. What I liked best about this man was not the answers he had—but the questions. He asked questions about the Bible, about classic literature, about our place in the universe. He would even jot questions in the margins of our papers. And I give him a lot of credit for helping me examine my own life. I'm telling you about him because I think each of us encounter people who make us think—sometimes painfully. And I feel, very strongly, that we should listen to their questions and suffer through that thinking. We may decide everything in our lives is just like we want it. But we may also decide to change something.

My second big "non-book" experience was in UMAS—the United Mexican American Students. Lost in what seemed like a rich Anglo campus, UMAS was an island of familarity: people who looked like me, talked like me, and *felt* like me. We shared our fears and hopes and hurts—and did something about them. We worked hard to deal with racism on campus, persuading the university to offer Chicano studies classes. But the more racism we experienced, the angrier we became. Some members made bombs. Two of those members died. And I remember asking myself: "Am I willing to go up in smoke over my anger? Or is there another way to make a difference?" We talked a lot about this, and concluded that two wrongs don't make a right. Most of us agreed that working *within* the system was the thing to do. We also agreed not to deny our Hispanic heritage: not to become "coconuts"—brown on the outside and white on the inside—but to look for every opportunity to bring *our* culture to a table of many cultures. That outlook has helped me a great deal as a manager, because it opened me to listening to all points of view. And when a group is open to all points of view, it usually chooses the right course.

The third experience I wanted to share from my college days was the time they came nearest to ending prematurely. During my freshman year, I received a call that my mother had been seriously injured in a traffic accident. Both of her legs were broken. So was her pelvis. My younger brother and sister were still at home. My father was unemployed at the time, and I was off at college. So who do you think was elected to take on the housework? Raise your hand if you think it was my father. No??? Does anybody think it was *me?* I am truly amazed at your guessing ability. Or is there something in our Hispanic culture that says the women do the housework? Of course there is. So I drove home from Boulder every weekend; shopped, cleaned, cooked, froze meals for the next week, did the laundry, you know the list. And the truth is, it did not occur to me until some time later that my father could have done some of that. I had a problem, but I was part of the problem. I *did* resist when my parents suggested I should quit school. It seemed better to try doing everything, than to give up my dream. And it was the better choice. But it was also very difficult.

Which reminds me of another experience. Would it be too much like a soap opera if I told you about a personal crisis? Anybody want to hear a story about myself that I've never before told in public? While still in college, I married my high school sweetheart. We were both completing our college degrees. My husband's family could not figure out why I was pursuing college instead of kids, but I was. However, it seemed like my schoolwork always came last.

One Saturday night I had come home from helping my Mom, dragged into our tiny married-student apartment, cooked a big dinner for my husband, and as I stood there washing the dishes, I felt a teardrop trickle down my face. Followed by a flood. Followed by sobbing. *Heaving.* If you ranked crying on a scale of 1 to 10, this was an 11. My husband came rushing in with that . . . you know . . . that "puzzled-husband" look. He asked what was wrong. Well, it took me awhile to figure it out, to be able to put it into words. When I did, they were 12 words: "I just realized I'll be doing dishes the rest of my life."

Now, if I thought you'd believe me, I'd tell you *my husband finished the dishes.* He did not. But we both did some thinking and talking about roles and expectations, and, over the years, have learned to share the domestic responsibilities. We realized that we were both carrying a lot of old, cultural "baggage" through life. *And so are you.*

I'm not going to tell you what to do about it. But I am going to urge you to realize it, think about it, and even to cry over the dishes, if you need to. You may be glad you did. As for me, *What have I learned from all this?* I've learned, as I suggested earlier, that Hispanic women have bought into a lot of myths, through the years. Or at least *I* did. And I want to tell you now, especially you younger women, the "five things I wish I had known" when I was 20, 25, even 30. In fact, some of these things I'm *still* learning—at 37. Now for that list of "five things I wish I had known."

First: I wish I had known that I—like most Hispanic women—was under-estimating my capabilities. When I first went to work for Mountain Bell, which has since become U.S. WEST Communications—I thought the "ultimate" job I could aspire to, would be district manager. So I signed up for the courses I knew would help me achieve and handle that kind of responsibility. I watched various district managers, forming my own ideas of who was most effective—and why. I accepted whatever responsibilities and opportunities were thrown my way, generally preparing myself to be district manager.

My dream came true. But then it almost became a nightmare. After only 18 months on the job, the president of the company called me and asked me to go interview with *his boss*—the president of our parent company. And the next thing I knew, I had been promoted to a job *above* that of district manager. Suddenly, I was stranded in unfamiliar territory. They gave me a big office at U.S. WEST headquarters down in Englewood, where I pulled all the furniture into one corner. In fact, I sort of made a little "fort." From this direction, I could hide behind the computer. From that direction, the plants. From over here, the file cabinet. Safe at last. *Until* a friend from downtown came to visit me. She walked in, looked around, and demanded to know: *"What is going on here?* Why was your door closed? Why are you all scrunched up in the corner?" I had all kinds of excuses. But she said: "You know what I think? I think you're afraid you don't deserve this office!"

As she spoke, she started dragging the plants away from my desk. For a moment, I was angry. Then afraid. Then we started laughing, and I helped her stretch my furnishings—and my confidence. And it occurred to me that had I pictured, from the beginning, that I could become an executive director, I would have been better prepared. I would have pictured myself in that big office. I would have spent more time learning executive public speaking. I would have done a lot of things. And I began to do them with my new, expanded vision of becoming an officer—which subsequently happened.

I just wish that I had known, in those early years, how I was underestimating my capabilities. I suspect that *you are, too.* And I wonder: *What are you going to do about it?*

Second: I wish I had known that power is not something others give you. It is something that comes from *within yourself . . .* and which you can then share with others.

In 1984, a group of minority women at U.S. WEST got together and did some arithmetic to confirm what we already knew. Minority women were woefully underrepresented in the ranks of middle and upper management. We had a better chance of winning the lottery! So we gathered our courage and took our case to the top. Fortunately, we found a sympathetic ear. The top man told us to take our case to *all* the officers. We did. But we were scared. And it showed. We sort of ''begged'' for time on their calendars. We apologized for interrupting their work. Asked for a little more recognition of our plight. And the first few interviews went terribly. Then we realized: we deserve to be on their calendars as much as anyone else does. We realized that under-utilizing a group of employees is not an interruption of the officers' work—it *is* the officers' work. We realized that we should not be asking for help—we should be *telling* how *we could help.* So we did.

And it worked. The company implemented a special program to help minority women achieve their full potential. Since then, several of us have moved into middle and upper management, and more are on the way. I just wish we had realized, in the beginning, where power really comes from. It comes from within yourself . . . and which you can then share with others. I suspect *you* need to be reminded of that, too. And I wonder: *What are you going to do about it?*

Third: I wish I had known that when I feel envious of others, I'm really just showing my lack of confidence in myself. A few years ago, I worked closely with one of my coworkers in an employee organization. She is Hispanic. Confident. Outgoing. In fact, she's so likeable I could hardly stand her! But as we worked together, I finally realized: She has those attributes; I have others. And I had to ask myself: do I want to spend the time it would take to develop her attributes, or enjoy what we can accomplish by teaming-up our different skills? I realized that is the better way. I suspect that you may encounter envy from time to time. And I wonder: *What are you going to do about it?*

Fourth: I wish I had realized that true success is never something you earn single-handedly. We hear people talk about ''networking'' and ''community'' and ''team-building.'' What they mean is an extension of my previous idea: We can be a lot more effective working in a group than working alone.

This was brought home to me when I was president of our Hispanic employees' organization at U.S. WEST Communications. I wanted my administration to be the best. So I tried to do everything myself, to be sure it was done right. I wrote the newsletter, planned the fund-raiser, scheduled the meetings, booked the speakers, everything. For our big annual meeting, I got the chairman of the company to speak. By then, the other officers of the group were feeling left out. Come to think of it, they *were* left out. Anyway, we were haggling over who got to introduce our big speaker. I was determined it should be me, since I so ''obviously'' had done all the work.

As it turned out, I missed the big meeting altogether. My older brother died. And I did a lot of painful thinking. For one thing: I was glad my team was there to keep things going while I dealt with my family crisis. But more important: I thought about life and death and what people would be saying if *I* had died. Would I prefer they remember that "good ol' Janice sure did a terrific job of arranging every last detail of the meeting"? Or that "we really enjoyed working with her"? "Together, we did a lot." All of us need to ask ourselves that question from time to time. And I wonder: *What are you going to do about it?*

Hispanic women in America have been victims of racism, sexism, and poverty for a long, long time. I know, because I was one of them. I also know that when you stop being a victim is largely up to you. I don't mean you should run out of here, quit your job, divorce your husband, farm out your kids, or run for President of the United States.

But I *do* mean that "whatever" you can dream, you can become. A couple of years ago, I came across a poem by an Augsburg College student, Devoney K. Looser, which I want to share with you now.

> *I wish someone had taught me long ago*
> *How to touch mountains*
> *Instead of watching them from breathtakingly safe distances.*
> *I wish someone had told me sooner*
> *That cliffs were neither so sharp nor so distant nor so solid as they*
> *seemed.*
> *I wish someone had told me years ago*
> *That only through touching mountains can we reach peaks called*
> *beginnings, endings or exhilarating points of no return.*
> *I wish I had learned earlier that ten fingers and the world shout more*
> *brightly from the tops of mountains*
> *While life below only sighs with echoing cries.*
> *I wish I had realized before today*
> *That I can touch mountains*
> *But now that I know, my fingers will never cease the climb.*

Please, my sisters, never, ever, cease the climb.
  Adelante Mujer!

RACIAL AND ETHNIC RELATIONS IN AMERICAN HIGHER EDUCATION[3]

Michael L. Williams

Michael L. Williams, Assistant Secretary for Civil Rights in the United States Department of Education, delivered this provocative speech to the 4th Annual Conference on Racial and Ethnic Relations in Higher Education, in San Antonio, Texas, in 1991.

On the wall of a church in England there is a sign that reads, "A vision without a task is but a dream, a task without a vision is drudgery, a vision and a task are the hope of the world." My comments this morning concern a vision, a task, and a hope for the future of American higher education.

The essence of a vision, as I use the term this morning, rests in its character as a moral view of not only the way the world should be, but also a way of describing the way the world is today. It's our vision of the world that sets the agenda for thought and action. As such, one's vision has a sense of causation. Policies, practices and behavior are based on our vision of the world.

Every educational system has its own unique vision—that special something that it tries to attain; that orders its conduct; and produces a certain type of individual. Aristocracies wanted gentlemen. Young Greeks and Romans were taught the classics. Early America—an agrarian society—commanded men and women who were hardworking and God-fearing. Students were taught the basics (reading, writing and arithmetic) during a school term dictated by the growing season. A remnant of that agrarian past exists to this day.

What's the vision of contemporary American education? What's its raison d'etre? Some may have other views, but let me posit the following. American education ought to be about the business of creating a people with the sentiment, knowledge, character and training to support a democratic society. In the process, we should be stretching our collective imagination as a nation to conquer mediocrity and to create and nurture new and innovative approaches. America 2000, announced by the President several weeks ago, is that kind of approach. Its purpose is to make "this land all that it should be." And we can achieve that goal by imbuing the young with a commitment to individual liberty and self-determination. The notion that each of us is part of a common culture has been part of the American educational vision for more than two centuries and must continue. This is true even though at times we have sorely missed the mark of the American promise. Segregated elementary schools and dual systems of higher education are sad reminders of a not too distant past. Sad compromises for which we pay today. It is a price we can no longer afford.

Yet, fundamentally, the American educational vision remains.

We are a country composed of individuals from a wide range of racial, ethnic and cultural backgrounds with increasing numbers of persons pursuing higher education. In 1988, the U.S. Department of Education reported that American college enrollment included 10.3 million whites, 1.1 million blacks, 680,000 Hispanics, 497,000 Asians, 98,000 Native Americans, and 361,000 students from foreign countries. In addition to the aggregate number of minority students attending college, the percent of college-age minority individuals attending institutions of higher education also increased. For example, the American Council on Education reported that college enrollment among black 18-24 year olds increased from 15.5 percent in 1970 to 23.5 percent in 1989.

Along with an increase in the number of minority individuals pursuing higher education and the recognition that changing demographics will usher in a colorization of the American workplace there is increased pressure on colleges and universities across the nation, both public and private, to become more diverse and culturally pluralistic. Pressure to diversify America's colleges is being exerted by many segments of the community. These segments include minority and non-minority persons, students, faculty and administrators alike. This broad based, top-down and bottom-up pressure to diversify colleges and universities undoubtedly reflects the sentiment that diversity concerns are not the special pleadings of particular interest groups but rather are nation-wide concerns that affect the very essence of academic communities.

That America's universities and colleges are being thrust into the forefront of diversity issues is not surprising. Dinesh D'Souza notes that of all American institutions, perhaps only the military brings people of such varied backgrounds into more intimate contact. However, universities are more than mirrors of society and social change. They often are a leading indicator. Thus, it is likely that other institutions will soon face issues similar to those which now confront colleges and universities. Moreover, with the position of forerunner comes a high level of responsibility. Other institutions will observe closely colleges and university's actions in addressing the issues which arise in connection with increased diversification.

Therein lies the task before American higher education. It is the task of educating an increasingly heterogeneous population in a manner consistent with the American vision of democracy. It is to lead the political institutions and corporate world through the maze of diversity. It is my hope that my brief remarks today will contribute to this important debate on diversity and to the associated re-examination of elements fundamental to university life—admissions, financial aid, curriculum, student activities, faculty appointments and promotion.

Because of higher education's elevated status and importance to the strength of our society and the advancement of the individual, we expect this debate to take place in an atmosphere conducive to free speech. The Supreme Court also has recognized the university's need to engage in free speech as fundamental to the functioning of our society. The preservation of this core American value is a responsibility that colleges and universities must strive to meet—indeed exceed.

President Bush stated recently that Americans debate in order to separate the good ideas from the bad ideas. The freedom to speak one's mind and engage in debate:

> . . . *defines and cultivates the diversity upon which our national greatness rests. It tears off blinders of ignorance and prejudice and lets us move on to greater things.*

The task before American higher education is educating an increasingly heterogeneous population in a manner consistent with the American vision of democracy. This task is made ever more difficult by America's past history of discrimination.

This is no small challenge. Diane Ravitch, educational researcher and author, suggests an interesting change has taken place. She says that this country:

> . . . *has become a multiethnic, multiracial country intensely aware of differences of every kind, a country in which almost everyone thinks of himself or herself as a member of a minority group. Having once been a society in which differences were shunned, accents studiously unlearned, and foreignness somewhat suspect, the United States has become a nation where people are seeking out their long-forgotten roots, learning ancestral languages, celebrating the traditions that their fathers and mothers rejected.*

Growing up in Midland, Texas, some three hundred miles west of here, I remember on hot days like this when we wanted something cool to drink, we asked for a Coke. It didn't matter our desired flavor. Grape, orange, cola, or even Mountain Dew. Everything was a Coke. Simplicity and overuse had their shortcomings. Particularly if you ended up with a beverage that didn't agree with your palate.

Discussions about diversity are similar. Diversity means different things to different people. What flavor of diversity do we want? I share the sentiment that increasingly diverse campuses will better serve all students. Colleges and universities can use academic freedoms accorded them to promote increased diversity. While recognizing the benefits of increased diversity, however, I am also somewhat troubled by the methods many campuses are using in their attempts to diversify. Emerging evidence suggests that two basic models of diversity are being advanced.

The first model, the exclusion model, focuses on numerical racial and proportionality, most notably in the area of student admissions. It also criticizes the existing dominant culture and intellectual canons. For some, the goal is to focus on limitations of Western culture and canons as opposed to focusing on supplementing existing curriculums with contributions from the qualities and traditions of non-Western cultures and canons. Further, the exclusion model allows the promotion of group self-isolationism and what Delegate Eleanor Holmes Norton once described as a "new separatism" rather than encouraging increased interaction among all students.

The exclusion model is inadequate for satisfying the vision of American higher education. It conflicts with core democratic principles, fails to achieve its stated goals, and, paradoxically, harms the very groups it attempts to serve.

The First Amendment protects, in part, the integrity of the marketplace of ideas. A marketplace where all individuals have the ability to speak their minds freely. Such freedom insures a continually creative and varied flow of viewpoints that can be brought to bear on a wide range of common issues and problems. The genius of such a marketplace is that good ideas and workable solutions can be distinguished from the bad on the basis of reasoned discourse, rational discussion, reflection, and the power of persuasion. The efficiency and utility of this marketplace as a mechanism for solving society's problems can only be enhanced by embracing ideas rooted in different cultures. This is not to say that there are no limitations on the bounds of open discussion in the academic environment.

The U.S. Supreme Court's decision in *Regents of the University of California v. Bakke* is the touchstone of any analysis of a university's interest in using its academic freedom to promote a diverse student body. In *Bakke,* the Court struck down, under Title VI of the Civil Rights Act of 1964, a medical school admissions policy that set aside a fixed percentage of each class for minority candidates. Justice Powell in his decisive opinion ruled that such a racial classification could not be justified as constituting valid "remedial action" in the absence of judicial, legislative or administrative findings of constitutional or statutory violations. Powell then further ruled that a university has an interest of constitutional dimension in using its academic freedom to promote a diverse student body contributing to a "robust exchange of ideas." While that interest can be sufficiently compelling to justify a university's consideration of race in its decision making, Powell wrote that it did not warrant the set-aside of admission slots to minority applicants because such was not necessary to achieve a diverse student body.

Powell's ruling assigns a premium to intellectual diversity that is distinguished from and does not automatically flow from numerical proportionality. That is to say that an individual's political or intellectual perspective is influenced but not dictated by his or her cultural, ethnic or racial background. It's trite but true. All blacks, and all Hispanics and all Asians do not think alike.

Another assumption of the exclusion model is that discrete groups can be accurately and fairly identified. In our increasingly heterogeneous society, how does one define an absolute minority group? How are individuals that arguably belong to more than one such group to be classified?

The exclusion model's skepticism of the dominant culture and canons is equally troubling. I agree that curriculums would be enhanced by becoming more diverse. However, instead of focusing on the positive contributions from numerous non-Western cultures, some proponents of the exclusion model focus instead on the limitations of Western work. Rather than explore avenues of accommodation, some proponents seek to supplant. Besides being an invitation to cultural fisticuffs, the exclusion model fails from its own internal weaknesses.

Provincialism has always been an enemy of the well-educated. Group isolationism and separatism conflict on their face with the goal of increased interaction among all students. An integral component of education includes exposure to and interaction with people whose perspective, culture or background differ from one's own.

Professor Allan Bloom commented on the self-separatism phenomenon in his book *The Closing of the American Mind*. Bloom writes:

> *Thus, just at the moment when everyone else has become a "person," blacks have become blacks. I am not speaking about doctrine, although there was much doctrine at the beginning, but about feeling. "They stick together" was a phrase often used in the past by the prejudiced about this or that distinctive group, but it has become true, by and large, of the black students. In general, the expectation of anything other than routine contact in classes or at campus jobs— usually quite polite—has vanished.*

Intellectual diversity and cultural differences are important resources that should be shared in order to better enable all students to learn from one another. While I understand the magnetic appeal to fellowship with persons who look like me and, while I have been drawn to such racial group activities as a student and as an adult, I fear that on many of our campuses this is being done at too great a cost. The purpose of education is to prepare students to live and work in a multi-ethnic, multi-racial society. Students must be able to walk in the mainstream, not stand on the sidewalk. Opportunities to learn that are not explored or taken advantage of are wasted. For our students to become intellectually fluent in today's increasingly global economy, exposure to and an understanding of a variety of cultures is essential.

Curiously, this resulting separatism is precisely what the original civil rights movement fought against. By focusing on differences and ignoring shared values, the exclusion model can lead to policies that set groups apart and prevent minorities from engaging in and enriching the larger culture. It also denies students in the larger culture the opportunity to interact with and learn from students that bring to a campus a different background or an alternative viewpoint. Moreover, efforts to increase minority student matriculation in the name of diversity on the one hand while simultaneously aiding those same students to cordon themselves off from the majority smack of a large dose of hypocrisy. In the thirty-seven years since the Supreme Court's heralded opinion in *Brown v. Board of Education* has our vision of equal educational opportunity been so turned on its head that we now want students educated separately?

Education institutions and all of their students, minority and non-minority, are impeded by policies which exacerbate indifference in the name of unity and undermine norms of fairness, debate and intellectual discourse. These components comprise the very foundation upon which the academe rests.

A second model for promoting diversity is the inclusion model. The inclusion model recognizes contributions from Western and non-Western cultures. This model not only celebrates elements which distinguish cultures but also celebrates elements shared by different cultures. In addition, the inclusion model, as the label suggests, seeks to integrate all ideas regardless of cultural origin into the marketplace of ideas. It assumes that ideas are generated by individuals rather than held uniformally by all members of a particular group. Once these ideas are admitted into this marketplace, the merits and contributions of all cultures can be discussed freely by all members of the academic community regardless of the member's racial, ethnic or cultural background. Finally, the inclusion model encourages active intellectual engagement and participation from individuals from all segments of the academic community.

The inclusion model's focus on the individual rather than the group is consistent with the Constitution's text and intent which expressly addresses itself to individuals, not ill-defined groups and mandates, but to fair representation, and not strictly proportional representation based on group identity. Clearly the two concepts are not interchangeable. And, clearly there is a growing disenchantment with counting by the numbers. America remains sensitive to its history of past injustice. In addition, America simply cannot accept any form of discrimination now or in the future. Despite this commitment, a recent poll suggests there is a general discomfort with establishing fixed quotas for minorities. Believing that such policies run counter to deep-seated convictions that equal rights belong to individuals, the once secure arm-in-arm civil rights consensus appears to be deteriorating.

By focusing on the ideas and expression of the individual and by celebrating elements that both distinguish and bind different cultures, the inclusion model effectively celebrates diversity without denigrating either Western or non-Western traditions. The active and reasoned engagement of all segments of an academic community in intellectual debate and discussion increases the utility and efficiency of the marketplace of ideas. It allows the university community to concentrate on scholarship and academic merit, which is the only currency that the academe is uniquely qualified to trade in.

The infusion of ideas from varied cultural origins into the academic marketplace of ideas will permit the important elements and contributions from all origins to rise through open, fair and reasoned debate. This cannot be achieved if whole segments of the community withdraw. Participation in intellectual debate and discussion by individuals from all segments of a university community will enable individuals to invest themselves in the academic community and will vastly enrich the debate itself and the creativity of the solutions it produces.

The sharing of ideas and exposure to different viewpoints, each with a human face, made possible by increased diversity will result in a reduction of bigotry and insensitivity and an increase in tolerance and understanding between and among minority and non-minority individuals. Such a result will reduce the isolation, inhospitable climate and alienation felt by many minority students on today's campuses. In particular, such a result hopefully will help eliminate the seeds of racial harassment. All students need to know that the schools they attend respect them as individuals with a wide variety of racial, ethnic and cultural backgrounds. This variety needs to be welcomed, explored and enjoyed.

The inclusion model permits minority students—indeed all students—to achieve increased self-realization and advancement. Educational institutions at all levels need to continue to include, welcome and nurture all students and not tolerate campuses which are indifferent or inhospitable to the needs of any student. The inclusion model permits this nation's colleges and universities to fulfill their role and obligation to serve as conduits for open debate and vehicles for individual betterment. This betterment is as crucial to individual self-fulfillment as it is to America's national interest.

That's the hope for America—keeping its eye on the vision of democracy and fashioning a campus community in its glow. We need not fear. For in the words of Audre Lorde,

When I dare to be powerful—to use my strength in the service of my vision—then it becomes less and less important whether I am afraid.

NOTES

1. Black Hawk, "Black Hawk's Farewell," *Literature of the American Indian,* Thomas E. Sanders and Walter W. Peek (Beverly Hills: Glencoe, 1973) 279–280.

2. Janice Payan, "Opportunities for Hispanic Women," *Vital Speeches of the Day* LVI (1990): 697–700.

3. Michael L. Williams, "Racial and Ethnic Relations in American Higher Education," *Vital Speeches of the Day* LVIII (1992): 174–177.

DOING RESEARCH ON A TOPIC   APPENDIX B

★ OUR ROLE AS RESEARCHERS ★

Research is a central and vital part of academic life. **It's as researchers, more than in any other function, that student and professor stand on common ground.** Doing research is your role and mine. Thus do we identify with one another in purpose. We are investigators who seek information, some of which may eventually generate knowledge or insight. Yes, to be a student is to conduct research, and as many instructors will testify, to be a teacher is to be a student. For the principal functions of all in the academic community are inquiring and learning.

Appendix B will discuss the following topics: finding, recording, and checking research materials.

FINDING MATERIALS

On many occasions for speaking, discussing, and writing, you'll draw the major part of your material from your own store of knowledge, but often you'll need new information and the support of authoritative data. Many times you can find much of the needed material in the library. Among other sources are correspondence, direct observation, and interviews or polls.

The Library

Are you well acquainted with the library on campus? Are you able to make it work for you? Do you fully appreciate its many offerings? Very likely a large number of college students would answer yes to one or more of these questions, but fewer will reply affirmatively to all three. The aim at this point, then, is to help you become better acquainted with basic library resources, so as to increase your academic power and effectiveness.

1. The card catalog. If you have avoided close contact with the card catalog, now is the time to realize its usefulness. The card catalog, a centrally located index of all books in the library, is housed in a cabinet of many drawers. Its index cards are arranged alphabetically in three ways: by author, by title, and by subject.

Let's illustrate use of the card catalog with a hypothetical example. Assume that you are exploring the subject of *the Vietnamese in America.* Remembering that you once heard a professor mention a book by Vuong Thuy, you decide to see if you can locate it or any others that he has written. So, you go to the drawer of the card catalog that would have a card or cards for an author named "Thuy." As the name is uncommon among American names, you quickly come to a card headed "Thuy, Vuong G." This is the card for his book *Getting to Know the Vietnamese and Their Culture.* Also on the card are the publisher's name, date of publication, classification number for locating the book on the library shelves, and other information.

After this start in your research, you shift your pursuit to subject cards, for you can't recall the names of other authorities on the Vietnamese in America. Going through alphabetically arranged headings, you look for subject headings like these: History of Indochina, Refugees, Vietnamese–Americans, Vietnamese Culture, and Vietnamese People. You begin to locate a few titles that relate to your subject. And for those that seem promising, you jot down authors, titles, *and* classification or call numbers, the information needed for finding the books on the shelves.

If you have in mind the name of a book but don't know the author, start looking through the cards for the title. Remember that *A, The,* and *An* are ignored in the alphabetizing. Thus, you would find the card for the book *A Comparison of American and Vietnamese Value Systems* by looking under *Comparison,* not *A.*

2. A computer catalog. Many libraries now provide researchers with computer access to titles of their books and periodicals. Such a system of locating source material is an electronic version of the card catalog, used with a keyboard that brings all pertinent information to a viewing screen. A major advantage is that **this catalog system supplies more information than the card catalog.** Besides giving title, author, publisher, date of publication, and so on, it will indicate where the item is located in the library and whether or not it's checked out.

3. The *Readers' Guide to Periodical Literature.* Known simply as the *Readers' Guide,* this index is of great value in locating magazine articles. About 175 magazines are included in the coverage. A set of bound yearly volumes is to be found on a shelf or table in a convenient location in the library. Arrangement in each volume is by subject and author.

If, for example, you want to find the most recent magazine articles on the subject of *censorship,* turn to the semimonthly issues of the *Readers' Guide,* those not yet bound in hard cover, and look under the appropriate alphabetically arranged listing. Try these, for instance: Censorship, Free Speech, Freedom of the Press, Obscenity, Government and the Press, Moving Picture Censorship. Or perhaps you've heard of an article and can recall only the author and probable year of publication, for example, one by Nadine Gordimer that you think was published in 1990. Thumb through the 1990 *Readers' Guide.* In the G's you'll find that Gordimer's essay (actually an excerpt of her speech) is in *Harper's* magazine: N '90,

281: 27+ (the November 1990 issue, volume 281, page 27+). It's called "Censorship and Its Aftermath."

4. **Specialized indexes.** Many other useful and more specialized indexes are available in the library: *Public Affairs Information Service* (PAIS), *Social Sciences Index, Education Index, Art Index, Book Review Digest,* and *Biography Index,* to name a few. Check to see if such a special index covering your topic is available.

5. **Newspaper indexes.** A particularly helpful resource is the index of the *New York Times.* Published regularly since 1913, it alphabetically categorizes the contents of that newspaper according to subject and names of people and organizations. But it's more than an index to the newspaper. For instance, it can serve as a general index to historical events. Assume that you want to verify that the President of the United States gave a speech on prison reform before Congress in a given year. Go to the volume for that year, turn to the president's name, and move down the columns until you find Messages to Congress. It's safe to say that no general newspaper in the country is more faithful than the *New York Times* in printing the texts of speeches on questions of national interest. It's quite probable, for example, that a speech by the president before Congress will be printed in full.

Some libraries have the National Newspaper Index, an index of items published recently in five major newspapers of the United States, including the *New York Times.* Depending on the library, this information is on either CD ROM (a computer file) or microfilm. Names and subjects are alphabetized.

Other newspaper and magazine indexes are available in many libraries. An increasing number are providing computer access.

6. **General reference works.** In the early stages of research, general references may be useful. They can help to get you started and perhaps suggest more specialized aids. Some representative types are here listed, along with two examples of each from the many works available.

Encyclopedias	*Encyclopaedia Britannica* and *Collier's Encyclopedia*
Biography	*Dictionary of American Biography* and *Who's Who in America*
Yearbooks	*World Almanac* and *Statistical Abstract of the United States*
Books of quotations	Bartlett's *Familiar Quotations* and *The Oxford Dictionary of Quotations*
Miscellaneous	*Books in Print* *Ulrich's International Periodical Directory*

7. **Specialized reference works.** Each academic discipline or field has special aids to enable the researcher to function effectively in that area. The list is at least as long as the number of fields. Here are some examples.

Education	*World Education Encyclopedia*
History	*Dictionary of American History*
Literature	*Literary History of the United States*
Drama	*Oxford Companion to the Theatre*
Music	*Grove's Dictionary of Music and Musicians*
Science	*McGraw-Hill Encyclopedia of Science and Technology*
Social sciences	*Encyclopedia of the Social Sciences*
Speech communication	*History of Speech Education in America*

8. Government publications. You may be amazed at the great variety of useful materials prepared and made available by the federal and state governments. To determine titles that bear on your topic, consult the current issues of the yearly bound volumes of the *Monthly Catalog of United States Government Publications.* See also the *Monthly Checklist of State Publications.* Very likely, the member of the House of Representatives from your district will be willing to help you secure federal documents.

Correspondence

Perhaps you need information that is accessible only by correspondence. If you're absolutely certain that published sources do not supply the information, contact the knowledgeable source by mail. Carefully design your letter to secure the usable material. Be clear; be brief. **State your questions so that it's easy for the source to help you, and with minimal effort.** A question like "How do you feel about pornographic films?" may land your letter in the wastebasket, whereas "What are your criteria for determining whether a film is pornographic?" has a reasonable chance of obtaining a response. The first question is general and ambiguous; it asks for an *impression.* The second is specific and clear; it's objective in intent and suggests to the addressee that you want a *reasoned answer.*

Be courteous, to the point of enclosing a self-addressed and stamped envelope.

For further guidance in shaping questions, see the section on interviewing that soon follows.

Direct Observation

Another way to acquire information is to investigate by direct observation of situations or conditions that relate to the topic. This may involve a field trip or an on-site inquiry. In a study of traffic hazards, for example, useful information might result from well-planned observations at a certain notoriously dangerous intersection in your community. Anyone studying alcoholism would find a meeting of Alcoholics Anonymous most rewarding.

Interviews and Polls

Interviews   Would an interview with an expert be likely to yield useful material on your topic? If so, follow the usual dictates of courtesy and expediency as you proceed. Plan all details, arrange for a meeting, be friendly but businesslike, and respect the respondent's schedule. Here are other suggestions:

1.   **From the first contact, by telephone or letter, build understanding and a climate of trust.** Be clear about your purpose, and attempt to stimulate the respondent's interest and involvement. Avoid asking questions that are likely to threaten the respondent and arouse defensive behavior. Work for conditions conducive to open and productive interaction.

2.   **Know the kind of response you want.** Do you want the respondent's general opinion on a certain idea or event? Do you want facts? Do you want a prediction? Do you want the respondent's position on an issue? Understand your goal.

3.   **Prepare your questions skillfully.** They should be brief, purposeful, easily understood, and shaped to elicit a specific response. Some may seek a yes-or-no answer, whereas others will be open-ended, to encourage an expanded response.

4.   **Follow up on a question that's inadequately answered.** For example, you might ask, "Could you give more details on . . . ?" or "Did you say 1994?" or "How does that relate to . . . ?"

5.   **Remember your purpose, always.** Keep your objectives, general and of-the-moment, uppermost in mind. If the interview strays off the subject, return to it as adroitly as possible.

6.   **Be professional and objective in your behavior.** Advocacy or argumentation on your part, or presentation of emotionally laden questions, can cause distractions. People who are challenged may decide not to cooperate. Withhold your personal views for other occasions, with other people.

7.   **Listen to the respondent.** This suggestion cannot be overemphasized. Observe both verbal and nonverbal reactions. Even though you may be thinking far ahead to future questions, understand the meaning of each response as it appears. Listen purposively and hard!

8.   **Respond to comments in ways that will help the respondent provide information.** Receive the answer given. Rephrase and clarify when indicated. Remember, too, that you're sending nonverbal messages to the respondent all the while. Ordinarily, your messages should say something like this: "Yes, I see. I understand your answer, I accept you and your answer for the information they provide; my role is not to judge you or your ideas; I am listening."

9.   **Record the information accurately.** There's a separate section below on recording materials; however, I would like to mention now the particular problem of recording data taken in an interview. Should you tape-record the interview? **A recording machine will threaten some**

interviewees and thus curb candor and spontaneity, but not always. You must decide if potential sensitivity, whether reflected in the interviewee's personality or inherent in the subject, will rule out use of a recorder. If you're in doubt, don't use it.

Should you take detailed notes? Again, you must assess the conditions. If your active pencil and lowered eyes are likely to detract from your purpose, use another method. Certainly, you can't copy everything verbatim. But if you've planned carefully and have arranged limited questions, you may be able to get accurate and ample data by taking brief written notes during the interview, which later will remind you of full responses. Immediately following the meeting, you can use these to facilitate retrieval of your copious mental notes.

Polls   You may need to secure reactions from a cross-section of people on a set of important questions. The answer is to poll them with a carefully drafted questionnaire, which you can either distribute to the selected group or present orally face to face.

For sound results, **the sample of people polled must be large enough to be significant** and in all other ways representative of the specific population. For example, results of a poll of only 15 students on the need to keep the library open on Saturday evenings probably are unusable. Also unusable would be the opinions of married students only. Both samples are unrepresentative.

Poor wording of questions will also reduce the reliability of your survey. Good questions are

1.   Clear, and understood in the same way by all respondents
2.   Calculated to get a concise and brief response
3.   Unbiased
4.   Unthreatening and nonargumentative, designed to encourage an honest and candid response
5.   Limited in number
6.   Easy to tabulate and interpret

Think ahead before you distribute your questionnaire, trying to anticipate every predicament. In your planning, be sure to include a full trial run of the entire process, from shaping questions, to recording responses, to tabulation and interpretation.

RECORDING MATERIALS

The Bibliography

To keep a record of references consulted, **researchers develop a bibliography as they proceed in their investigations.** The bibliography

> Muzny, Charles C. *The Vietnamese
> in Oklahoma City: A Study in
> Ethnic Change.* New York: AMS
> Press, 1989.

is a list of sources on the topic and should include all the books, encyclopedia articles, issues of magazines and newspapers, and pamphlets consulted or used, as well as citations of correspondence and interviews or polls.

The Bibliography Card

As you do your research, prepare a card for each source of data, each bibliographic item. This will be a master card on which you will note all the essential bibliographic information. If the source is a book, record the author's name, title of the work, publisher, and place and date of publication; if a magazine, note the author, title of the article, title and volume of the magazine, date of publication, and inclusive page numbers. (See Figures B-1 and B-2.) For correspondence or interviews, prepare a card with this kind of notation: "Personal Correspondence/Interview with John Milton, December 2, 1993."

Whether or not your instructor requires a full bibliography, the set of **master bibliography cards will be essential in helping you control your research and keep track of your sources.**

Note Taking

With the bibliography card as a complete record of author, title, and publication data, prepare note cards on relevant and usable pieces of material found in the source. Prepare one card for each item or subtopic. These can be cards of 3 by 5 inches, 4 by 6 inches, or larger. Since you have a master bibliography card for each source, the note cards need not include

Lam, Andrew. "My Vietnam, My
America." <u>The Nation</u> 10 Dec. 1990:
724-26.

full bibliographic data, only the minimum identification, the last name of
the author and an abbreviated title. *But do record the appropriate page
numbers accurately.*

Most note cards fall into one of four categories.

1. Direct quotation. As you look into a topic, you often want to take
down the exact words of a given source. Record them carefully.

**If you don't need all the words in a piece of material, use an ellip-
sis to show the omitted part**: three dots for the omission of a beginning
or middle portion of a sentence and four dots for omissions of the end of
a sentence or of whole sentences.

Mazny, C. <u>The Vietnamese</u>   Vietnamese
<u>in Okla. City</u>   Values in
                 America
"In the areas of dating, engagement,
and marriage, there were some
behavioral changes ... but no
changes in values ...."
                              p. 185

> Liu, W. <u>Transition</u>
> Hostility to Vietnamese in America
>
> Principal sources of:
> 1. Fear of job displacement
> 2. Concern about money spent to facilitate resettlement
> 3. Cultural prejudice
>   pp. 67-69

For accuracy in accounting for a quotation that continues on to another page, use a slash to show where one page stops and the other starts. (See Figure B-3.)

2. Summary outline. Use this kind of note when you need to record the main points of an item. List broadly the points, topics or arguments treated, and so forth; or record a synopsis or overview of the covered information. (See Figure B-4.)

3. Indirect quotation. A restatement of the source material in your own words is an indirect quotation. Although usually a condensed version

> Thuy, V. <u>Getting to Know the Vietnamese</u>
> Religion
>
> Nearly 90% of the Vietnamese are Buddhists; approx. 10% are Roman Catholic.   pp. 7-12
>
> [but the representation of Roman Catholicism is much higher among those who came to the U.S.]

of the original, it may amount to a sentence, a paragraph, or a full card or more.

If the original material is lengthy and if you include all the topics as organized, the resulting compact statement is called an *abstract,* a condensation of the essential thought.

4.   Reaction. You may want in some way to respond to the material, as an example, to note a personal judgment of its worth, to mention its possible use, or to suggest a counterargument. When placing such commentary on a note card, keep it—*your* idea—separate from the source material by using *brackets.* **In research work, brackets indicate intrusion of the mind of the researcher.** *Never* use parentheses; they are for other purposes. (See Figure B-5.)

Whether you follow one or a combination of such note-taking forms, a conscientious and scholarly manner is necessary. Carefully note the source so that you can give due credit later. Accuracy is a second vital consideration. Some people seem to be accurate almost naturally, whereas others need to give themselves constant reminders of the necessity of being careful in recording data. To save the time of having to return and check something, get full and correct information before leaving the source: names, dates, page numbers, titles, places of publication, and so on.

Sometimes tedious but often deeply satisfying, participation in the pursuit of knowledge through research is an activity of great importance. Without the basic skills, one remains rather helpless, a spectator on the sidelines of academic life. The strength and vigor of your scholarly work depend on gaining experience in research. Learning the fundamentals can be very rewarding and make all the difference in raising your level of success and enjoyment at school. You can do it for yourself— and come to know that you belong in the role of scholar.

CHECKING MATERIALS

The task of research is not finished until the collected materials are evaluated. At the least, you should ask three basic questions: (1) Do I have enough material? (2) Are all pieces relevant to my topic? (3) Are all data reliable?

Sufficiency

As you anticipate the paper, discussion, or speech for which you are gathering data, try to determine if you have enough material. Do you have a quantity sufficient to support your ideas or draw significant conclusions? It's better to have an excess than a shortage, to avoid pressured, last-minute trips to the library.

Consider whether you have looked at all angles and exhausted all necessary topics and sources.

Relevance

Test the materials for applicability. Are the collected ideas, examples, statistics, and quotations fully related to the theme and purpose of your planned work? Further, do the data bear on every anticipated aspect of the project and all its possible turns? A discussion, for example, occasionally may get off onto related side roads. As you examine your materials, try to take into account all possible contingencies and needs.

Reliability

The most thorough check of materials should be for reliability, the tests of reasonableness, consistency, and trustworthiness. Are the data sound by standards of good reasoning? Are they internally consistent; that is, do conclusions agree with ideas and evidence from which they are drawn? As you have extracted the data, do they keep the meaning and intent of their source? Do you have full faith in them? Do you have any reason to question the source? Will they be convincing to those who hear or read them? These questions represent some of the inquiries essential to the testing of materials for reliability.

For additional guidance on checking materials for specific use in speeches, consult Chapter Nine, ''Thinking Critically.''

LOOKING BACK

Competence in research is fundamental to your work as a scholar because your main purpose is to inquire and to learn. Available to you are libraries, knowledgeable people, and other sources of useful information. As a researcher, you must know how to find material, properly record it, and gauge its sufficiency, relevance, and reliability.

To be a student is to be a researcher, an active participant in a process of inestimable value both to the individual and to humankind.

GLOSSARY

A

Acceptability   In reference to language use: fitness for audience and occasion.

Accommodation   Adjustment to others' backgrounds and needs, and so on.

Action step   In persuasion, the final phase of the speech to motivate response; step 5 of the motivated sequence pattern.

Adaptation   The act of suiting a message to the audience, for example, through lively language.

Affective bases of error   In critical thinking, a reference to unfavorable intrusion of emotions.

After-dinner speech   Traditionally, a banquet speech that capitalizes on humor for effect but with an emerging serious purpose.

Age   A factor to be considered in learning about an audience.

Aids   Nonverbal supporting material for ideas of speeches, visual or audio.

Alienation   State of being apart, estranged; a feature of the human condition.

Alliteration   In language use, the repetition of initial sounds, usually consonants: "Tim talked turkey to the tough guy."

Allness fallacy   An error in thinking, not accounting for exceptions to a generalization, as an example, "All women want children."

Ambiguity   Vagueness or indistinctness: an obstacle to critical thinking.

Analogy   A figure of speech or mode of reasoning involving comparison of phenomena, for example, "A college curriculum is very much like a supermarket—a huge store with shelves and shelves of nourishing items to choose from."

Analysis   A breakdown of an idea or statement, to determine its parts, for example, of the thesis of a speech to derive main heads.

Ancestry   Lineage and background, especially of family; a factor to be used in learning about an audience.

Announcement   A short speech to report on an event, often including information on who, where, when, why, and so on.

Antonym   A word meaning the opposite, as an example, *love* opposing *hate*.

Apathy   Lack of interest or emotion; unconcern.

Appeal   Factor in effecting persuasion, for example, emotional appeal.

Apprehension   Fear in speaking publicly.

Argumentation   A form of public speaking involving the presentation of arguments for a thesis, with an emphasis on use of reasoning.

Articulation   A reference to operations of the lips, teeth, tongue, and palate to form words and phrases; the final step in the physiological process of producing meaningful sound units.

Assertive   The quality of being forthright and confident in expression of one's views.

Attention   First step in the motivated sequence pattern for organizing speeches; the act of keeping one's mind closely focused on an idea.

Attitude   An assumed position or way of looking at things, for example, a liberal attitude on supporting education.

Audience   The person or persons with whom one speaks, listeners.

Audience dynamics   The complex, ever-changing psychological, attitudinal, and other states represented in an audience.

Audience psychology   The cognitive, emotional, and behavioral characteristics of an audience; the study of audiences.

Authority   A quoted source, testimony, or like reference used in support of an idea.

B

Background   Information on a speaker's or audience's family history, culture, ethnic identity, experiences, and other relevant factors.

Backing   Supporting material used to develop an idea; in Stephen Toulmin's theory on reasoning, evidence to support warrants.

Begging the question   Building an argument from an unestablished assumption, as an example, "Of course the U.S. can no longer compete in the world auto market, so let's help GM, Chrysler and Ford die peacefully."

Behaviors   Acts of speakers and listeners, for example, in responding to a point.

Beliefs   Convictions or points of view.

Belongingness and love needs   A category in psychologist Abraham Maslow's hierarchy of human needs.

Bibliography card   In research, a master card for a source, for example, book: includes author, title, publisher, place of publication, and date.

Biographical order   A structuring of main heads for a speech about a person, for example, Early Life, Goals, and Accomplishments.

Body   The largest part of the speech, coming after the thesis, composed of 2–4 main heads.

Brainstorming   A discovery process featuring a free, unrestricted naming of possibilities, for example, of subjects for a speech or discussion.

C

Card catalog   Cabinet of cards on library holdings, indexed by author, subject, and title.

Case method   Basis for discussion, motivated by information relevant to a given situation, for example, a description of working conditions in the packaging department of a specific company.

Causation   The act of producing an effect; reference to a mode of reasoning.

Cause and effect   A method of structuring main heads of a speech.

Centrism   An orientation based on the feeling that one's group, ideas, or feelings, and so on, are superior to others'.

Channel   The means of sending a message, as an example, in direct interaction as opposed to written form.

Chart   A sheet of information for use as a visual aid in public speaking; may be held, fixed to a surface, or flipped as the speech unfolds.

Choice   An option or decision of communicators, for example, in preparing messages or responding.

Civility   Respectful behavior, sensitivity and courtesy; arising from a sense of community.

Civilization   The state of human society, as advanced culturally, scientifically, politically, and so forth.

Claim   In Stephen Toulmin's theory, the conclusion to a line of reasoning.

Clarity   In language use, the quality of clearness.

Classification   Type of definition involving categorizing, for example, a horse is a four-legged mammal.

Climactic order   Arrangement of a speech's main heads according to increasing degree of importance or dramatic quality.

Climax   In language use, a strategy for progressively building the intensity of a line of thought to an exciting or forceful ending.

Code   A system of symbols for communication.

Cognitive bases of error   In critical thinking, a reference to mental lapses, especially in processes of perceiving, knowing, or judging; related to fallacies in thinking.

Cohesion   State of being together or connected, as in sharing a heritage of idea; central to the condition of identification.

Cohesiveness   Spirit or quality of interdependence and unity, as represented in a well-functioning discussion group.

Color and variety   Types of appeals with which to enliven speeches.

Commonalities   Individuals' specific shared interests, experiences, attitudes, beliefs, and so forth.

Common ground   Like commonalities, bases of communication through shared properties and views.

Common properties   Like common ground and commonalities, things held in common: outlooks, traits, attributes, personal or cultural perspectives, and so on.

Communication   Interaction with others to influence their thinking or behavior, involving use of verbal and nonverbal language symbols.

Communication breakdown   A point of failure in achievement of purpose in interaction; loss of effectiveness.

Communication skills   Abilities that equip one to interact effectively.

Communicative relationship   The state of the union jointly created by speaker and audience.

Communicative spirit   A mood or temper contributing to effectiveness in communication.

Comparison   A type of example that points up similarities; see Analogy.

Complementors   Nonverbal behaviors that add meaning to a message, as an example, a snapping of the fingers.

Comprehend   To grasp an idea.

Computer catalog   Library tool used in research to identify and locate sources of data.

Concepts   A general idea or abstract notion.

Conclusion   In a four-part speech, the last phase; the end point in reasoning, the judgment or decision reached.

Concreteness   A quality of things or events that can be perceived by the senses; preciseness.

Confidence   A state characterized by personal security or faith in self.

Confirmation   Validation, for example, of self-worth or personal point of view.

Confrontational   Descriptive of directness in presenting argument or in reacting to others, usually in opposition; may be descriptive of defiance.

Confusion   Lack of clarity; in communication, a result of the intrusion of noise.

Congruence   A quality of behavior revealing consistency with one's beliefs and attitudes, unity of one's outlooks and actions.

Connotation   An individual, subjective meaning of a word or idea.

Constraint   A controlling or limiting force, such as one's upbringing as it influences current behavior.

Contention   A stated belief or premise.

Context   Features of the whole situation or environment relevant to an event or act.

Contrast   A type of example that points up differences in things or ideas.

Conversation   Informal speech communication; a norm for public speaking, as in speaking conversationally.

Convince   To establish belief or to prove.

Coordinate points   In outlining, heads that are of equal weight or status.

Cosmopolitan dimension   Reference to a state of personal security and open-mindedness that allows for mature interaction with others of varying backgrounds, views, or orientations; the opposite of provincialism, sexism, racism, and so forth.

Counterpersuasion   The response to a persuasive message; rebuttal.

Credibility   A speaker's believability or reliability, as perceived by the audience; ethos.

Criteria   A type of definition involving imposition of qualifying tests, for example: "To be defined as a candidate for entry into the law school, one must have made formal application, submitted letters of reference, paid the standard fee, and . . . ."

Criteria for solution   The tests established by which to measure any proposed solution to a problem under discussion by a group.

Critical thinking   Speakers' and listeners' application of tests to determine validity and trustworthiness of thinking processes and materials; specifically, the checking of conclusions, premises and ideas, conceptions, judgments, opinions, evidence, and sundry data.

Criticism   Commentary on speeches, including commendable features and those needing improvement.

Cultural identity   One's traits and patterns of behavior that reflect influences of a particular culture, of a particular family, ethnic environment, or group with distinct values, and so on.

D

Data   In speech preparation and analysis, the content of speeches, both generalizations and specific materials.

Debate   A form of argumentation involving the clash of opposing ideas.

Decode   To determine the meaning of the language of a message.

Deduction   Reasoning from principle, from a general premise to a conclusion.

Defensiveness   Self-protective behavior; can be counterproductive in communication.

Definition   The meaning of a word or term, as determined by classification, example, etymological fact, or negation, and so forth.

Delivery   The presentation or giving of a public speech.

Democratic heritage   Events, documents, speeches, memories of great deeds, and so on, that remind us of the values of self-government or democratic foundations of the nation.

Denotation   The objective, dictionary meaning of a term.

Description   The result of the process of describing; one function of an example as used by speakers, as opposed to the narrative.

Development   In speechmaking, the building or supporting of an idea, giving meaning and force to it.

Dewey discussion pattern   A structure for reflective thinking as adapted for use in group problem-solving; a conception of philosopher John Dewey.

Dialogue   Interchange of ideas in conversational form.

Difference and distance   Marks of the separation of people from one another; aspects of the human condition that motivate communicative behavior.

Direct interaction   Face-to-face speech communication, as opposed to written communication or communication through the media.

Direct pattern   A deductive structure for organizing speeches; the method of stating the point to be made before developing it.

Discipline   A branch of study, for example, speech communication or history; personally imposed controls on behavior, as in conforming to time limits of speeches or making purposeful preparations for speaking.

Discussion   Organized group speech communication for the purpose of solving a problem or acquiring information.

Display   A visual supporting aid comprised of objects put together in a meaningful pattern, design, or scene.

Disrespectful language   Usages that insult people or groups; for example, in reference to race, religion, physical condition, or sexual orientation.

Distraction   Any stimulus that draws attention away from a message.

Diversified language   Variety in usage.

Diversity   A condition of society in the United States, hence a quality of audiences, as an example, regarding ethnicity and gender.

Dubious premise   An unsound generalization on which a line of reasoning is built, a source of fallacy.

Duration   In voice production, the length of time that a vowel sound lasts, such as the so-called "drawl" that involves giving vowels longer duration.

E

Effectiveness   Success in accomplishment of purpose in speaking, the achievement of identification of speaker and audience.

Either-or fallacy   The so-called dysjunctive reasoning error, allowing only two choices or alternatives, when others should be taken into account.

Elliptical messages   Partially developed messages or ideas, allowing the audience to "fill in," to complete the idea.

Empathy   Feeling as the other person feels.

Encode   To select language to convey a message.

End   The general objective of a speech, as opposed to specific purpose or thesis.

Enforcement of an idea   The speaker's establishment of the point at hand, the making of the point.

Entertain   A general objective in speaking involving the creation of pleasure, often through use of humor.

Enthymeme   A form of deductive reasoning used in speaking; a practical syllogism that deals in probabilities and is usually stated with fewer than the formal three premises (any omitted premise is implied, expected to be added by the audience).

Esteem needs   To do with personal status and adequacy; a category in psychologist Abraham Maslow's hierarchy of human needs.

Ethics   A topic dealing with people's treatment of others, whether humanely or abusively, respectfully or disrespectfully.

Ethnic and cultural background   Identity of people reflecting learnings or customs derived from experiences in a specific family, racial or religious group, a group representing a given nationality or common language, and so forth.

Ethnocentrism   An attitude of superiority as regards one's ethnic identity.

Ethos   In speech communication, a speaker's credibility: a factor of highly significant influence on the outcome of a speech.

Etymology   Definition involving reference to a term's origin and/or development.

Euphemism   A word or phrase that is less offensive or threatening than another, used to soften an expression, for example, "The killer of those children was a *misguided soul.*"

Evidence   In argumentation and persuasion, the material used to support or prove points.

Example   A sample or case in point, the most common material used by speakers to develop ideas; a form of definition.

Exchange   An interaction of people in communication.

Experience   A variable in communication; the influential and formative result of learnings, travels, observations, social encounters, jobs held, and so on, that contributes to effectiveness in communication.

Explanation   A statement of explication or simplification, used to clarify or interpret; a primary process.

Extemporaneous mode   A method of controlling and presenting ideas by adhering to a physical or mental outline and conversational norm, as opposed to speaking from manuscript or from verbatim memorization.

Eye contact   In speaking, the act of looking at the audience, observing responses and interacting.

F

Fabricated story   A made-up narrative for use in humorous speaking.

Fact   One kind of thesis or discussion question; something verifiable, a thing that has actually happened.

Fallacy   An error in reasoning, an obstacle to critical thinking.

False analogy   An erroneous comparison, a fallacy and obstacle to critical thinking.

False issue   Not a real point in conflict, as an example, a political candidate contending that her stand on abortion explains her failure to be elected, while the real issue may have been something else.

Familiarity   A quality of speech content that may facilitate securing and holding audience attention.

Family culture   One factor that speakers take into account as they seek identification with listeners.

Fatigue and discomfort   Two of the many forces against identification.

Faulty causation   A fallacy of causal reasoning, an obstacle to critical thinking.

Faulty generalizing   A fallacy and an obstacle to critical thinking, such as the hasty generalization that three cases of flu in a community means the start of an epidemic.

Faulty sign reasoning   A fallacy and an obstacle to critical thinking involving incorrect interpretation of something observed, for example, in concluding that the locked door of the "Mom-and-Pop" store means that they, too, have been robbed today. (Maybe it's a religious holiday for the proprietors, or the daughter's getting married.)

Fear   In speaking, a felt threat to personal security; apprehension.

Feedback   The messages sent back from audience to speaker, indicating the status of the interaction, usually mostly nonverbal.

Feelings   A variable in speech communication, such as a speaker's or listener's emotions related to a chosen subject that may affect the handling or reception of the message.

Feltboard   A visual aid on which to place material for viewing by an audience.

"Flight or fight" option   The choice of a person who feels threatened in a speaking situation.

Flip chart   A visual aid with pages of material that are "flipped" in accord with development of ideas.

Formal identification   Identification of speaker and audience resulting from certain forms given to a speech, for example, the motivated sequence form fits patterns of human thinking and thus facilitates formal identification with listeners.

Forum   The part of a speech occasion in which the audience is invited to participate.

Functional value in language use   A measurement of practical utility, such as its suitability or adaptability.

G

Gender   Male and female; a factor in audience understanding.

General data   Ideas or thought structure of a speech, as opposed to specific data or materials.

General education   Interpreted here as education that contributes to areas of personal development beyond those specific to a course in speech communication, as an example, organizational skills that can be applied to numerous situations in life.

Generalization   A broad statement or premise, for example, an undeveloped point in a speech outline; inductive reasoning, involving the drawing of a conclusion from a collection of related pieces of evidence, as an example, "In driving around town, I noticed that many people were decorating their cars; there must be a parade planned for today."

General objective   The broad goal or general end of a speech, as opposed to the specific purpose or thesis.

General semantics   The study of the relationship between language symbols and reality and the improvement of language use.

Gesture   In speaking, a movement of the body, which may help to provide emphasis or other meaning, or it may be a distraction.

Giving the speech   The act of presenting the message.

Good audience   Listeners who are purposeful, self-assured, attentive, and watchful and who operate with the expectation that speakers' messages will be marked by sound reasoning, fairness, and consistency.

Graph   A visual aid used to lay out information, such as statistical data—for example, a bar graph or pie graph.

Grounds   In Stephen Toulmin's theory, an observation that's the starting point in a line of reasoning.

Grounds of inherent appeal   A foundation on which to communicate a message to an audience.

H

Hasty generalization   The reaching of a conclusion without sufficient evidence; a fallacy and obstacle to critical thinking.

Hearing   Physiological function of receiving sound waves, such as, of another's voice, as opposed to listening which involves comprehending, interpreting, and finding meaning.

Human condition   The state of being apart from others, at a distance and different from; the force motivating acts of communication.

Humor   Funny or witty comment and narratives that are useful in communicating.

Hyperbole   Exaggeration for effect, as an example, "I walked a thousand miles today."

Hypercritical outlook   Faultfinding or overly judgmental attitude, a problem in listening well.

Hypothetical examples   Illustrations or instances that are not actual, often introduced with words like, "Let's assume that you win the lottery. . . ."

I

Ideal Solution Form   A sequence of questions used as the structure of a small group discussion, with the answer to one question leading to another, and so forth.

Ideas   Concepts; the main thoughts or points of a speech: thesis, main heads, and subheads.

Identification   Unity of speaker and audience, a sharing of relevant thoughts or perspectives; common ground or harmony in belief or feeling; a bridging of gaps that separate and a reconciliation of differences; the goal of communicators.

Identity   One's individuality, especially as reflective of personality, goals, habits, attitudes, and background: ethnic, cultural, educational, political, religious, and various orientations; how one is different from another person.

Illustration   A relatively detailed example; type of verbal supporting material.

Impatience   Restiveness or unquietness that becomes a problem in listening.

Imperative   An urgency or "command" that is not be to denied; in communication, the force that motivates one to connect with others, to identify with them.

Impromptu speeches   Those given without prior preparation, put together on the spur of the moment.

Incongruence   Behavior that is inconsistent with one's beliefs or attitudes, for example, suppression of a feeling of personal pride.

Indifference   Inactivity or apathy, a problem in listening.

Indirect plan   An inductive method of organizing a speech; the "upside down plan," in which the headings *follow* the supporting material.

Indistinctness   Lack of clarity in articulation.

Individualism   Extreme exaltation of self; assumption of personal privilege, distinction, and entitlement that precludes reciprocity and fairness in interaction; an obstacle to critical thinking.

Individuality   One's self as marked by personal characteristics that are distinct from another's.

Influence   The power of affecting, as in persuasion.

Inform   A category of speech; an expository message, one to clarify or explain a thing, event, process, or place, and so on.

Insecurity   Lack of confidence or feeling of personal threat, for example, regarding public speaking; may be a problem in listening well.

Insensitivity   Lack of awareness or nonresponsiveness, such as, regarding others' feelings or backgrounds.

Insertion   The addition of an extra sound in a word, as an example, ath-*uh*-lete; a problem of articulation.

Instance   A form of example, a short, undetailed case in point.

Interaction   In speech communication, an exchange: conversation, discussion, or public speech.

Interests and attitudes   Factors to consider in audience analysis.

Interpersonal dimension   To do with certain relational and behavioral aspects of any speaking situation or form of speech communication: elements of trust, sensitivity, openness, fear and anxiety, conflict, emotional climates, self-concept, congruence, and so on.

Interpersonal sensitivity   Awareness of essential relational and behavioral aspects in any speaking situation; see Interpersonal dimension.

Interviews and polls   Methods of gathering information for use in speaking, planned conversations with knowledgeable people and other systems of asking questions and securing data.

Intrapersonal dimension   To do with a communicator's interior speech, talking with oneself, for example, to make a choice or decision.

Introduction   The first part of a speech; the short speech to introduce a speaker.

Irony   A figure of speech in which the intended meaning is opposite to that indicated by the words used, as an example, "We had a lovely afternoon," said the Tigers' manager after his team lost to the A's by a score of 15–1.

Issue   A point of controversy or dispute suggesting an opposing view and grounds for debate, such as a town's *need* of a new sewer system (need being the issue).

K

Kinship   A factor in identification, representing significant properties of self, idea, belief, feeling, and so on, shared by communicators.

Knowledge   A variable in communication: what a person knows, as a factor in effectiveness.

L

Lack of confidence   Personal insecurity, as it influences outcome in communication.

Lack of design   Specifically, a problem in listening, for example, a listener's functioning without a plan to visualize the speaker's purpose and structure.

Language   A system of verbal and nonverbal symbols used in communication.

Leadership   In reference to the function of guidance and direction in small group discussion.

Lecture panel   A form of small group discussion involving structured but informal interaction in a group of four to seven people, with an individual set speech preceding or following.

Line of reasoning   A logical case for a point of view; a pattern of thinking relevant to an idea or issue.

Linguistic behavior   Patterns of language use, for example, as they may vary among cultures.

Listeners' mental frames   Fixed perceptions, attitudes, and so forth, that dictate listeners' responses, such as when listeners may be constrained to discount any speaker's appeals to raise taxes.

Listener's purpose   The goal(s) of the audience member in a given speaking situation.

Listening   The mental function of *perceiving* a message, as opposed to hearing which is the physiological function of *receiving;* includes the perceiving of nonverbal elements of messages as well as verbal.

Liveliness   A quality of language that appeals to the senses and has a certain vitality.

Logical appeal   Logos; proof derived through force of reasoning or good sense.

M

Main heads   The principal points of the body of a speech, two to four recommended.

Major premise   The principal generalization in a syllogism or enthymeme, for example, the categorical statement "All members of the club use the volleyball court" ("and since Nancy is a member . . . ," continues the reasoning to a conclusion).

Manuscript reading   Presentation of the speech word-for-word from the printed page.

Materials   Specific supporting data: visual and audio aids, examples, statistics, and quotations, as opposed to ideas or thought structure which are general data.

Maturity   In communication, a reference to a self-respecting, audience-respecting, purposeful and prepared speaker, and to the "good audience."

Meeting of minds   Identification, a sharing of views.

Memorization   Presentation of the speech by verbatim recall.

Mental dampening   Limited use of mental powers and an obstacle to critical thinking, characterized by apathy or indifference.

Message   A speaker's statement, particularly a speech or talk.

Metaphor   A figure of speech in which, for effect, something is named as something else, such as, "Political machinery must be kept well-oiled."

Methods   Strategies used by speakers and members of discussion groups to communicate effectively.

Minor premise   The second part of a syllogism or enthymeme, for example, the statement that follows the major premise, "All members of the club use the volleyball court,"—"Nancy is a member of the club" (minor premise).

Misarticulation   A miscue in articulation, arising from substituting one sound for another, omitting certain sounds, inserting extra sounds, or misplacing an accent; a possible distraction.

Misplacement of an accent   An articulation problem involving giving stress to the wrong syllable or sound, for example, "HOtel."

Mispronunciation Not a fault of articulation but an utterance that deviates from a community, regional, or other pronunciation standard, as an example, "myoon-uh-CIP-al" for municipal.

Model A representation of something, such as, a small airplane held up as a visual aid to support an idea in a speech; something offered as a standard, for example, the text of a successful speech; a structural design used to explain a process, for example, a communication model.

Modes of proof The classical three: logical (logos), emotional (pathos), and personal or ethical (ethos).

Motivated sequence The five-part pattern of speech organization invented by Alan H. Monroe: attention, need, satisfaction, visualization, and action.

Motivation In persuasion, strategic efforts used to effect positive audience response; the motivation to communicate arises in response to the human condition of interpersonal separation.

Multicultural Descriptive of an increasing number of American audiences in which diversity in background is typical, such as in native language, ethnicity, religion, gender, physical attribute, sexual orientation, and so on.

Mutuality "Togetherness" or unity in thought, for example, between speaker and audience.

Mutually exclusive Separate and distinct, as an example, in the nonoverlapping, "sovereign" main heads in the body of a speech.

N

Narcissistic mental operations and conditions As opposed to the favorable, those unfavorable personal states and behaviors that affect negatively the creation of identification and lead to problems in listening: for example, preoccupation, apathy, highly individualized perception; forms of subjectivity, such as untoward self-interest.

Narrative A story, for example, as told by a speaker to interest listeners.

Narrowing The process of deriving a speaking topic from a subject.

Need The second part of Alan H. Monroe's motivated sequence outline, the section laying out the problem.

Need-plan-benefits A structure for use in discussing or debating questions of policy; the stock issues of policy questions.

Negation Definition indicating what a term is not, as an example, "A house is not a home nor is it a . . . ."

Newspaper indexes An alphabetical compilation of articles and other reported events that appear in newspapers, such as, of the *New York Times* which reports on speeches and serves as a record of national and world events.

"Noise" Any intrusion that distorts or blocks the communication of a message, for example, threatening content, loud music outside, self-preoccupation or worry.

Nomination speech A speech to name one as a candidate for office.

Nonrepresentative instance In the inductive process, a case that doesn't fit the pattern; for example, the one case out of thirty bank failures that can't be explained as caused by bad loans. That case cannot be lumped together with the others.

Nonverbal communication Elements other than words that contribute to the shaping of meaning in messages, such as, bodily movements, scent, jewelry, sounds, clothing, and vocal intonations.

Note-taking in research   The systematic recording of materials gathered in support of a speech, paper, or other scholarly project.

O

Objectives of a class in speech communication   Sought-after gains such as mastery of principles of speech communication and increased self-assurance.

Objectivity   The ability to view an event apart from self-bias or needs of self.

Observation in research   On-site inquiry, such as occurring during a field trip.

Occasion   Any speaking situation or special event for speaking, for example, a particular ceremony or celebration.

Omission   The articulation problem of leaving out certain sounds, such as dropping the "r" from library or February: "libary" and "Febuary."

Oral mode   A reference to peculiarities of the act of speech communication, as opposed to written communication.

Orator   A public speaker, but often used now to connote a speaker guided by a grand or formal manner.

Organization   The structure or order of ideas, their arrangement and relationships, for example, of a speech or small group discussion.

Orientation   A reference to one's nature or inclination, such as, sexual nature.

Outline   In public speaking, a formal layout of the thought structure of a speech, including designation of coordinate and subordinate elements.

Overhead projector   A device for projecting onto a screen selected images to support ideas in speeches.

"Owning" an idea   Truly knowing and thereby *possessing* a thought, to the point of being confident in the "giving" of it in a public speech: "If you really own it, you're free to give it"; an argument for selecting a fitting speech subject or material.

P

Panel   Small group discussion form, four to seven participants around a table or seated in a partial circle who have organized their discussion but interact freely with one another.

Parallel structure   In language use, phrases or clauses set against each other in a balanced relationship, for example, "I laughed, I cried, I said goodbye."

Participant observer   An active participant in a small group discussion who at the same time evaluates processes and procedures.

Partition of a speech   A preview of the main heads that follows the statement of the thesis, an optional procedure.

Patterns of behavior   Regular, rather unvarying ways of doing, a person's characteristic acts.

Perception of a message   A process involving interpretation of relevant stimuli picked up by the senses.

"Performing"   Presenting speeches somewhat mechanically or "by the numbers," as opposed to interacting extemporaneously and adjusting one's behavior in response to others' reactions.

Personal appeal   Ethos or the effect of the speaker's character, knowledge, and good will; one of the three general modes of proof.

Personification   The figure of speech that gives human qualities to inanimate objects, such as, "The motor hummed."

Persuasion   The speech act designed to influence beliefs or behavior.

Physical materials   Visual and audio aids for supporting ideas of speeches, as opposed to strictly verbal supporting materials.

Physical setting   The place of the speaking: room, hall, auditorium, stadium, and so on.

Physiological needs   Human requirements of food, water, and shelter, and so on; a category in psychologist Abraham Maslow's hierarchy of needs.

Pitch   The characteristic of sound as it relates to the musical scale, a vocal attribute.

Policy   One kind of thesis or discussion question, that dealing with a system or plan.

Power of the spoken word   The effect of speech on an audience or on society.

Practical art   For example, speaking to get things done; the discipline of rhetoric, including theory on discovering ideas, selecting among ideas, supporting ideas, arranging them, and using appropriate language and methods of delivery.

Practice in speaking   Rehearsal.

Precept   A guiding principle or lesson.

Precise language   Explicit, definite, or exact words and phrases.

Preoccupation   The act of giving attention to one's personal concerns to the detriment of listening and identifying.

Presentation speech   A message to present an award or bestow another such honor.

Primary processess   Rhetorical methods often used before, or along with, the development of an idea, to provide needed cohesion, emphasis, or meaning: transitions, definition, repetition and restatement, explanation.

Principle as a form of reasoning   A type of thinking that proceeds from a premise; deduction, for example, in the form of an enthymeme.

Principles of speech communication   The essential practical and interpersonal elements of public speaking.

Probability   Likelihood, as opposed to certainty, infallibility, or inevitability.

Problem–solution   An order of analysis, a pattern of arrangement for speeches.

Pronunciation   The act of pronouncing words or phrases (judged by a social or dictionary standard).

Proof   Evidence and reasoning to back up an idea.

Proposal   What a speaker proposes, for example, as revealed in the thesis.

Provincial nature   The human tendency to be occupied with local events or personal concerns.

Psychological appeal   Pathos or emotional appeal in speaking, as an example, to an audience's feelings about terrorism.

Public speaking   Speechmaking, the formal act of preparing and presenting a message to an audience, as opposed to conversation or speaking in a group discussion panel.

Purpose   Specific aim, the thesis statement.

Q

Qualifier   In Stephen Toulmin's theory on reasoning, a phrase that limits the extent of the claim.

Quality   A characteristic of sound, related to resonation.

Quotation and authority   A quoted source or authoritative reference used in support of an idea, testimony.

R

Rapport   Close, agreeable relationship in communication.

Readers' Guide to Periodical Literature   Index of articles of about 175 magazines, found in the library.

Reason   A structural order for organizing argumentative speeches; an argument for a case.

Reasoning   Use of mental processes to think, to make inferences and draw conclusions, and so on.

Receiver   The one receiving the message or for whom it is intended.

Reciprocal influence   The effect of communicators on one another, such as of speaker and listener.

Reciprocity   Mutuality of involvement or exchange.

Reference groups   Primary groups in one's life, for example, family and school friends.

Refutation   The act of rebutting a point or answering back, as an example, to reveal an error.

Regulators   Nonverbal messages used by a speaker to direct listeners, such as pointing or looking to the back of the room to draw attention there.

Rehearsal   The act of practicing a speech.

Reinforce   To bolster or make stronger, for example, through restatement.

Relationship   The state of being involved together, for example, as speaker and listener.

Repeaters   Nonverbal messages that reinforce a verbal message through repeating, such as, after saying "Just one time," the speaker raises one finger.

Repetition and restatement   Primary processes that provide useful redundancy.

Research on a topic   The organized process of gathering material to use in a public speech or small group discussion.

Reservation   In Stephen Toulmin's system of reasoning, the statement that constitutes a rebuttal to the claim, noting exceptions or limits.

Resistance   An unwillingness to participate in communication, a force against identification.

Respectful language   Words and phrasings that acknowledge human dignity and avoid abuses such as racism or sexism.

Response   A reaction to the message, feedback to the speaker.

Responsible persuasion   Ethical speaking, characterized by honesty and fairness, with respect for the listeners.

Rhetoric   The study of human communicative interaction, particularly to do with processes of purposeful and planned symbolic influence on listeners, for example, through choice of organizational pattern or mode of development of ideas; conceptualized in this book with reliance on Aristotelian, Burkeian, and other theory, such as on effectiveness and speaker–listener identification.

Rhetorical question   A question posed by the speaker but to which no immediate answer is sought or expected.

Rhetorical value   The functional use of a given message element or kind of language, that promises to provide the desired effect.

Role   One of a person's many identities to be assumed and used strategically in speaking, such as the role of mediator, counselor, or activist.

Round numbers   Numerical data expressed in approximate units rather than exactly, for example, 700 rather than 693.

Rules   Constraints on a communicator's behavior, such as of societal or family origin.

S

Safety needs   To do with protection, security, and tranquility; a category of psychologist Abraham Maslow's hierarchy of human needs.

Satisfaction   The part of Alan H. Monroe's motivated sequence outline that takes up solutions to the expressed need.

Selective perception   Perceiving certain qualities, objects, or conditions, and so on, while ignoring or denying the existence of others.

Self   One's physical, mental, and emotional characteristics, those patterns of behavior, interests, temperament, attitudes, values, and motives that distinguish one person from another; the "somebody" as met and responded to by others—audiences—in the communicative process of identification.

Self-absorption and self-preoccupation   References to the inability to attend to others, their ideas and needs, and so forth, as opposed to the ability to empathize; a problem in communication, such as in listening.

Self-acceptance   Appreciation of one's own being, coming from self-awareness.

Self-actualization needs   The basis of creativity, high level personal growth, maturity, and so on; a category in psychologist Abraham Maslow's hierarchy of human needs.

Self-assurance and self-esteem   Conditions represented by feelings of personal security and confidence; being happy and pleased with oneself.

Self-awareness   The condition of being perceptive about one's self, self-knowledge.

Self-protection   Defensiveness, for example, as seen in being apprehensive regarding public speaking.

Semantic confusion   A problem of language usage, particularly as related to the fact that words have differing meanings in people's minds.

Sender   The one who presents a message.

Sense-appealing language   Language that paints word pictures, helping listeners to visualize form, texture, color, and so forth.

Sensitivity in communication   Awareness and appreciation of differences among people as audiences.

Separation   In reference to the human condition, of being apart from others, varied and different.

Sexual orientation   A person's sexuality, for example, heterosexual or homosexual.

Share   To give of one's ideas and feelings, that is, offering something of the self, fundamental to communication.

Sign reasoning   Coming to a conclusion through observation of relevant indicators.

Simile   A figure of speech making a comparison and introduced with *like* or *as,* for example, "He drove like a maniac."

Situation   The setting or environment for speaking, with relevant characteristics of time, place, occasion, and other impinging features.

Skill in communication   One of the variables in the communicative process.

Small group discussion   Organized communicative interaction among a limited number of participants to answer a question or solve a problem.

Sociability   The responsiveness of people to others' messages, a social sense suggesting availability for identification with others.

Social action   A reference to speech as a social act, of people affecting one another as they relate through assumption of roles and thus "do things" to and with each other.

Social agreement   An understanding developed over time by a community of people that a given term or other language usage is to mean this or that or is restricted to employment in a given situation; social code.

Social good   A standard of community values by which policies, ideas, or behaviors, and so on, are to be measured; related to social necessity or what is required to provide for community welfare.

Society   A body of individuals living as members of a community; reference to a large cultural group, nation, or all humans.

Source   In research, a person, book, document, and so forth, providing information.

Spatial order   The analysis of a thesis into main heads relating to space or placement, for example, according to position in space, location, and layout or in reference to distance, regions, or zones, and so on.

Speaker–audience environment   The communicative situation and all of its relevant features.

Speaking notes   A convenient and unobtrusive brief abstraction of the speech outline for use in giving the speech, often placed on a small card.

Specific data   Supporting material for speeches and discussions, as opposed to ideas or thought structure, evidence for backing main heads.

Specific purpose   The thesis.

Speciousness   The quality falsely suggesting that a statement or message is logical, correct, or genuine, and so on.

Speech   A public address or message prepared for an audience; purposive speech communication, usually more organized and more formal than conversation; the study of speech communication.

Speech communication   The study of all forms of oral interaction: public speaking, conversation, debate, discussion, oral interpretation of literature, and so on.

Speechmaking   The act of composing and giving speeches.

Spoken word   In reference to speaking in society, its place, power, and uses.

Standard language   Representative of the usual language choices of educated people.

Statistics   Numerical data to support ideas of speeches, quantitative material.

Stereotyping   A fixed or conventional conception of a group, person, or idea that allows for no individuality; often in reference to race, gender, sexual orientation, physique, and so forth.

Stimulus   Something that arouses or stimulates a response, such as a speaker's emotional appeal.

Strategies of communication   Methods chosen by speakers to be effective, as examples, a purposefully chosen organizational pattern or supporting quotation.

Subject   A broad area of thought, such as agriculture, from which speakers choose topics, for example, milking cows by hand.

Subjectivity   The inability to separate oneself or one's feelings from things or events.

Subordinate point   A subhead or division of a point.

Substandard language   Socially unacceptable modes of expression.

Substitute   A nonverbal message to replace a verbal, such as a smile that says, "Well done."

Substitution   A problem in articulation in which one sound is replaced by another, for example, *d* substituted for *th* in "that."

Summary   A recapitulation of the main points of a speech.

Support for ideas   Physical and verbal materials to back up ideas in speeches: visual and audio aids, examples, statistics, and quotations.

Syllogism   A form of classical deductive logic.

Symbol   A conventional representation of something, such as, the word *fish* standing for an aquatic creature, as agreed upon by users of English.

Symposium   In speech communication, a group of oral presentations made at an event, usually unified by a theme.

Synecdoche   A figure of speech in which the part stands for the whole, or less often, the whole standing for the part, for example, "I need your voice in my campaign."

Synonyms   Words or terms that mean the same thing, such as, *automobile* and *car.*

T

Talk   Informal word for a short speech.

Testing ideas   Evaluating the quality of a thought, particularly as regards logicality and good sense.

Theory   A systematic formulation conceived to explain certain phenomena, to make predictions, and to put to practice, for example, Burkeian theory of identification.

Thesaurus   A book of synonyms and antonyms; from the Greek, meaning "treasury."

Thesis   The specific purpose statement, the second of the four major parts of a speech.

Time   One of the major structures for ordering main heads of speeches, chronological patterning.

Topic   A small division of a subject, well-narrowed to allow for adequate treatment in a speech.

Transition   A rhetorical method used by a speaker to show the relationships among the unfolding thoughts of a speech, to demonstrate connections of the ideas *and* distinctions among them.

Trigger words   Words or terms provoking defensive response, thereby hampering communication.

Trust   Firm belief and confidence in another person's reliability, honesty, faithfulness, competence, and so on.

Two-way act   In speech communication, a reference to the interaction of speaker and listener, the speaking and responding.

U

Unity   The condition of being together in spirit, idea, or feeling; identification, the fundamental goal of communication.

Unity of form   A reference to the shaping of all main heads of a speech to conform to a single theme, such as, chronologically *or* spatially.

V

Value A type of thesis or discussion question, for example, "Why are general education requirements a part of the curriculum?"

Values A variable in the process of communication, individuals' conceptions of the good that figure into their communicative interactions.

Variables in speech communication Factors influencing outcome in a communicative interaction: participants' knowledge, experience, values, ethnic and cultural background, communicative skills, and feelings.

Variety in language use Alteration and diversification in usage, to enhance the appeal of messages, for example, through use of synonyms and varied phrasings.

Verbal materials Supporting data for speeches and discussions, consisting mainly of words: examples, statistics, and quotations.

Verbatim Word for word, as in exact memorization.

Visualization In Alan H. Monroe's motivated sequence outline, the step in which the speaker pictures for the audience the good effects of a proposed solution and/or the bad effects should the problem be allowed to continue.

Vocal characteristics Features of voice production: pitch, volume, duration, and quality.

Vocal variety Desired variation in vocal expressiveness in response to the ideas of a message, such as pitch variety.

Volume Loudness of the voice.

W

Warrant In Stephen Toulmin's theory of reasoning, the pivotal point that allows the reasoner to make a claim or draw a conclusion.

Welcome The kind of speech offered to receive a visitor.

NAME INDEX

Mead, George Herbert, 29
Menander, quoted, 46
Mink, Patsy, 9
Mitrovich, George S., 165; quoted, 147
Monet, Claude, 117
Monroe, Alan H., 192–193
Moore, George, quoted, 45

N
Nader, Ralph, 9, 46
Nehru, Jawaharlal, 8
Neibuhr, Reinhold, quoted, 199
Nichols, Marie Hochmuth, quoted, 169

P
Padrow, Ben, quoted, 204
Payan, Janice, 354; quoted, 372–378
Paz, Octavio, quoted, 25
Penn, C. Ray, 112, 164; quoted, 104, 140
Peterson, Owen, 274
Picasso, Pablo, 117
Pissaro, Camille, 117
Plautus, quoted, 392
Prior, Matthew, quoted, 139

Q
Quintilian 29; quoted, 39–40

R
Raspberry, William, 163
Reagan, Ronald, 351; quoted, 350
Red Jacket, 84
Reed, David, 113, 232; quoted, 109, 215
Renoir, Pierre Auguste, 117
Riis, Jacob, 8
Robinson, Mary, 343–344, 347, 350, 352; quoted, 348, 349
Rockefeller, Jay, 147
Romulo, Carlos P., 8; quoted, 218
Roosevelt, Eleanor, 8
Roosevelt, Franklin Delano, 8; quoted, 153
Rosenfeld, Lawrence B., 298
Roybal, Edward R., 274; quoted, 255
Runkel, Howard W., 353; quoted, 141, 355–359

S
Sanger, Margaret, 8
Sarbanes, Paul, 8
Satanta, 8
Saxe, J. G., quoted, 397
Schurz, Carl, 8
Seide, Michael, quoted, 224
Selden, John, quoted, 152
Sequoyah, 8
Shakespeare, William, 136, 151
Shaw, George Bernard, quoted, 151–152
Sinatra, Frank, 74
Sisley, Alfred, 117
Smith, Howard K., quoted, 108
Socrates, quoted, 32
Springer, Cecile M., 204; quoted, 108, 187
St. Augustine, quoted, 197
Stone, Lucy, 8
Sullivan, Louis W., 149, 165; quoted, 151
Sutherland, George, quoted, 83

T
Taner, Julie, 353; quoted, 360
Tennyson, Alfred, quoted, 118
Therow, Lester, 156
Thuy, Vuong G., 388
Tien, Chang-Lin, 349, 350, 352; quoted, 343–344, 347–348
Tijerina, Reies, 9
Tomlinson, H.M., quoted, 243
Tompkins, Phillip K., 14, 203
Toulmin, Stephen, 221–223, 231
Towne, Neil, 298
Tubman, Harriet, 8
Tutu, Desmond, quoted, 249
Twain, Mark, 344; quoted, 264

V
Van Gogh, Vincent, 184

W
Warren, Earl, quoted, 152
Washington, Booker T., 8, 298; quoted, 296, 297
Webster, Daniel, 8
Welch, Bruce L., 191
Whately, Richard, 29

SUBJECT INDEX

Audience, 3, 38, 61, 312, 321–322
    adaptation to, 23–24, 46–50, 66, 103,
        155, 167, 171, 173–175, 178, 181–
        185, 189, 221, 230, 260, 270, 271,
        272, 279, 288–290, 297, 312,
        351
        see also Common ground, Iden-
            tification, *and* Unity in com-
            munication
    analysis of in persuasion, 171, 173–
        175, 181–185
    critical thinking and, 209, 227, 229
    diversity of, 4–5, 9–14, 23–25, 28–
        29, 230, 303
    dynamics of, 95–96, 261–262, 264,
        278, 280, 281–286, 341
    eye contact with, 59, 122, 236–237,
        282, 283, 285–286, 297, 312, 324,
    as influence on subject choice, 46–
        50
    intruding conditions in, 95–98, 240–
        243
        see also Noise in communication
    welfare of, 296
Audio aids, developing ideas with,
    115–120, 123–124, 137
Australia, 51–52
Averages, 132–133

B

Backgrounds of listeners and speech
    communication, 4, 9–14, 23, 28–29,
        48–51, 155, 181–182, 231
    African American, 10, 48, 146, 149,
        260, 266
    Age, 9, 47–48, 181, 248, 259, 331
    Asian-Pacific, 10, 48, 181–182, 226,
        260, 339
    cultural and ethnic, 4, 21–22, 48,
        106, 181, 199, 212, 228, 243–244,
        248, 259, 260, 331
    gender as, 13, 48, 55, 181, 212, 228,
        243, 259
    Hispanic, 10, 48, 54
    Irish American, 10
    Native American, 54, 83–84
    physical/mental, 9, 13, 259
    racial, 9, 13, 228, 259
    religious, 13, 181, 228, 243, 248, 259
    sexual orientation as, 9, 48, 243, 248,
        259

Vietnamese, 11, 388
    see also Audience, Culture, *and*
        Diversity
Bartlett's Familiar Quotations, 389
Begging the question, 226
Belongingness and love needs, 178,
    179
Bibliography in research, 392–393
Bibliography card in research, 393
Biography as an order of analysis, 82
Biography Index, 389
Bodily action in speaking, 236–237,
    279, 280–285, 286, 294, 296, 297,
    324
Body of a speech, 65, 73–82, 101, 189,
    192, 339, 341, 342–343
    see also Analysis of the thesis *and*
        Main heads
Book Review Digest, 389
Books in Print, 389
Brainstorming, 45–46, 301, 304, 309,
    312

C

Cairns, Queensland, 51
Call to Arms speech, 221
Card catalog of the library, use of in
    research, 387–388
Case method in small group discus-
    sion, 308, 311, 333
Causation
    faulty reasoning and, 225, 227
    reasoning by, 214–215, 225
Cause and effect as order of analysis, 81
CD ROM, 389
Censorship, 388–389
Centrism, 228
China, 87
Choice in communication, 12, 13, 27,
    32, 38, 39, 44–51, 168, 229, 236, 238,
    242, 246, 249, 273, 278, 279, 280,
    296–297
Civil disobedience, 256
Civility in communication, 10, 12–14,
    38–39, 168, 238, 259, 331
Clarity in language use, 103, 194, 253,
    262–265, 273
Classification, definition by, 107
Climax
    in language use, 269
    as order of analysis, 81

Cohesion, 98–103, 110–112

Collier's Encyclopedia, 389

Color and variety in persuasion, 184

Columbia Encyclopedia, 137

Combined patterns of organization, 192, 342–343

Common ground, 14, 23–25, 171–173, 179–185, 188, 199, 387
- and definition, 108
- in the introduction to a speech, 69–70
- in the use of language, 107, 253, 261–262
- *see also* Adaptation to audiences, Identification, *and* Unity in communication

Communication
- as audience study, 5
- and civility, 10, 12–14, 38–39, 168, 238, 259, 331
- critical thinking in, 209, 213, 220–221, 224, 228, 229, 230–232
- defensiveness in, 31–33, 49, 183, 230, 242–243, 246, 264, 280
- definition of, 24
- and diversity, 4–5, 9–14, 23–25, 28–29, 230, 303
  - *see also* Audience
- empathy in, 13, 96, 249, 250, 259
- as facilitated by the democratic heritage, 9, 10, 169–170
- feedback in, 20, 21, 25, 33, 36, 245, 250, 279, 281–282, 286, 303
- and the human condition, 4–5, 12–14, 17, 23–25, 37, 39, 199, 229, 243, 248, 327
- and identification, 4–5, 10, 12–14, 17, 23–25, 30, 37, 38–39, 66, 70–72, 93, 97, 168–169, 171–173, 199, 242, 257, 296, 321,
- and identity, 14, 25–26, 31, 32, 169, 230, 243, 260, 279, 284–285, 287, 303, 329
- maturity in, 31, 32, 35, 230, 238, 243, 245, 246, 249, 259, 277, 296–297, 303
- model of, 21
- motivation for, 4–5, 23–24, 32, 34, 39, 70, 196
- need for accommodation in, 12, 13, 49–50, 66, 145, 174, 176–177, 181–186, 254
- noise in, 22–23, 96–98, 105, 110, 244–245, 247, 250, 280
  - *see also* Error, bases of in critical thinking; *and* Identification, forces against
- nonverbal elements, in 20, 21, 30, 115, 116–133, 168, 173, 236, 248–249, 257, 280–284, 285, 286, 297
- process of, 20–25, 237–238, 256–257
- risks/rewards and, 33, 36, 170, 227–228, 238–239, 243, 249, 257, 280, 297, 329, 333
- sensitivity/insensitivity in, 27, 28–29, 31, 38–39, 48, 171, 197, 228, 230, 231, 241, 243, 248, 249, 284, 329, 331, 332, 392
- unity in, 4–5, 10, 12–14, 34–35, 39, 71, 194, 199, 230, 255, 262
- uses of, 25–27
- values and, 10, 12, 13, 21, 22, 178–182, 243, 262
- variables in, 17, 21–22, 39, 243
- *see also* Speech communication

Comparison
- examples to show, 142–144
- *see also* Analogy

Complementors as nonverbal strategies, 281

Computer catalog, use of in library research, 388

Conclusion
- to an impromptu speech, 340
- to speeches generally, 65, 82–85, 189, 192, 198, 341, 343
- summary in, 82–83, 86, 101, 340

Concreteness in persuasion, 184

Confucianism, 86–88

Confusion, as a force against identification, 97, 98

Congruence/Incongruence in communication, 33–34, 155, 263, 272, 279, 283, 285, 294, 303, 329
- and subject choice, 45

Connotation/denotation, 98, 253, 260–261, 264

Constitution of the United States, 10, 254, 339

Contrast, examples to show, 144

improvement of, 30, 279, 280, 290–294, 297

manuscript reading, in 59, 279

and maturity in communication, 277, 280, 297

memorization in, 58, 279

nonverbal strategies in, 277, 280–284

in persuasion, 167, 174, 184, 196, 198

and pronunciation, 277, 288–292

and reception of feedback, 281–282

rehearsal for, 33, 60, 61, 103, 277, 294–296

the self in, 277, 278, 279–280, 283, 284–285, 294, 296, 297, 346

as a step in speech composition, 277, 278, 279

and understanding of ideas, 285

the voice in, 277, 280–285, 297

see also Nonverbal elements in communication

Democratic heritage and process

in facilitation of communication, 9, 10, 169–170

and listening, 239, 246

as part of the common culture, 10, 12

and persuasion, 167, 169–171, 197, 198

Description, 139

Development of ideas, 115–165, 279, 338

as related to delivery, 281, 282, 296, 297

verbal, 115, 135–165

with visual and audio aids, 115–133

Dewey's (John) reflective thinking and discussion pattern, 301, 307, 309–310, 312–320

Dictionary of American Biography, 389

Dictionary of American History, 390

Difference and distance, and the human condition, 4–5, 10, 12–14, 17, 23–25, 37, 39, 199, 229, 243, 248, 327

see also Diversity

Direct interaction, speaking as, 93, 94, 110, 237–238, 271, 279 280, 281–286

Direct observation in research, 390

Direct plan of organization, 189–190, 192–193, 343

Discussion, small group, 301–335, 352

adaptation of four-part method to, 310

brainstorming and, 301, 304, 309, 312

case method in, 308, 311, 333

cohesiveness in, 328, 329, 331, 332, 333, 334

criteria for solution in, 309

vs. debate, 306, 327, 331

definition of, 302

Dewey pattern of, 301, 307, 309–310, 312–320

formality of, 329

formats of, 301, 311–322, 332, 333

see Lecture panel, Panel, *and* Symposium

forum of, 321–322, 333

goals, 301, 302–304

ideal solution form of, 301, 310–311, 312

impromptu speaking in, 325

interaction in, 301, 302–303, 304, 309–310, 312–320, 321–325, 328–332

interpersonal problems affecting, 301, 303, 325–327, 332, 333

see also "Don't Ask Me!"; "Following Orders!"; "Flying Blind!"; "Mob Rule"; "I Won't Play!"; "Sounds of Different Drummers"; "Where're We Goin'?"; *and* "Who Am I, Anyway?"

leadership in, 301, 309, 312, 313, 320, 321, 324, 326, 329–330, 332–333, 334

making a point in, 301, 323–325, 333, 340

materials for, 301, 320, 322–323, 325, 331, 333, 387–397

narrowing subjects of to topics, 301, 304–305, 312, 332, 334

organization of, 301, 308–311, 312, 313–321, 324, 332, 333

participant observer in, 329

private vs. public, 311, 322

research for, 313, 322–323, 331, 387–397

connotation/denotation, 98, 253, 260–261, 264
defined, 257–258
and definition, 105–108
encoding, 20, 21, 244
euphemisms of, 106, 264, 265
in facilitating identification, 253, 260, 261–271, 272, 273
    see also Acceptability of language use, Clarity, Liveliness, and Variety
figurative, 254, 265–268, 273
for the ear, 271
formal vs. informal, 253, 258, 260, 272
functional values of, 253, 260
improvement in use of, 30, 253, 271–274
and influence of the occasion, 195, 196, 262, 270, 271, 272, 273
limitations of, 118–119
and listening, 261–262, 271, 272, 273
oral vs. written, 94, 271
in persuasion, 167, 174, 184, 187, 193–196, 198
respectful vs. disrespectful, 253, 259–260
in small group discussion, 332
as a social agreement, 253, 257–260, 270
standard vs. substandard, 260, 270, 272, 273
structures of, 269–270
    see also Alliteration, Climax, Loose construction, Parallelism, Periodic construction, and Rhetorical question
use of one's own, 253, 271, 272, 273
see also Verbal elements of speech communication
Latin America, 351
Leadership in small group discussion, 301, 309, 312, 313, 320, 321, 324, 326, 329–330, 332–333, 334
Lecture-panel in small group discussion, 301, 311, 321
Lectures on Rhetoric and Belles Lettres of Hugh Blair, 29, 62
"Let me direct you" as nonverbal strategy, 282–283

Library, use of in research, 387–390
Lincoln's (Abraham) debates with Stephen A. Douglas, 26
Listeners
    age of, 8, 47–48, 181, 248, 259, 331
    attitudes and interests of, 29, 47, 48–50, 171, 172, 181, 182–183, 229, 260, 278, 282, 296, 312, 333
    backgrounds of, 4, 9–14, 23, 28–29, 48–51, 155, 181–182, 231, 260
    culture and ethnicity of, 48, 243, 248
    expectations of, 66, 265
    fears of, 49–50
    gender of, 48, 243
    and influence on subject choice, 46–50
    interacting with, 61, 265, 273, 278, 279, 290
    needs of, 66, 75, 242–243, 285–286
    questions for, 246–250
    as speakers, 249–250
    see also Audience
Listening, 30–31, 34, 36, 38–39, 56, 99, 109, 235–251, 331, 391
    active, 237, 246, 248–250
    choice in, 12, 236, 238, 242, 246, 249
    in completing enthymemes, 220–221
    defensiveness and, 243, 246
    defined, 236–237
    and diversity, 243, 248
    empathy in, 249, 250
    goals of, 235, 239–240
    and the good audience, 235, 245–250
    vs. hearing, 235, 236
    improvement of, 30–31, 230–232, 235, 243–250
    interactive dimension of, 237–239, 242, 250, 282–284, 324
    and language use, 261–262, 271, 272, 273
    malfunctioning of, 235, 240–243, 250
    to nonverbal messages, 236, 248–249
    and objectivity vs. subjectivity, 207, 209, 212–213, 230, 231, 260

National Newspaper Index, 389

National origin and language use, 259

Native American background and speech communication, 54, 83–84

NBC Handbook of Pronunciation, quoted 289–290

Need (problem) step of the motivated sequence speech, 192, 193

Need-Plan-Benefits, as order of analysis, 82

Needs and motivation theory, 178–181
see also Belongingness and love needs, Esteem needs, Physiological needs, Safety needs, Self-actualization needs, *and* Maslow, Abraham H.

Negation, definition by, 108

New York Times Index, 389

New Zealand, 139

Noise in communication, 22–23, 96–98, 105, 110, 244–245, 246, 247, 250, 280
see also Fallacies in reasoning *and* Narcissism

Nominating speech, 337, 338, 345–346, 351

Nonrepresentative instance, 214, 225, 392

Nonverbal elements in communication, 20, 21, 30, 115, 116–133, 168, 173, 236, 248–249, 257, 277, 280–284, 285, 286, 297
and six strategies, 282–284

Notes, speaking, 60, 85–86, 295
model of, 87
preparation and use of, 60, 85–86, 286
vs. the speech outline, 65, 85, 86

Note taking in research, 393–396
and bibliography card, 393, 394
and direct quotation card, 394–395
and indirect quotation card, 395–396
and reaction card, 395–396
and summary outline card, 395

''Now hear this!'' as nonverbal strategy, 282

O

Objective, general of a speech, 43, 52–55, 58, 61

Objectives, of the speech class, 29–39

Objectivity, 37
in critical thinking, 207, 209, 211–213, 230, 331
definition of, 211
and listening, 212
and speaking, 212
vs. subjectivity, 207, 209, 211–213, 230, 231, 260–261

Observation in research, 390

Occasion
demands of, 155, 196, 244–145, 288–89, 305, 337, 338, 337–352
as influence on language use, 195, 196, 262, 270, 271, 272, 273
as influence on subject choice, 50–51
see also Situation *and* Special occasions

Omission, 291

Oral mode vs. written, 94, 271

Organization of small group discussion, 301, 308–311, 312, 313–321, 324, 332, 333

Organization of speeches, 65–90, 174, 224, 278, 312, 338, 342–343
of the announcement, 340–341
benefits of, 66, 188–189
combined patterns of, 192, 342–343
direct patterns of, 189–190, 192–193, 343
indirect plan of, 190–192, 342–343, 346
and the introduction, 69–73, 86, 189–192, 339, 341
and listeners' expectations, 66
motivated sequence plan of, 192–193
outlining and, 66–69
for persuasion, 167, 174, 184, 188–193, 198, 199
as related to purpose, 77, 82
as related to thinking, 189
and the speech outline, 66–85

Othello of Shakespeare's play, 136

Outlines
of the announcement, 340–341
coordinate points of, 67–68
familiarity with, 295
headings and indentations of, 67

as a social act, 17, 19–20, 24, 28, 39, 169, 173–174, 257, 303
uses of, 6–12, 13, 17, 25–27
vs. writing, 94, 271
see also Speech communication
Special occasions, speeches for, 50–51, 337–352
see also Acceptance speech, After-dinner speech, Announcement, Impromptu speech, Introduction speech, Nominating speech, Response to a welcoming speech, Presentation speech, *and* Welcoming speech
Speech communication
apprehension in, 18, 31–33, 38, 45, 120, 227, 228, 280
choice in, 12, 13, 27, 32, 38, 39, 44–51, 168, 229, 236, 238, 242, 248, 249, 273, 278, 279, 280, 296–297
cosmopolitan dimension in, 35
and critical thinking, 30, 230–232
demands of a class in, 35–39
dimensions of, 18–20, 24–25, 26–27, 29–30
as a discipline, 30–31, 60, 284
dynamics of a class in, 28–29
general objectives of, 43, 52–55, 58, 61
and improvement of education, 35
maturity in, 31, 32, 35, 230, 238, 243, 245, 246, 249, 259, 277, 296–297, 303
nonverbal elements of, 20, 21, 30, 115, 116–133, 168, 173, 236, 248–249, 257, 277, 280–284, 285, 286, 297
objectives of class in, 29–39
occasions for, 50–51, 337–352
situations in, 17, 27–29, 39, 184, 186, 288–289
use of notes in, 60, 85–86, 295
variables in, 17, 21–22
see also Communication *and* Speaking
Speeches
model outlines of, 86–90, 110–112, 130–133, 157–164, 190–191, 201–203

model texts of:
"Running Free," 159–161
"Trumpet Mutes," 353, 360
"Black Hawk's Farewell Address," 354, 370–371
"Making Lincoln Live," 353, 355–359
"Opportunities for Hispanic Women," 354, 372–378
"The Other 99 Percent of the Population," 353, 363–369
"Racial and Ethnic Relations in American Higher Education," 354, 379–385
"What is an Average?", 353, 361–362
of symposia, 320–321
Sperry Corporation, 238–239, 251
Spoken word, power of, 38
Statistical Abstract of the United States, 389
Statistics, 118, 135, 136, 146–150, 155, 158–163, 176, 339
checking and handling, 148–150, 198, 245, 312, 320, 325, 332, 342
defined, 146
Stereotypes, 227, 228, 259–260
see also Allness fallacy
Stock issues, 79–80
Subjectivity
in critical thinking, 207, 209, 212–213, 230
definition of, 211
and listening, 209, 212, 213, 230, 231, 260, 261
vs. objectivity, 207, 209, 211–213, 230, 231, 260–261
and speaking, 212, 213, 287
Subjects
choosing, 32, 43, 44, 45–51, 58, 59, 61, 224, 278, 338–339
narrowing to topics, 43, 51–52, 58, 305, 332
samples of, 61–62, 199–200
for small group discussion, 301, 304–305, 312, 332, 333, 334
vs. topics, 51
Substitutes as nonverbal strategies, 281
Substitution, 290
Syllogism, 219, 220, 231

Symbols in communication, 20, 236, 253, 256–257, 261, 273
Symposium in small group discussion, 301, 311, 320–321
Synecdoche, in language use, 265, 267

T

Thesaurus, 23, 103, 264
Thesis
    analysis of, 73–82, 86, 136, 175–176, 183–184, 189, 190–192, 200–201, 338, 339, 341, 342–343
    checking weaknesses of, 56–57
    definition of, 55, 56
    and the four-part speech, 43, 55–58, 65, 71, 72, 73, 83, 101, 183, 189, 190, 192, 278
    of impromptu speeches, 339
    and the introduction, 72–73
    for persuasion, 175–176, 189, 197
    phrasing, 56–58, 61, 73, 86, 278
Thinking, 189, 208, 229, 230, 231
    see also Critical thinking
"This is my feeling about it" as nonverbal strategy, 282
"This is what I mean" as nonverbal strategy, 284
Time as an order of thesis analysis, 78
Time limits on speaking assignments, 37–38
Topic as an order of thesis analysis, 80–81
Topics
    definition of, 51, 56
    narrowing subjects to, 43, 51–52, 58, 61, 305, 332
    shaping theses from, 55–58
    vs. subjects, 51
Toulmin's (Stephen) reasoning system, 207, 221–223, 231
Transition
    conjunctions as, 100
    function of in listening, 99, 248–249
    through nonverbal action, 282–283
    value and use of as a primary process, 93, 98–103, 110–112, 321, 345
Trinity College, 343–344, 349
Trust in communication, 19, 34, 99, 228, 284, 297, 328, 330–331, 391

U

Ulrich's International Periodical Directory, 389
United States Marine Corps, 346
Unity in communication, 4–5, 10, 12–14, 34–35, 39, 71, 194, 199, 230, 255, 262
    see also Common ground *and* Identification
University of California, 343, 347, 349

V

Value
    as the issue, 80
    thesis and discussion questions of, 175–176, 301, 306–307, 308
Values
    and norms in communication, 10, 12, 13, 178–181, 262
    as variables in communication, 21–22, 182, 243, 279
Variables in communication, 17, 21–22, 39, 243
Variety in language use, 195, 253, 262, 268–270, 273
Verbal elements of speech communication, 30, 82, 83, 168, 253–274
    in developing ideas, 115–116, 118, 135–165, 320, 339
    in effecting identification, 137, 155, 261–271
    see also Common ground
    in wording transitions, 103
    see also Language
Vietnam, 87
    people of, 11, 388
    war in, 264
Visual aids
    developing ideas with, 115–123. 124–133, 137, 176, 280, 284, 339
    in effecting identification, 119
    holding attention with, 119
Visualization step of motivated sequence speech, 192–193
Vital Speeches of the Day, 90, 112–113, 146, 164–165, 204, 232, 274
Vocal folds, 286–287
Voice in speaking, 277, 280–285, 286–288, 294, 296, 297

PHOTO CREDITS

Chapter 12: page 276, © Joel Gordon 1991; page 283, © David J. Sams/Texas Inprint; page 289, Terry M. Smith; page 295, © Joel Gordon 1989

Chapter 13: page 300, © Joel Gordon 1990; page 313, Michael Amador/Texas Inprint; page 322, Photo provided by California State University, Hayward; page 330, © Joel Gordon 1990

Chapter 14: page 336, © Joel Gordon 1991; page 340, © Joel Gordon 1989; page 347, NASA Photo; page 349, Peg Skorpinski